Municipal Council Johnstown

Standing Rules and By-Laws

Of the Municipal Council of the District of Johnstown from 1842 to 1849

Municipal Council Johnstown

Standing Rules and By-Laws
Of the Municipal Council of the District of Johnstown from 1842 to 1849

ISBN/EAN: 9783337158699

Printed in Europe, USA, Canada, Australia, Japan

Cover: Foto ©Suzi / pixelio.de

More available books at **www.hansebooks.com**

STANDING RULES

AND

BY-LAWS

OF THE

MUNICIPAL COUNCIL

OF THE

DISTRICT OF JOHNSTOWN.

FROM 1842 TO 1849 INCLUSIVE.

TORONTO:
PRINTED AT THE "LEADER" STEAM PRESS, 63 KING STREET EAST.

1866.

STANDING RULES.

I. That the Municipal Council do meet at 9 o'clock in the forenoon, and if at that hour there is not a Quorum, the Warden may take the Chair and adjourn to a certain hour on the same or the following day.

II. That whenever the Warden is obliged to adjourn the Council for want of a Quorum, the hour at which such adjournment is made and the names of the Councillors present, shall be inserted in the Minutes.

III. That immediately after the Warden shall have taken the Chair, the Minutes of the preceding day shall be read by the Clerk, to the end that any mistake therein may be corrected.

IV. That the Warden shall preserve good order and decorum, and shall decide questions of order, subject to an appeal to the Council.

V. That every Councillor, previous to his speaking, shall rise from his seat, and address himself to the Warden.

VI. That when a Councillor is speaking, no other member of the Council shall hold discourse to interrupt him.

VII. That a Councillor called to order by the Warden shall sit down, unless when permitted to explain; and when two or more members rise at once, the Warden or person presiding (subject to an appeal of the Council, if demanded) shall name the member who is first to speak.

VIII. That no Councillor shall speak more than once on the same question, without leave of the Council, except the mover, who shall have a right to reply.

IX. That upon a division on any question in the Council, the names of those who vote for, and of those who vote against the question, shall be entered upon the Minutes, if any Councillor require it.

X. That no question shall be debated or put, unless the same be in writing and seconded.

XI. That all questions shall be put in the order in which they are moved.

XII. That every motion, when seconded, shall be read by the Warden.

XIII. That every By-Law shall be introduced by a motion for leave, specifying the object of it—or by a motion to appoint a Committee to prepare and bring it in—or by an order of the Council on the report of the committee.

XIV. That every By-Law shall receive three several readings at length, each on different days, previous to its being passed, except on urgent occasions.

XV. That the time of each meeting, and of the passing of every By-Law shall be certified on the back thereof by the Clerk.

XVI. That every Member of the Council, who shall introduce a Bill, Petition, or Motion, upon any subject, which may be referred to a Select Committee, shall be one of the Committee, without being named by the Council.

XVII. That all persons whose interest or property may be affected by any proposed By-Law, may appear in person, or by Agent before the Council or Committee appointed to consider the By-Law.

XVIII. That Petitions and other papers addressed to the Council shall be presented by a Councillor in his place, immediately after the reading of the minutes, who shall be answerable to the Council that they do not contain improper or impertinent matter. All such petitions and papers shall be read by the Clerk, when present.

XIX. That the mode of appointing Special or Standing Committees shall be for each Councillor in his place to name one, which shall be written down by the Clerk. Those who have most voices shall be taken successively until the number agreed on is completed.

(Signed),   W. MORRIS,
Warden.

By-Laws of District Council.

No. I.—BY-LAW

Of the Municipal Council of the District of Johnstown See Con. Stats. U. C., Cap. 54 & 55.
relating to Statute Labor.—Passed February 9, 1842.

———

No. II. BY-LAW

Of the Municipal Council of the District of Johnstown to regulate the appointment of Surveyors of Highways. —Passed February 12, 1842.

The Council of the District of Johnstown duly See Con. Stats. U. C., Cap. 54 Sec. 243,
assembled in Council in the Town of Brockville, on
Saturday, the Twelfth day of February, in the year of
Our Lord One Thousand Eight Hundred and Forty-two,
by virtue of an Act passed in the fourth and fifth years
of the reign of Her Majesty Queen Victoria, entitled
"An Act to provide for the better internal government
of that part of this Province which formerly consituted
the Province of Upper Canada, by the establishment of
Local or Municipal authorities therein," do ordain and
enact the following By-Law, and it is hereby enacted,
That the persons hereinafter named, be appointed Surveyors ap-
Surveyors of Highways, within the several and respective pointed.
Townships of this District, having the same powers and Powers, &c., of
authority, and subject to the same responsibilities, Surveyors.
regulations, and requirements, as the Surveyors of
Highways heretofore appointed by the Justices of the
Peace, under and by virtue of an Act passed in the 50th
year of the reign of His late Majesty, King George III.,
entitled "An Act to provide for the laying out, mending

and keeping in repair the public Highways and Roads in this Province, and to repeal the laws now in force for that purpose."

For the Township of

Elizabethtown..... ....William K. Glazier.
Yonge.......... .... John Morris.
Augusta...........Philemon Pennock and Alex. M'Millan:
Edwardsburgh........John M'Ilmoyle and Levi Adams.
Bastard........... .James Scofield and James Eaton.
Kitley........Christopher Gunnis and George Hornick.
Oxford...............................Tyrus Hurd.
Elmsley................. ....John Riddle.
Leeds...............................Humphrey Young.
Lansdowne, ... Surasten Soper
South Crosby......................Henry B. Marvin.
Wolford...... ....John L. Read and Samuel Ferguson.
South Grower,................. ....
North Crosby ....James Bilton.

Duration of office.
SECTION 2. That the several and respective Surveyors of Highways herein before appointed, and their several and respective successors in office as such Surveyors of Highways, shall respectively continue in office as such Surveyors, until removed therefrom by resolution of the District Council, or by the removal from the Township, or the incapacity of the person appointed.

W. MORRIS, *Warden.*

***

No, III.—BY-LAW

Seo Con. Stat. U. C., Cap. 51. *To define the duties of Surveyors of Highways and for other purposes therein mentioned.—Passed May* 14. 1842.

The Municipal Council of the District of Johnstown, duly assembled at the Town of Brockville, on the Fourteenth day of May, in the Year of Our Lord One Thousand Eight Hundred and Forty-two, under and by virtue of a certain Act of the Legislature of the Province, passed in the former and fifth year of Her Majesty's Reign, entitled "An Act to provide for the better internal government of that part of this Province which formerly constituted the Province of Upper Canada, by the establishment of local or Municipal authorities therein," do ordain, and it is hereby ordained and enacted, That all and every of the persons appointed Surveyors of Highways for the Townships ot Elizabeth- town, Yonge, Bastard, Kitley, South Elmsley, Leeds, Lansdowne, South Crosby, North Crosby and South Burgess, in the said District, under and by virtue of a certain By-law passed at the last session of this Council entitled "By-law of the Municipal Council of the District of Johnstown, to regulate the appointment of Surveyors of Highways," shall be taken and considered as having been appointed such Surveyors of Highways in and for the County of Leeds, and that all and every of the persons appointed by the said By-Law for the Townships of Augusta, Edwardsburgh, Oxford, Wolford, and South Gower, in the said District, shall be considered as having been appointed such Surveyors of Highways in and for the County of Grenville. *Appointed for Counties.*

SECTION 2. That the said Surveyors, before entering upon their duty, shall take and subscribe the Oath of *Oath of Office.* office, pointed out by the second section of the Provincial Statute 50 Geo. III. cap. 1, and deposit the same in the office of the District Clerk; and after having been once sworn in this manner, they may continue to discharge their duty from year to year during their continuance in office.

SECTION 3. That in all applications for the laying out of any new, or altering of any old road, or roads, eight days' previous notice shall be given by such Surveyors, *Notice of application.* before the sitting of the Council, at which the report of the survey is intended to be made.

SECTION 4. That no Surveyor of Highways shall receive any allowance for attending the Council, unless his Report shall be made at the opening of the Council, *Report of Surveyor.* nor unless his conduct shal have been conformable to law, nor unless his report shall be made in the form following, that is to say:—

District of Johnstown, } To the Municipal Council of said
    To Wit: District in Council assembled:
I, ————, Surveyor of the Highways in and for the County of ———— in the said District, beg leave to report: that on application in writing made to me by twelve freeholders of the said County of ———— bearing date the ———— day of ———— in the year one Thousand Eight Hundred and ———— stating as follows: (here insert the petition verbatim with names of freeholders): I proceeded to examine the same, which I have surveyed, and laid out as follows, that is to say,

8

(here insert the description of the road as surveyed). and I have made the said road —— feet in width. I have further to state that I gave due public notice of this survey according to law, by affixing a copy of this report in *three* of the most public places next adjacent to the place where the aforesaid survey has been made. Dated at —— this —— day of —— in the year of our Lord one thousand eight hundred and——.

Surveyor of Highways for the County of——.

Duty of Surveyor SECTION 5. That every Surveyor of Highways shall carefully enter in his report the requisition of the Freeholders *verbatim*, and act strictly according to it in making his report, and shall see that it is in conformity to the Statute, according to the words of which "The requisition is to state that any public highway or road in the neighborhood as the said freeholders now in use, is inconvenient and may be altered, so as better to accommodate Her Majesty's subjects and others travelling thereon, or that it is necessary to open a new highway or road."

Description of Road. SECTION 6. That every such Surveyor shall lay down in the blank space left for that purpose, an accurate description of the new road intended to be laid out, or of the proposed alteration of the old road, giving the length and courses as correctly as possible, and stating whether the survey is marked out by blazes on trees, or with red chalk, or by stakes planted on the open ground.

Notice of Report. SECTION 7. That the width of the road shall be stated in the survey, and exact copies of the report affixed in at least two public places near the road surveyed.

SECTION 8. That every report shall be accompanied by a plan or diagram, and shall be personally presented to the Council by the Surveyor making any such survey, which shall be referred to the Committee on Roads with **Powers of Road Committee.** power to confirm, annul or modify the Report on enquiry into the necessity of establishing any such road or not, and to make such report thereon to the Council as the said Committee may conceive proper, and in case any opposition shall be made to any survey, it shall be the duty of the party making such opposition to show before the said Committee that two days' notice of such opposition has been given before the sitting of the Council, to the Surveyor, who shall notify the petitioners of such opposition, so that they may be prepared to sustain their application for the establishment of such road.

SECTION 9. That no road hereafter to be laid out shall be more than sixty-six, nor less than forty feet in. width, and on the alteration of any road, the new road shall not be laid out of a less width than the. old one. *Width of Road.*

SECTION 10. That in all cases the Surveyors of Highways shall mention in their reports and mark on their diagrams, the distance of all parallel roads, or roads nearly parallel, whether opened or not, from the one intended to be reported, or of other roads in the vicinity, noticing the termination of such road or roads required to be laid out, so that the Council or Committee thereof may be enabled to judge of the necessity of establishing the same. *Parallel Roads.*

SECTION 11. That in all cases in which claims are made for compensation for land taken for roads established by the Council, the applicants for such compensation shall appear on the first day of the Session next after the establishment of such road or roads, to support their claim, on its being reported by the Surveyor of Highways according to law, and in order that the Council may know who are the parties to support any road so confirmed, Surveyors are required in their reports, when copying the petition for the alteration of an old road, or the laying out of a new one, to enter the names of the petitioners therein, and to give said petitioners notice that a compensation is claimed, so that they may also attend on the first day of the sitting of the Council next after the notice of such claim, given to the Surveyor of Highways. *Notice of Compensation.*

SECTION 12. That all claims for compensation for lands taken for roads established by the Council, shall, when lawfully reported by the Surveyor of Highways, be also referred to the Committee on Roads, who after investigating the same, shall report to the Council what sum, if any, shall be allowed to the claimant, and whether the road is of a public or private nature, no order shall issue to open the same until the amount, if any, awarded by the said Committee after such compensation, shall be paid by the said petitioners; but in case they shall find that the road so established is of a public nature, then the amount fixed on for such compensation shall be paid out of the funds of the District, and it shall be the duty of the Treasurer, and. he is hereby required to pay the same on the certificate of the District Clerk. *Payment of compensation.*

SECTION 13. That no Licensed Land Surveyor shall be employed by the Surveyor of Highways, unless by special order of the Council, on its being shown that it *Land Surveyors when to be employed.*

is necessary or useful to obtain the aid of such Land Surveyor in laying out or altering any road or highway.

Old roads, sale of land. SECTION 14. That with respect to the sale of Land through which any old road may have passed, and other duties of Surveyors of Highways, reference must be had to the Provincial Statutes 50 Geo. 3, chap 1, and 4 Geo. 4, chap 10.

Forms of Notice, &c. SECTION 15. That the following forms shall be used in all surveys and claims for compensation for land taken for roads;

NOTICE OF OPPOSITION TO SURVEY.

To Mr ——, Surveyor of Highways in and for the County of ——, Take notice that I oppose the survey of the road made by you over my land, being Lot (or part of Lot as case may be) No. —— in —— concession of ——, and that I shall appear before the District Council at its next meeting for that purpose. Dated the —— day of ——, 184 .

NOTICE TO PETITIONERS OF OPPOSITION TO SURVEY.

To—— : Take notice that——————has this day given me notice that he intends to oppose the survey of the road made on your petition over his land, being Lot (or part of Lot as case may be) No.——in ——concession of ——, and that he will appear before the District Council at its next meeting for that purpose. Dated the —— day of ——, 184 .

—— ——,
Surveyor of Highways, for the County of ——

NOTICE OF COMPENSATION CLAIMED.

To Mr ——, Surveyor of Highways for the County of —— : Take notice that I shall apply to the next District Council for compensation for the road laid out by you over my land, being Lot (or part of Lot as case may be) No. —— in —— concession of ——, and that I claim the sum of £—— for the land taken for said road, of which you are required to give notice to the petitioners and report this, my claim, to the said Council at its said meeting.

—— ——.
Dated the —— day of —— 184 .

NOTICE TO BE GIVEN TO PETITIONERS FOR COMPENSATION.

To ———— : Take notice that ———— has this day given me notice that he intends to apply to the next District Council for compensation for the road laid out by me on your petition over his land, being Lot (or part of Lot as the case may be) No. ——— in ——— concession of ————, a copy of which notice is hereunto annexed.

————————,

Surveyor of Highways for the County of ——.

REPORT TO THE COUNCIL OF CLAIM FOR COMPENSATION.

To the Municipal Council of the District of Johnston, in Council assembled:

I, ————, Surveyor of Highways in and for the County of——, beg leave to report that ———— claims the sum of £—— for the land taken for the road surveyed by me on Lot (or part of Lot as the case may be) No.—— in ——— concession of —— which was reported and confirmed at the last meeting of the Council. Copies of the notices of compensation claimed given to me by the said ————, and of mine to the petitions are hereunto annexed:

————————

Surveyor of Highways for the County of ——.

W. MORRIS, Warden.

No. IV. BY-LAW,

To provide for the vacating of the seats of Members of the District Council in certain cases.—Passed November 11, 1842.

See 12 Vic., Cap. 81.
See Con. Stat. U. C., Cap. 54.

No. V. BY-LAW,

To provide for the filling up of vacancies in certain Township or Parish Offices.—Passed August 11, 1842.

See 12 Vic., Cap. 81.
See Con. Stat. U C., Cap. 54.

No. VI. BY-LAW,

Relating to the opening of Roads.

See Con. Stat. U. C. Cap. 54.

Preamble. Whereas many highways in this district upon which statute labor has been done or public moneys expended, are obstructed, and whereas the allowance originally made by Government for public highways, are in many places unopened and impassable, and whereas it is desirable that all such roads should be opened to the public travel and convenience: Be it therefore ordained and enacted, and it is hereby ordained and enacted, by the Municipal Council of the District of Johnstown duly assembled at the Town of Brockville, on the fourteenth day of May, in the year of our Lord one thousand eight hundred and forty-two, that all Roads and Highways allowed and granted by the Executive Government, or upon which any public moneys or statute labor may have been expended, previous to the year of our Lord one thousand eight hundred and ten, by resolution, adoption of a Report, enactment of a By-law, or other **What declared Highways.** decision of this Council, declared a public road and Highway, shall be, to all intents and purposes, and for all public use and convenience, considered a public road and highway, and as such shall not be obstructed or impeded by any person or persons whatever.

SECTION 2. That whenever any such road may be unopened or obstructed as aforesaid, it shall and may be lawful for the Overseer of Highways for the Division in **Overseer to direct Statute Labor to be done.** which any such road may be situated, to order and direct any amount of the statute labor within the Division for which he may be Overseer of Highways, to be expended thereon, as in his discretion he may think fit.

Certificate of Clerk. SECTION 3. That a certificate from the Clerk of the District, duly signed by that officer, signifying that such road hath been declared a public road and highway, by the Municipal Council of this District, shall be deemed good and sufficient authority for the Overseer of the Division in the removal of obstructions, or in the opening of any such road as aforesaid, or in the expenditure of the statute labor thereon as aforesaid.

W. MORRIS, Warden.

No. VII. BY-LAW,

To regulate the mode of opening of new Roads, the closing See Con. Stat. U. *of old ones, and the altering of their course and direc-* C., Cap. 54. *tion.—Passed May 14, 1842.*

Whereas much public injury may be done, and private Preamble. interests affected, by the opening of new roads, or by the closing of roads already allowed or travelled, or by altering or diverting of their course without due public notice being given : Be it therefore ordained and enacted, and it is hereby ordained and enacted by the Municipal Council of the District of Johnstown, duly assembled at the Town of Brockville, on the fourteenth day of May, in the year of our Lord one thousand eight hundred and forty-two, that no new road or highway shall be opened and declared to be a public highway and road, nor shall any Government allowance, or other established or public Highway be closed, nor shall any alteration be made in the course or direction of any such Government allowance, or other public or established road or highway, without such opening or closing or alteration, as aforesaid, shall be requested by requisition from twelve freeholders Requisition of 12 of the District, duly signed and presented to a Surveyor Freeholders. of Highways requiring such opening, closing, or alteration aforesaid, nor until such opening, closing, or alteration as aforesaid, shall have been duly examined and reported upon by such Surveyor of Highways, which examination and report thereon, duly attested on oath or affirmation, shall be laid before the Council of the District and filed with the public papers and records of the same.

W. MORRIS, Warden.

No. VIII. BY-LAW,

Of the Municipal Council of the District of Johnstown, to See Con. Stat. U. *regulate the appointment and duties of Pound-Keepers.* C., Cap. 54 Sec. *—Passed February 11, 1842.* 243, 359 and 360.

No. IX. BY-LAW,

Sec 12 Vic. 61,
Sec. 156. *Of the Municipal Council of the District of Johnstown, to enable the Clerk of the Council to issue Subpœnas in certain cases.*

Preamble.

The Council of the District of Johnstown duly assembled in Council in the Town of Brockville, on Saturday, the twelfth day of February, in the year of our Lord one thousand eight hundred and forty-two, by virtue of an Act passed in the fourth and fifth years of the reign of Her Majesty Queen Victoria, entitled "An Act to provide for the better internal government of that part of this province, which formerly constituted the Province of Upper Canada, by the establishment of Local Municipal authorities therein," do ordain and enact the following By-Law, and it is hereby enacted, that when ever any claimant or respondent in any cause may require the attendance of any person or party to appear before this Council or any Committee thereof to testify and declare the truth, according to his knowledge, in any matter or any thing that may be brought before the said Council, or any Committee thereof, it shall and may be

Clerk's power to issue.

lawful for the Clerk of this Council to issue to any person applying therefor a Subpœna requiring the attendance of such person or party, as the case may be.

SECTION 2. That if any person or party shall neglect

Fine for refusing to obey subpœna Fee.

or refuse to obey such subpœna, he shall be fined any sum not less than Five Shillings, nor more than Five Pounds, in the discretion of the Justice or Justices before whom such witness or witnesses may be cited to appear.

SECTION 3. That the Clerk may charge to the party

Fee.

applying for the same, the sum of One Shilling and Three Pence, for every such Subpœna which he may issue as aforesaid.

SECTION 4. That all fines that may be imposed under the provisions of this By-Law, together with all sums that may be paid for Subpœnas, shall be paid to the Treasurer of the District, and shall go into and form part of the general revenues thereof, subject to the control,

Application of Fines.

direction, and application of the District Council.

SECTION 5. That in all cases in which witnesses shall have duly appeared to give evidence before this Council, or before any Committee thereof, either voluntarily or in obedience to a Subpœna duly issued and served, the Council or Committee (as the case may be) before whom

they shall appear to give evidence, shall order and direct
such witness or witnesses to be paid for his, her, or their Payment of witnesses.
loss of time and expenses, such sum or sums of money
as the Council or Committee (as the case may be) shall
deem just and equitable, which order the party or parties
upon whom it shall be made are hereby required and
directed to obey.

W. MORRIS, Warden.

No. X. BY-LAW,

Relating to certain fees. See By-Law No. 106.

The Municipal Council of the District of Johnstown
duly assembled in Council in the Town of Brockville, on
the fourteenth day of May, in the year of our Lord one
thousand eight hundred and forty two, under and by
virtue of a certain Act of the Legislature of this Province,
passed in the 4th and 5th years of the reign of Her
Majesty Queen Victoria, entitled "An Act to provide
for the better internal government of that part of this
Province which formerly constituted the Province of
Upper Canada by the establishment of Local or Municipal
Authorities therein," do ordain and enact the following
By-law, and it is hereby enacted, That each and every
Councillor of the District, and also every Justice of the
Peace for the District of Johnstown, shall at all seasonable
hours, and upon proper application, have free access to Councillors, &c., may search without fee.
the books, plans, records, and other documents, in the
hands or keeping of the Clerk of the District Council,
and also of the Treasurer of the District, without fee or
charge of any kind for any such access or investigation.

SECTION 2. That any person, other than a member of
the District Council, or a Justice of the Peace as aforesaid
who may require any such search, access or investigation
of, or to, the books, plans, records, or documents, in the
hands of the District Clerk, or District Treasurer, as
aforesaid, shall pay for every such search, access, or
investigation, the sum of One Shilling, to be paid at the Fee for search.
time of making such search or investigation as aforesaid.

SECTION 3. That all fees and emoluments collected by
the Clerk of the District, or the Treasurer of the District,
under and by virtue of this By-law, be paid to the last
named officer, and be by him placed to the public credit How to be applied.
to and for the general uses and purposes of the District.

W. MORRIS, Warden.

No. XI. BY-LAW

Sec Con. Stat. U. C, 61 Sec. 213.

Of the Municipal Council of the District of Johnstown relating to the breach or violation of any By-law.

The Council of the District of Johnstown duly assembled in Council in the Town of Brockville on Saturday the twelfth day of February, in the year of our Lord one thousand eight hundred and forty-two, by virtue of an Act passed in the 4th and 5th years of the reign of Her Majesty, Queen Victoria, entitled "An Act to provide for the better internal government of that part of this Province which formerly constituted the Province of Upper Canada by the establishment of Local or Municipal Authorities therein," do ordain and enact the following By-law, and it is hereby enacted, That for any breach or violation of any By-law now enacted, or that may hereafter be enacted by this Council, the person convicted thereof shall suffer and pay a penalty, not more than *Amount of Fine.* Five Pounds nor less than Five Shillings, in the discretion of the Court ordering the conviction, together with all reasonable costs incurred.

W. MORRIS, Warden.

No. XII. BY-LAW,

To refund certain monies therein mentioned.

Preamble. Whereas it hath been made to appear in evidence before a Select Committee of the Municipal Council of the District of Johnstown, appointed for that purpose, that certain sums of money had been paid through mistake, and in ignorance of the facts relating thereto, to the Treasurer of the said District of Johnstown, and whereas certain sums of money have been received by certain Collectors of the public rates and assessments in the notes of a certain Institution known and designated as the "Suspension Bridge Bank," which Institution at the time the said notes were so received as aforesaid, was legally authorized to issue them, and was then considered good and solvent, but has since failed and become solvent: Be it therefore ordained and enacted, and it is hereby ordained and enacted by the Municipal Council of the District of Johnstown duly assembled at the Town of Brockville, on the fourteenth day of May, in the year of Our Lord one thousand eight hundred and forty-two, That out of any funds paid to and for the public uses of the District of Johnstown and remaining unappropriated in the hands of the Treasurer, that officer be authorized to pay to the persons hereinafter mentioned, or to allow them in their accounts with the District (if any such they may have) the several and respective sums hereinafter mentioned :—

To Daniel Phillips, late Collector for the Township of Yonge, the sum of Three Pounds and Five Shillings. *Parties to whom refunded.*

To Thomas Smith, Collector of the Township of Edwardsburgh, the sum of One Pound and Fifteen Shillings.

To William Cughan, of the Township of Yonge, Three Pounds and Five Shillings.

To Nicholas Hopkins, Collector for the Township of Elizabethtown, the sum of Sixteen Pounds Three Shillings and Five Pence Half-penny.

To Christopher Gunnis, Collector for the Township of Kitley, the sum of Nine Shillings and Two-pence.

To Alexander Morris, Esquire, of the Town of Brockville, the sum of Two Pounds.

To Adiel Sherwood, Esquire, late Treasurer of the District, the sum of Five Pounds.

To James Kerker, of Gananoque, the sum of Nine Shillings.

To the Treasurer of the District of Johnstown, the sum of Fifteen Pounds, to make good to him that sum advanced to defray the expense of removing and conveying the destitute Insane persons hitherto maintained at the expense of the District to the temporary Lunatic Asylum at Toronto.

W. MORRIS, Warden.

No. XIII.—BY-LAW.

Relating to Collectors of Rates in arrears for Taxes collected by them. *See Con. Stat. U. C., Cap. 54.*

Whereas it appears that the Magistrates of the District of Johnstown in General Quarter Sessions assembled at the Town of Brockville by adjournment, on the fourth day of May, in the year of our Lord one thousand eight hundred and forty-two, have, under and by virtue of *Preamble.*

B

the thirty-eighth section of the Statute of the late Province of Upper Canada, 1 Victoria, chap. 21, issued Distress Warrants against certain Collectors of Rates and their sureties, who appeared by the List of the Treasurer of said District, prepared and placed before the said Court on the day and year aforesaid to be in arrears for rates due to the said District; And whereas the said Magistrates have expressed a doubt whether they still retain the powers contained in the said section of the said Statute, and in order to remove such doubt; Be it therefore ordained and enacted, and it is hereby ordained and enacted by the Municipal Council of the District of Johnstown in Council assembled on the fourteenth day of May, in the year of our Lord one thousand eight

Warrants issued by Quarter Sessions confirmed. hundred and forty-two, That the issuing of said Warrants by the said Court of Quarter Sessions be confirmed and declared valid, and that the said Court are hereby empowered to proceed in the collection of said rates so in arrears as aforesaid, under and by virtue of said Warrants.

SECTION 2. That in future said Court of General Quarter Sessions of the Peace of the said District, shall **Authority of Justices.** have full power and authority under and by virtue of the said section of the said Statute 1 Victoria, chap 21, to issue Distress Warrants against all such Collectors of Rates, and their sureties as may hereafter appear to be in arrear for the same time.

W. MORRIS, WARDEN.

No. XIV.—BY-LAW

To regulate certain Salaries and Allowances.—Passed 14th May, 1842.

(Repealed; see By-law No. 186, sec. 13.)

No. XV.—BY-LAW

See 12 Vic. Cap. 81. *To regulate the Bonds of certain Township Officers.* **See Con. Stat. U. C,, Cap. 54.** *—Passed May* 14, 1842.

No. XVI.—BY-LAW

To regulate the mode in which certain deductions may be made from the Township Assessments.—Passed May 14, 1842.

See Con. Stat. U. C., Cap. 54.

No. XVII.—BY-LAW

To provide for the payment of certain monies applicable to Roads.

See By-Law No. 72.

See Con. Stat. U. C., Cap. 54.

Whereas many sums of Public Money paid by Justices of the Peace to Overseers of Highways, Town Clerks, and other Public Officers, are unexpended and unaccounted for: Be it therefore ordained and enacted, and it is hereby ordained and enacted by the Municipal Council of the District of Johnstown, in Council assembled, the eleventh day of August, in the year of our Lord one thousand eight hundred and forty-two, That all sum or sums of money made to any Overseer of Highways within this District, for the purpose of being expended on the Public Highways, shall be paid over by every such Overseer of Highways to the Clerk of the Township in which he shall be an Overseer of Highways, within thirty days after its receipt by such Overseer. *Preamble.*

How monies to be expended.

SECTION 2. That it shall be the duty of every such Town Clerk once in every year, that is to say, on or before the first day of May, to apply to and to receive from the Treasurer of the District, all monies that may be then in the hands of that Officer, collected for wild land assessment, and applicable to the Roads and Bridges within the Township for which he shall be Clerk. *Town Clerk to receive monies.*

SECTION 3. That every Town Clerk within the District shall make a quarterly return of all monies paid into his hands, for public use and purposes, to the Councillor or Councillors (as the case may be) representing the Township for which he may be Clerk, setting forth by whom paid, and for what purpose particularly. *Returns to be made.*

SECTION 4. That all monies paid into the hands of any Township Clerk within this District, for the making or repairing of any Public Highway within the same, be paid over by every such Clerk to the order of the Councillor or Councillors (as the case may be) representing each and every Township in the Council *Monies to be paid to Councillors.*

of the District, to be by him or them expended within six months in the making or repairing of the Public Highways within the Township.

W. MORRIS, Warden.

No. XVIII.—BY-LAW

To regulate the mode and manner of payments of all sums by the Treasurer of the District.

Preamble. Whereas it is necessary for the future to pursue one settled and uniform practice in the payment of all sums required for the public use and purposes of the District: Be it therefore ordained and enacted, and it is hereby ordained and enacted by the Municipal Council of the District of Johnstown, duly assembled at the Town of Brockville on the fourteenth day of May, in the year of our Lord one thousand eight hundred and forty-two, That from and after the passing of this By-Law, no sum or sums of Money shall be paid by the Treasurer of the **How payments allowed.** District, or allowed to that Officer in his accounts with the public, unless it shall have been first certified by the Clerk of the District, that the said sum or sums as aforesaid were duly passed and ordered to be paid by the Council of the District.

Certificate of Clerk. SECTION 2. That upon the production to the Treasurer of any order, with the certificate of the Clerk as aforesaid, that officer be authorized, and is hereby authorized and required to pay the amount pursuant to the order and certificate, and which amount may appear therein to have been ordered and directed as aforesaid.

Acquittance to Treasurer. SECTION 3. That the production by the Treasurer of any such order and certificate as aforesaid, shall be considered by the District Auditors as a full discharge to the Treasurer for the payment from the public funds of whatsoever sum or sums may be contained in such order and certificate, and shall be allowed by such Auditors to the Treasurer in his account with the public.

W. MORRIS, Warden.

No. XIX.—BY-LAW

Of the Municipal Council of the District of Johnstown relating to certain duties of the Treasurer.

The Council of the District of Johnstown, assembled in Council in the Town of Brockville, on Saturday, the fourteenth day of May, in the year of our Lord one thousand eight hundred and forty two, by virtue of an Act passed in the 4th and 5th years of the reign of Her Majesty Queen Victoria, entitled "An Act to provide for the better internal government of that part of this Province which formerly constituted Upper Canada, by the establishment of Local or Municipal Authorities therein," do ordain and enact the following By-Law, and it is hereby enacted, That the Treasurer of the Johnstown District shall and may close the respective accounts relating to Township Assessments made in the year of our Lord one thousand eight hundred and forty-one, for the Townships of Augusta, Bastard, Burgess, Elmsley, Edwardsburgh, Kitley, rear of Leeds and Lansdowne, Marlborough, Montague, North Gower, North Crosby, Oxford, South Crosby, South Gower, Wolford and Yonge, by entries in the said accounts, remitting the balance due from each Township as *uncollectable*, and thereupon shall and may cancel or deliver up the Collector's Bonds for the same respectively. *(margin: Treasurer to close accounts with Collectors.)*

SECTION 2. That the several payments which have heretofore been made by the said Treasurer of orders passed by this Council shall be deemed and taken to be valid and legal. *(margin: Certain pay'nts confirmed.)*

W. MORRIS, Warden.

No. XX.—BY-LAW

Relating to the Assessment of the District of Johnstown for the year 1842.—Passed Aug. 11, 1842.

(Expired by Limitation)

22

No. XXI.—BY-LAW

To provide for the Assessment of Wild Lands in certain Townships therein mentioned.—Passed August 11, 1842.

(Repealed; see By-Law No. 61.)

No. XXII.—BY-LAW

Relating to the Governing Boundary of the Township of Edwardsburgh.

Preamble. Whereas the inhabitants of the Township of Edwardsburgh have, by petition, represented the great loss, uncertainty, and inconvenience they are subjected to, in consequence of having no accurate or ascertained Governing Boundary Line for that Township; And whereas it is important to effect an object so necessary and desirable, to procure the concurrence of the Eastern District in making a survey to ascertain such Governing Boundary Line as aforesaid; Be it therefore enacted and ordained, and it is hereby enacted and ordained by the Municipal Council of the District of Johnstown, assembled at the Town of Brockville, on the fourteenth day of May, in the year of our Lord one thousand eight hundred and forty-two, That John Bogert, Esquire, be authorized **Application for Mandamus.** and empowered to apply to Her Majesty's Court of Queen's Bench, in that part of this Province formerly called Upper Canada, for a Mandamus or Writ of Prerogative, requiring the Justices of the Peace to shew cause why they should not appoint an Agent for and on behalf of that District, to meet a similar officer for and on behalf of the Johnstown District, in order that such survey may be completed according to law.

Treasurer to pay expenses. Section 2. That the just, legal and necessary expenses attending such application, and arising thereout or therefrom, be paid by the Treasurer of the District, out of the general funds in his hands unexpended and unappropriated.

W. MORRIS, Warden.

No. XXIII.—BY-LAW

*For establishing a Public Highway in the Ninth Conces-
sion of the Township of North Crosby.*

Whereas a Road has been surveyed and laid out by James Bilton, Surveyor of Highway in and for the Township of North Crosby, commencing at the Town line of the Township of Bedford, and running from thence in a straight course with the side line between lots numbers twelve and thirteen in the ninth Concession of North Crosby, to a post, and marked as the centre of a road, on or near the said side line or road leading from the said Township of Bedford, and from thence to a post planted and marked on the ninth Concession line of the said Township of North Crosby, from thence on the old road, and in a direct line to a beech post, planted and marked in the centre of the road formerly travelled, to another post planted and marked in a line with the said old road, leading to the head of the West Rideau Lake; and whereas the said road will be of public benefit and advantage: Be it therefore enacted and ordained, and it is hereby enacted and ordained by the Municipal Council of the District of Johnstown, duly assembled at the Town of Brockville, on the fourteenth day of May, in the year of our Lord one thousand eight hundred and forty-two, That the said road, so surveyed and laid out by the said James Bilton as aforesaid, be declared and established, and it is hereby declared and established, as a Public Highway and Road. *(Preamble and description.)* *(Established as a Public Highway.)*

W. MORRIS, Warden.

No. XXIV.—BY-LAW

To establish a Road in the Township of South Gower.

Whereas a Road laid out by John R. Christie, Surveyor of Highways in and for the County of Grenville, commencing in the Township of South Gower, at a post marked A, planted on the line in the open ground, west side of the main road that runs between lots 6 and 7, in the fourth Concession of the said Township, and thence in a course nearly parallel with the concession line west-south-west, crossing lots 7 and 8 to a post marked *(Preamble.)* *(Description.)*

B, planted in the open ground near the Bridge crossing Beache's Mill-Pound upon lot 9, and from thence to the main road running between South Gower and Oxford, the length of the road surveyed being about one hundred and seventy rods, has been reported by him to the Council: Be it therefore ordained and enacted, and it is hereby ordained and enacted by the Municipal Council of the District of Johnstown, in Council assembled, the eleventh day of August in the year of our Lord one thousand eight hundred and forty-two, That the said

Confirmed. above described road be confirmed, and the same is hereby confirmed.

W. MORRIS, WARDEN,

No. XXV.—BY-LAW

To establish a road in the Township of Elizabethtown

Preamble. Whereas a Road laid out by Thomas Hill, Surveyor of Highways in and for the County of Leeds, commencing at the concession road between the ninth and tenth concession of Augusta to a post marked B, between lots numbers one and two in the tenth concession of Elizabethtown, thence to a post marked D, on lot number

Description. two, thence commencing at the School House, at a post marked E, on lot number four, thence to a Cedar post marked F, between lots numbers five and six, thence to the middle of lot number six to a post marked G, the boundaries or posts being all planted on the south side of the said road, and which road is forty feet in width, has been examined by and reported upon to the Municipal Council of the District of Johnstown by the said Thomas Hill: Be it therefore ordained and enacted, and it is hereby ordained and enacted by the Municipal Council of the said District, in Council assembled, at the Town of Brockville, on the eleventh day of November, in the year of our Lord one thousand eight hundred and forty-two, That the said above described road be approved of and confirmed, and it is hereby approved of and

Confirmed. confirmed.

W. MORRIS, WARDEN.

No. XXVI.—BY-LAW

To establish a Road in the Township of Wolford.

Whereas Samuel Ferguson, Surveyor of Highways **Preamble.** in and for the County of Grenville, has been petitioned by twelve freeholders of the said County to lay out a certain Road in the Township of Wolford; and whereas the said Samuel Ferguson has surveyed and laid out the said road pursuant to such petition, as follows: commencing at the front of the fourth concession be- **Description.** tween lots numbers 10 and 11, running between said lots until it intersects the fifth concession line, then east down said concession line half a mile, and from thence across lot number nine in the fifth concession, and from thence on as straight a line as the best land for making a road will permit, until it intersects the Prescott road at the residence of Robert Hair on lot number one in the ninth concession of the Township of Oxford: Be it therefore ordained and enacted by the Municipal Coun- cil of the District of Johnstown, in Council assembled at the Town of Brockville, in the year of our Lord one thousand eight hundred and forty-two, That the said **Declared a Pub-** above described road be, and the same is hereby declared **lic Highway.** to be a public road and highway.

W. MORRIS, Warden.

No. XXVII.—BY-LAW

To establish a Road in the Township of Oxford.

Whereas Tyrus Hurd, Surveyor of Highways in and **Preamble.** for the County of Grenville, has been petitioned by twelve freeholders of the said County to lay out a certain Road in the Township of Oxford; and whereas the said Tyrus Hurd has surveyed and laid out the said Road pursuant to such petition, as follows: commencing at **Description.** the public Highway on the north side of the south branch of the River Rideau, between lots numbers 16 and 17, in the fourth concession of the Township of Oxford, aforesaid, thence running along the side line south thirty-six degrees, east thirty-two rods to the fourth concession line, thence along the said line in the fifth concession thirty-one rods and half rod, then south

forty-eight degrees east, along the south side of the
south branch ninety-seven rods, opposite the falls, thence
north fifty-four degrees, east twenty-two rods to the
centre of number seventeen in the fifth concession,
thence south thirty-six degrees, east through the centre
of the fifth, sixth and seventh concessions of Oxford;
Be it therefore ordained and enacted, by the Municipal
Council of the District of Johnstown, in Council assembled, at the Town of Brockville, on the eleventh day of
November in the year of our Lord one thousand eight
hundred and forty-two, That the said above described

Declared a Pub-lic Highway. road be, and the same is hereby declared to be a public
road and highway.

W. MORRIS. WARDEN.

No. XXVIII.—BY-LAW

To establish a Road in the Township of Oxford.

Preamble. Whereas Tyrus Hurd, Surveyor of Highways in and
for the County of Grenville, has been petitioned by
twelve freeholders of the said County to lay out a certain Road in the Township of Oxford; and whereas the
said Tyrus Hurd has surveyed and laid out the said Road

Description. pursuant to such petition, as follows: commencing at the
side road between lots numbers 15 and 16 in the centre of
the fifth concession of Oxford, running north fifty-four
degrees, east across lot number 16, then north thirty-six
degrees, west twenty-nine rods, between lots numbers
sixteen and seventeen, then north forty-four degrees,
east forty-one rods, or until it intersects the road on the
south-east side of the branch or falls: Be it therefore
ordained and enacted by the Municipal Council of the
District of Johnstown in Council assembled at the Town
of Brockville, on the eleventh day of November in the
year of our Lord one thousand eight hundred and forty-

Declared a Pub-c Highway. two, That the said above described Road be, and the
same is hereby declared to be a Public Road and
Highway.

W. MORRIS, WARDEN.

No. XXIX.—BY-LAW

To close a Road in the Township of Elizabethtown.

Whereas William K. Glazier, Surveyor of Highways Preamble.
for the County of Leeds, has been petitioned by
twelve freeholders of the said County to close a certain
Road in the Township of Elizabethtown, and whereas
the said William K. Glazier has examined the said
road pursuant to such petition, as follows: commencing
at a point where the side line at the centre of lot number Description.
thirty-three in the fourth concession of Elizabethtown
intersects the concession line between the fourth and
fifth concessions of said Township, thence south westerly
about seven chains to the centre of the Creek, thence
southerly about seventeen chains and fifty links, to
where it intersects the new road near to the limit
between lots numbers 33 and 34, and at about the distance
of seventeen chains and eighty-six links from the rear
of said concession: Be it therefore ordained and enacted
by the Municipal Council of the District of Johnstown,
in Council assembled at the Town of Brockville on the
eleventh day of November, in the year of our Lord one
thousand eight hundred and forty-two, That the said
above described road be, and the same is hereby declared Declared closed.
closed.

W. MORRIS, Warden.

No. XXX.—BY-LAW

To establish a Road in the Township of Oxford.

Whereas a road laid out by Tyrus Hurd, Surveyor Preamble.
of Highways for the County of Grenville, leading from
Burritt's Bridge to Merrickville, across lot number one
in the first concession of Oxford, commencing at the
west side line and running north seventy-five degrees, Description.
east one hundred and twenty rods, and marked by
stakes or posts in the open line, the said road being
forty-five feet in width, has been reported by him, the
said Tyrus Hurd, as necessary for the public use and
convenience: Be it therefore ordained and enacted, and
it is hereby ordained and enacted by the Municipal Council of the District of Johnstown, in Council assembled,

Confirmed.

at the Town of Brockville, on the eleventh day of November, in the year of our Lord one thousand eight hundred and forty-two, That the said road laid out by the said Tyrus Hurd, as above described, be confirmed, and the same is hereby confirmed.

W. MORRIS, Warden.

No. XXXI.—BY-LAW!

To establish a Road in the Township of Oxford.

Preamble.

Whereas Tyrus Hurd, Surveyor of Highways in and for the the County of Grenville, has been petitioned by twelve freeholders of the County to lay out a certain Road in the Township of Oxford; and whereas the said Tyrus Hurd has surveyed and laid out the said Road

Description.

pursuant to such petition, as follows: commencing on the east side of the Public Highway, that is, leading from Kemptville to Prescott, then north forty-seven degrees, east eighty-one rods and an half rod, along a certain street laid down in the Village of Kemptville on lot number 27, in the third concession, then north fifty-four degrees, east fourteen rods, which intersects the above mentioned road: Be it therefore ordained and enacted by the Municipal Council of the District of Johnstown, in Council assembled, at the Town of Brockville, on the eleventh day of November, in the year of our Lord one thousand eight hundred and forty-two, That the said above described road be, and

Declared a Public Highway.

the same is hereby declared to be a public road and highway.

W. MORRIS, Warden.

No. XXXII.—BY-LAW

To establish a Road in the Township of Oxford.

Preamble.

Whereas Tyrus Hurd, Surveyor of Highways in and for the County of Grenville, has been petitioned by twelve freeholders of the said County to lay out a certain Road in the Township of Oxford; and whereas the said

Tyrus Hurd has surveyed and laid out the said Road pursuant to such petition as follows: commencing at the south side of the south branch of the River Rideau, on lot number 28, in the third concession, at the water's edge, then south thirty-six degrees, east thirty-nine rods, then north forty-nine degrees twenty-five rods and an half rod, across a Creek where a Mill Dam has been erected by Alfred Holmes and M. Barns, then south thirty-eight degrees, east eight rods and an half rod, on the east side of said Creek, then south fifty-eight degrees, east twenty-eight rods and an half rod, then south forty-nine degrees seventeen rods to the public highway, that leads from Kemptville to South Gower: Be it therefore ordained and enacted by the Municipal Council of the District of Johnstown, in Council assembled, at the Town of Brockville, on the eleventh day of November, in the year of our Lord one thousand eight hundred and forty-two, That the said above described Road be, and the same is hereby declared to be a public Road and Highway. *Description,* *Dec'ared a Public Highway,*

W. MORRIS, WARDEN.

No. XXXIII.—BY-LAW

To establish a Road in the Township of Lansdowne.

Whereas Humphrey Young, Surveyor of Highways in and for the County of Leeds, has been petitioned by twelve freeholders of the said County to survey and lay out a Road in the Township of Lansdowne; and whereas the said Humphrey Young (having first given due notice according to law) did proceed to examine, survey, and lay out the said Road pursuant to the prayer of the said petition; and whereas, the said Surveyor of Highways has been examined on oath before a Committee of the Council appointed for that purpose, and has declared the opening and establishing of the said Road to be necessary and convenient for the public use. Be it therefore enacted by the Municipal Council of the District of Johnstown, in Council assembled, at the Town of Brockville, on the eleventh day of November, in the year of our Lord one thousand eight hundred and forty-two, That the said Road commencing at a post marked R, on the north side, planted in the side line between the Road and lot number 19, in the third conces- *Preamble.* *Description.*

sion of the Township of Lansdowne, at about sixty-eight chains and fifty links from the front of the said third Concession, thence north eighty-two degrees and fifty minutes, east magnetically about twenty-nine chains and seventy-five links to a post marked R on the west and north sides, thence parallel to the side line in said concession about fifty-three chains and sixty links to the allowance for Road in rear of said third concession, which said described **Established as a Public Highway.** road is forty feet in width, be established, and the said Road is hereby established as a public Road and Highway.

W. MORRIS, Warden.

No. XXXIV.—BY-LAW

To establish a Road in the Township of Escott.

Preamble.
Whereas James Brooker, Surveyor of Highways in and for the County of Leeds, has been duly petitioned by twelve freeholders of the District to survey and lay out a road in lieu of some parts of the Town line dividing the townships of Lansdowne and Escott, in consequence of such parts being inpracticable and unfit for a road ; and whereas the said James Brooker has complied with the prayer of said petition, and surveyed and laid out a road according to the **Description,** following description ; that is to say : commencing at the water edge on the River St. Lawrence, at the Town line, at a post planted on the east side of the said line, marked R on the east side, from thence running west of north four rods nine feet to a post marked R, from thence north-easterly thirteen rods to a post marked R, from thence running nearly the same direction to a post planted twenty-one rods distant, from thence running west of north to a blazed stump seven rods, thence west by north west to a Beech tree marked R twenty-one rods, from thence to a Hemlock standing in the Town line, marked R, thirteen rods more or less, from thence along the Government allowance, or Town line, eight rods south of a Road leading to Larue's Mills, at a post planted on the west side of the allowance for Road, and marked R as aforesaid, thence running west of north thirteen rods to a post planted, thence running parallel with said allowance to a post planted twelve rods distant and marked R on the east side, from thence north of east, eighty feet more or less, to the aforesaid Town line

thence along said line to the commencement of the second range, thence running east of north ten rods to a post planted and marked R on the west side, from thence in the same direction to a post planted eight rods distant, from thence west of north seven rods to the Town line, thence along said Town line to a hemlock tree twenty-five rods from John M'Culloch's clearing, and marked R, from thence running east of north to a tree marked R twelve rods, from thence to the aforesaid Town line eight rods more or less, which said road is forty feet in width : Be it therefore enacted, and it is hereby ordained and enacted by the Municipal Council of the District, of Johnstown, in Council assembled, at the Town of Brockville, on the eleventh day of November, in the year of our Lord one thousand eight hundred and forty-two, That the said above described Road be approved of and confirmed as a public Road and Highway. Confirmed as a Public Highway.

W. MORRIS, Warden.

No. XXXV.—BY-LAW

To close a certain Road in the Township of North Crosby.

Whereas James Bilton, Surveyor of Highways in and Preamble. for the County of Leeds, has reported to the Council of the district of Johnstown, that in pursuance of a requisition to him presented by twelve freeholders of the said County, he has examined the Government allowance for road com- Description. mencing at the part of the seventh concession of the township of North Crosby, and running to the ninth concession between lots numbers 12 and 13 in the said Township of North Crosby, and that he the said James Bilton, Surveyor of Highways as aforesaid, has condemned the said allowance for road : be it therefore enacted, and it is hereby enacted and ordained by the Municipal Council of the District of Johnstown, in Council assembled, at the Town of Brockville, on the eleventh day of November, in the year of our Lord one thousand eight hundred and forty-two, That the Government allowance as above described, is hereby con- Condemned as demned as unfit for public use, travel or convenience. unfit for public use.

W. MORRIS, Warden.

No. XXXVI.—BY-LAW

To establish a Public Highway in the Townships of Bastard and South Crosby.

Preamble.

Description.

Whereas a Road has been surveyed and laid out by Henry B. Marvin, Road Surveyor in and for the County of Leeds, commencing at the Town line in the Township of Bastard, that is to say: commencing or leaving the Portland Road at the angle between lots numbers 27 and 28 in the third concession of the Township of Bastard, on the allowance for road between the second and third concessions, thence on the aforesaid allowance to the Township line between Bastard and South Crosby, thence from the termination of the said allowance for road angling across the corner of lot number 22 in the first concession of the said Township of South Crosby, nearly a southerly direction to a post planted near the said line between lots numbers 21 and 22 in the said first concession of South Crosby, thence running easterly across a part of said lot number 21 in the first concession of South Crosby, leading to the public road to Newboro', where there is a post planted at the north-west side of said new road; and that the said road be made forty feet wide: Be it therefore enacted and ordained, and it is hereby enacted and ordained by the Municipal Council of the District of Johnstown, duly assembled at the Town of Brockville, on the eleventh day of November, in the year of our Lord one thousand eight hundred and forty-two, That the said road so surveyed and laid out by the said Henry B. Marvin, as aforesaid, be declaired and established, and it is hereby declared and established as a public highway and road.

Established as a public highway.

W. MORRIS, Warden.

No. XXXVII.—BY-LAW

To establish a Road in the Township of Leeds.

Preamble.

Description.

Whereas a Road laid out by Surasten L. Soper, Surveyor of Highways in and for the County of Leeds, commencing at a post planted in the open ground near the west side line of lot number 3 in the eighth concession of the Township of Leeds, at Henry Wiltse's Landing on the bank of the Rideau Canal, and running from thence easterly across said lot to a small flow of water on the line between numbers three and four to a point of rocks on said line, then forming part of a small circle around the point of rocks on number four, about ten rods distant on to lot number three, from thence running south along the said line to a post planted within sixty feet of the flow of water in front of said lot, then easterly along the side of said flow of water to a ridge of land near the centre of lot number four, forming a point into the flow of water, thence south across said flow of water, to a post planted as the centre of the road, and intersecting the main travelled road leading to Kingston, the width of two and a half lots west from a side road leading to the ninth concession, and east of a road running nearly parallel across the corner of lot number three in the seventh concession to the Rideau Canal, has been examined by and reported on to the Municipal Council of the District of Johnstown, by him, the said Surasten L. Soper: Be it therefore ordained and enacted, and it is hereby ordained and enacted by the Municipal Council of the said District, in Council assembled, at the Town of Brockville, on the eleventh day of November, Confirmed. in the year of our Lord one thousand eight hundred and forty-two, That the said above described road be approved of, and the same is hereby approved of and confirmed.

W. MORRIS, Warden.

No. XXXVIII.—BY-LAW

To establish a Road in the Township of Yonge, formerly Escott.

Whereas John Morris, Surveyor of Highways in and Preamble. for the County of Leeds, has been petitioned by twelve freeholders of the said County, to lay out a certain Road in the Township of Yonge, formerly Escott; and whereas the said John Morris has surveyed and laid out the same road pursuant to such petition, as follows: commencing from the Queen's Highway in rear of the eighth concession Description. of the Township of Yonge, formerly Escott, running fifty-four rods between lots numbers twenty-two and twenty-three, until obstructed by a ledge of rocks called Briar-hill, from thence, to avoid said obstruction, running forty rods easterly round a certain point of said ledge, bearing

C

southerly until it strikes the above mentioned line between numbers twenty-two and twenty-three in the eighth concession aforesaid, from thence running along said line six rods to a white birch tree which is blazed on four sides, from thence south-westerly three hundred and forty-two rods across numbers twenty-two and twenty-one, following the blaze to the west side of number twenty-one, from thence following an old road across number twenty to the extremity of high rock point, and which road is forty feet wide : Be it therefore ordained and enacted, and it is hereby ordained and enacted by the Municipal Council of the said District, in Council assembled, at the Town of Brockville, on the seventeenth day of February, in the year of our Lord one thousand eight hundred and forty-three, That the above described road be approved of and confirmed, and it is hereby approved of and confirmed.

Confirmed.

W. MORRIS, WARDEN.

·No. XXXIX.—BY-LAW

To establish a Road in the Township of South Crosby.

Preamble.

Whereas Henry B. Marvin, Surveyor of Highways in and for the County of Leeds, has been petitioned by twelve freeholders of the said County to lay out a Road in the Township of South Crosby; and whereas the said Henry B. Marvin has surveyed and laid out the said road, pursuant to such petition, as follows, that is to say : commencing on lot number eleven in the first concession of South Crosby, at the road leading from the Beverly Lake, ten chains and seventy links from the side line between lots numbers eleven and ten in said concession ; thence angling across lots numbers eleven and ten in a straight line to the front of the second concession ; thence directly in the old track across number ten to the front of the third concession to a post planted two chains and thirty-eight links from the south-east corner of lot number ten, standing on the corner of number nine, and marked as north-west side of road, and from thence on to the Long Falls, which said road is forty feet in width : Be it therefore ordained and enacted, and it is hereby ordained and enacted by the Municipal Council of the said District, in Council assembled, at the Town of Brockville, on the

Description.

35

seventeenth day of February, in the year of our Lord one
thousand eight hundred and forty-three, That the above
described road be approved of and confirmed, and it is Confirmed.
hereby approved of and confirmed.

W. MORRIS, Warden.

No. XL.—BY-LAW.

*To establish a Road in the Township of Yonge,
formerly Escott.*

Whereas James Brooker, Surveyor of Highways in and Preamble.
for the County of Leeds, has been petitioned by twelve
freeholders of the said County to lay out a certain Road
in the Township of Yonge, formerly Escott; and whereas
the said James Brooker has surveyed and laid out the
said Road pursuant to such petition, as follows: com- Description.
mencing in the centre of lot number seventeen, in the
fourth concession, and running westerly on a line of
blazed trees to a hemlock tree marked R, one hundred
and forty-seven rods, more or less; from thence west by
south to the Town line, seven hundred and twenty rods
more or less, and then connecting itself with the sixth
concession of Lansdowne, and which road is fifty feet in
width: Be it therefore ordained and enacted, and it is
hereby ordained and enacted by the Municipal Council of
the said District, in Council assembled, at the Town of
Brockville, on the seventeenth day of February, in the
year of our Lord one thousand eight hundred and forty-
three, That the above described road be approved of and Confirmed.
confirmed, and the same is hereby approved of and
confirmed.

W. MORRIS, Warden.

No. XLI.—BY-LAW.

To establish a Road in the Township of South Crosby.

Whereas Henry B. Marvin, Surveyor of Highways in Preamble.
and for the County of Leeds, has been petitioned by
twelve freeholders of the said County to lay out a certain
Road in the Township of South Crosby; and whereas the

Description.

said Henry B. Marvin has surveyed and laid out the said
road pursuant to such petition, as follows, that is to say :
commencing two chains and thirty-eight links from the
south-east corner of lot number ten, in the third concession of South Crosby, on the corner of lot number nine in
said concession, thence across number ten, to a post
marked as the north side of the road, in a westerly course,
thence angling southerly in a straight course, to the allowance for road in front of fourth concession, by a stone
standing on its end, inclining easterly, about three feet
in height, and marked as the north-cast side of the road,
thence along the concession eastwardly to a post one
chain and thirty-eight links from the corner of lot number
nine in the fourth concession, thence across the corner of
number ten, and then along the side line between nine
and ten in said concession, to an ash tree marked as the
south-east side of road, thence angling across number nine
to a maple tree marked as centre of road, thence in a
straight line to a beech tree near the concession line, in
front of the Fifth Concession, marked as the north-west
side of road, thence leading southerly across lots numbers
nine and eight in the Fifth Concession, through the
Tamarack Swamp, thence angling across lot number seven
in said concession, and six in the sixth concession, in a
straight line to Jones' Falls, to a pine stump marked as
south-east side of road, which said road is forty feet wide :
Be it therefore ordained and enacted, and it is hereby
ordained and enacted by the Municipal Council of the
said District, in Council assembled, at the Town of Brockville, on the seventeenth day of February, in the year of
our Lord one thousand eight hundred and forty-three,

Confirmed.

That the above described road be approved of and confirmed, and it is hereby approved of and confirmed.

W. MORRIS, WARDEN.

No. XLII.—BY-LAW

To establish a Road in the Township of North Crosby.

Preamble.

Whereas James Bilton, Surveyor of Highways in and
for the County of Leeds, has been petitioned by twelve
freeholders of the said County to lay out a certain Road
in the Township of North Crosby; and whereas the said

James Bilton has surveyed and laid out the said road pursuant to such petition, as follows, that is to say: commencing at the ninth concession line in North Crosby, **Description.** and running on the side line between lots numbers nine and ten in the eighth concession to the post between said lots on the said concession; then running from the post on the rear of the seventh concession between lots numbers nine and ten, and following the said line between said lots to the front of the seventh concession to a post there planted and marked, and which road is forty feet in width: Be it therefore ordained and enacted by the Municipal Council of the said District, in Council assembled, at the Town of Brockville, on the seventeenth day of February, in the year of our Lord one thousand eight hundred and forty-three, That the above described road be approved of and confirmed, and it is hereby approved of and **Confirmed.** confirmed.

W. MORRIS, Warden.

No. XLIII.—BY-LAW

To impose Fines in certain cases.

See Con. Stat. U. C., Caps. 54 & 55.

Whereas it is expedient and necessary to impose a fine **Preamble.** on persons refusing or neglecting to perform the duties of the following offices: Be it therefore ordained and enacted, and it is hereby ordained and enacted by the Municipal Council of the District of Johnstown, duly assembled at the Town of Brockville, on the seventeenth day of February, in the year of our Lord one thousand eight hundred and forty-three, That from and after the first day of January, which will be in the year of our Lord one thousand eight hundred and forty-four, any person duly elected to either of the following offices who shall neglect or refuse to serve therein, without giving just cause (which cause is to be decided by the Court before whom the issue shall be tried) to the contrary, or who shall refuse to take and subscribe the oath of declaration required by law, shall forfeit and pay the fines and penalties hereinafter mentioned, that is to say:

	£	s.	d.
For refusing to serve as District Councillor,	10	0	0
As District Auditor	5	0	0
As Township Clerk	2	10	0
As Township Assessor	5	0	0

Fines.

As Township Collector...................... ..... 5 0 0
As Surveyor of Highways.................... 2 0 0
As Overseer of Highways......... .... 1 0 0
As Poundkeeper............................. 1 0 0

For neglecting to take or subscribe, the oath or declaration of Office:

	£	s.	d.
As Township Clerk	1	0	0
As Township Assessor...................	1	0	0
As Township Collector.......	2	0	0
As Surveyor of Highways.	0	10	0
As Overseer of Highways	1	0	0

No person to hold more than one office. SECTION 2. That no one person shall be allowed to fill more than one of the offices hereinafter named, viz: Town Clerk, Assessor or Collector.

W. MORRIS, WARDEN.

No. XLIV.—BY-LAW

Relating to the Assessment of the District of Johnstown for the year 1843.—Passed February 17, 1843.

(Expired by Limitation.)

No. XLV.—BY-LAW

See 6 Vic. Cap. 6.
See 18 Vic., Cap. 11.
See Con. Stat. Can., Cap. 49.

Relating to the inspection of Pot and Pearl Ashes.

Preamble. Whereas by an Act of the Provincial Legislature passed in the sixth year of Her Majesty's reign, entitled " An Act to regulate the Inspection of Pot and Pearl Ashes," the Municipal Council of the District of Johnstown in Council assembled, are authorized and empowered to appoint three fit, proper and skilful persons to act as a Board of Examiners, according to the provisions and conditions of the said above recited Statute: Be it therefore ordained and enacted by the Municipal Council of the District of Johnstown, in Council assembled, at the Town of Brockville, on the seventh day of February, in the year of our Lord one thousand eight hundred and forty-three, That Henry **Members of the Board.** Jones, Billa Flint, and William Matthie, do form a Board of Examiners.

SECTION 2. That any person or persons applying for the situation of Inspector to the Board of Examiners as aforesaid, shall pay the said Board of Examiners the sum of two pounds ten shillings, which said sum or sums so paid shall be equally divided amongst the said Board of Examiners, which said sum or sums so paid, shall be in full compensation for their services. *Fees to be paid.*

W. MORRIS, WARDEN.

No. XLVI.—BY-LAW

To establish a Road in the Township of Burgess.

Whereas James Eaton, Surveyor of Highways in and for the County of Leeds, has been duly petitioned according to law, by Peter Cole, and thirteen others, Freeholders of the said County of Leeds, to examine, lay out, and survey a certain Road in the Township of Burgess (South,) in the said County, and whereas the said James Eaton has examined, laid out and surveyed the said Road, pursuant to the prayer of the said Petition, as follows, that is to say : commencing where a post has been planted on the west side of the Government Road, leading from Portland to Oliver's Ferry, marked A, near the centre of Lot number nine in the second Concession of Burgess as aforesaid, from thence running a westerly course to a Picket planted near the Mill of Peter Cole ; thence to the allowance for road between lots six and seven, or nearly the rear of the aforesaid Concession, to where a post has been planted marked B, thence running along the allowance for road to the corner post between the second and third Concessions, from thence running a northerly course to Elias Chamberlain's, on the bank of the Rideau Lake, and which said Road is forty feet in width; Be it therefore ordained and enacted, and it is hereby ordained and enacted by the Municipal Council of the District of Johnstown, in Council assembled, at the Town of Brockville, on the eleventh day of May, in the year of our Lord one thousand eight hundred and forty-three, that the said road as above described, laid down and Surveyed, be approved of and confirmed, and the same is hereby approved of and confirmed. *Preamble. Description. Confirmed.*

W. MORRIS, WARDEN.

No. XLVII.—BY-LAW

To establish a Road in the Township of Elizabethtown.—
Passed May 11th, 1843.

(Repealed: see By-Law No. 75, Sec. 2.)

No. XLVIII.—BY-LAW

To establish a certain Road in the Township of Oxford.

Preamble.

Whereas Edward Mix, Surveyor of Highways in and for the County of Grenville, has been duly petitioned by Emaliel Dake, and eleven others, Freeholders of the said County of Grenville, to examine, lay out, and survey a certain road in the Township of Oxford, in the said County, and whereas the said Edward Mix has examined, laid out, and surveyed the said Road, pursuant to the prayer of the said petition, as follows, that is to say: commencing on the Road side at a Stone Monument fourteen chains seventy six links from lot number twenty-seven to lot number twenty-eight in the third Concession in the Township of Oxford aforesaid, running North thirty-six degrees West to the front of said Concession, from thence continuing through the second concession on the side line between lots twenty-eight and twenty-nine, one half of the road on each lot; from thence continuing said road from the rear of the first Concession to the middle, in the centre of lot number twenty-nine, to a post marked A, then north fifty-six degrees east to a post marked B, planted on the bank of the south Branch of the River Rideau, which said Road is forty feet in width: Be it therefore ordained and enacted, and it is hereby ordained and enacted by the Municipal Council of the District of Johnstown, in Council assembled, at the Town of Brockville, on the eleventh day of May, in the year of our Lord one thousand eight hundred and forty-three, that the said road as above described, laid down, and surveyed, be approved of and confirmed, and the same is hereby approved of and confirmed.

Description,

Confirmed.

W. MORRIS, Warden.

41

No, XLIX.—BY-LAW

To close a Road in Elizabethtown.

Whereas the Trustees of the Victoria Macadamized Preamble. Road, leading from Brockville to St. Francis, have decided that the formerly travelled road running through the farms of Sylvester Wright, Esquire, Smith King, Increase Smith, Description. and John Taylor, all in the fourth Concession of the Township of Elizabethtown, has become unnecessary for public use and convenience, and whereas doubts have arisen as to the power of the said Trustees to close any part of said formerly travelled Road; and whereas the aforesaid John Taylor has by Petition to this Council, bearing date the eighth of this May instant, humbly prayed that he may be allowed to enclose so much of the said formerly travelled road as crosses his farm, being part of lot number twenty-one in the fourth Concession in the said Township of Elizabethtown; and whereas the said John Taylor has by his petition as aforesaid, re-presented that he is willing to accept of the said old or formerly travelled road as aforesaid, as in lieu of, and as in full compensation for all loss and damage he may have sus-tained by reason of the said Victoria Macadamized Road passing through his Farm as aforesaid: Be it therefore enacted by the Municipal Council of the District of Johnstown duly assembled at the Town of Brockville, on the eleventh day of May, in the year of our Lord one thousand eight hundred and forty-three, That so much of the said formerly travelled road as passes through the lands of the said John Taylor on lot number twenty-one in the fourth Concession of Elizabethtown, be, and the Declared un-
necessary for same is hereby declared to be unnecessary for public use, public use. travel or convenience.

SECTION 2. And be it further enacted by the authority aforesaid, that the said John Taylor be at liberty to John Taylor al- enclose so much of the said formerly travelled road as lowed to enclose passes through his land in the said fourth Concession of part of the road. Elizabethtown, the same being in lieu of, and as in full compensation for all damages, loss and disadvantage he may have sustained for, or by reason of the construction of the said Victoria Macadamized Road, through his said premises as aforesaid.

W. MORRIS, WARDEN.

ᵛⁱNo. L.—BY-LAW

To establish a Road in the Township of Wolford.

Preamble. Whereas Samuel Fergusson, Surveyor of Highways, in and for the County of Grenville, has been petitioned by Stephen H. Merrick, and thirteen others, Freeholders of the said County, to examine, survey, and lay out a certain Road in the Township of Wolford, in the said County of Grenville, and whereas the said Samuel Fergusson has reported to a Committee of this Council, that he has, in pursuance to the prayer of said Petition, and in accordance with law, duly examined, surveyed and laid out **Description.** the said road, as follows, that is to say: commencing in the centre of lot number four in the first concession of the said Township of Wolford, at a post marked II, from thence running to a Hemlock tree marked A, on lot number six, from thence to the centre of lot number eight, and from thence to the first Concession line of Wolford, and which said road is forty feet in width: Be it therefore ordained and enacted by the Municipal Council of the District of Johnstown, in Council assembled, on the eleventh day of May, in the year of our Lord one thousand eight hundred and forty-three, that the said road as above indicated and described, be approved of and confirmed, **Confirmed.** and the same is hereby approved of and confirmed as a public Road and Highway.

W. MORRIS, Warden.

No. LI.—BY-LAW

To establish a Road in the Township of Bastard.

Preamble. Whereas James Eaton, Surveyor of Highways in and for the County of Leeds, has been petitioned by Joseph Polke, and twelve others, Freeholders of the said County, to examine, survey, and lay out a certain road in the Township of Bastard in the said County, and whereas the said James Eaton has reported to a select Committee of the Municipal Council of the District, that he has, in pursuance of the prayer of the said petition, and in accordance with law, examined, surveyed and laid out the said **Description.** road as follows, that is to say: commencing at the west side line of lot number fourteen in the second concession of Bastard, where a post has been planted marked C; thence across said lot to where a post has been planted marked D, distant about three rods from the Bridge across Shelden Creek, the said post to indicate and mark the west side of the said road, which runs a northerly course, and is nearly parallel with the road formerly travelled, and which said road is forty feet in width: Be it therefore ordained and enacted by the Municipal Council of the District of Johnstown, in Council assembled, on the eleventh day of May, in the year of our Lord one thousand eight hundred and forty-three, that the said road as above indicated and described, be approved of and confirmed, **Confirmed.** and the same is hereby approved of and confirmed as a public Road and Highway.

W. MORRIS, Warden.

No. LII.—BY-LAW

To establish a Road in the Township of Augusta.

Whereas Philemon Pennock, Esquire, Surveyor of Highways, in and for the County of Grenville, has been petitioned by Samuel J. Bellamy, Esquire, and fifteen **Preamble.** others, Freeholders of the said County of Grenville, to examine, survey, and lay out a certain road in the Township of Augusta, in the said County, and whereas the said Philemon Pennock, Esquire, has reported to a select Committee of this Council, duly appointed for that purpose, that he has, in pursuance to the prayer of the said petition, and in accordance with law, examined, surveyed, and laid out the said road, as follows, that is to say: commencing at a certain post planted on the north east side of the lower Rideau Road, on lot number nineteen in the **Description.** ninth Concession of the said Township of Augusta, on the north side of the said south Branch, and about thirteen chains therefrom, from thence following the direction of the said south Branch, in a north east course across part of lot number nineteen and the intervening lots, to lot number eight in the said ninth Concession, which said Road is fifty feet in width: Be it therefore ordained and enacted, by the Municipal Council of the District of Johnstown, duly assembled on the eleventh day of May, in the year of our Lord one thousand eight hundred and forty-three, That the said road as above indicated and described, be approved of and confirmed, **Confirmed.** and the same is hereby approved of and confirmed as a public road and highway.

W. MORRIS, Warden.

No. LIII.—BY-LAW

To establish a Road in the Township of Edwardsburgh.

Preamble.

Description.

Whereas Levi Adams, Surveyor of Highways, in and for the County of Grenville, has been petitioned by twelve Freeholders of the said County to lay out a certain road in the Township of Edwardsburgh; and whereas the said Levi Adams has surveyed and laid out the said Road pursuant to such petition, as follows: commencing at lot ten in the fifth concession of said Township, following the direction of the old survey until it intersects the allowance of Road between numbers six and seven, then thirty-five degrees east of north across number four, five and six, then seventy-five degrees east of north across lots numbers two and three, then fifty-five degrees east of north until it intersects the Town line—said road to be fifty feet in width: Be it therefore ordained and enacted by the Municipal Council of the District of Johnstown in Council assembled, at the Town of Brockville, on the fourteenth day of November, in the year of Our Lord one thousand eight hundred and forty-three, That the said above described Road be, and the same is hereby declared to be a public Road and Highway.

Declared a Public Road.

(Signed,)

OGLE R. GOWAN, Chairman.

No. LIV.—BY-LAW

To establish a Road in the Townships of Leeds and Lansdowne (in front.)

Preamble.

Description.

Whereas Humphrey Young, Surveyor of Highways in and for the County of Leeds, has been petitioned by twelve Freeholders of the said County, to lay out a certain Road in the Townships of Leeds and Lansdowne; And whereas the said Humphrey Young has surveyed and laid out the said road pursuant to such petition, as follows: commencing at a Beech Post planted on the north side of the road and at about the centre of lot number twenty-four in Lansdowne marked R I. on the south side; thence north seventy degrees, west thirteen chains fifteen links to a post marked R II.; thence north eighty-seven degrees, west seven chains fifty links to a post marked R III.; thence south eighty-eight degrees, west eleven chains fifty

links to a post marked R IV.; thence south eighty-four
degrees, west eleven chains fifty links to a post marked
R. V.; thence west eleven chains twenty-four links to a
post marked R VI.; thence north sixty-three degrees,
west seven chains twelve links to an Elm tree marked
R VII; thence south eighty degrees, west four chains
sixty links to a post marked R VIII.; thence north seventy
chains seven degrees, west seven chains ninety links to a
post marked R IX; thence north fifty-five degrees, west
twelve chains eighty links to a Hemlock tree marked R X.;
thence south seventy-four degrees, west three chains twenty
links to a Hemlock tree marked R XI.; thence north sixty
degrees, west six chains fifty links to a Hemlock tree
marked R XII.; thence north seventy-five degrees, west
seven chains to a Hemlock tree marked R XIII.; thence
north-westerly and westerly across the creek and along the
south side on the high land about nine chains to a post
marked R XIV.; thence north eighty-five degrees, west
seven chains fifty links to a post marked R XV.; thence
south forty five degrees, west two chains to a Poplar tree
marked R XVI.; thence about south seventy degrees, west
thirteen chains to a maple tree marked R XVII.; thence
south eighty degrees, west twenty-three chains fifty links
to a post marked R XVIII., at the Road mentioned in the
above petition, and I have made the said Road sixty-six
feet in width and on the south side of the said posts which
are marked with red chalk: Be it therefore ordained and
enacted and it is hereby ordained and enacted by the
Municipal Council of the District of Johnstown in Council
assembled, at the Town of Brockville, on the fifteenth day
of November, in the year of our Lord one thousand eight
hundred and forty-three, That the above described road be
approved of and confirmed, and it is hereby approved of Confirmed.
and confirmed to be a Public Highway and Road.

(Signed,)
OGLE R. GOWAN, Chairman.

No. LV.—BY-LAW

*To establish a Road in the Townships of Leeds and Lans-
downe (in front.)*

Whereas William Robinson, Surveyor of Highways in Preamble.
and for the County of Leeds, has been petitioned by twelve
Freeholders of the said County to lay out a certain Road

Description. in the Townships of Leeds and Lansdowne : and whereas the said William Robinson has surveyed and laid out the said Road, pursuant to such petition, as follows, that is to say : commencing between lots numbers seven and eight at a post on the Concession line between the third and fourth concessions, marked R on the north side of said post; thence running across lot number eight in the fourth Concession, and half of number nine by a line of marked trees on the north side of said line to a post marked R on south side of said post, the course being a little north of east round a large swamp being on said Concession line, the distance one hundred and thirty-three rods, thence bearing south to said concession line thirty-three rods to a post marked R on west and south side of said post. The width of said Road to be sixty feet : Be it therefore ordained and enacted by the Municipal Council of the District of Johnstown, in Council assembled, at the Town of Brockville, on the fifteenth day of November, in the year of our Lord one thousand eight hundred and forty-**Declared a Public Road.** three, That the above described Road be and the same is hereby declared to be a Public Road and Highway.

(Signed,)

OGLE R. GOWAN, CHAIRMAN.

No. LVI—BY-LAW

Relating to a Road leading through the Township of Wolford.—Passed November 15, 1843.

(Repealed ; see Bylaw No. LXII.)

No. LVII.—BY-LAW

To establish a Road in the Township of Yonge.

Preamble. Whereas John Morris, Surveyor of Highways, in and for the County of Leeds, has been petitioned by twelve freeholders of the said County to lay out a certain Road in the Township of Yonge ; and whereas the said John Morris has surveyed and laid out the said Road pursuant to such petition, as follows : commencing on the front of

the fifth concession running between lots numbers fifteen Description.
and sixteen, following the line in or about sixty rods to a
post planted in the open field on number fifteen in said
concession; from thence to to a Cherry tree on the bank
of the Creek near the Mill; from thence bearing north
easterly until it intersects the now travelled road on number fourteen in said concession; said Road to be fifty feet
in width: Be it therefore ordained and enacted and it
is hereby ordained and enacted by the Municipal Council
of the District of Johnstown, in Council assembled, at the
Town of Brockville, on the fifteenth day of November, in
the year of our Lord one thousand eight hundred and
forty-three, That the above described Road be approved Confirmed.
of and confirmed to be a Public Highway and Road.

(Signed,)

OGLE R. GOWAN, Chairman.

No. LVIII.—BY-LAW

To establish a Road in the Township of Elizabethtown.—
Passed February 14th, 1844.

(Repealed; see By-law No. LXXV., Sec. 2.)

No. LIX.—BY-LAW

To establish a Road in the Township of Leeds.

Whereas Humphrey Young, Surveyor of Highways in Preamble.
and for the County of Leeds, has been petitioned by
twelve freeholders of the said County to lay out a certain
Road in the Township of Leeds; And whereas the said
Humphrey Young has surveyed and laid out the said
Road pursuant to such petition as follows: commencing Description.
at a Beech stump at about twenty-five chains from the
front of the said concession, and marked on the north side
R; thence due East twenty-eight chains to a Maple
tree; thence north fifty degrees, east twenty chains to a
Hemlock tree; thence north fifty-five degrees, east ten
chains to a Maple tree; thence north eighty degrees, east
ten chains to a Maple tree; thence east eighty chains to
a Birch tree; thence south fifty degrees, east ten chains

to a Beech tree; thence north-easterly twenty-four chains to a Beech tree, where it intersects the South Lake Road, the above lines being marked by marking the trees on two sides, and the trees mentioned in the above, marked with red chalk on the north side of said Road, being one chain wide: Be it therefore ordained and enacted by the Municipal Council of the District of Johnstown, in Council assembled, at the Town of Brockville, on the fourteenth day of February, in the year of our Lord one thousand eight hundred and forty-four, **Declared a Public Road.** That the said above described Road be, and the same is hereby declared to be a public road and highway.

OGLE R. GOWAN, Chairman.

[L.S.]

No. LX.—BY-LAW

To establish a Road in the Townships of Leeds and Lansdowne (in front.)

Preamble

Whereas William Robinson, Surveyor of Highways in and for the County of Leeds, has been petitioned by twelve freeholders of the said County to lay out a certain Road in the Township of Leeds and Lansdowne in front; And whereas the said William Robinson has surveyed and laid out the said Road pursuant to such petition, as follows, that is to say : commencing at the water's edge **Description.** in Landon's Bay, on said broken front, at a post between lots numbers seven and eight marked R, on the south side of said post, then running an easterly course across lots numbers eight and nine on said broken front, and the half of number ten, to a post by a line of marked trees marked R on the south side of said post, the distance being two hundred and fifteen rods ; from thence running south of east round a ledge of rocks to a post planted on the line between lots numbers ten and eleven marked R, on the south side of said post, the distance being fifty-two rods ; from thence running an easterly direction by a line of blazed trees across lots numbers eleven, twelve and part of thirteen, two hundred and twenty-two rods to a black oak tree, standing near the water side, marked on four sides, called Night's Bay ; thence across said Bay ten rods to a Pine Tree marked on four sides, from thence running a north-easterly course one hundred and forty-seven rods across

the remaining part of thirteen and fourteen to a post near
the line between fourteen and fifteen marked R on the
south side of said post, from thence in the same direction
across lot number fifteen, eighty-one rods, to a post on the
scaling line between lots numbers fifteen and sixteen
marked R on the south side of said post; from thence on
the north side of said scaling line, nineteen rods to a post
near an offset on said scaling line, the offset running north
forty-four rods, in consequence of striking a large Marsh
near John Crea's; thence along a north-easterly direction
sixty-one rods across lot number sixteen running along
the old Road leading from John Findlay's Mill to a post
on the line between lots numbers sixteen and seventeen
marked R on the south side; from thence running the
same direction fifty-five rods to a post marked R on the
South side, where it intersects the road leading from
Trickey's Point to the main road, and the width of said
road to be forty feet: Be it therefore ordained and enacted
by the Municipal Council of the District of Johnstown, in
Council assembled, at the Town of Brockville, on the
fourteenth day of February, in the year of our Lord, one
thousand eight hundred and forty-four, That the above Declared a Pub-
described road be and the same is hereby declared to be a lic Road.
Public Road and Highway.

OGLE R. GOWAN, Chairman.

[L. S.]

No. LXI.—BY-LAW

*To repeal a By-law, entitled " By-Law to provide for the
Assessment of Wild Lands in certain Townships
therein mentioned.*

Whereas it is expedient to repeal a By-Law passed by Preamble.
the Municipal Council of the District of Johnstown, entitled
" By-Law to provide for the Assessment of Wild Lands in
certain Townships therein mentioned": Be it therefore
ordained and enacted, and it is hereby ordained and
enacted by the Municipal Council of the District of
Johnstown, in Council assembled, at the Town of Brock-
ville, on the fifteenth day of February, in the year of our Repeal of By-law
Lord one thousand eight hundred and forty-four, That No. 21.
the said By-law be, and the same is hereby repealed.

D

SECTION 2. That the surplus of Taxes is paid to the District Treasurer under the said By-Law, above the amount which would have been payable under the Statute Laws of Upper Canada, shall, by the said Treasurer, be placed at the credit of the Taxes hereafter payable under the said Statute Laws, on the Lands on which the same were paid, and that the remainder of the Tax received under such By-Law, shall by the said Treasurer be carried into account, and applied in the same way as if such By-Law had not been passed.

How taxes paid to be disposed of.

OGLE R. GOWAN, CHAIRMAN.

[L. S.]

No. LXII.—BY-LAW

To repeal By-Law No. fifty-six, entitled " By-Law relating to a Road leading through the Township of Wolford."

Preamble.

Whereas a certain By-Law was passed by the Municipal Council of the District of Johnstown, on the Fifteenth day of November, in the year of our Lord one thousand eight hundred and forty-three, entitled "By-Law relating to a Road leading through the Township of Wolford," and whereas it is necessary to rescind the said By-law: Be it therefore ordained and enacted, and it is hereby ordained and enacted by the Municipal Council of the District of Johnstown, in Council assembled at the Town of Brockville, on the fifteenth day of February, in the year of our Lord one thousand eight hundred and forty-four, That the said By-Law be rescinded, and it is hereby rescinded.

Repeal of By-law No. 56.

OGLE R. GOWAN, CHAIRMAN.

[L. S.]

No. LXIII.—BY-LAW

To establish a Road in the Township of Kitley, and close another Road in the said Township.

Preamble.

Whereas Hugh Kernahan, Surveyor of Highways in and for the County of Leeds, has been petitioned by twelve Freeholders of the said County to lay out a certain Road in the Township of Kitley; And whereas the said Hugh

Kernahan has surveyed and laid out the said Road pursuant to such petition, as follows: commencing at the centre of Lot number twelve on the allowance for Road *Description.* between Lots numbers twelve and thirteen; thence north fifty-four degrees, east between the front and rear half of the said Lot number twelve, to the Rideau Road on said Lot, the width of the Road is to be sixty feet, and all to be taken off the rear half of said Lot; And whereas it is necessary to condemn and close the old Road, which may otherwise be known, as follows: commencing on Lot number twelve in the fourth concession of the said Township of Kitley, on the rear of said Concession near the School-house, until it strikes the centre of said Concession; thence on the front of rear half of said Lot: Be it therefore ordained and enacted, and it is hereby ordained and enacted by the Municipal Council of the District of Johnstown, in Council assembled at the Town of Brockville, on the fifteenth day of February, in the year of our Lord one thousand eight hundred and forty-four, That the above described Road, as laid out by the said Hugh Kernahan as aforesaid, be approved of and *Confirmed as a* confirmed, and it is hereby approved of and confirmed to *Public Road.* be a public highway and Road, and the old Road as aforesaid be condemned and closed, and it is hereby condemned *Old road closed.* and closed.

OGLE R. GOWAN, CHAIRMAN.

[L. S.]

No. LXIV.—BY-LAW

To establish a Road in the Township of Kitley.

Whereas Hugh Kernahan, Surveyor of Highways in *Preamble.* and for the County of Leeds, has been petitioned by twelve freeholders of the said County to lay out a certain *Part repealed,* road in the Township of Kitley; And whereas the said *see By-law No.* Hugh Kernahan has surveyed and laid out the said Road *84* pursuant to such petition as follows: commencing at a *Description.* Cedar post marked with red chalk, placed near the centre of Lot number thirteen in the fifth concession of Kitley near the School House adjoining the premises of Hugh Kernahan; thence on the west half of said Lot number thirteen to a post planted on the limits between lots numbers thirteen and fourteen; thence along said limits last

mentioned south thirty-six degrees, east to the rear of said
Concession; thence on said Concession over Irish Creek
to a post planted at the line between Lots number eleven
and twelve in front of the sixth Concession of Kitley,
thence south thirty-six degrees, east along said line
between eleven and twelve to the rear of said Concession;
thence on said Concession line to the centre of Lot
number twelve in the seventh Concession of said Township; thence south thirty-six degrees, east through the
centre of the said Lot number twelve to the Rideau Road;
thence westerly along the Rideau Road to the allowance
for Road between Lots numbers twelve and thirteen;
thence along said allowance through the eighth, ninth and
part of the tenth Concessions to an Elm tree; thence
easterly in a straight line across number twelve and about
twenty rods of number eleven to the town line of Elizabethtown at the intersection of the Road leading to Peter
Cole's, the width of the said Road to be sixty feet, and the
above description applies to the centre thereof: Be it
ordained and enacted, and it is hereby ordained and
enacted, by the Municipal of the District of Johnstown,
in Council assembled at the Town of Brockville, on the
fifteenth day of February, in the year of our Lord one
thousand eight hundred and forty-four, That the above
described Road be approved of and confirmed, and it is
Confirmed.   hereby approved of and confirmed to be a Public Highway and Road.

OGLE R. GOWAN, Chairman.

[L. S.]

No, LXV.—BY-LAW

*Relating to the salary of the Clerk of the District Council.
Passed February 15, 1844.*

(Repealed; see By-law No. 186.)

No. LXVI.—BY-LAW

*Relating to the Assessment of the District of Johnstown for
the year 1844.—Passed February 15, 1844.*

(Expired by Limitation)

No. LXVII.—BY-LAW

To establish a Road in the Township of Edwardsburgh.

Whereas John McIlmoyle, Surveyor of Highways in *Preamble.*
and for the County of Grenville, has been petitioned by
twelve freeholders of the said County to lay out a certain
Road in the Township of Edwardsburgh, and whereas the
said John McIlmoyle has surveyed and laid out the said
Road pursuant to such petition as follows, viz: commenc- *Description.*
ing at the nine mile Road between numbers six and seven
in the centre of third concession of Edwardsburgh and at
a post planted in the open ground marked with red chalk
for the centre of the said Road; then running an easterly
course across number six and to the centre of number five
to a Hemlock tree marked C R for the centre of said Road,
then a straight course until it strikes the north bank of the
Black Creek, then along the said bank until it intersects
the allowance of road between Edwardsburgh and
Matilda, and the said road is forty feet in width : Be it therefore ordained and enacted by the Municipal Council of the
District of Johnstown in Council assembled at the Town
of Brockville, on the Fifteenth day of May, in the year of
our Lord one thousand eight hundred and forty-four, That *Declared a Pub-*
the said above described Road be and the same is hereby *lic Road.*
declared to be a Public Road and Highway.

OGLE R. GOWAN, CHAIRMAN.

[L. S.]

No. LXVIII.—BY-LAW

To establish a Road in the Township of Elizabethtown.

Whereas William K. Glazier, Surveyor of Highways in *Preamble.*
and for the County of Leeds, has been petitioned by
twelve freeholders of the said County to lay out a certain
Road in the said Township of Elizabethtown, and whereas
the said Wm. K. Glazier has surveyed and laid out the
said Road pursuant to such petition as follows, viz: commencing at a stake planted on the north side of the old *Description.*
Road opposite C. Leggo's House ; thence in a north easterly course until it intersects the Macadamized Road
at a point where a stake is planted crossing a part of lot
number sixteen and the west half of lot number fifteen in

the second concession of Elizabethtown, and the above mentioned stake is intended for the centre of the Road, and the said road is fifty-eight feet in width : Be it therefore enacted and ordained by the Municipal Council of the District of Johnstown in Council assembled, at the Town of Brockville, on the fifteenth day of May, in the year of our Lord one thousand eight hundred and forty-

Declared a Public Road. four, That the above described Road be, and the same is hereby declared to be a Public Highway.

OGLE R. GOWAN, Chairman.

[L. S.]

No. LXIX.—BY-LAW

To establish a Road in the Township of Yonge, formerly Escott.

Preamble. Whereas Benjamin Warren, Surveyor of Highways in and for the County of Leeds, has been petitioned by twelve freeholders of the said County to lay out a certain Road in the Township of Yonge, formerly Escott; And whereas the said Benjamin Warren has surveyed and laid out the said road pursuant to such petition as follows :

Description. commencing on the front of the third concession of Yonge, formerly Escott aforesaid, on the east line of lot number nineteen ; thence west-south-west to the side road between lots numbers eighteen and nineteen ; thence west-south-west on a line of blazed trees on the south side of said road to near the residence of William Pepper, at or near the west side line of lot number fifteen ; thence south-west to the west side of Lot number thirteen, twenty rods from the concession, more or less ; thence west-south-west to the west side of lot number eleven to a post marked R with red chalk : from thence south-south-west on a line of pickets on the north side of said road to the said third concession road now in use, twenty rods more or less, from the west line of lot number nine : the width of said road to be sixty feet, and the length is nine hundred rods more or less, passing on the north side of said line from the commencement to the west side of lot number eleven, and from thence on the south side to the concession road at lot number nine : Be it therefore enacted and ordained by the Municipal Council of the District of Johnstown, in Council assembled at the Town of Brockville, on the fifteenth day of May, in the year of our Lord one thousand eight hundred and forty-four, That the above described Road be, and the same is hereby declared to be a Public Highway and Road. Declared a Public Road.

OGLE R. GOWAN, Chairman.

[L. S.]

No. LXX.—BY-LAW

To establish a Road in the Township of Yonge, formerly Escott.

Whereas Benjamin Warren, Surveyor of Highways in and for the County of Leeds, has been petitioned by twelve freeholders of the said County, to lay out a certain Road in the Township of Yonge, formerly Escott; and whereas the said Benjamin Warren has surveyed and laid out the said road pursuant to such petition as follows: commencing on the Road now in use on the line of the fourth Concession of the said Township at the west end of the bridge on said Concession; thence west-north-west to a post marked R with red chalk four rods, more or less; thence south-south-west to the Concession line eight rods, more or less; thence along the said concession to lot number seventeen, thirty rods from the west line of said lot; thence west-by-north on a line of blazed trees and pickets on the north side of said road to a post planted on lot number fifteen marked R with red chalk; thence west-south-west to the west line of lot number eleven on a line of pickets and blazed trees to a beech tree marked R; thence south-south-west on a line of blazed trees on the east side of said road to the Concession, twenty rods from the west line of lot number ten, more or less; the width of said Road to be fifty feet, and the length is nine hundred and sixty rods: Be it therefore enacted and ordained by the Municipal Council of the District of Johnstown, in District Council assembled at the Town of Brockville, on the fifteenth day of May, in the year of our Lord one thousand eight hundred and forty-four, That the above described Road be, and the same is hereby declared to be a public highway and road. Preamble. Description. Declared a Public Road.

OGLE R. GOWAN, Chairman.

[L. S.]

No. LXXI.—BY-LAW

To establish a Road in the Township of Yonge, formerly Escott.

Preamble.

Whereas Benjamin Warren, Surveyor of Highways in and for the County of Leeds, has been petitioned by twelve freeholders of the said County to lay out a certain Road in the Township of Yonge, formerly Escott; And whereas the said Benjamin Warren has surveyed and laid out the said Road pursuant to such petition as follows:

Description.

commencing at the third Concession Road on lot number twenty-one, six rods from the line between lots numbers twenty-one and twenty-two, from a post marked R with red chalk; thence north-north-east twelve rods, more or less, across the line between lots numbers twenty-one and twenty-two; thence on the west side of lot number twenty-two on a line of pickets on the west side of said Road one hundred and twenty rods, more or less, to a post marked R; thence on the east side of lot number twenty-one on a line of pickets on the east side of said Road, twenty-five rods, more or less; thence west and by north twenty-five rods to the bridge over Jones' Mill Pond; thence on the road now in use to the Concession; thence to the Town line between Yonge, and Yonge formerly Escott; the width of the said road to be forty feet and the length eight hundred rods, more or less: Be it therefore enacted and ordained by the Municipal Council of the District of Johnstown, in District Council assembled at the Town of Brockville, on the fifteenth day of May, in the year of our Lord one thousand eight hundred and forty-four, That the

Declared a Public Road.

above described Road be, and the same is hereby declared to be a Public Highway and Road.

OGLE R. GOWAN, CHAIRMAN.

[L. S.]

No. LXXII.—BY-LAW

See By-Law No. 17.

To extend the provisions of a By-law, entitled "By-law to provide for the payment of certain monies applicable to Roads.

Preamble.

For the accommodation of the Public and of the several Township Clerks in the District of Johnstown: Be it enacted and ordained, and it is hereby enacted and ordained by the Municipal Council of the District of Johnstown in Council assembled, the fifteenth day of May, in the year of our Lord one thousand eight hundred and forty-four, That any District Councillor of any Township, or union of Townships, in the District, shall be authorised and empowered to act as an Agent for the Township Clerk of his Township, or union of Townships, and as such to receive from the Treasurer of the District, and grant receipts for any money in the hands of such Treasurer, collected from wild land assessments and applicable to the Roads and Bridges of such Township, or union of Townships, and that all payments of such money by the said Treasurer heretofore made, or hereafter to be made, to any such District Councillor shall be deemed legal and valid.

Town Clerk to receive monies.

SECTION 2. That the money so received, or which may hereafter be so received, by any District Councillor, shall by him (if not already so paid,) be forthwith paid over to the Township Clerk of his Township ; and shall be expended and accounted for in the manner provided by a By-law of the Municipal Council of the Johnstown District, entitled " By-law to provide for the payment of certain monies applicable to Roads."

Councillors to pay to Clerks.

OGLE R. GOWAN, CHAIRMAN.

[L. S.]

No. LXXIII.—BY-LAW

To establish a Road in the Township of Leeds.

Whereas Surastin L. Soper, Surveyor of Highways in and for the County of Leeds, has been petitioned by twelve freeholders to lay out a certain Road in the Township of Leeds ; and whereas the said Surastin L. Soper has surveyed and laid out the said Road pursuant to such petition as follows : commencing at a post in the open ground at the foot of the hill on the road leading from S. Haskins' to Gananoque, on lot number twelve in the seventh Concession of Leeds, then running northerly across part of lots numbers twelve and thirteen to a hill near the side line, then making a small angle north-easterly across lots numbers fourteen and fifteen to a Beech tree marked on four sides for the centre of the road ; then easterly across lot number sixteen to a Basswood tree standing on the Concession line : and the said road to be

Preamble.

Description.

forty feet in width: Be it ordained and enacted, and it is hereby ordained and enacted by the Municipal Council of the District of Johnstown, in Council assembled, at the Town of Brockville, on the fifteenth day of May, in the year of our Lord one thousand eight hundred and forty-four, That the above described Road be approved of and confirmed to be a public Highway and Road.

Confirmed.

OGLE R. GOWAN, Chairman.

[L. S.]

No. LXXIV.—BY-LAW

To establish a Road in the Township of Yonge.

Preamble.

Whereas John Morris, Surveyor of Highways in and for the County of Leeds, has been petitioned by twelve freeholders of the said County to lay out a certain Road in the Township of Yonge; and whereas the said John Morris has surveyed and laid out the said Road pursuant *Description.* to such petition, as follows: commencing at the side line between lots numbers sixteen and seventeen in the eighth Concession of the Township of Yonge aforesaid, where a Road has been laid out across numbers fifteen and sixteen, following the now travelled road near the Lake, to lot number nineteen in said concession, to a post planted on the south side of the road, from thence in a straight line to a post planted on lot number twenty-two in the seventh Concession, from thence in a straight line to a post planted on lot number twenty-six in said Concession, from thence in a straight line to a post planted on lot number twenty-three in the ninth Concession of Yonge, formerly Escott; from thence in a straight line to a post planted near the bridge on lot number twenty-two in said Concession; from thence to the Town-line of Lansdowne to meet the twelfth Concession line: the above mentioned monuments are on the south side of said Road, and the width of said Road to be fifty-five feet: Be it therefore ordained and enacted by the Municipal Council of the District of Johnstown, in Council assembled, at the Town of Brockville, on the fifteenth day of May, in the year of our Lord one thousand eight hundred and forty-four, That the said above described Road be, and the same is hereby declared *Confirmed.* to be a Public Road and Highway,

OGLE R. GOWAN, Chairman.

[L. S.]

No. LXXV.—BY-LAW

To establish a Road in the Township of Elizabethtown.

Whereas William K. Glazier, Surveyor of Highways in Preamble. and for the County of Leeds has been petitioned by twelve freeholders of the said County to lay out a certain Road in the Township of Elizabethtown; and whereas the said William K. Glazier has surveyed and laid out the said Road pursuant to such petition, as follows, viz: com- Description. mencing at a post planted and marked C, on the division line between lots numbers nineteen and twenty in front of the seventh Concession of Elizabethtown aforesaid, nearly parallel with the side road in the sixth Concession; thence following the side line thirty chains seventy-three links, being a north-westerly course, to a post marked B; thence north sixty-two chains twenty-one links to a post planted and marked D, on the west side of lot eighteen, crossing lot number nineteen and Commons; thence a north-westerly course thirty-seven chains seventy-two links to a post planted and marked E, on lot number seventeen, on the north side of Pearson's Mill-stream, crossing lot number eighteen and part of seventeen; thence a north-westerly course to the Concession Road in rear of lot seventeen, being four chains twenty-eight links to a post planted and marked A, nearly parallel with the side Road in the eighth Concession: the above described Posts are intended for the centre of the Road: the width of said Road to be forty feet: Be it therefore ordained and enacted by the Muni- cipal Council of the District of Johnstown, in Council assembled, at the Town of Brockville, on the fifteenth day of August, in the year of our Lord one thousand eight hundred and forty-four, That the said above described Declared a Pub- Road be, and the same is hereby declared to be a Public lic Road. Road and Highway.

SECTION 2. And whereas it is expedient to rescind two By-laws passed by this Council, relative to the said Road: the first passed on the eleventh day of May, 1843, entitled "A By-law to establish a Road in the Township of Elizabethtown;" and the other passed on the fourteenth day of February, 1844, entitled "A By-law to establish a Road in the Township of Elizabethtown:" Be it enacted By-Laws Nos. 47 that the two above recited By-laws be rescinded, and the and 68 repealed. same are hereby repealed and rescinded.

JOHN HOLDEN, CHAIRMAN.

[L. S.]

No. LXXVI.—BY-LAW

To establish a Road in the Townships of Kitley and Elizabethtown.

Preamble.

Whereas John Jelly, Surveyor of Highways in and for the County of Leeds, has been petitioned by twelve Freeholders of the said County, to lay out a certain Road in the Townships of Kitley and Elizabethtown, and whereas the said John Jelly has surveyed and laid out the said Road, pursuant to such petition, as follows: commencing

Description.

at the north side of the Rideau Road, at a post marked R, and planted about fifteen feet from the eastern limit of lot number twelve in the eighth Concession of Kitley; thence in a direct line nearly parallel with the side line, to a post marked R, and planted in the front of the ninth Concession of said Township, on the boundary line between lots numbers eleven and twelve in the ninth concession; thence along said boundary line to within ten rods of the rear of said Concession; thence easterly across [the south-eastern corner of lot number eleven in said Concession, and across the north-eastern corner of lot number twelve in the tenth Concession of said Township, to a point ten rods from the front of said Concession, on the side line between lots numbers eleven and twelve in the said tenth Concession; thence along said side line to within forty rods of the Town-line between Kitley and Elizabethtown; thence southeasterly across the south rear corner of lot number eleven in said tenth Concession of Kitley, to an Ironwood tree marked R, at the said Town-line; thence on the allowance for road between lots numbers twenty-four and twenty-five to the front of the eleventh Concession of Elizabethtown; thence across the north-eastern corner of lot number twenty-five in the tenth Concession of said Township, to a post marked R, and planted on the allowance for road, being about thirty-five rods from the rear of said Concession; thence along the allowance for Road to the Road passing Samuel Hanna's; thence to a post marked R in front of said Concession; thence along the allowance for Road between lots numbers twenty-four and twenty-five in the ninth Concession, to a post marked R, on the south side of a creek near John Haskin's shop; thence to a Post about twenty-eight rods from the rear of the eighth Concession; thence south-westerly about thirty rods to a post marked R; thence to Mud Creek Bridge; thence along the Road now travelled to a post marked R, about sixteen rods from the front of said Concession; thence to

a post marked R, about sixteen rods from the rear of the
seventh Concession; thence along the allowance for a road,
to a post planted in the centre of said Road about eight
rods from the front of said Concession; thence to a post
marked R, and planted in the centre of the road now
travelled, about eight rods from the rear of the sixth Concession; thence along the road now travelled, through the
remainder of the sixth, and part of the fifth Concession, to
where it intersects the Perth Road, near Bigelow's tavern.
The said Road is laid out sixty feet wide in Kitley, and
fifty feet wide in Elizabethtown; the posts planted to be
in the centre of said Road, and marked on two sides with
red chalk: Be it therefore ordained and enacted by the
Municipal Council of the District of Johnstown in Council
assembled, at the Town of Brockville, on the fifteenth day
of August, in the year of our Lord one thousand eight
hundred and forty-four, That the above described road Declared a Pub-
be, and the same is hereby declared to be a Public Road lic Road.
and Highway.

JOHN HOLDEN, Chairman.

[L. S.]

———

No. LXXVII—BY-LAW.

To establish a Road in the Township of Oxford.

Whereas Edward Mix, Surveyor of Highways in and for Preamble.
the County of Grenville, has been petitioned by twelve
freeholders of the said County, to lay out a certain Road
in the Township of Oxford; and whereas the said Edward
Mix has surveyed and laid out the Road pursuant to such
petition, as follows: commencing on the upper side of lot Description.
number sixteen in the first Concession of the Township of
Oxford, aforesaid, at a cedar post marked R number one,
planted two chains sixty links from the water's edge, at a
place known by the name of The Catchall, and running a
north-easterly course about forty-five rods to a cedar post
marked R number two, planted by the side of a large
Hemlock stump, about forty-five feet from the banks of
said river, then a little more northerly to a cedar post
marked R number three, planted at the south end of the
Bridge crossing Wild Meadow Creek, and from the north
end of said Bridge in a more easterly direction, to a post
marked R number four, planted on the allowance for road

between lots numbers twenty and twenty-one, five chains eighty links south easterly of the stone monument erected by order of the Boundary Line Commissioners; thence along said allowance to a post marked R number five, planted one chain twenty links south-easterly of said monument; then running in a line parallel with the base line to the lower side of lot number twenty-two; then running a north-easterly course to a cedar post marked R number six, and R number one planted at or near the side line between lots numbers twenty-four and twenty-five; said posts are all planted on the south side of the said Road, and marked with red chalk; and the line through the woods is marked out by blazes on trees; and the said Road is forty feet in width : Be it therefore ordained and enacted by the Municipal Council of the District of Johnstown, in Council assembled at the Town of Brockville, on the fifteenth day of August, in the year of our Lord one thousand eight hundred and forty-four, That the said

Declared a Public Road. above described Road be, and the same is hereby declared to be a Public Road and Highway.

JOHN HOLDEN, CHAIRMAN.

[L. S.]

No. LXXVIII.—BY-LAW

To establish a Road in the Township of Oxford.

Preamble. Whereas Edward Mix, Surveyor of Highways in and for the County of Grenville, has been petitioned by twelve freeholders of the said County to lay out a certain Road in the Township of Oxford; and whereas the said Edward Mix has surveyed and laid out the said Road pursuant to such petition as follows: commencing at a cedar post *Description.* marked R number six and R number one, planted on the side line between lots numbers twenty-four and twenty-five in the first Concession of the Township of Oxford, aforesaid, and at the termination of a Road just surveyed by the said Edward Mix, from the Catchall to the lower side of the aforesaid lot number twenty-four, and running in a north-easterly direction to the centre of said lot number twenty-five; then a more northerly course to a post marked R number two, planted on the upper side of lot number twenty-six, four chains fifty-five links in

front of the base line; then north-easterly to a post in
front of Alexander Beckett's house; then easterly along
the bank of the Rideau River to the road leading from
said river to Kemptville, between lots numbers twenty-six
and twenty seven; said posts are all planted on the south
side of the said road, and marked with red chalk, and the
line through the woods by blazes on trees; and the width
of the said Road to be forty feet: Be it therefore ordained
and enacted by the Municipal Council of the District of
Johnstown, in Council assembled at the Town of Brockville, on the fifteenth day of August, in the year of our
Lord one thousand eight hundred and forty-four, That the **Declared a Pub-**
said above described Road be, and the same is hereby **lic Road.**
declared to be a Public Road and Highway:

JOHN HOLDEN, Chairman.

[L. S.]

No. LXXIX,—BY-LAW

To establish a Road in the Township of South Crosby.

Whereas Henry B. Marvin, Surveyor of Highways in **Preamble.**
and for the County of Leeds, has been petitioned by twelve
freeholders of the said County to lay out a certain Road
in the Township of South Crosby; And whereas the said
Henry B. Marvin has surveyed and laid out the said road
pursuant to such petition, as follows, viz: commencing at **Description.**
the south-west corner of lot number thirteen in the third
Concession of South Crosby aforesaid, and leading across
the corner of said lot in a circular form directly in the old
track, the distance of eight chains; thence turning westward on to the allowance for a road between the third and
fourth concessions of said Township, and continues on the
same to a Maple stump at the foot of the hill on lot
number fourteen, marked as north side of the road; thence
angling westward on to the old track to an Elm tree,
marked as north side of road; thence north to a post
near the point of a hill marked north side of road;
thence angling westward along the foot of said hill;
again intersecting the old track near the side line
between lots numbers fourteen and fifteen in the fourth
Concession, at an Elm tree marked north side of Road;
said Road to be forty feet in width: Be it therefore
ordained and enacted by the Municipal Council of the

District of Johnstown, in Council assembled, at the Town of Brockville, on the fifteenth day of August, in the year of our Lord one thousand eight hundred and forty-four, *Declared a Public Road.* That the above described road be, and the same is hereby declared to be a Public Road and Highway.

JOHN HOLDEN, Chairman.

[L.S.]

No. LXXX.—BY-LAW

To establish a Road in the Township of Augusta.

Preamble. Whereas Philemon Pennock, Surveyor of Highways in and for the County of Grenville, has been petitioned by twelve freeholders of the said County to lay out a certain Road in the Township of Augusta; And whereas the said Philemon Pennock has surveyed and laid out the said *Description.* road pursuant to such petition, as follows, viz: commencing at the now travelled road across the fifth Concession of said Township, on the south side of lot number nineteen, and from the said road, on the north side of the line dividing lots numbers nineteen and twenty, to the allowance or Concession road between the fifth and sixth Concessions in Augusta aforesaid—a distance of about seventy rods, more or less; the above described road commences at a Cedar post marked R, and terminates at another Cedar post marked R, and in the centre of the said new road, and by planting stakes in the intermediate space, a distance of seventy rods, more or less also; which said road is forty feet wide: Be it therefore ordained and enacted by the Municipal Council of the District of Johnstown, in Council assembled, at the Town of Brockville, on the fifteenth day of August, in the year of our Lord one thousand eight hundred and forty-four, That the above described Road be and the same is hereby *Declared a Public Road.* declared to be a Public Road and Highway.

JOHN HOLDEN, Chairman.

[L. S.]

No. LXXXI.—BY-LAW

To establish a Road in the Township of Yonge, formerly Escott.

Whereas Benjamin Warren, Surveyor of Highways in Preamble. and for the County of Leeds, has been petitioned by twelve freeholders of the said County to lay out a certain road in the Township of Yonge, formerly Escott: And whereas the said Benjamin Warren has surveyed and laid out the said Road pursuant to such petition, as follows: commencing at the western extremity of the established Road, Description. known as the Road leading to Peter Trickey's Mill in the fifth Concession of said Township, from a post planted on the south side of said Road on lot number twenty-one marked R with red chalk; from thence on a line of blazed trees a south-west course across part of lot number twenty-one; thence on a line of pickets to the line between lots numbers twenty-one and twenty to a post on said line marked R; thence on a line of pickets across lot number twenty to a post planted between said lot number twenty and lot number nineteen, on a line of blazed trees across lot number nineteen to the allowance for a side road between lots numbers nineteen and eighteen; thence on said allowance to the Concession in front of said fifth Concession ninety rods more or less, the whole of said road being and running a south-westerly course, and to be forty feet in width: Be it therefore ordained and enacted by the Municipal Council of the District of Johnstown, in Council assembled, at the Town of Brockville, on the fifteenth day of August, in the year of our Lord one thousand eight hundred and forty-four, That the above Declared a Pub- described Road be, and the same is hereby declared to be lic Road. a Public Road and Highway.

JOHN HOLDEN, Chairman.

[L. S.]

No. LXXXII.—BY-LAW

To establish a Road in the Township of Bastard.

Whereas James Schofield, Surveyor of Highways in and Preamble. for the County of Leeds, has been petitioned by twelve freeholders of the said County to lay out a certain Road in the Township of Bastard; and whereas the said James

E

Description. Schofield has surveyed and laid out the said Road pursuant to such petition, as follows, viz: commencing on the side line between lots numbers sixteen and seventeen in the eighth Concession, where the Road leading from the Stone School-house to Beverly intersects said line; thence running parallel with the said side line to intersect the Concession line between the eighth and ninth Concessions in the Township of Bastard aforesaid; said Road is laid out on the eastern side of the above mentioned side line, and to be one chain wide; Be it therefore ordained and enacted, and it is hereby ordained and enacted by the Municipal Council of the District of Johnstown, in Council assembled, at the Town of Brockville, on the fifteenth day of August, in the year of our Lord one thousand eight hundred and forty-four, That the said Road as above described, laid down, and surveyed, be approved of and confirmed, and the same is hereby

Confirmed. approved of and confirmed.

JOHN HOLDEN, Chairman.

[L. S.]

No. LXXXIII.—BY-LAW

See Con. Stat. U. C., Cap. 65. *To remove doubts concerning the performance of Statute Labor by persons not assessed.—Passed August 14, 1844.*

(Repealed; see 13 and 14 Vic., ch. 66.)

No. LXXXIV.—BY-LAW

To repeal a part of By-law number sixty-four, entitled "By-Law to establish a Road in the Township of Kitley."

Preamble. Whereas a certain By-law was passed by the Municipal Council of the District of Johnstown, on the fifteenth day of February, in the year of our Lord one thousand eight hundred and forty-four, entitled "*By-law to establish a Road in the Township of Kitley,*" and whereas it is **Part By-law No. 64 repealed.** necessary to rescind a part of the said By-law: Be it therefore ordained and enacted, and it is hereby ordained and enacted by the Municipal Council of the District of Johnstown, in Council assembled, at the Town of Brockville, on the fifteenth day of August, in the year of our Lord one thousand eight hundred and forty-four, That the following portion of said By-law be rescinded, and it is hereby rescinded, viz: "Thence westerly along the Rideau Road to the allowance for Road between lots numbers twelve and thirteen, thence along said allowance through the eighth, ninth and part of the tenth Concession to an Elm tree; thence easterly in a straight line across number twelve and about twenty rods of number eleven to the Town-line of Elizabethtown, at the intersection of the Road leading to Peter Cole's."

JOHN HOLDEN, Chairman.

[L. S.]

No. LXXXV.—BY-LAW

For raising, levying, and collecting of Assessed Rate from the inhabitants of sundry School Districts within the District of Johnstown.

Whereas by an Act passed by the parliament of this Preamble. Province in the fourth and fifth years of Her Majesty's Reign, entitled "*An Act to provide for the better internal Government of that part of this Province which formerly constituted the Province of Upper Canada, by the establishment of Local or Municipal authorities therein,*" it is amongst other things enacted that the Municipal Council of the District may cause an Assessment to be made and collected from the inhabitants providing for the establishment of, and a reasonable allowance for the support of schools; and whereas applications have been made to this Council, by the Trustees duly and legally appointed for several School Districts, praying that a local tax or assessment, may be levied on such Districts, for the purpose of education within the same: Be it therefore enacted by the Municipal Council of the District of Johnstown, assembled at the Town of Brockville, on Thursday, the fifteenth day of August, in the year of our Lord one thousand eight hundred and forty-four, That for the purpose of education, that is to say, for the erection, repair, and completion of certain School Houses, now required to be built, erected or repaired, in certain School Districts hereinafter mentioned, there shall be raised, and levied upon all real and personal property therein, the following sums:—

In the Township of Yonge, formerly Escott,

Sums to be levied. In School District Number Twenty-six, the sum of Thirty pounds.

In the Township of Bastard,

In School District Number One the sum of Twenty Pounds.

In the Township of Yonge,

In School District Number Three, the sum of Fifty Pounds.

In School District Number Seven, the sum of Thirty Pounds.

In the Township of Oxford,

In School District Number Ten, the sum of Ten Pounds.

How rated and collected: SECTION 2. That the said sums be rated equally upon all the assessed property in each of the said School Districts respectively, and be levied and collected by the Collectors of the several Townships hereinbefore named, within the School Districts aforesaid, in the same manner as is now by law provided, and be by them paid to the Superintendents of the several Townships, under the provisions and restrictions of the twelfth section of an Act passed by the Parliament of this Province, on the ninth day of December, in the year of our Lord one thousand eight hundred and forty-three, entitled "*An Act for the establishment and maintenance of Common Schools in Upper Canada.*"

JOHN HOLDEN, CHAIRMAN.

[L. S.]

No. LXXXVI.—BY-LAW

For the purpose of raising a Sum for the payment of the District and Township Superintendents of the District of Johnstown for 1844.—Passed August 15, 1844.

(Expired by Limitation.)

No LXXXVII.—BY-LAW

To establish a Road in the Township of South Gower.

Whereas John Byce, Surveyor of Highways in and Preamble.
for the County of Grenville, has been petitioned by twelve
freeholders of the said County, to lay out a certain Road
in the Township of South Gower; and whereas the said
John Byce has laid out and surveyed the said Road pursuant to such petition as follows: commencing on the line
between lots numbers six and seven in the third conces- Description.
sion about one hundred rods from the front of said concession at a post planted on the open ground on the north
side of the road now in use, marked A with red chalk;
then running a little to the west from the parallel line
about sixty-six rods to a post marked B with red chalk
in the open ground; then a little south about fourteen
rods to a post in the open ground marked C with red chalk,
being on a line or nearly so between lots numbers seven
and eight, then leaving the old road running a more westerly
course about eighty-two rods to a post planted in the open
ground marked D with red chalk; then a little south to a
post planted in the open ground marked E with red chalk,
about seventy-eight rods; then seventy-four rods to a post
planted in the open ground marked F with red chalk;
thence to a Beech tree marked G with red chalk, about
eighty rods; thence to a post on Oxford line marked H,
about forty-five rods, being about one hundred rods from
the front of said concession; the said road is surveyed
forty feet wide: Be it therefore ordained and enacted by
the Municipal Council of the District of Johnstown, in
Council assembled at the Town of Brockville, on the
thirteenth day of November, in the year of our Lord one
thousand eight hundred and forty-four, That the said Declared a Pub-
above described road be and the same is hereby declared lic Road.
to be a Public Road and Highway

JOHN HOLDEN, Chairman.

[L. S.]

No. LXXXVIII.—BY-LAW

*To establish a Road in the Township of Edwardsburgh,
and to close an old Road in the same Township.*

Whereas Levi Adams, Surveyor of Highways in and Preamble.
for the County of Grenville, has been petitioned by twelve

freeholders to lay out a certain Road in the Township of Edwardsburgh; and whereas the said Levi Adams has surveyed and laid out the said Road pursuant to such **Description.** petition as follows: commencing at the corner post of the division line of lot number thirty-six in the seventh concession of the Township of Edwardsburgh aforesaid: thence following the direction of said centre line until it intersects the allowance for road in rear of said lot, and the said road to be forty feet in width: Be it therefore ordained and enacted by the Municipal Council of the District of Johnstown, in Council assembled at the Town of Brockville, on the thirteenth day of November, in the year of our Lord one thousand eight hundred and **Declared a Pub-** forty-four, That the said above described Road be, and **lic Road.** the same is hereby declared a Public Road and Highway.

SECTION 2. And whereas it is expedient to close an old Road in the vicinity of the said above described Road established by an order of the Quarter Sessions in the month of February, in the year of our Lord one thousand eight hundred and forty-one: Be it therefore enacted by **Old road closed.** the authority aforesaid, that the said old Road be condemned and closed, and it is hereby condemned and closed.

JOHN HOLDEN, CHAIRMAN.

[L. S.]

No. LXXXIX.—BY-LAW

To establish a Road in the Township of Yonge.

Preamble. Whereas Benjamin Warren, Surveyor of Highways in and for the County of Leeds, has been petitioned by twelve freeholders of the said County to lay out a certain Road in the Township of Yonge; and whereas the said Benjamin Warren has surveyed and laid out the said Road pursuant to such petition as follows: commencing at a **Description.** post planted on the concession line between lots numbers fourteen and fifteen and on the line between the broken front and first Concession of the Township of Yonge, aforesaid; from thence on the south side of said line ninety rods, more or less, to a post planted on said line marked R; from thence angling to the north of said concession line a westerly course on a line of pickets twenty rods, more or less, to a post planted on lot number sixteen marked R on the south side; from thence

71

on a line of pickets and blazed trees, a southerly course
to the concession line thirty rods, more or less, to a post
planted between lots numbers sixteen and seventeen
marked R with red chalk; from thence along the said
concession line to the centre of lot number seventeen;
angling thence a north-westerly course from a post planted
in rear of the dwelling of Harmon Guile to another planted near the concession line; thence on the road now in
use across the west half of lot number seventeen; thence
on the south side of said concession line across lot number
eighteen in the broken front where it intersects the side
road running between lots numbers eighteen and nineteen;
the said Road is laid out forty feet in width: Be it therefore ordained and enacted by the Municipal Council of
the District of Johnstown, in Council assembled at the
Town of Brockville, on the thirteenth day of November,
in the year of our Lord one thousand eight hundred and
forty-four, That the above described Road be, and the Declared a Pub-
same is hereby declared to be a public Road and Highway. lic Road.

JOHN HOLDEN, Chairman.

[L.S.]

No. XC.—BY-LAW

To establish a Road in the Township of Augusta.

Whereas Philemon Pennock, Surveyor of Roads in and Preamble.
for the County of Grenville, has been petitioned by twelve
freeholders of the said County to lay out a certain Road
in the Township of Augusta; and whereas the said Philemon Pennock has surveyed and laid out the said road
pursuant to such petition, as follows: commencing at the
rear of the ninth concession in the Township of Augusta Description.
aforesaid, at the centre of lot number ten at a Cedar post
planted and marked R; and the said surveyor has planted
another Cedar post marked as above, in the centre of the
said Road, at the distance of twenty chains from each
other, to where it terminates on the road leading from
Thomas Hutton's to the lower Rideau Road, and through
the ninth concession; the length of the said new road is
one hundred chains running about twenty-five degrees east
of south through the centre of said lot, and that the width
of the said new Road is forty feet: Be it therefore ordained and enacted by the Municipal Council of the Dis-

trict of Johnstown, in Council assembled at the Town of Brockville, on the thirteenth day of November, in the year of our Lord one thousand eight hundred and forty-four, That the above described road be, and the same is hereby declared to be a public Road and Highway.

Declared a Public Road.

JOHN HOLDEN, Chairman.

[L.S.]

No. XCI.—BY-LAW

To establish a Road in the Township of Bastard.

Preamble.

Whereas James Eaton, Surveyor of Highways in and for the County of Leeds, has been petitioned by twelve freeholders of the said County, to lay out a certain road in the Township of Bastard; and whereas the said James Eaton has surveyed and laid out the said Road pursuant to such petition, as follows: commencing on the Road

Description.

leading from Portland to Smith's Falls, at a Maple tree blazed on four sides between lots numbers nine and ten in the second concession of the Township of Bastard aforesaid; thence running equally on each of said lots to the corner post between the first and second concessions; thence running to a post planted on lot number 9 marked B first concession, supposed to have been about thirty rods of the line between lots numbers eight and nine in said concession; thence taking a northerly course to the Town line between Bastard and Burgess, to a post between lots numbers four and five in the first concession of the Township of Burgess aforesaid; then taking a north-westerly course until it intersects the Road leading from New Boyne to Gile's Mill, the blazed trees and stakes on the said surveyed road are intended to indicate the centre thereof, and the said Road is to be forty feet in width: Be it therefore ordained and enacted by the Municipal Council of the District of Johnstown in Council assembled, at the Town of Brockville, on the thirteenth day of November, in the year of our Lord one thousand eight hundred and forty-four, That the above described Road be, and the same is hereby declared to be a public Road and Highway.

Declared a Public Road.

JOHN HOLDEN, Chairman.

[L. S.]

No. XCII.—BY-LAW

To establish a Road in the Township of Bastard.

Whereas James Eaton, Surveyor of Highways in and **Preamble.**
for the County of Leeds, has been petitioned by twelve
freeholders of the said County to lay out a certain Road
in the Township of Bastard; And whereas the said James
Eaton has surveyed and laid out the said road pursuant to
such petition as follows: commencing at a corner post **Description.**
between lots numbers twelve and thirteen in the eighth
concession of the Township of Bastard aforesaid; running
thence on the Government allowance to a post which has
been planted at a swamp which intersects the said Government allowance; then turning on the south side of the
said post, and running an easterly course until it intersects
the old Road that runs angling across lot number twelve;
the said road to be sixty feet width up to the said post;
from thence to where it intersects the said road to be forty
feet in width: Be it therefore ordained and enacted by
the Municipal Council of the District of Johnstown, in
Council assembled, at the Town of Brockville, on the
thirteenth day of November, in the year of our Lord one
thousand eight hundred and forty-four, That the said above **Declared a Pub-**
described road be, and the same is hereby declared to be **lic Road**
a public Road and Highway.

JOHN HOLDEN, CHAIRMAN.

[L. S.]

No. XCIII.—BY-LAW

To establish a road in the Township of Wolford.

Whereas Michael Kelly, Surveyor of Highways in and **Preamble**
for the County of Grenville, has been petitioned by twelve
freeholders of said County, to lay out a certain Road in
the Township of Wolford; And whereas the said Michael
Kelly has surveyed and laid out the said Road pursuant
to such petition as follows: commencing near the centre
of lot number four on the first concession line, where a post **Description.**
is planted in the centre of the Road; thence in a south-
westerly course to a post planted and marked in the centre
of the Road near the end of the Beaver Meadow Bridge
one hundred and eighty rods; thence across said Bridge

to a post planted and marked in the centre of the road forty-four rods; thence to a Beech tree, blazed, in the centre of the road, one hundred and thirty-six rods : thence to a Birch tree, blazed, in the centre of the road, forty rods; thence to a Hemlock tree, blazed, seventy-eight rods; thence along the line between E. Collar's, Esq., and Hugh Mageever's on the east side of the said line until it intersects the road in front of the first concession about one hundred and sixty rods, the said road is forty feet in width: Be it therefore ordained and enacted by the Municipal Council of the District of Johnstown in Council assembled at the Town of Brockville, on the thirteenth day of November, in the year of our Lord one thousand eight hundred and forty-four, That the said above described

Declared a Public Road. road be, and the same is hereby declared to be a public Road and Highway.

JOHN HOLDEN, Chairman.

[L. S.]

No. XCIV.—BY-LAW

For the raising, levying, and collecting of an Assessment Rate from the Inhabitants of sundry School Districts within the District of Johnstown.

Preamble. Whereas by an Act passed by the Parliament of this Province, in the fourth and fifth year of Her Majesty's reign, entitled "*An Act for the better internal Government of that part of this Province which formerly constituted the Province of Upper Canada, by the establishment of Local or Municipal Authorities therein,*" it is amongst other things enacted, that the Municipal Council of the District may cause an Assessment to be made and collected from the inhabitants, providing for the establishment of and a reasonable allowance for the support of schools; And whereas applications have been made to this Council, by the Trustees duly and legally appointed for several School Districts, praying that a Local Tax or Assessment may be levied on such Districts for the purposes of Education within the same: Be it therefore ordained and enacted by the Municipal Council of the District of Johnstown assembled at the Town of Brockville, on Thursday, the fourteenth day of November, in the year of our Lord one thousand eight hundred and forty-four, That for the purposes of Education, that is to say : for the erection, repair, and completion of certain School Houses, now required to be built, erected, or repaired in certain School-Districts hereinafter mentioned, there shall be raised and levied for the present year upon all real and personal property therein, the following sums, clear of the expenses of levying and collecting, namely :—

In the Township of Oxford,

In School-District number fourteen, the sum of fifteen Pounds.

Sums to be levied.

In the Township of Edwardsburgh,

In School-District number sixteen, the sum of twenty-five Pounds.

SECTION 2. That the said sums be rated equally upon all the assessed property in each School-District respectively, by the Clerk of the Peace, and be levied and collected by the Collectors of the several Townships hereinbefore named within the School Districts aforesaid, in the same manner as is now by law provided, and be by them paid to the Superintendents of the several Townships, under the provisions and restrictions of the twelfth section of an Act passed by the Parliament of this Province, on the ninth day of December, in the year of our Lord one thousand eight hundred and forty-three, entitled *"An Act for the establishment and maintenance of Common Schools in Upper Canada."*

How rated and collected.

SECTION 3. That the said sums shall be rated on the Collector's Rolls of the said Townships respectively for the next year, and be collected by the Collectors appointed for the said last mentioned year.

Collectors' Rolls.

JOHN HOLDEN, CHAIRMAN.

[L.S.]

No. XCV—BY-LAW

See Con. Stat. U. C., Cap. 54.

To repeal part of By-Law passed on the fourteenth day of May, in the year of our Lord one thousand eight hundred and forty two, entitled " By-Law to define the duty of Surveyors of Highways, and for other purposes therein mentioned."

The Municipal Council of the District of Johnstown, duly assembled at the Town of Brockville, on the fourteenth day of November, in the year of our Lord one thousand eight hundred and forty-four, under and by virtue of a certain Act of the Legislature of this Province passed in the fourth and fifth years of Her Majesty's reign, entitled *" An Act to provide for the better internal Government of that part of this Province which formerly constituted the Province of Upper Canada, by the establishment of Local and Municipal Authorities therein,"* do ordain and it

Sec. 4 and part sec. 8 of By-law No. 3 repealed.

is hereby ordained and enacted, That the fourth section and so much of the eighth section as relates to the personal attendance of Road Surveyors upon this Council, of a certain By-Law passed by this Council on the fourteenth day of May, in the first year aforesaid, shall be, and are hereby repealed.

SECTION 2. That in future all Reports of Road Surveyors shall be in the form following, that is to say :

Form of report. *District of Johnstown,* I ———————, Surveyor of *to wit :* Highways in and for the County of ———, in the said District, being duly sworn, do declare that on application in writing made to me by twelve freeholders of said County of ———, bearing date the —— day of ———, in the year ——, stating as follows (here insert the petition verbatim, with names of freeholders): I proceeded to examine the same, which I have surveyed and laid out as follows, that is to say (here insert the description of road as surveyed): and I have made the said road —— feet in width. I do further declare that I gave due public notice of this survey according to law, by affixing a copy of this Report, in three of the most public places next adjacent to the place where the aforesaid survey has been made.

Dated at ———, this —— day of ——, 18 .

—— ———,
Surveyor of Highways for the County of ———.

Sworn before me the —— day of ———, 18 .

Which Report may be sworn to before any Justice of the Peace for the District.

SECTION 3. That in future no compensation shall be allowed to any Road Surveyor for attendance upon this Council, unless so required to attend by a Resolution or By-Law of the Council. *No compensation for attendance.*

JOHN HOLDEN, CHAIRMAN.

[L. S.]

No. XCVI.—BY-LAW

To determine the number of Councillors to go out of office, according to the provisions of the Municipal Council Act.

Whereas at the Session of this Council held in the month of November, in the year of our Lord one thousand eight hundred and forty-two, it consisted of a number of Councillors divisible into three equal parts, and it was not then necessary to pass any By-Law to determine the number to go out of office according to the statute; but from the increase since of the inhabitant Householders and Freeholders in certain Townships, and the election of two additional Councillors, this Council now consists of a number of Councillors not divisible into three equal parts, and it is therefore necessary to fix and determine the number to go out of office at the end of this and the two following years respectively: Be it therefore ordained and enacted by the Municipal Council of the District of Johnstown, in Council assembled at the Town of Brockville, on the fourteenth day of November, in the year of our Lord one thousand eight hundred and forty-four, That on the first Monday in January next, seven Councillors shall go out of office; on the first Monday in January thereafter, nine; and the remaining Councillors on the first Monday in January which will be in the year of our Lord one thousand eight hundred and forty-seven, so that at the end of three years from January last none of the Councillors now composing this Council shall remain in office. *Preamble.* *Number to go out at certain periods.*

JOHN HOLDEN, CHAIRMAN.

[L. S.]

78

No. XCVI.—BY-LAW

See Con. Stat. U. C., Cap. 54. *To complete the authority of the several Overseers of Roads in the District of Johnstown.—Passed February 12, 1845.*

No. XCVII.—BY-LAW

To establish a new Road, and to close an old one in the Township of South Gower.

Preamble. Whereas John Byce, Surveyor of Highways in and for the County of Grenville, has been petitioned by twelve freeholders of the said County, to lay out a certain Road in the Township of South Gower; and whereas the said John Byce has surveyed and laid out the said Road pursuant to such petition, as follows: commencing at the **Description.** south side of the Road between the Townships of Mountain and South Gower, in the fifth concession of the last named Township, immediately opposite to the Road running westerly through the sixth concession of Mountain aforesaid; thence running a little to the south of west across lots numbers one, two, and about three-fourths of the way across lot number three, to a gate on the south side of the old road; the distance of the new survey being about two hundred and thirty rods, and the Road to be forty feet in width, and on the north side of the line; And whereas it is necessary to condemn and close the old road, which may be otherwise known as follows: commencing at the township line between Mountain and Gower aforesaid, and extending through the south half of lot number one and number two in the fifth concession of South Gower aforesaid, until it intersects the new road: Be it therefore ordained and enacted, and it is hereby ordained and enacted by the Municipal Council of the District of Johnstown, in Council assembled at the Town of Brockville, on the twelfth day of February, in the year of our Lord one thousand eight hundred and forty-five, **New road con-** That the above described Road, as laid out by the said **firmed.** John Byce as aforesaid, be approved of and confirmed, and it is hereby approved of and confirmed to be a public Highway and road, and that the old road, as aforesaid, be condemned and closed, and it is hereby condemned and **Old road closed.** closed.

W. S. MACDONALD, Chairman.

[L.S.]

No. XCVIII.—BY-LAW

To establish a Road in the Township of Yonge.

Whereas Benjamin Warren, Surveyor of Highways in Preamble. and for the County of Leeds, has been petitioned by twelve freeholders of the said County, to lay out a Road in the Township of Yonge; and whereas the said Benjamin Warren has surveyed and laid out the said Road pursuant to such petition as follows: commencing in front of the sixth concession of Yonge, formerly Description. Escott, at a post planted on the Town line, at the south-east angle of lot number twenty-four; thence on the east side of said line, eighteen rods more or less, passing a ledge of rocks; from thence angling to the south-west of said line to the allowance for a Road on the Escottside of the line; thence along said allowance to a post planted on the aforesaid line marked R on the south side; from thence on a line of blazed trees, a north-east course to the centre of lot number twenty-six in the Township of Yonge, to a post marked R; thence on a line of blazed trees a north-east course to a Beech tree blazed on two sides and marked R where it intersects the present travelled Road leading to Charleston, one hundred rods more or less from the Concession line in rear of the fourth Concession, passing on the south side of said Monuments, across lot number twenty-six; the width of said Road to be forty feet: Be it therefore ordained and enacted, and it is hereby ordained and enacted by the Municipal Council of the District of Johnstown, in Council assembled at the Town of Brockville, on the twelfth day of February, in the year of our Lord one thousand eight hundred and forty-five, That the above described Road be approved of and confirmed, and it is hereby approved of and con- Confirmed. firmed to be a public Highway and Road.

W. S. MACDONALD, Chairman.

[L. S.]

No. XCIX—BY-LAW.

To establish a Road in the Township of Yonge.

Whereas Benjamin Warren, Surveyor of Highways in Preamble. and for the County of Leeds, has been petitioned by twelve freeholders of the said County to lay out a certain

Description. Road in the Township of Yonge; and whereas the said Benjamin Warren has surveyed and laid out the said road pursuant to such petition as follows: commencing on the line between lots numbers seventeen and eighteen in the fourth Concession of the Township of Yonge, from a post planted on the south side of the present travelled Road, marked R, known by the Road to Dr. Week's; from thence west-south-west to the centre of lot number eighteen; thence on a straight line to another post planted in the open ground, where it intersects the present travelled Road, twenty-five rods more or less from the west line of lot number eighteen; the above mentioned monuments are on the south side of said road, and the width of said Road is forty feet: Be it therefore ordained and enacted, and it is hereby ordained and enacted by the Municipal Council of the District of Johnstown in Council assembled at the Town of Brockville, on the twelfth day of February, in the year of our Lord one thousand eight hundred and forty-five, That the above described Road be approved of and confirmed, and it is hereby approved of and confirmed to be a public highway **Confirmed.** and road.

W. S. MACDONALD, Chairman.

[L. S.]

No, C.—BY-LAW

To close an old Road in the Township of Bastard.

Preamble. Whereas James Eaton, Surveyor of Highways in and for the County of Leeds, has been petitioned by fourteen freeholders of the said County to examine an old Road in the Township of Bastard, and to report thereon; and whereas the said James Eaton has examined the said Road, and has reported to this Council that the same is useless and unnecessary for public travel or convenience: Be it therefore ordained and enacted by the Municipal Council of the District of Johnstown, in Council assembled at the Town of Brockville, on the twelfth day of February, in the year of our Lord one thousand eight hundred and forty-five, That the said Road, to wit: the **Description.** Road leading from the front of the first concession in the township of Bastard, across lot number twenty-five to the town-line of Burgess, be condemned and closed, and it is **Closed.** hereby condemned and closed.

W. S. MACDONALD, Chairman.

[L. S.]

No, CI.—BY-LAW

To establish a Road in the Township of Augusta.

Whereas Philemon Pennock, Surveyor of Highways in **Preamble.** and for the County of Grenville, has been petitioned by twelve Freeholders to lay out a certain road in the township of Augusta; and whereas the said Philemon Pennock has surveyed and laid out the said Road pursuant to such petition, as follows: Commencing at a Cedar post planted **Description.** in the centre of the old Road between lots numbers nine and ten to the centre of the old Road, thirty-eight chains; thence on the old Road across lots numbers twelve and part of lot number thirteen to a Cedar stump marked R; thence on the south side of the old Road seventy-three chains, until it crosses the old Road on lot number fourteen; thence on the north side of the old Road thirtythree chains; thence on the old Road to the line between lots numbers seventeen and eighteen; thence on the south side of the old Road twenty chains; thence on the old Road to the Rideau Road; the said new Road is marked out by a line of pickets planted thereon, and is surveyed fifty feet in width: Be it therefore ordained and enacted by the Municipal Council of the District of Johnstown, in Council assembled at the Town of Brockville, on the thirteenth day of February, in the year of our Lord one thousand eight hundred and forty-five, That the said above described Road be approved of and confirmed, and it is hereby approved of and confirmed to be a public Road **Confirmed.** and Highway.

W. S. MACDONALD, Chairman.

[L.S.]

———

No. CII.—BY-LAW

To establish a Road in the Township of Elizabethtown.

Whereas John Jelly, Surveyor of Highways in and for **Preamble.** the County of Leeds, has been petitioned by twelve freeholders of the said County, to lay out a certain Road in the Township of Elizabethtown; and whereas the said John Jelly has surveyed and laid out the said Road pursuant to such petition as follows: commencing where a post has been planted on a line between the seventh and

F

Description. eighth concessions, being the corner post or boundary between lots numbers five and six in the eighth concession of Elizabethtown aforesaid, and running parallel with the allowance for a side road between lots numbers six and seven in the said eighth concession, to where it intersects the road leading from Pearson's Mills to Bellamy's Mills in Augusta; the side line between lots numbers five and six are in the centre of the said Road, and the said Road is laid out forty feet in width; Be it therefore ordained and enacted by the Municipal Council of the District of Johnstown, in Council assembled at the Town of Brockville, on the twelfth day of February, in the year of our Lord one thousand eight hundred and forty-five, That the said above described Road be approved of, and the same is hereby approved of and confirmed as a Public Road

Confirmed. and Highway.

W. S. MACDONALD, CHAIRMAN.

[L S.]

No. CIII.—BY-LAW

Relating to the Salary of the District Auditors.—Passed February 13, 1845.

(Repealed; see By-Law No. 186.)

No. CIV.—BY-LAW

For raising, levying and collecting an Assessed Rate from the Inhabitants of sundry School Districts within the District of Johnstown.

Preamble. Whereas by an Act passed by the Parliament of this Province, in the fourth and fifth years of Her Majesty Queen Victoria's reign, entitled *"An Act for the better internal Government of that part of this Province which formerly constituted the Province of Upper Canada, by the establishment of Local or Municipal Authorities therein,"* it is amongst other things enacted, that the Municipal Council of the District may cause an Assessment to be made and collected from the Inhabitants, providing for

the establishment of and a reasonable allowance for the
support of schools; And whereas applications have been
made to this Council, by the Trustees duly and legally
appointed for several School Districts, praying that a Local
Tax or Assessment may be levied on such Districts for the
purpose of education within the same: Be it therefore
ordained and enacted by the Municipal Council of the
District of Johnstown, assembled at the Town of Brockville, on Thursday, the thirteenth day of February, in the
year of our Lord one thousand eight hundred and forty-
five, That for the purpose of Education, that is to say: for
the erection, repair and completion of certain School
Houses now required to be built, erected or repaired in
certain School districts hereinafter mentioned, there shall
be raised and levied for the present year upon all real
and personal property therein, the following sums, clear
of the expenses of levying and collecting, namely :—

In the Township of Elizabethtown,

In School-District number nineteen, the sum of twenty
Pounds. Sums to be levied.

In the Township of Kitley,

In School-District number fifteen, the sum of fifty
Pounds.

Section 2. That the said sums be rated equally upon
all the assessed property in each School-District respectively, by the Clerk of the Peace, and be levied and collected by the Collectors of the several Townships hereinbefore named within the School Districts aforesaid, in
the same manner as is now by law provided, and be by
them paid to the Superintendents of the several Townships, under the provisions and restrictions of the twelfth
section of an Act passed by the Parliament of this
Province, on the ninth day of December, in the year of
our Lord one thousand eight hundred and forty-three,
entitled " *An Act for the establishment and maintenance
of Common Schools in Upper Canada.*" How rated and collected.

W. S. MACDONALD, Chairman.

[L. S.]

No. CV.—BY-LAW

To provide for certain information being furnished to Township Assessors.]

Preamble.

Treasurer to furnish lists of lots.

Whereas it is expedient for the information and guidance of each Township Assessor that he should be furnished by the District Treasurer with a schedule or list showing the quantity of land in each lot and broken lot in the Township for which such Assessor is elected : Be it therefore enacted and ordained by the Municipal Council of the District of Johnstown, duly assembled at the Town of Brockville, on the thirteenth day of February, in the year of our Lord one thousand eight hundred and forty-five, That the District Treasurer shall furnish for each Township Assessor of the District a schedule or list showing the number of acres of land, as nearly as he can in each lot and broken lot in the Township for which such Assessor is appointed ; and the said Treasurer shall be

Compensation.

allowed the sum of four pounds Currency per annum out of the District Treasury for furnishing the said schedules or lists each year.

How delivered to Assessors.

SECTION 2. Be it further enacted, That the said schedules or lists shall be delivered by the District Treasurer to the Clerk of the Peace, and by that officer delivered to the Assessors respectively with the Township Assessment Rolls.

W. S. MACDONALD, CHAIRMAN.

[L. S.]

No. CVI.—BY-LAW

To regulate the future payment of office contingencies of the District Treasurer.

Preamble.

Whereas it is expedient to repeal a By-Law of the District Council of the District of Johnstown, entitled *"By-Law to regulate certain fees,"* so far as relates to the District Treasurer, and to make provision for the payment of any office contingencies, which the District Treasurer may be entitled hereafter to charge against the District for Stationery, Postages, Candle-light, or Fuel: Be it therefore ordained and enacted, and it is hereby ordained

Part of By-law No. 10 repealed,

and enacted, That the said By-Law be, and the same is hereby repealed so far as relates to the District Treasurer.

And be it further enacted, That the District Treasurer shall be allowed, and he is hereby authorized to charge and receive for his use and benefit, the sum of one shilling and three pence for every search in the plans, books and papers in his office, from any person requiring such search, except a District Councillor of this District, which sum shall be in full for all future charges or claims on the part of the said District Treasurer against the District of Johnstown or District Council, for Stationery, Postage, Candlelight, or Fuel for his office. *Fees in lieu of contingencies.*

W. S. MACDONALD, Chairman.

[L. S.] .

No. CVII.—BY-LAW

Relating to the Assessment of the District of Johnstown for the year 1845. Passed February 13, 1848.

(Expired by Limitation.)

No. CVIII.—BY-LAW

To establish a Road in the Township of North Crosby.

Whereas James Bilton, Surveyor of Highways in and for the County of Leeds, has been petitioned by twelve freeholders of the said County to lay out a certain Road in the Township of North Crosby; and whereas the said James Bilton has surveyed and laid out the said Road pursuant to such petition, as follows: commencing at the centre of lot number four in the fifth Concession of the Township of North Crosby aforesaid, running through the centre of said lot to the sixth Concession, to a post planted in the centre of said lot, and the said Road is surveyed forty feet wide: Be it therefore ordained and enacted by the Municipal Council of the District of Johnstown, in Council assembled at the Town of Brockville, on the fourteenth day of May, in the year of our Lord one thousand eight hundred and forty-five, That the said above described Road be approved of and confirmed, and it is hereby approved of and confirmed as a public Highway and Road. *Preamble* *Description.* *Confirmed.*

OGLE R. GOWAN, Chairman.

[L. S.]

No. CIX.—BY-LAW

To establish a Road in the Township of Bastard.

Preamble. Whereas James Eaton, Surveyor of Highways in and for the County of Leeds, has been petitioned by twelve freeholders of the said County, to lay out a Road in the Township of Bastard; and whereas the said James Eaton has surveyed and laid out the said road pursuant to such petition as follows: commencing sixteen rods from a **Description.** creek on lot number eight in the third concession in the Township of Bastard aforesaid, where a Cedar post marked A is planted, running to the corner post on the centre of said lot number eight, forty rods a south-east course, said post divides the said lot between William Rogers and James Gardiner; thence on a line between the said William Rogers and James Gardiner, up to the said line between lots number eight and seven, fifty-four rods a north-east course, to where a Cedar post is planted and marked B, where it intersects the Portland Road leading to New Boyne—the said road is laid out on the east side of the first mentioned post; from thence it runs equally between the farms of William Rogers and James Gardiner, until it intersects the Portland Road, and the said Road is surveyed forty feet wide: Be it therefore ordained and enacted by the Municipal Council of the District of Johnstown in Council assembled at the Town of Brockville, on the fourteenth day of May, in the year of our Lord one thousand eight hundred and forty-five, That the above described Road be approved of and confirmed, and the same is hereby approved of and confirmed as a public **Confirmed.** Highway and Road.

OGLE R. GOWAN, Chairman.

[L. S.]

No. CX.—BY-LAW

To establish a Road in the Township of Bastard.

Preamble. Whereas James Eaton, Surveyor of Highways in and for the County of Leeds, has been petitioned by twelve freeholders of the said County to lay out a certain Road in the Township of Bastard; and whereas the said James Eaton has surveyed and laid out the said Road pursuant

to such petition as follows: commencing on the second Description.
concession line of the Township of Bastard aforesaid,
thirty-two rods from the corner post between lots numbers
twenty-five and twenty-six, where a Cedar post is planted,
marked R; running thence a south-easterly course to the
hill at Samuel Poole's Orchard, ninety-seven rods, where
a Cedar post is planted marked R; thence southerly to
the side-line between lots numbers twenty-six and twenty-
seven, where a Cedar post is planted marked R; thence
along said side line to the third Concession of said Township of Bastard; the said Road is laid out on the east side
of the above mentioned posts, and is surveyed forty feet
wide: Be it therefore ordained and enacted, and it is
hereby ordained and enacted by the Municipal Council of
the District of Johnstown, in Council assembled at the
Town of Brockville, on the fourteenth day of May, in the
year of our Lord one thousand eight hundred and forty-
five, That the above described Road, as laid out by the
said James Eaton as aforesaid, be approved of and confirmed, and it is hereby approved of and confirmed to be Confirmed.
a public Highway and Road.

OGLE R. GOWAN, CHAIRMAN.

[L. S.]

No. CXI.—BY-LAW

*To establish a Road in the Townships of Kitley and
Elizabethtown.*

Whereas John Jelly, Surveyor of Highways in and for Preamble.
the County of Leeds has been petitioned by twelve freeholders of the said County, to lay out a certain Road in
the Townships of Kitley and Elizabethtown; and whereas
the said John Jelly has surveyed and laid out the said
Road pursuant to such petition, as follows: commencing
at the Town-line between the Townships of Wolford and Description.
Kitley, at a Cedar post marked R, near the dwelling of
William Ashmore, on the east side of lot number four, in
the tenth Concession of Kitley aforesaid; thence nearly
south-west seventy-nine rods and eight feet to a Beech
tree marked R; thence south twenty degrees, west two
hundred and thirty-one rods and eight feet to a Cedar
post marked R, on the Division-line in the centre of the
Road near William Bates's House; thence nearly south-

west sixty-one rods and nine feet to a post planted on the side line between lots numbers six and seven in the tenth Concession of Kitley aforesaid; thence south twenty degrees, west two hundred and twenty-two rods to a Cedar post marked R, in the centre of the present travelled Road, on the west side of lot number eight in the said tenth Concession of Kitley; thence south one hundred and seventy-eight and a half rods to a Cedar post marked R, on the side line between lots numbers twenty-one and twenty-two in the eleventh Concession of Elizabethtown aforesaid; thence south twenty degrees, east one hundred and five rods and three feet to a Cedar post on the front of said eleventh concession; thence to a Cedar post marked R, one hundred and four rods and nine feet, to within five rods of Joseph Powell's Barn; thence south ten degrees, east two hundred and sixty rods to a Cedar post marked R; thence south one hundred and eighty-eight and a half rods to a Cedar post in front of lot number twenty-four in said tenth Concession of Elizabethtown; the above mentioned posts are marked on two sides with red chalk, and are all planted in the centre of said Road, which said Road is laid out forty feet in width: Be it therefore ordained and enacted, and it is hereby ordained and enacted by the Municipal Council of the District of Johnstown, in Council assembled at the Town of Brockville, on the fourteenth day of May, in the year of our Lord one thousand eight hundred and forty-five, That the above described Road be approved of and confirmed as a public Highway and Road, and it is hereby approved of and confirmed as a Public Highway and Road.

Confirmed.

OGLE R. GOWAN, Chairman.

[L. S.]

No. CXII.—BY-LAW

To establish a Road in the Township of Yonge, formerly Escott.

Preamble. Whereas Benjamin Warren, Surveyor of Highways in and for the County of Leeds, has been petitioned by twelve Freeholders of the said County to lay out a certain Road in the Township of Yonge, formerly Escott; And whereas the said Benjamin Warren has surveyed and laid out the said Road pursuant to such petition as follows:

commencing at the water's edge at or near the centre of Description. lot number twenty, broken front of the Township of Yonge, formerly Escott, aforesaid, or the Gray's landing, from a post planted near the water's edge; from thence a north-west course four rods more or less, to another post marked R with red chalk; from thence a west course ten rods more or less, to another post planted in the open ground marked R on two sides; from thence north-north-west on a line of blazed trees to a post planted and marked R with red chalk, where it intersects the public Highway on the front Road twenty rods more or less from the water's edge; the width of said Road to be forty feet: Be it therefore ordained and enacted, and it is hereby ordained and enacted by the Municipal Council of the District of Johnstown, in Council assembled at the Town of Brockville, on the fourteenth day of May, in the year of our Lord one thousand eight hundred and forty-five, That the above described Road be approved of and confirmed, and it is hereby approved of and confirmed as a public Road Confirmed. and Highway.

OGLE R. GOWAN, Chairman.

[L. S.]

No. CXIII.—BY-LAW

To establish a Road in the Townships of North Crosby and South Crosby.

Whereas James Bilton, Surveyor of Highways in and Preamble. for the County of Leeds, has been petitioned by twelve freeholders of the said County, to lay out a certain Road in the Townships of North and South Crosby; and whereas the said James Bilton has surveyed and laid out the said Road pursuant to such petition, as follows: commencing on the Town line between the Townships of North and Description. South Crosby, at a Cedar post marked and planted six hundred and eighty-three feet from the corner post in rear of lot number twenty-seven, in the fourth Concession of South Crosby aforesaid, opposite to the store of Benjamin Tett, Esquire, and adjoining the land of said lot conveyed to John Kilborn, Esquire; thence running south eighty degrees fifteen minutes, east across lots numbers twenty-seven and twenty-six in the said fourth Concession of South Crosby, and in front of parts of said lots owned by

John Kilborn, Benjamin Tett, and Edward Webster, eighty and one quarter rods to the north-east corner of the Barn of David B. Stevens, situated on said lot number twenty-six; the said Road is laid out sixty feet wide, the posts planted and marked thereon are on the west side of said Road; the said Road is continued further: commencing at a Hemlock post marked and planted in the centre of the public highway now travelled, upon lot number two in the fourth Concession of North Crosby aforesaid, near the north corner of the Hospital situate on said lot number two in the fourth Concession of North Crosby aforesaid; thence north-easterly across said lot one hundred and fifty rods more or less, until it intersects the side line between lots numbers two and three at a Hemlock post marked and planted thereon; thence along the said side line north fifty-four degrees, east taking twenty feet from lot number two, and twenty feet from lot number three to the front of the said fourth Concession line; said road is laid out forty feet wide, and the above description and posts are marked and planted on the centre thereof: Be it therefore ordained and enacted, and it is hereby ordained and enacted by the Municipal Council of the District of Johnstown, in Council assembled at the Town of Brockville, on the fourteenth day of May, in the year of our Lord one thousand eight hundred and forty-five, That the above described Roads be approved of and confirmed, and they are hereby approved of and con-

Confirmed. firmed as public Roads and Highways.

OGLE R. GOWAN, Chairman.

[L. S.]

No. CXIV.—BY-LAW

To establish a Road in the Townships of Lansdowne and Leeds.

Preamble. Whereas Surasten L. Soper, Surveyor of Highways in and for the County of Leeds, has been petitioned by twelve freeholders of the said County to lay out a certain Road in the Townships of Lansdowne and Leeds; and whereas the said Surasten L. Soper has surveyed and laid out the said Road pursuant to such petition as follows: commencing at a post marked R at the end of a Road running from the Long Point Road across lot letter A in the seventh Concession of Lansdowne aforesaid, on the Town line between Leeds and Lansdowne; thence running south-westerly in a direct line across lot number twenty-four in the eighth Concession of the Township of Leeds aforesaid to a post marked R; thence westerly to a post planted on the seventh Concession line; angling thence in a south-westerly course to a post planted near the Beaver Meadow; thence in a southerly direction on a line of blazed trees, to intersect the road leading to the Gananoque Road, across lot number sixteen in the seventh Concession of Leeds aforesaid; the above mentioned posts and blazed trees are in the centre of said Road, and the said Road is laid out forty feet in width: Be it therefore ordained and enacted, and it is hereby ordained and enacted by the Municipal Council of the District of Johnstown, in Council assembled at the town of Brockville, on the fourteenth day of May, in the year of our Lord one thousand eight hundred and forty-five, That the above described Road be approved of and confirmed, and it is hereby approved of and confirmed as a public Highway and Road. *Description.* *Confirmed.*

OGLE R. GOWAN, Chairman.

[L. S.]

No. CXV.—BY-LAW

To establish a Road in the Township of Elizabethtown, and to close an old Road in the same Township.

Whereas the Government allowance for a Road, originally surveyed and laid out between lots numbers six and seven in the fifth Concession of the Township of Elizabethtown, has been found impracticable for public use and travel; and whereas Archibald M'Dougall, proprietor of lot number seven in the said fifth concession of Elizabethtown, has given and laid off for the public travel, use, and convenience, a Road on the west side of his said Lot number seven, which is now, and has been for some years past the public travelled Road: Be it therefore ordained and enacted by the Municipal Council of the District of Johnstown, in Council assembled at the Town of Brockville, on the fourteenth day of May, in the year of our Lord one thousand eight hundred and forty-five, That the said Government allowance for a Road between lots numbers six and seven in the said fifth Concession be closed as unnecessary for public use, travel, and convenience. *Preamble.* *Description.* *Allowance closed.*

And be it further enacted by the authority aforesaid,
That the said Archibald M'Dougall be permitted to
enclose, use, and occupy the said Government allowance
in lieu of the Road given by him on the west side of said
lot number seven as aforesaid.

Arch. McDougall allowed to use allowance.

OGLE R. GOWAN, Chairman.

[L. S.]

No. CXVI.—BY-LAW

To establish a Road in the Township of Leeds.

Preamble.

Whereas Surasten L. Soper, Surveyor of Highways
in and for the County of Leeds, has been petitioned by
twelve freeholders of the said County to lay out a certain
Road in the Township of Leeds; and whereas the said
Surasten L. Soper has laid out and surveyed the said
Road pursuant to such petition as follows: commencing
at a stone Monument on the shore of Crippen Lake near
Thomas Tye's House, near the centre of the front half
of lot number twenty-two in the ninth Concession of the
Township of Leeds, aforesaid, running south-easterly to a
post planted in the open ground near the centre of the
front half of lot number twenty-three; thence east to a
post planted near the side line between lots numbers
twenty-three and twenty-four in the said ninth Concession;
then north-easterly on a line of pickets across lot number
twenty-four, aforesaid, to the Town line on a bearing to
intersect the allowance for a Road between the eighth and
ninth Concessions of the Township of Lansdowne, which
runs to the Long Point Road; the above mentioned
Monuments are intended for the centre of the said surveyed Road, and the said Road is surveyed forty feet wide:
Be it therefore ordained and enacted by the Municipal
Council of the District of Johnstown, in Council assembled
at the Town of Brockville, on the fourteenth day of May,
in the year of our Lord one thousand eight hundred and
forty-five, That the above described Road be approved of
and confirmed, and it is hereby approved of and confirmed
as a Public Highway and Road.

Description,

Confirmed.

OGLE R. GOWAN, Chairman.

[L. S.]

No. CXVII.—BY-LAW

For Raising, Levying and Collecting an Assessed Rate from the Inhabitants of School District number Twelve, in the Township of Yonge.

Whereas by an Act passed by the Parliament of this Preamble. Province, in the fourth and fifth years of Her Majesty Queen Victoria's reign, entitled *"An Act for the better internal Government of that part of this Province which formerly constituted the Province of Upper Canada, by the establishment of Local or Municipal Authorities therein,"* it is amongst other things enacted, that the Municipal Council of the District may cause an Assessment to be made and collected from the inhabitants, providing for the establishment of and a reasonable allowance for the support of schools; And whereas application has been made to this Council, by the Trustees duly and legally appointed for School District number Twelve, in the Township of Yonge, praying that a Local Tax or Assessment may be levied on such District, for the purpose of education within the same: Be it therefore ordained and enacted by the Municipal Council of the District of Johnstown, assembled at the Town of Brockville, on the fourteenth day of May, in the year of our Lord one thousand eight hundred and forty five, That for the purpose of Education, that is to say: for the erection, repair and completion of a certain School House now required to be built in School District number twelve, in the Township of Yonge, hereinafter mentioned, there shall be raised and levied for the present year upon all real and personal property therein, the following sum, clear of the expenses of levying and collecting, namely:

In the Township of Yonge,

In School District number twelve, the sum of fifty Sum to be levied. Pounds.

Section 2. That the said sum be rated equally upon all How rated and the assessed property in said School District by the Clerk collected. of the Peace, and levied and collected by the Collector of the said Township hereinbefore named within the School District aforesaid, in the same manner as is now by law provided, and be by him paid to the Superintendent of the said Township, under the powers and restrictions of the twelfth section of an Act passed by the Parliament of this Province, on the ninth day of December, in the year of our Lord one thousand eight hundred and forty-three, entitled "*An Act for the establishment and maintenance of Common Schools in Upper Canada.*"

OGLE R. GOWAN, CHAIRMAN.

[L. S.]

No. CXVIII.—BY-LAW

To establish a Road in the Township of South Crosby.

Preamble.

Whereas Henry B. Marvin, Surveyor of Highways in and for the County of Leeds, has been petitioned by twelve freeholders of the said County to lay out a certain Road in the Township of South Crosby; and whereas the said Henry B. Marvin has surveyed and laid out the said Road pursuant to such petition, as follows: commencing at a post planted in front of the fourth Concession of South Crosby aforesaid, seven chains and eighty links from the north corner of lot number twenty in said Concession, marked west side of Road and running directly on the old track across the fourth Concession to a post in front of the fifth Concession of South Crosby aforesaid, fifty links east from the middle of lot number twenty in the fifth concession; then along the concession line, the distance of two chains to a post on the west side of the Road; thence angling south ten degrees, west two chains and fifty links to a post planted on the west side of said road; thence in a parallel direction with the side line the distance of twelve chains seventy-seven links to a post on the west side of said road; thence south thirty-five degrees, west the distance of thirteen chains to a post on the west side of said Road; thence south ten degrees, west ten chains and fifty links to a post planted on the west side of said Road at the centre of the fifth Concession aforesaid, on the side line between lots numbers nineteen and twenty; thence along said line to the front of the sixth Concession of said Township, and the said Road is surveyed forty feet in width: Be it therefore ordained and enacted, and it is hereby ordained and enacted by the Municipal Council of the District of Johnstown, in Council assembled, at the Town of Brockville, on the fifteenth day of May, in the year of our Lord one thousand eight hundred and forty-

Description.

five, That the said above described Road be approved of and confirmed, and the same is hereby approved of and confirmed. confirmed as a Public Highway and Road.

OGLE R. GOWAN, CHAIRMAN.

[L. S.]

No. CXIX.—BY-LAW

To ensure the punctual Attendance of Members.

Whereas much inconvenience and delay to Public Business often arises, owing to the absence of members of this Council: Be it therefore enacted and ordained, and it is enacted and ordained by the Municipal Council of the District of Johnstown, in Council assembled at the Town of Brockville, on the fifteenth day of May, in the year of our Lord one thousand eight hundred and forty-five, That any Councillor who shall absent himself from his duty at any meeting of this Council, without leave first had and obtained, or without a sufficient apology being offered for such absence, (such apology to be in writing, and approved of by the Warden or Chairman,) shall for every such absence, forfeit and pay a sum of money of not more than twenty shillings, nor less than five in the discretion of this Council, which penalty shall be imposed at the next quarterly meeting of the Council. And be it enacted and ordained as aforesaid, That all fines and penalties that may be imposed and inflicted under and by virtue of this By-law, shall go into and form part of the general revenues of the District, applicable to District purposes.

OGLE R. GOWAN, CHAIRMAN.

[L. S.]

No. CXX.—BY-LAW

To establish certain Roads in the District of Johnstown.

Whereas Philemon Pennock, Surveyor of Highways in and for the County of Grenville, has been petitioned by twelve freeholders of the said County to lay out a certain Road in the Township of Augusta, and in pursuance of such

Petition the said Philemon Pennock has surveyed and laid out the said Road as follows : commencing at the Prescott Road on the rear of lot number five in the fifth Concession of Augusta aforesaid, two Cedar posts planted forty feet asunder ; from thence west twenty degrees, south fifty-one chains to a post marked R ; from thence west ten degrees, south seventy-three chains to a post marked R ; from thence west ten degrees, north eighty-eight chains to the line between lots numbers ten and eleven ; from thence on the said line thirteen chains ten links to the allowance between the fifth and sixth Concessions, on the said allowance twenty chains ; from thence west one hundred and ten chains to a post marked R in the sixth Concession ; from thence west thirty degrees, south to the lower Rideau Road in the sixth Concession aforesaid. The said Road is marked out by blazes on trees in the woods, and by stakes planted in the open ground : it is three hundred and eighty-one chains and ten links in length, and is surveyed forty feet wide.

Description of Road in Augusta.

And whereas Edward Mix, Surveyor of Highways in and for the County of Grenville, has been petitioned by twelve freeholders of the said County to lay out a certain Road in the Township of Oxford : and in pursuance of such petition the said Edward Mix has surveyed and laid out the said Road, as follows : commencing at a stone Monument planted on the front of the ninth Concession of Oxford aforesaid, on the west line of the east half of lot number eighteen in said ninth concession, and running along said west line to a stone Monument planted at the rear of the ninth Concession aforesaid ; and the said Road is laid out forty feet wide.

Description of Road in Oxford.

And whereas John Riddell, Surveyor of Highways in and for the County of Leeds, has been petitioned by twelve freeholders of the said County to lay out a certain road in the Township of Elmsley as follows : following the Post Road from Smith's Falls towards Lombard's to the allowance for side Road between lots numbers six and seven, in the fourth Concession of Elmsley aforesaid, where a Maple tree is blazed on four sides, standing on said allowance ; from thence following said allowance forty rods, to a small Hemlock tree blazed on four sides ; thence westerly along a line of blazed trees and pickets to an Ash stump standing near where the old path crosses a spring brook in Kinney's clearing, fifty rods ; thence northerly along a line of pickets and blazed trees to the aforesaid allowance,

Description of Road in Elmsley.

forty-two rods; thence following the allowance as said side
Road ninety rods, to a Maple tree blazed on four sides;
thence northerly along a line of blazed trees thirty-two
rods, to a Cedar tree blazed on four sides; thence westerly
along a line of blazed trees to the Concession line, fifty-
two rods; then following said Concession to the allowance
or side Road between lots number six and seven in the
fifth Concession; thence along said side Road to a stake
standing near the water's edge; thence northerly fourteen
rods, to a Stone Monument on the Government Land;
thence easterly along the Government Land to Poole-
malee; And the said Road is laid out forty feet in width,
where it does not cross the Government allowance, the
blazed trees and pickets are in the centre of said Road.

And whereas Henry B. Marvin, Surveyor of Highways
in and for the County of Leeds aforesaid, has been petitioned by twelve freeholders of the said County, to lay
out a road in the Townships of Bastard and South Crosby;
commencing at a post on the bank of Henderson Lake,
near Joseph Slack's house, marked east side of Road;
from thence to a post on the Town line between South
Crosby and Bastard aforesaid, marked west side of
Road, the distance of five chains and forty-five links;
thence along said line to the side line between lots
numbers two and three in South Crosby aforesaid:
thence along the side line the distance of twelve chains
and forty-five links, to a post marked east side of Road;
thence angling nearly south, and running a straight line
across lots numbers two and one in the first Concession
of said Township of South Crosby, and a part of number one in the second Concession of said Township, to a
post on the point of a large hill on the east side of the
Road; from thence in a straight line to a post at the edge
of Cedar swamp, marked east side of Road, and then
through said swamp to the Township line between South
Crosby and Leeds, the distance of seven chains from the
corner of lot number twenty-two in the eleventh Concession of the Township of Leeds, aforesaid; thence along
said line to the Road leading from Lyndhurst to the
Whitefish. And the said Road is surveyed forty feet wide.

Description of Roads in Bastard & South Crosby.

Be it therefore ordained and enacted by the Municipal
Council of the District of Johnstown, in Council assembled,
at the Town of Brockville, on the thirteenth day of
August, in the year of our Lord one thousand eight
hundred and forty-five, That the said above described

G

Confirmed as Public Roads.

Roads be respectively approved of and confirmed, and they are hereby approved of and confirmed as public Roads and Highways.

RICHARD F. STEELE, Warden.

No. CXXI.—BY-LAW

To close a Road in the Township of Oxford.

Preamble.

Whereas Edward Mix, Surveyor of Highways in and for the County of Grenville, has been been petitioned by twelve freeholders of the said County to examine an old Road and report thereon; and whereas the said Edward Mix has examined the said Road and has reported to this Council that the same is useless and unnecessary for public travel and convenience: Be it therefore ordained and enacted, and it is hereby ordained and enacted by the Municipal Council of the District of Johnstown, in Council assembled at the Town of Brockville, on the thirteenth day of August, in the year of our Lord one thousand eight hundred and forty-five, That the road commencing at what

Description.

is called the Branch road; thence running between lots numbers twenty-three and twenty-four in the third Concession of the Township of Oxford until it intersects the Concession in the rear of said lots, opposite to Thomas Shipman's, be condemned and closed, and the same is

Closed.

hereby condemned and closed.

RICHARD F. STEELE, Warden.

No. CXXII.—BY-LAW

To establish a Model School in the District of Johnstown.

Preamble.

Whereas it is desirable and necessary for the interest of the inhabitants of this District that a Model School should be established for the training and education of Teachers within the same: Be it therefore ordained and enacted, and it is hereby ordained and enacted by the Municipal Council of the Johnstown District, in Council assembled at the Town of Brockville, on the thirteenth day of August, in the year of our Lord one thousand eight hundred and

forty-five, That a sum not exceeding one hundred pounds Sum to be levied.
be levied and collected upon all the rateable property
liable to assessment within this District, for the purpose of
establishing and endowing a Model School within this
District.

SECTION 2. That the Clerk of the District be authorized
and directed to draw up and deliver to the several Town-
ship Collectors an Assessment Roll apportioning such rate How to be appor-tioned.
for this year.

RICHARD F. STEELE, WARDEN.

No. CXXIII.—BY-LAW

To close a Road in the Township of Bastard.

Whereas James Eaton, Surveyor of Highways in and for Preamble.
the County of Leeds, has been petitioned by twelve freeholders of the said County to examine and condemn the
Road running on lot number twelve in the eighth concession of the Township of Bastard, so far as it runs parallel Description.
with the Government allowance, up to where a cedar post
is planted at a swamp: Be it therefore ordained and
enacted by the Municipal Council of the District of Johnstown, in Council assembled on the twelfth day of February,
in the year of our Lord one thousand eight hundred and
forty-six, That the Road as above described be condemned
and closed, and it is hereby condemned and closed as un- Closed.
necessary for public travel or convenience.

RICHARD F. STEELE, WARDEN.

[L. S.]

No. CXXIV.—BY-LAW

To establish certain Roads in the District of Johnstown.

Whereas Henry B. Marvin, Surveyor of Highways in Preamble.
and for the County of Leeds has been petitioned by twelve
freeholders of the said County, to lay out a certain Road
in the Townships of Bastard and South Crosby; and in
pursuance of such petition the said Henry B. Marvin has

surveyed and laid out the said Road as follows: commencing on lot number twenty-nine in the Township of Bastard, at the three corners of the Beverly Road, and running on a straight line to the east corner of lot number nine in the first concession of South Crosby, the corner post of said lot being the south side of the road; thence running directly on the side line between lots numbers eight and nine, three-fourths of the distance across said Concession, to a post planted on the south side of the Road; thence angling westward and running on a straight line to the east corner of lot number nine in the second concession of the Township of South Crosby aforesaid, which said Road is laid out forty feet in width.

Description of Road in Bastard & South Crosby.

And whereas the said Henry B. Marvin has been petitioned by twelve freeholders of the County of Leeds, to lay out a certain Road in the Township of South Crosby; and in pursuance of such petition, the said Henry B. Marvin has surveyed and laid out the said Road as follows; commencing at the Lampson Road on lot number fourteen in the fifth concession of South Crosby, four chains from the allowance for a Road on the rear of said concession; thence in a westerly course round the point of the hill to the said allowance for a Road, the distance of eight chains, where a tree is marked as north side of Road; thence along said allowance to the foot of a hill sixteen chains from the east corner of lot number fifteen in the sixth concession of said Township; thence angling north-west and running in a circular form round the point of the hill the distance of two chains and seventy-five links to the allowance for a Road; thence along said allowance to a post planted on lot number sixteen in the fifth concession of said Township, near the foot of the hill; thence turning north-west and running in a circular form round the hill the distance of thirteen chains to the said allowance for a Road; thence along the said allowance to the foot of a hill at the west side of Black Creek swamp; thence turning north and running round the point of the hill to the allowance, the distance of three chains and fifty-five links; thence along the allowance to the side line between lots number nineteen and twenty to the fifth concession of South Crosby aforesaid, and the said Road is laid out sixty-six feet in width.

Description of Road in South Crosby.

Be it therefore ordained and enacted by the Municipal Council of the District of Johnstown, in Council assembled at the Town of Brockville, on the twelfth day of

February, in the year of our Lord one thousand eight Confirmed a
hundred and forty-six, That the above described Roads be Public Roads.
respectively approved of and confirmed as Public Roads
and Highways.

RICHARD F. STEELE, Warden D. J.

[L. S.]

No. CXXV.—BY-LAW

To establish a Road in the Township of Augusta.

Whereas Philemon Pennock, Surveyor of Highways in Preamble.
and for the County of Grenville, has been petitioned by
twelve freeholders of the said County to lay out a certain
Road in the Township of Augusta; and whereas the said
Philemon Pennock has surveyed and laid out the said
Road pursuant to such petition, as follows: commencing Description.
on the north side of a Creek running across lots numbers
thirty-five and thirty-six in the fourth Concession of the
said Township of Augusta; from thence fifteen chains
from the bank of said Creek on the line between lots
numbers thirty-five and thirty-six, and from thence east
two chains and thirty-nine links to the travelled Road
leading from Moses Read's to the rear of the Township
which said Road is laid out forty feet in width, which width
may be distinguished by Cedar posts planted on either
side of it at the commencement and at its termination:
Be it therefore ordained and enacted, and it is hereby
ordained and enacted by the Municipal Council of the
District of Johnstown in Council assembled, at the Town
of Brockville, on the twelfth day of February, in the
year of our Lord one thousand eight hundred and forty-
six, That the above described Road be approved of and
confirmed, and it is hereby approved and confirmed to be Confirmed.
a public Highway and Road.

RICHARD F. STEELE, Warden, J. D.

[L. S.]

No. CXXVI.—BY-LAW

To provide for the payment of the residue of the debt for the
New Gaol and Court House of the District of Johnstown.

Preamble.

Whereas it is expedient to relieve the inhabitants of the District of Johnstown from further direct taxation, on account of the debt incurred for the erection of the New District Gaol and Court House, by providing for the payment out of the Common District fund of the amount now remaining unpaid : And whereas there remains, and is now owing, a residue of such debt and interest to Paul Glasford, Adiel Sherwood, William Freeland, Alexander Morris and John Weatherhead, Esquires, payable on or before the tenth day of May next, the sum of five hundred and fifty-three pounds and six shillings and ten pence currency.

Debt £553 16s. 6d.

Section 1. Be it therefore ordained and enacted, and it is hereby ordained and enacted by the District Council of the District of Johnstown, assembled at the Town of Brockville on the twelfth day of February, in the year of our Lord one thousand eight hundred and forty-six, That, in addition to the New Gaol and Court House monies in the District Treasury applicable to the payment of such debt, the District Treasurer shall apply out of the monies now or hereafter in his hands for Common District purposes such a sum as with such New Gaol and Court House monies shall be sufficient to pay the said debt of five hundred and fifty-three pounds and six shillings and ten pence, and shall pay over the same to the said Paul Glasford, Adiel Sherwood, William Freeland, Alexander Morris and John Weatherhead, Esquires, in full satisfaction of the balance of the said debt and interest owing to them on account of monies loaned by them to the District for the erection of the said new Gaol and Court House.

How to be paid.

Section 2. And whereas from such payment being made out of the Common District Fund there may not remain or come into the District Treasury from ordinary sources, during the present year, a sufficient amount of money to meet the current expenses of the District until the usual Assessments for the year shall become available, and it is desirable to provide for such a contingency : Be it therefore further ordained and enacted, and it is hereby ordained and enacted, That the District Treasurer shall and may, and is hereby authorized and empowered if he shall think it expedient or necessary so to do, to borrow

Treasurer to borrow money for current expenses.

from any person or persons, body corporate or bank, willing to loan the same at a rate of interest or discount not greater than six per centum in advance from time to time, such sum or sums of money not exceeding in the whole five hundred pounds currency, as he may consider necessary to meet any deficiency of the Common District fund to pay and discharge the current expenses of the District; which shall by him be applied in the same manner as other monies coming into his hands for Common District purposes.

SECTION 3. And be it further ordained and enacted, and it is hereby ordained and enacted, That such money shall be borrowed upon a Promissory Note or Notes to be made by the District Treasurer and countersigned by the Clerk of the District Council of this District, who shall affix thereto the seal of the said Council; which note or notes shall be made payable at such place and day (not exceeding six calendar months) as such Treasurer shall consider advisable; and such note or notes shall be paid and ratified by the said Treasurer out of the monies which shall come into his hands applicable to common District purposes. *How borrowed.*

RICHARD F. STEELE, WARDEN.

[L. S.]

No. CXXVII.—BY-LAW

For regulating the duties of the District Superintendent of Common Schools, and for other purposes.

The Municipal Council of the District of Johnstown, duly assembled at the Town Hall of Brockville, on the twelfth day of February, in the year of our Lord one thousand eight hundred and forty-six, do ordain, and it is hereby ordained and enacted, That all monies raised, levied or collected, (except those raised for the purpose of paying the several Teachers of the Common Schools their proportion of the School Funds,) within this District, for the support or maintenance of Education, or of any matter or thing relating thereto, be paid by the Collectors or officer receiving the same to the Superintendent of Education for the District, who shall pay over the same to the several Superintendents and other Educational Officers in the same ratio and proportion as they are now by law entitled to receive the same. *How monies raised to be paid*

SECTION 2. That all Township Superintendents shall make a true and faithful return according to the requirements of the twenty-sixth section of the Act passed on the ninth of December, 1843, and entitled "*An Act for the establishment and maintenance of Common Schools in Upper Canada.*"

Township Superintendents to make returns.

SECTION 3. That the District Superintendent shall annually, (to wit) on the first day of February in each year, transmit to the Clerk of this Council a true and faithful statement of all monies by him received for the purpose of education, together with a true and faithful statement in detail of how the same has been expended, to whom paid and for what purpose, particularly setting forth the balances (if any) remaining in his hands, and he shall also set forth in detail a clear and succinct account of the returns made by all Township Superintendents of the monies by them received and how expended, and to whom paid.

Annual statement of District Superintendent.

SECTION 4. That for the purposes of this By-law, the District Superintendent shall have free access to all returns made or to be made by the several Township Superintendents, School Trustees, and other educational officers, and he shall have power to demand and receive from each and every such Township Superintendent, Trustee, and other School Officer, all such further information touching the Schools of the District, and the appropriation of all monies connected therewith, as to him may seem advisable, to the end that he may be enabled to report fully and annually on the said first day of February, on the state of education within the District, and upon all matters connected therewith, for the information of this Council.

Powers of District Superintendent.

SECTION 5. That the Model School of the District be established at Frankville, in the Township of Kitley, and be subject to the same Superintendencies and review of the said District Superintendent as the other Schools of the District.

Model School.

SECTION 6. (Repealed : see By-law No. 186.)

Salary of District Superintendent, see By-law No. 148.

SECTION 7. That the Township Collectors retain only the per centage allowed by Statute, out of the aggregate of the whole Assessments collected by them, whether the Assessment be for the District, School, or other purposes.

Collectors' per centage.

RICHARD F. STEELE, WARDEN, D. J.

[L.S.]

No. CXXVIII.—BY-LAW

To provide for the publication of Lists of Lands in Arrears for Taxes.

Whereas it is provided by the second section of an Act *Preamble.* passed at the last Session of the Provincial Legislature, entitled, *" An Act to provide for the collection of arrears of Taxes in the District of Johnstown, and for other purposes"* that the District Treasurer should cause a copy of the list or lists of lots, part lots, pieces and parcels of land, and the amount due upon the same respectively to the times therein stated to be published (together with a notice specifying the intent of such publication) six several times *How to be pub-* in such Newspaper published in the District as might be *lished.* named by the Municipal Council; this Council, duly assembled at the Town of Brockville, on the twelfth day of February, in the year of our Lord one thousand eight hundred and forty-six, do therefore name the paper published in this District, and called *The Statesman*, as the Newspaper in which the said Treasurer shall cause the copy of the said list or lists to be published in accordance with the said Act.

SECTION 2. And whereas the said list or lists would obtain a greater circulation if the same were inserted in both Newspapers published in this District; it is therefore ordered that the said Treasurer do likewise cause the same to be published in the Newspaper of this District, called *The Recorder*, and shall pay the expense of such last *In Recorder* publication out of any unexpended monies which shall *newspaper also..* come into his hands as Treasurer, applicable to common District purposes.

RICHARD F. STEELE, WARDEN, D. J.

[L. S.]

No. CXXIX.—BY-LAW

Relating to the Assessment of the District of Johnstown for the year 1846.—Passed February 12, 1846.

(Expired by Limitation.)

No. CXXX.—BY-LAW

To establish a Road in the Township of Elizabethtown.

Preamble

Whereas John Jelly, Surveyor of Highways in and for the County of Leeds, has been petitioned by twelve freeholders of the said County, to lay out a certain Road in the Township of Elizabethtown; and whereas the said John Jelly has surveyed and laid out the said Road pursuant to such petition, as follows: commencing at a Cedar post on the east side of the Highway and on the west side of James Coleman's Dwelling House on the front part of lot number thirty-one in the third concession of the said Township of Elizabethtown, and running a south-easterly course twenty-two chains and twenty-seven links, more or less, to a Cedar post near the foot of the Mountain on the north side, and on lot number thirty-one in the second concession of Elizabethtown; thence ten chains more or less in a south-west course to a Hemlock sapling marked R; thence nine and a half chains and fifteen links more or less, to a post on the side line between lots numbers thirty-one and thirty-two in the said second concession of Elizabethtown; thence on the east side of said side line to the front of the second concession; thence from a Cedar post in the rear of lot number thirty-one in the first concession of Elizabethtown south-easterly by a Beech tree marked R, seven and a half chains and twenty-four links, more or less, to the centre line of said lot number thirty-one in the first concession; thence on the east side of said line to a Cedar post within forty-feet of a certain ledge or point of rock on said lot number thirty-one; thence south-easterly to a post on the east side of lot number thirty-one within eighty rods of the main Road; thence on the allowance between lots numbers thirty and thirty-one, until it intersects the main road; the said posts are all planted on the west side of said road and marked with red chalk, which said road is laid out forty feet in width: Be it therefore ordained and enacted, and it is hereby ordained and enacted by the Municipal Council of the District of Johnstown, in Council assembled, at the Town of Brockville, on the twelfth day of February, in the year of our Lord one thousand eight hundred and forty-six, That the above described road be approved of and confirmed, and it is hereby approved of and confirmed to be a public Road and Highway; Provided that this By-Law shall not be in force until all damages which may here-

Description.

Confirmed.

after be awarded by this Council, shall be first paid by the Proviso. parties applying for the establishment of the said Road.

RICHARD F. STEELE, Warden, D. J.

[L. S.]

No. CXXXI.—BY-LAW

For raising levying, and collecting of an Assessed Rate from the inhabitants of sundry School-Districts within the District of Johnstown.

Whereas by an Act passed by the Parliament of this Preamble. Province, in the fourth and fifth years of Her Majesty Queen Victoria's reign, entitled "*An act for the better internal Government of that part of this Province which formerly constituted the Province of Upper Canada, by the establishment of Local or Municipal Authorities therein,*" it is amongst other things enacted, that the Municipal Council of the District may cause an Assessment to be made and collected from the inhabitants, providing for the establishment of and a reasonable allowance for the support of Schools; And whereas applications have been made to this Council, by the Trustees duly and legally appointed for several School-Districts, praying that a Local Tax or Assessment may be levied on such Districts, for the purpose of Education within the same: Be it therefore ordained and enacted by the Municipal Council of the District of Johnstown assembled at the Town of Brockville, on Thursday, the twelfth day of February, in the year of our Lord one thousand eight hundred and forty-six, That for the purpose of Education, that is to say: for the erection, repair and completion of certain School Houses now required to be built, erected or repaired in certain School Districts hereinafter mentioned, there shall be raised and levied for the present year upon all real and personal property therein, the following sums, clear of the expenses of levying and collecting, namely:

In the Township of Kitley,

In School-District number fifteen, the sum of fifty Sums to be levied. pounds.

In the Township of Yonge,

In School District number twelve, the sum of fifty pounds.

In the Township of Oxford,

In School-District number fourteen, the sum of fifteen pounds.

How rated and collected.

SECTION 2. That the said sums be rated equally upon the assessed property in each School District respectively by the Clerk of the Peace, and be levied and collected by the Collectors of the several Townships hereinbefore named within the School Districts aforesaid, in the same manner as is now by law provided, and be by them paid to the Superintendents of the several Townships under the provisions and restrictions of the twelfth section of an Act passed by the Parliament of this Province, on the ninth day of December, in the year of our Lord one thousand eight hundred and forty-three, entitled "*An Act for the establishment and maintenance of Common Schools in Upper Canada.*"

RICHARD F. STEELE, WARDEN, **D. J.**

[L. S.]

No. CXXXII.—BY-LAW

To establish a Road in the Township of Lansdowne.

Preamble.

Whereas John Robinson, Surveyor of Highways in and for the County of Leeds, has been petitioned by twelve freeholders of the said County, to lay out a certain Road in the Township of Lansdowne; and in pursuance of such petition the said John Robinson has surveyed and laid

Description.

out the said Road as follows: commencing in the centre of lot number four, on the allowance for said Road, at a post between the third and fourth concessions marked R on the south side of said post; thence running across the east half of lot number four in a north-easterly direction round a swamp till it strikes said Road between lots numbers four and five on the concession line, distance fifty-one rods and a half to a post marked R on the south side; thence along said concession line till it intersects the old survey between six and seven, to a post fifteen rods south of said concession line, marked R on the south side fixed by the old survey; thence along the south side of said swamp in an easterly direction till it intersects said concession line about the centre of lot number seven to a post marked R on the south side, distance being thirty-two

rods; thence along said concession line till it intersects
the old survey to a post planted between eight and nine;
thence along the old survey on the centre of lot number
eleven on said concession line, to a post marked R on the
south side; thence a north-easterly course round a ledge
of rocks laying on said concession line to a post marked
R on the south side on said concession line, distance being
twenty-four rods; thence along said concession line till
it intersects the Kidd Road between eleven and twelve;
which said Road is laid out sixty feet in width: Be it
therefore ordained and enacted, and it is hereby ordained
and enacted by the Municipal Council of the District of
of Johnstown, in Council assembled at the Town of Brockville, on the twelfth day of August, in the year of our
Lord one thousand eight hundred and forty-six, That the
above described Road be approved of and confirmed, and
it is hereby approved of and confirmed to be a Public Confirmed.
Highway and Road.

OGLE R. GOWAN, Chairman.

[L. S.]

No. CXXXIII.—BY-LAW

To establish a Road in the Township of Bastard.

Whereas James Eaton, Surveyor of Highways in and Preamble.
for the County of Leeds, has been petitioned by twelve
freeholders of the said County to lay out a certain Road
in the Township of Bastard; and in pursuance of such
petition the said James Eaton has surveyed and laid out
the said road as follows: commencing at Chipman's
School House on the Portland Road leading to Smith's Description.
Mill, where a Cedar post is planted marked R; from
thence a south-westerly course to the side road between
lots numbers eighteen and nineteen, and crossing the said
Road where a Cedar post is planted on the west side of
said side road marked R, a distance of sixty-nine rods;
thence a south-west course to Amos Giles' barn yard gate,
where at or near a cedar post is planted, marked R, a
distance of twenty-six rods, where a bend is made in the
Road owing to the said Giles' buildings; thence a south-
west course to a ledge at or near Alexander Acheson's new
barn, where a bend is again made owing to the ledge and barn
where a Cedar post is planted and marked R, a distance of

one hundred and seventy-three rods; thence still a south-west course to the supposed line between Edward Connelly and Hiram Giles, where a Cedar post is planted marked R, a distance of one hundred and sixty-two rods; from thence till it intersects the Portland Road leading to Phillipsville, where a Cedar post is planted marked R, still a south-west course; the said Road to be on the south side of said posts, and which is laid out forty feet in width: Be it therefore ordained and enacted, and it is hereby ordained and enacted by the Municipal Council of the District of Johnstown, in Council assembled at the Town of Brockville, on the twelfth day of August, in the year of our Lord one thousand eight hundred and forty-six, That the above described road be approved of and confirmed, and it is hereby approved of and confirmed to be a Public Highway and Road.

Confirmed.

OGLE R. GOWAN, Chairman.

[L. S.]

No. CXXXIV—BY-LAW

To Tax certain School-Districts within the District of Johnstown.

Preamble.

Whereas applications have been made to the Municipal Council of the District of Johnstown, by the Trustees duly and legally appointed for several School-Districts, praying that a local tax or assessment may be levied on such School-Districts for the purposes hereinafter mentioned: Be it therefore ordained and enacted by the Municipal Council of said District, assembled at the Town of Brockville, on the twelfth day of August, in the year of our Lord one thousand eight hundred and forty-six, That for the purpose of Education, that is to say, for the erection, repair, and completion of certain School-Houses now required to be built, erected, repaired, or completed, and for the purchase of land for sites for School-Houses in certain School Districts hereinafter mentioned, there shall be raised and levied for the present year, upon all real and personal property therein, the following sums, clear of the expenses of levying and collecting, namely:

In the Township of North Crosby,

Sums to be levied.

In School District number four, the sum of fifty pounds, for the erection of a School-House therein.

In the Township of Escott,

In School District number twenty-six, the sum of twelve pounds ten shillings, for the completion of the School-House therein.

In the Township of Yonge.

(Repealed: see By-Law No. 149.)

In the Township of Elizabethtown,

In School District number seventeen, the sum of fifty pounds, for the erection of a School-House therein.

SECTION 2. That the said sums be rated equally upon the assessed property in each School District respectively by the Clerk of the Peace, and be levied and collected by the Collectors of the several Townships hereinbefore named within the School Districts aforesaid, in the same manner as is now by law provided. *How rated and collected.*

OGLE R. GOWAN, CHAIRMAN.

[L. S.]

No. CXXXV.—BY-LAW

To establish a road in the Township of Wolford.

Whereas Michael Kelly, Surveyor of Highways in and for the County of Grenville, has been petitioned by twelve freeholders of the said County, to lay out a certain Road in the Township of Wolford; and whereas the said Michael Kelly has surveyed and laid out the said Road pursuant to such petition, as follows: commencing at the west end of Olmstead's Bridge, and running due west three chains and fifty-nine links to an Ironwood tree, blazed and marked R, the Road being on the south side of said Ironwood tree; thence south fifty-four degrees, west eight chains and ninety-one links, along the line between Haskins' and Olmstead's, twenty feet on each side of said line till it intersects the Town line between Wolford and Kitley; the said Road to be forty feet in width: Be it therefore ordained and enacted, and it is hereby ordained and enacted by the District Council of *Preamble.* *Description.*

the District of Johnstown, in Council assembled at the Town of Brockville, on the eighth day of October, in the year of our Lord one thousand eight hundred and forty-six, That the above described Road be approved of and confirmed, and it is hereby approved of and confirmed as a public Road and Highway.

Confirmed.

OGLE R. GOWAN, Chairman.

[L. S.]

No. CXXXVI.—BY-LAW

To establish a Road in the Township of Bastard.

Preamble.

Whereas James Eaton, Surveyor of Highways in and for the County of Leeds, has been petitioned by twelve freeholders of the said County to lay out a certain Road in the Township of Bastard; and whereas the said James Eaton has surveyed and laid out the said Road pursuant to such petition as follows: commencing at John Morris's south-west gate-post on the concession line in front of his dwelling-house, and in rear of lot number twenty-three; from thence to a Cedar post marked R, planted thirty rods from said gate, and twelve feet from the concession line on said lot number twenty-three; thence a straight line to a Cedar post marked R, planted in rear of lot number twenty-two, and opposite to a bridge crossing a precipice caused by rocks; from thence to a Cedar post marked R, planted on the concession line a distance of eighteen rods from the last named post on said lot, adding twelve feet to the width of the concession road at the first post marked R, and at the second post at the bridge, forty-two feet in width: Be it therefore ordained and enacted, and it is hereby ordained and enacted by the Municipal Council of the District of Johnstown, in Council assembled at the Town of Brockville, on the eighth day of October, in the year of our Lord one thousand eight hundred and forty-six, That the above described Road be approved of and confirmed, and the same is hereby approved of and confirmed as a Public Road and Highway.

Description.

Confirmed.

OGLE R. GOWAN, Chairman.

[L. S.]

No. CXXXVII.—BY-LAW

To establish a Road in the Township of North Crosby.

Whereas James Bilton, Surveyor of Highways in and Preamble. for the County of Leeds, has been petitioned by twelve freeholders of the said County to lay out a certain Road in the Township of North Crosby; and whereas the said James Bilton has surveyed and laid out the said Road pursuant to such petition, as follows : commencing at a post marked Street on the Highway in the village of Description Westport, and runs to the Rideau Lake; said Road is staked out on both sides, and is marked and laid out fifty feet in width : Be it therefore ordained and enacted, and it is hereby ordained and enacted by the Municipal Council of the District of Johnstown in Council assembled at the Town of Brockville, on the eighth day of October, in the year of our Lord one thousand eight hundred and forty-six, That the said above described road be approved of and confirmed, and it is hereby approved of and confirmed as a Confirmed. public Road and Highway.

OGLE R. GOWAN, Chairman.

[L. S.]

No. CXXXVIII.—BY-LAW

To establish a Road in the Township of North Crosby.

Whereas James Bilton, Surveyor of Highways in and for Preamble. the County of Leeds, has been petitioned by twelve freeholders of the said County, to lay out a certain Road in the Township of North Crosby; and whereas the said James Bilton has surveyed and laid out the said Road pursuant to such petition as follows: commencing at a Beech post marked and planted on lot number twelve in Description. the seventh concession of North Crosby aforesaid, where the old Road runs to the Mill of Mr. James Rorison; thence from the said Post across said lot and across the Mill-Pond, north-west across lots numbers thirteen, fourteen, fifteen, sixteen and seventeen to a Basswood stump marked as a post on the side line between lots number seventeen and eighteen in said Township; the line of said Road is blazed on trees on the west side of the Road, and is marked with red chalk, which said Road is laid out

H

fifty feet in width: Be it therefore ordained and enacted, and it is hereby ordained and enacted by the Municipal Council of the District of Johnstown, in Council assembled at the Town of Brockville, on the eighth day of October, in the year of our Lord one thousand eight hundred and forty-six, That the above described Road be approved of and confirmed, and the same is hereby approved of and confirmed as a public Road and Highway.

Confirmed.

OGLE R. GOWAN, Chairman.

[L. S.]

No. CXXXIX.—BY-LAW

To establish a Road in the Township of Bastard.

Preamble.

Whereas James Eaton, Surveyor of Highways in and for the County of Leeds, has been petitioned by twelve freeholders of the said County to lay out a certain Road in the Township of Bastard; and whereas the said James Eaton has surveyed and laid out the said Road pursuant to such petition, as follows: commencing in front of the

Description.

third concession line, or road, at where a post is planted that divides lot number sixteen where a Cedar post marked R is planted, twenty feet on the north-east side from the said post; from thence a side line course, a distance of thirty-five rods along the centre of said lot where a Cedar post marked R has been planted, the Road running equally upon each half of said lot number sixteen up to the post; thence a south-east course and turning on the south side of said post, and crossing the one half of lot number sixteen, and about three-fourths of lot number fifteen, where it intersects the Road leading to New Boyne, where I have planted a Cedar post marked R; the said Road to be on the south-east side of the two last named posts, which said Road is laid out forty feet in width: Be it therefore ordained and enacted, and it is hereby ordained and enacted by the Municipal Council of the District of Johnstown, in Council assembled at the Town of Brockville, on the eighth day of October, in the year of our Lord one thousand eight hundred and forty-six, That the above described Road be approved of and confirmed, and

Confirmed.

it is hereby approved of and confirmed to be a public Road and Highway.

OGLE R. GOWAN, Chairman.

[L. S.]

No, CXL.—BY-LAW

To establish a Road in the Township of North Crosby.

Whereas James Bilton, Surveyor of Highways in and Preamble. for the County of Leeds, has been petitioned by twelve freeholders of the said County, to lay out a certain Road in the Township of North Crosby; and whereas the said James Bilton has surveyed and laid out the said Road pursuant to such petition, as follows : commencing at a Maple stump squared and marked as a post on lot number Description. seventeen, in the first concession of North Crosby aforesaid, and runs across lots numbers seventeen, eighteen and nineteen, a north-west course, and from thence runs lengthways of lot number twenty, in the second Concession of the said Township of North Crosby, to the road laid out leading from Westport to Perth: the said line of Road is blazed and marked with red lead, and is laid out forty feet in width, and is on the west side of said line : Be it therefore ordained and enacted, and it is hereby ordained and enacted, by the Municipal Council of the District of Johnstown, in Council assembled at the Town of Brockville, on the eighth day of October, in the year of our Lord one thousand eight hundred and forty-six, That the said Road as above described be approved of and confirmed, and it is hereby approved of and confirmed as a public Road and Confirmed. Highway.

OGLE R. GOWAN, Chairman.

[L. S.]

No. CXLI.—BY-LAW

To establish a Road in the Townships of Bastard and North Crosby.

Whereas James Eaton, Surveyor of Highways in and Preamble. for the County of Leeds, has been petitioned by twelve freeholders of the said County to lay out a certain Road in the Townships of Bastard and South Burgess : commencing on the line between Burgess and Bastard, at the line between Description. lots numbers twenty-two and twenty-three, where a post marked R is planted twenty feet from said line, and being on the west side of said Road : from thence a side line course until it intersects the second concession line or road, where a cedar post marked R is planted twenty feet from the above named line and on the west side of said road, running equally on each of said lots numbers twenty-two and twenty-three, from the front to the rear of said lots, which said road is laid out forty feet in width : Be it therefore ordained and enacted, and it is hereby ordained and enacted, by the Municipal Council of the District of Johnstown, in Council assembled at the Town of Brockville, on the eighth day of October, in the year of our Lord one thousand eight hundred and forty-six, That the above described Road be approved of and confirmed, and it is hereby approved of and confirmed as a Public Road and Highway.

Confirmed.

OGLE R. GOWAN, Chairman.

[L. S.]

No. CXLII.—BY-LAW

See By-law No. 2, County Council.

To compensate Councillors for their attendance at the Meetings of the Municipal Council of the District.

Preamble.

Whereas by the third Section of the ninth Victoria, chapter forty, entitled " *An Act to amend the Laws relative to District Councils in Upper Canada,*" it is enacted, " That it shall be lawful for any District Council in its discretion, by any By-law to be passed for that purpose, to allow to each member of such Council a sum not exceeding six shillings and three pence for each day he shall actually sit in Council, to be paid out of the District Funds in such manner, and on such conditions as shall be directed in such By-law :" Be it therefore ordained and enacted, and it is hereby ordained and enacted by the District Council of the District of Johnstown, in Council assembled at the Town of Brockville, on the seventh day of October, in the year of our Lord one thousand eight hundred and forty-six, That at this present Session of the Council, and at every subsequent session hereafter to be held (provided such Sessions do not exceed four in any one year,) the Clerk of the Council for the time being shall duly enter the names of each and every Councillor, for each and every day he shall actually sit in Council, and

Certificate of Clerk.

shall certify the same at the end of each Session, which certificate shall be countersigned by the Warden or Chairman, who shall have presided at the Session of the Council for which any such certificate was given, and after being so countersigned shall be deemed and taken to be a true statement of the number of days the Councillor receiving the same had actually sat in Council, at any such Session, as aforesaid.

Section 2. And be it enacted by the authority aforesaid, That for each and every day so certified as aforesaid, the Councillor in whose favor it shall be given shall be entitled to receive from the Treasurer of the District, the sum of six shillings and three pence for each and every day so **Sums allowed** certified, as aforesaid, and the Treasurer of the District is hereby authorised and required, upon the production and delivery to him of every such certificate, to pay to the Councillor or to his authorised agent producing the same, the sum of six shillings and three pence, for each and every day it shall appear by such certificate that such Councillor had actually sat in Council, and such certificate shall be taken as a proper Voucher from such Treasurer, and be allowed and credited to that officer in his account with the District.

OGLE R. GOWAN, Chairman.

[L. S.]

No. CXLIII.—BY-LAW

For regulating the places for holding the Township Meetings, and for providing for the erection of Town Halls in the several Townships of the District. **See 12 Vic., Cap 80. See 12 Vic. Cap. 61. See Con. Stat. U. C., Cap. 54.**

Whereas much uncertainty has arisen as to the places at which the several respective Township Meetings for the **Preamble.** annual Election of Township and Parish Officers should be held; and whereas, owing to such uncertainty, no suitable accommodations have been provided for the decent and orderly holding of such meetings, and much inconvenience has been experienced by the people attending such meetings; and whereas by the second section of the ninth of Victoria, chapter forty, entitled "*An Act to amend the Laws relative to District Councils in Upper Canada,*" it is amongst other things enacted "that each District Council shall have power by By-Law or By-laws to be passed from time to time, to fix the site of Town Halls, and the place for holding the Township Meetings in each or any Township of the District, and all Township Meetings authorised by law, shall thereafter be held at the places so appointed, and not elsewhere": Be it therefore ordained and enacted by the Municipal Council of the District of Johnstown, assembled at the Town of Brockville, on the eighth day of October, in the year of our Lord one thousand eight hundred and forty-six, That from and after the first day of January next, which will be in the year of our Lord one thousand eight hundred and forty-seven, the several and respective Township Meetings in and for the District of Johnstown, for the election of Township and Parish Officers, shall be held annually, according to law, at the following places, that is to say :—

For the Township of Leeds and Lansdowne, (in front).

(Repealed; see By-Law No. 154.)

In the Township of Escott,

Places where Town Meetings to be held. At Vanstondale, being on lot number twelve in the second concession of Escott.

For the Township of Yonge,

At Mackintosh, being on lot number fifteen in the fifth concession of Yonge.

For the Township of Elizabethtown,

At New Dublin, being on lot number twenty in the sixth concession of Elizabethtown.

For the Township of Augusta,

At Stone's Corners, being on lot number thirty in the third concession of Augusta.

For the Township of Edwardsburgh,

At Spencerville, being on lot number twenty-six in the sixth concession of Edwardsburg.

For the Township of South Gower, and all that part of the Township of North Gower being south of the Rideau river.

On lot number three in the fifth concession of South Gower.

For the Township of Oxford,

At Kemptville, being on lot number twenty-seven in the third concession of Oxford,

For the Township of Wolford,

At Merrickville, on lot number nine, in Broken Front concession A, of Wolford.

For the Township of Kitley,

At Brandenburgh, formerly called Frankville, on lot number twenty-one in the eighth concession of Kitley.

For the Township of Bastard,

(Repealed; see By-law No. 168.)

For the Township of South Crosby,

At Marvin's School House, on lot number seventeen, in the first concession of South Crosby.

For the Township of North Crosby,

At Westport, on lot number ten, in the seventh concession of North Crosby.

For the Township of South Burgess,

(Repealed; see By-law No. 180.)

For the Rear of Leeds and Lansdowne,

. At Lyndhurst.

For the Township of Elmsley,

At Lombardy, on lot number nineteen in the second concession of Elmsley.

And be it further ordained and enacted, and it is hereby ordained and enacted, That whenever the Freeholders and inhabitant Householders of any Township within the said District, assembled at any annual Township or Parish Meeting, held pursuant to law, at any of the places aforesaid, shall determine by a majority of the votes of such Freeholders and inhabitant Householders then and there assembled, to purchase or erect a suitable building to be called the "Town Hall" of the Township, for the accommodation of the public, at such Township Meetings as aforesaid, or for the use and purposes of a public school house, public library, court room, or such other useful or necessary purpose or purposes as may be determined on by the Trustees hereinafter named, or by a majority of them ; it shall be the duty of the Township Clerk of every such Township as aforesaid, and he is hereby authorised and required to certify the fact of such decision under his hand to the District Clerk within twenty days after such election and decision as aforesaid, and such District Clerk shall lay the said notice before the District Council at its next ensuing meeting, and thereupon it shall be the duty of the Council to levy and assess upon the rateable property of every such Township as aforesaid, a competent amount for the erection of every such Hall, and for all other necessary expenses appertaining to its erection, comfort, convenience and preservation.

How Town Hall to be provided.

And be it enacted by the authority aforesaid, That the Councillor or Councillors (as the case may be) representing any such Township in the Municipal Council of the District for the time being, together with the Township Clerk for the time being, shall be the Trustees of every such Town Hall in their several and respective Townships, and as such Trustees shall have perpetual succession, and shall have the care, custody, control, possession, management and preservation of every such building or hall, together with all the property, grounds and appurtenances thereunto attached or belonging.

Councillors to be Trustees.

And be it enacted by the authority aforesaid, That if any Town Clerk shall neglect or refuse to notify in writing to the District Clerk for the time being, the fact of the Township Meeting having decided by a majority of votes then and there assembled, within twenty days after the holding of such Township Meeting, he shall for every such neglect or refusal forfeit and pay the sum of five pounds, together with all lawful costs appertaining to his conviction.

Penalty.

OGLE R GOWAN, Chairman.

[L. S.]

No. CXLIV.—BY-LAW

To establish certain Roads in the District of Johnstown.

Whereas John Robinson, Surveyor of Highways in and *Preamble.* for the County of Leeds, has been petitioned by twelve freeholders of the said County, to lay out certain Streets and Lanes, or Alleys, in Gananoque, on the east side of the Gananoque River; and in pursuance of such petition, the said John Robinson has surveyed and laid out the said Streets and Lanes as follows: commencing on the Queen's Highway in Gananoque on the north side where it inter- *Description of Streets in Ganan-* sects with Stone street; from thence along Stone street, *oque.* northerly nine hundred feet to North street, to a post marked R; from thence easterly along North street, one thousand three hundred and sixty feet, to William street, to a post marked R; from thence southerly along William street nine hundred feet to the Queen's Highway: And then commencing on North street where it intersects with Charles street, and from thence southerly across Brock and Garden streets and the Queen's Highway, one thousand five hundred and forty feet to Sydenham street, to a post marked R; then easterly along Sydenham street two hundred and forty feet, to a post marked R to the end of said street; then commencing on William street where it intersects with Brock street; from thence easterly along Brock street across Charles and Stone streets one thousand six hundred and eighty feet to a post marked R, where it intersects with West street; thence southerly along West street three hundred and eighty feet to a post marked R, where it intersects with Garden street; thence easterly along Garden street, across Stone, Charles and William streets two thousand three hundred and forty feet to a post marked R, to where it intersects with James street; from thence southerly along James street two hundred and sixty feet to the Queen's Highway; then commencing on the north side of the Queen's Highway, where it intersects with Stone street; from thence southerly two thousand one hundred and sixty feet to the River Saint Lawrence; then commencing on the east side of Stone street, where it intersects with Pine street; from thence easterly along Pine street one hundred and eighty feet to the end of said street to a post marked R; then commencing on the easterly side of Stone street, where it intersects with John street; from thence along John street three hundred and sixty feet to the end of said street to a post marked R; then commencing on the easterly side of Charles street, where it intersects with Pine street; from thence easterly two hundred and forty feet to the end of said street to a post marked R; then commencing on William street where it intersects with North alley; from thence westerly along North alley across Charles street one thousand three hundred and sixty feet to Stone street, to a post marked R; then commencing on West street, where it intersects with Garden alley; from thence easterly along Garden alley, across Stone and Charles streets to William street, one thousand six hundred and eighty feet to a post marked R; then commencing on James street, where it intersects with Cooper alley; from thence westerly along said alley across William, Charles and Stone streets, two thousand two hundred and twenty feet to the end of said alley, to a post marked R; then commencing on the Queen's Highway where it intersects with Cowan alley; from thence northerly along said alley two hundred and sixty feet to Garden street, to a post marked R; then commencing on Stone street where it intersects with Oak alley; from thence easterly along said alley across Charles street to the end of said alley nine hundred feet to a post marked R; then commencing on Charles street where it intersects with Spruce alley; from thence easterly along said alley to the end, two hundred and twenty feet to a post marked R; then commencing on Stone street where it intersects with Manse alley; from thence easterly along said alley to the end three hundred and sixty feet to a post marked R; then commencing on Stone street where it intersects with South alley; from thence easterly along said alley to the end three hundred and sixty feet to a post marked R; which said streets are laid out sixty feet in width, and the alleys are laid out twenty feet in width:

And whereas Benjamin Warren, Surveyor of Highways in and for the County of Leeds, has been petitioned by twelve freeholders of the said County to lay out a certain Road in the Township of Escott; and in pursuant of such petition the said Benjamin Warren has surveyed and laid out the said Road as follows: commencing on lot number four in broken front Concession of the Township of Escott, on the present travelled Road twenty-five rods more or less from the west line of said lot, at a black Oak tree blazed on three sides, and marked R on the south side: from thence on a line of blazed trees an east-south-east course, to a post at or near the line between lots numbers four and five in the said Concession of the said Township of Escott: from thence on a line of blazed trees

Description of Road in Escott.

and posts, an east course, across lot number five in said Concession to a post planted between lots numbers five and six in said Concession; thence on a line of blazed trees and posts, an east south-east course across lots numbers six, seven, eight, nine, ten, eleven, twelve, thirteen, fourteen, fifteen and sixteen, to a post planted between said lots numbers fifteen and sixteen, marked R on the south side: thence on a line of blazed trees east-south-east across the west of lot number seventeen in said Concession of said Township, to an Oak tree marked R, where it intersects the present travelled Road north of the Dwelling of Stephen Elliot, and is to be on the South side of said line: and which said Road is laid out forty feet in width.

And whereas John Jelly, Surveyor of Highways in and for the County of Leeds has been petitioned by twelve freeholders of the said County of Leeds, to lay out a certain Road in the Township of Elizabethtown; and in pursuance of such petition the said John Jelly has surveyed and laid out the said Road as follows: commencing at a Beech tree marked Description of R on two sides on the north side of the highway and on the Road in Eliza-east side of lot number twenty-two in the first Concession bethtown. of Elizabethtown; thence a south-westerly course seven chains more or less to a post sixty feet north of a point of rock on said lot number twenty-two; thence a straight course south-westerly thirteen chains more or less to a post on the north side of the present travelled Road; the said posts being on the north side of said Road, and are all marked R with red chalk on two sides,—which said Road is laid out sixty feet in width.

And whereas Edward Mix, Surveyor of Highways in and for the County of Grenville, has been petitioned by twelve freeholders of the said County to lay out a Road in the Township of Oxford: and in pursuance of such petition the said Edward Mix has surveyed and laid out the said Road as follows: commencing at a stone monu- Description of ment marked RR, planted on the line in front of the Road in Oxford. fourth concession of said Township, in the centre of lot number three in said fourth Concession and running along said centre line to the rear of said concession; thence continuing the same course about one hundred rods more or less in the fifth concession of the said Township of Oxford to its junction with the Prescott Road at another stone monument marked R R: which said Road is laid out forty feet in width,—twenty feet of which is to be taken from each side of the line.

Be it therefore ordained and enacted by the Municipal Council of the District of Johnstown, in Council assembled at the Town of Brockville, on the fourth day of February, in the year of our Lord one thousand eight hundred and forty-seven, That the above described Roads be respectively approved of and confirmed as Public Roads and Highways.

Confirmed as Public Roads.

OGLE R. GOWAN, Warden.

[L. S.]

No. CXLV.—BY-LAW

See By-law No 231, County Council.

Of the Municipal Council of the District of Johnstown, setting aside the sum of Three Hundred Pounds to pay the interest on a certain sum of money therein mentioned.—Passed February 5, 1847.

(Repealed : see By-law County Council No. 4.)

No. CXLVI.—BY-LAW

To authorise the Assessment and Collection of Rates for the general purposes of the Johnstown District for the year 1847.—Passed February 5, 1847.

(Expired by Limitation.)

No. CXLVII.—BY-LAW

To Assess the Inhabitants of the District of Johnstown for the support and maintenance of Common Schools therein, for the year 1847.—Passed February 5, 1847.

(Expired by Limitation.)

No. CXLVIII.—BY-LAW

To fix the Salaries of the District Officers mentioned therein.—Passed February 5, 1847.

(Repealed ; see By-law No. 186.)

No. CXLIX.—BY-LAW

To repeal part of By-Law No. 134, entitled " By-Law to Tax certain School Districts within the District of Johnstown."

Whereas by a certain By-Law passed by the Municipal Council of the Johnstown District, on the twelfth day of August, in the year of our Lord one thousand eight hundred and forty-six, it is amongst other things provided, that there shall be raised and levied for the said year, upon real and personal property therein, in School District number thirteen, in the Township of Yonge, the sum of one hundred pounds for the erection of a School House therein, and to purchase land as a site for the same ; And whereas it is necessary to repeal so much of the said By-Law as relates to the said tax on the said School District number thirteen, in the Township of Yonge, aforesaid : Be it therefore ordained and enacted, and it is hereby ordained and enacted by the said Council of the Johnstown District, aforesaid, assembled at the Town of Brockville on the fifth day of February, in the year of our Lord one thousand eight hundred and forty-seven, That so much of the said By-Law No. 134 as relates to the said Tax on said School District number thirteen in Yonge, aforesaid, be repealed, and the same is hereby repealed.

OGLE R. GOWAN, Warden.

No. CL.—BY-LAW

To indemnify the late Treasurer.—Passed February 5,1847.

1. Be it enacted by the Council of the District of Johnstown, That the Auditors of the District of Johnstown be and are hereby authorised to audit and acquit the accounts of Andrew N. Buell, Esquire, late Treasurer of this

District, so soon as he shall report to them, or either of them, that his books and accounts are ready for such audit and inspection; and that upon their auditing, inspecting and acquitting said books and accounts, and that upon

For delivery of books, &c., to his successor.

and after the delivery by the said Andrew N. Buell, Esquire, to the said James L. Schofield, Esquire, duly appointed Treasurer of this District, of the books, papers and monies, of and belonging to the said District, which then may be in the possession of him, the said Andrew N. Buell, the Clerk of this Council be, and is hereby authorised to deliver up to the said Andrew N. Buell his bond or security or the due administration of his said office of Treasurer, and the Council will indemnify and save harmless the said Andrew N. Buell from any loss or damage that he may at any time hereafter sustain, and from any cost he may at any time be put to by reason of his the said Andrew N. Buell's so having delivered up the said books, papers and monies of the Treasury of this District to the said James L. Schofield, and indemnify the said Clerk for any act done under this By-Law.

OGLE R. GOWAN, Warden,

No. CLI.—BY-LAW

To assess the Inhabitants of certain School Sections in the District of Johnstown.—Passed February 8, 1847.

1. Be it enacted by the District Council of the District of Johnstown, That there be raised and levied on the assessed rateable property, of the inhabitants of School Sections hereinafter mentioned in the said District, the several sums of money required for the said School Sections for the following purposes, (clear of all charges of assessing and collecting,) namely:—

Sums to be levied in.

Yonge.

In School Section No. 13, in the Township of Yonge.

The sum of one hundred pounds for the purpose of erecting and completing the School House commenced therein, and paying for the site of the same.

Bastard:

In School-Section No. 7, in the Township of Bastard.

The sum of one hundred pounds, for the purpose of erecting and completing a School-House therein.

In School-Section No. 9, in the Township of Augusta. Augusta.

The sum of fifty pounds, for the purpose of erecting and completing a School-House therein.

In School-Section No. 4, in the Township of North Crosby. North Crosby.

The sum of forty pounds, for the purpose of completing the School-House therein.

In School-Section No. 9, in the Township of Elmsley. Elmsley.

The sum of fifty pounds, for the purpose of erecting and completing a School-House therein.

In School-Section No. 2, in the Township of South Crosby. South Crosby.

The sum of sixty pounds, for the purpose of erecting a School-House therein.

In School-Section No. 1, in the Township of Augusta. Augusta.

(Repealed; see By-Law No. 172.)

And the said sums so to be raised and levied, shall be apportioned on the said property in the said School Sections respectively, according to the values assigned to the same by law, and shall be placed on the Collectors' Rolls by the Clerk of the Peace: Provided always, that the sum to be raised and levied in each School Section aforesaid, shall not in any year exceed two pence in the pound on the assessed value of the said property in every such School Section, until the said several sums shall be fully raised and levied as aforesaid. How levied.

2. That the said sums shall be collected by the respective Collectors of the several Townships in which the said School-Sections are situated, in like manner as any other tax for said District, but shall be paid over by them to the District Superintendent of Common Schools, within the period fixed by law for the payment of rates collected in each year to the Treasurer. How collected.

3. That it shall be the duty of the Assessors of the several Townships, in which the said several Sections are respectively situated, to return to the Clerk of the Peace a list of all the rateable property in each of the said School Duties of Assessors.

Sections with the names of the rateable inhabitants therein, duly attested in the same manner and at the same time as they are required to make the Annual Assessment Returns for the respective Townships.

OGLE R. GOWAN, Warden.

No. CLII.—BY-LAW

To expend certain monies granted for Roads and Bridges in the District of Johnstown.

Preamble.

Whereas by a certain resolution of the District Council of the District of Johnstown, the sum of eight hundred pounds has been set apart for Roads and Bridges therein; and whereas it is necessary to divide the said sum among the several Townships in the said District: Be it therefore ordained and enacted, and it is hereby ordained and enacted by the Municipal Council of the District of Johnstown in Council assembled, on the eighth day of February, in the year of our Lord one thousand eight hundred and forty-seven, That the Councillor or Councillors for the respective Townships in said District, are hereby authorized to receive from the Treasurer of said District, and expend on Roads and Bridges in his or their respective Townships, the several sums of money as hereinafter mentioned, viz:—

Sums granted to Townships.

	£	s	d
Elizabethtown,	68	17	9
Augusta,	68	17	9
Yonge,	68	17	9
Escott,	30	0	0
Bastard,	68	17	9
Kitley,	68	17	9
Elmsley,	20	0	0
Leeds and Lansdowne, in front,	68	17	9
Leeds and Lansdowne, in rear,	30	0	0
South Crosby,	30	0	0
North Crosby,	30	0	0
Burgess,	10	0	3
Edwardsburgh,	68	17	9
Oxford,	68	17	9
South Gower,	30	0	0
Wolford,	68	17	9

OGLE R. GOWAN, Warden.

No. CLIII.—BY-LAW

To Assess the Inhabitants of the Johnstown District for the maintenance of the District Model School for the year 1847.—Passed February 8, 1847.

(Expired by Limitation.)

No. CLIV.—BY-LAW

To repeal so much of By-law No. 143 as enacts that the Annual Township Meeting in the front of Leeds and Lansdowne shall be held at Landonville.—Passed February 9, 1847.

Whereas it would be more convenient for the inhabitants of the front of Leeds and Lansdowne if the annual Township Meeting should be every alternate year held at the Village of Gananoque: Be it enacted, That so much of the said By-law No. 143 as enacts that the said Annual Township Meeting for the front of Leeds and Lansdowne be held at Landonville, on lot number eleven, in the second concession of Lansdowne, be repealed and the same is hereby repealed. *Preamble.*

Part By-law No. 143 repealed.

And be it ordained, That the said Annual Township Meeting for the said Township of the front of Leeds and Lansdowne be held alternately at the Village of Gananoque and at Landonville aforesaid; that is to say, the said Annual Township Meeting for the said Township for the year 1848 shall be held at Gananoque, and the year following at Landonville, and so on alternately during the continuance of this By-law. *Meeting alternately at Gananoque and Landonville.*

OGLE R. GOWAN, WARDEN.

No. CLV.—BY-LAW

To empower the respective Township Councillors to direct the laying out and performance of Statute Labor.—Passed February 9, 1847. *See Con. Stat. U. C., Caps. 54 & 55.*

Whereas by an Act of the Legislature of the Province of Canada, passed in the ninth year of Her Majesty's Reign, entitled *"An Act to amend the Laws relative to* *Preamble.*

J

District Councils in Upper Canada," that it shall and may be lawful for any District Council by By-law to empower the landholders in the District to compound for the Statute labor by them respectively performed, for any term not exceeding five years, at any rate not exceeding two shillings and six pence, currency, for each day's labor, and at any time before the labor compounded for ought to be performed, and by such By-law to direct to what Officer in each Township such commutation money shall be paid, and how such money shall be applied and accounted for, and to regulate by By-law the manner and the divisions in which the Statute labor shall be performed, or to empower the respective Township Councillors to direct the laying out and performance thereof; And whereas it is necessary to pass such a By-law: Be it therefore ordained and enacted, That the District Councillors in their respective Townships shall have all the powers and authority possessed by the Township Wardens under an Act of the Legislature of the late Province of Upper Canada, passed in the first year of Her Majesty's Reign respecting the compounding for Statute labor, or concerning any contract or agreement entered into with any person residing in the Township respecting Statute labor.

Councillors to have powers of Township Wardens.

SECTION 2. And be it ordained, That any landholder in the District may compound for Statute labor for which he or she is liable to perform, for any term not exceeding five years, and for any rate not exceeding two shillings and six pence, currency, for each day's labor, and at any time before the labor compounded for ought to be performed; and that at any dispute arising between any Township Councillor and the party so compounding, respecting any contract or agreement, shall and may be settled in the manner pointed out in the forty-third and forty-fourth clauses of the aforesaid Act, passed in the fifth year of Her Majesty's Reign, entitled "*An Act to alter and amend sundry Acts regulating the appointments and duties of Township Officers.*"

Landholders may compound.

SECTION 3. And be it ordained and enacted, That all money paid as commutation money for Statute labor shall be paid to the Road Overseer of the Division, to be by him paid over and accounted for in the manner prescribed by the eighth Section of By-law number one.

Commutation money to be paid to Overseer.

SECTION 4. Be it ordained and enacted, That all the powers and authority heretofore vested in the Justices of the Peace, acting for their respective Divisions by the twentieth section of said Act, the first of Victoria, chapter twenty-first, shall and may be vested in the respective Township Councillor or Councillors, as the case may be, so far as the said powers and authority appertain to, or are connected with the laying out of Road divisions, the appropriation, control, management, and distribution of Statute labor within the several and respective Townships.

Power of Justices vested in Councillors.

SECTION 5. Be it enacted, That the respective Township Councillors respresenting any Township in the Municipal Council of the District, or any one of them, shall have full power and authority to superintend and direct the manner in which Statute labor shall be performed, and they, or any one of them, are hereby authorised and empowered, should they see fit, to order and direct the Overseers of Highways, or any one of them, to lay out the Statute labor on any Road or part of a Road within their respective divisions.

Their powers as to labour.

SECTION 6. And be it ordained, That should the Overseers of Highways, or any one of them, receive no orders before the first day of June in any year from the Councillor or Councillors who represent the Township in which he resides, respecting the laying out of the Statute labor, then and in that case it shall be the duty of the said Road Overseer or Overseers, and he or they are hereby ordered and required to lay out the Statute labor in his or their division to the best of his or their abilities, in any manner that shall appear to him or them the most conducive to the public good.

How to be laid out.

SECTION 7. And be it ordained and enacted That it shall be the duty of the Overseers of Highways in their respective divisions, and they are hereby authorised and required (without receiving any order for that purpose) to demand from every male inhabitant within the limits of his division, of the age of twenty-one years and upwards, not assessed on the Assessment List of the Township, the performance of two days' Statute labor, or commute for the same at the rate per day allowed by the Statutes of the Province.

Parties not assessed to pay money in lieu.

OGLE R. GOWAN, WARDEN.

No. CLVI.—BY-LAW

To require the Office of the District Treasurer to be held in the Court House of the District.—Passed February 9, 1847.

Preamble.

Whereas a certain Room in the Court House of this District has been set apart by this Council for the office of the District Treasurer: and whereas it is desirable and necessary that the said Office should be held in and kept in the said Room: Be it therefore enacted by the Council of the District of Johnstown, That from and after the passing of this By-law, the Treasurer of the District of Johnstown do open and keep open his office as such Treasurer in said Room so set apart in the said Court House, and shall be kept open and attended for the **Office hours,** business of the District during the usual office hours, namely, from ten to three o'clock each day, (Sundays and Public Holidays excepted.)

OGLE R. GOWAN, Warden.

No. CLVII.—BY-LAW

To provide for the Custody of certain Books the property of the District.—Passed February 9, 1847.

(Repealed: see By-law County Council No. 20.)

No. CLVIII.—BY-LAW

To establish certain Roads in the District of Johnstown.

Preamble.

Whereas Edward Mix, Surveyor of Highways in and for the County of Grenville, has been petitioned by twelve freeholders of the said County to lay out a certain Road in the Township of Oxford, and in pursuance of such petition, the said Edward Mix has surveyed and laid out **Description of** the said Road as follows: commencing at a stone monu- **Road in Oxford.** ment (marked R. I.) planted on the Road side near the School-House, on lot number three, in the ninth concession of the Township of Oxford, and running in a northwesterly direction about eighty rods to another Stone monument (marked R. II.) planted on the lower side of lot number two, and about the middle of the aforesaid concession, then at a right angle from the said line to the centre of said lot number two to another stone monument (marked R. III.) planted on the division line between Chauncey Bishop and Moses McAllister, and thence to the front of the said Concession on the division line between the aforesaid Bishop and McAllister; which said Road is laid out forty feet in width,—twenty feet from each side of the monuments.

And whereas Edward Mix, Surveyor of Highways in and for the County of Grenville, has been petitioned by twelve freeholders of the said County, to lay out all the unestablished Streets in the Village of Kemptville, on lots Nos. 26 and 27 on both sides of the Branch, and on 28 on the south side of the Branch, and in pursuance of such petition the said Edward Mix has surveyed and laid out as follows: commencing with James street one chain 48½ links south of the side line between lots Nos. 27 and 28, and running north 36°, west 1 chain 56 links to Water street, and from Water street north 51° 45 min., west to the rear of the Village plot. Lydia street commences at the rear of the Village, 20 rods from James street, runs south 51° 45 min., east to the south branch. Henry street commences at the water's edge and runs to the rear of the village plot, five chains from and in a parallel line with Lydia street. Fanny street commences at the water's edge and runs along the side of Village lot No. 1 to Clothier street, and in a parallel line with Henry street. Water street commences on Henry street, two chains from the water's edge, and runs north 38° 15 min., east to the side line between 27 and 28. Clothier street lies four chains from, and parallel with Water street, from the side line between 27 and 28 to West street, and from West street to the side line between 26 and 27, a little more southerly. Oxford street lies four chains back from Clothier street, and runs south 38° 15 min., west from the lower to the upper side of 27. North street lies 4 chains back from Oxford street and in a parallel line with it, from the side line between 27 and 28 to West street. The above streets are on lot No. 27, on the north side of the Branch, and are of the following widths: Water street, North street, James street, and Henry street are each 40 feet in width. Lydia street and Clothier street are each 50 feet in width. Oxford street is 66 feet in width, and Fanny street is 44 links wide. Harriet street commences

Description of Streets in Kemptville.

at a post on the south east side of the Road leading up
the Branch, about 436 feet south of the side line between
26 and 27, and runs east 43 ° 33 min., south to the south
Branch, and is 39 feet wide. Alfred street commences
350 feet from, and runs in a parallel line with Harriet
street, to the Creek, and is 39 feet in width. Water street
commences on Harriet street, 200 feet from the Main
Road, and runs in a parallel line with it to Alfred street,
and is 35 feet in width. The above streets are on lot No.
26, on the north side of the branch. Reuben street commences about 289 feet from the water's edge, at the south
end of the bridge, on the Prescott Road, runs at right-
angle from the Road to the side line between 26 and 27.
Water street commences about 165 feet from the water's
edge, and runs a right-angle from the Prescott Road to
William street. William street commences at the water's
edge, about 361 feet from the Prescott Road, and runs to
Asa street, and from Asa street to Mary street in the same
direction, but is known by the name of Thomas street.
Joseph street commences at the water's edge, about 364
feet from William street, and runs parallel with the Prescott Road to Vanbury's Road. Rideau street commences
on the Prescott Road, about 363 feet from Asa street, and
runs in a parallel line with it to Thomas street. Mary
street commences about 760 feet from Asa street, and
runs parallel with it to Joseph street. All the above
streets are on the south side of the Branch, on lot No. 27,
and are each of them 40 feet in width, except Water street,
which is only 36 feet wide. Jack street commences at
the angle of the Road crossing Barn's Mill-dam, on lot
No. 28, on the south side of the Branch, and runs to the
Vanbury Road to a Cedar post (marked R) and is 40 feet
in width.

And whereas Edward Mix, Surveyor of Highways in
and for the County of Grenville, has been petitioned by
twelve Freeholders of the said County to lay out a
new road in the Township of Oxford; and in pursuance of such petition, the said Edward Mix has
surveyed and laid out the said Road as follows: com-
Description of Road in Oxford. mencing at a stone monument planted on the allowance
for road between lots numbers 15 and 16 in the second
Concession, and crossing the north-east corner of said lot
No. 15, at an angle of about forty degrees to another
stone monument planted at the rear of the first Concession,
on the allowance for road between lots numbers 15 and
16, in the aforesaid first Concession, (there being at this

place an offset of about eight rods;) which said Road is laid out sixty feet in width.

And whereas Benjamin Warren, Surveyor of Highways in and for the County of Leeds, has been petitioned by twelve freeholders of the said County to lay out a certain road in the Township of Escott, and in pursuance of such petition the said Benjamin Warren has surveyed and laid out the said Road as follows: commencing on the present travelled Road on the front of the third Concession of Escott, from a post planted on the north side of said Road, at or near the centre of lot number fourteen in the aforesaid concession of Escott, east of the dwelling of Thomas Donavon; from thence on a line of blazed trees a west-south-west course across the west half of said lot; thence on a line of pickets and blazed trees a straight course across lot number thirteen, passing the north of the dwelling of James Donnahugh, to a post planted on the line between lots numbers thirteen and twelve; thence on a line of pickets and blazed trees to a straight course across lot number twelve, passing to the south of the dwelling of James Brennan, and also the dwelling of William Flinn, where it intersects the present travelled road, at a post planted four rods east of the line, between lots numbers twelve and eleven; the aforesaid monuments are on the north side of the said road,—which said road is laid out forty feet in width.

Description of Road in Escott.

And whereas John Byce, Surveyor of Highways in and for the County of Grenville, has been petitioned by twelve freeholders of the said County, to lay out a certain Road in the Township of South Gower; and in pursuance of such petition the said John Byce has surveyed and laid out the said Road as follows: commencing at the front of the second concession on the line between lots numbers 2 and 3, at a post of Cedar marked A with red chalk; then following said line about 250 rods to a post of Cedar marked B, on the Road running from Mountain's line to Heck's Corners, between lots numbers 6 and 7,- which said Road is laid out forty feet in width.

Description of Road in South Gower.

And whereas William Fraser, Surveyor of Highways in and for the County of Grenville, has been petitioned by twelve freeholders of the said County, to lay out a certain Road in the Township of Edwardsburgh, and in pursuance of such petition the said William Fraser has surveyed and laid out the said Road as follows: commencing at a post between the first and second concessions of the Township of Edwardsburgh, in the centre of lot number 20, running north twenty-four degrees, west twenty-three chains to a post; thence south sixty-six degrees, west nine chains fifty links to the side line between lots numbers 20 and 21; thence south sixty degrees, west nine chains seventy-two links, to the centre line of said lot; thence south twenty-seven degrees, west eleven chains fifty links to the line between lots numbers 21 and 22; thence south fifty degrees, west nine chains seventy-six links to the centre of said lot : thence south sixty degrees, west across the west half of said lot, and the whole of lot number 23, to a post on the side line of lots numbers 23 and 24; thence north twenty-four degrees west, and twenty-four degrees east, fourteen chains eighty-seven links, intersecting said concession line; thence westerly along said concession line, six chains thirty links, to a post on the line between Nelson Wright and Johnston Parks; from thence south twenty-four degrees, east on the line between the said Nelson Wright and the said Parks to the Queen's Highway on the River Sr. Lawrence,—which said Road is laid out forty feet in width.

Description of Road in Edwardsburgh.

Be it therefore ordained and enacted by the Municipal Council of the District of Johnstown, in Council assembled, at the Town of Brockville, on the eighth day of October, in the year of our Lord one thousand eight hundred and forty-seven, That the said above described Roads be respectively approved of and confirmed as Public Roads and Highways.

Confirmed as Public Roads.

OGLE R. GOWAN, Warden.

[L. S.]

No. CLIX.—BY-LAW

See By-law No. 231, County Council.

Of the Municipal Council of the District of Johnstown, setting aside the Sum of Six Hundred Pounds to pay the interest of a certain Sum therein mentioned.—Passed October 8, 1847.

(Repealed : see By-Law No. 4 County Council.)

No. CLX.—BY-LAW

To Assess the Inhabitants of certain School Sections in the District of Johnstown.—Passed October 8, 1847.

1. Be it enacted by the District Council of the District of Johnstown, That there be raised and levied on the assessed rateable property of the inhabitants of the School Sections hereinafter mentioned, in the said District, the several sums of money required for the said Sections, for the following purposes (clear of all the charges of collecting), namely: *Sums to be levied in.*

In School-Section No. 22, in the Township of Elizabeth-town. Elizabethtown

The sum of thirty pounds currency, for the purpose of building a School-House therein.

In School-Section No. 6, in the Township of Bastard. Bastard.

The sum of eighty-five pounds, currency, for the purpose of purchasing a site for a School-House and erecting a House thereon.

In School-Section No. 13, in the Township of Yonge. Yonge.

The sum of seventy-five pounds, currency, over and above the sum already assessed on the said Section for the present year, and now being levied by the Collector, for the purpose of erecting and completing a School-House therein, and paying for the site of the same.

In School-Section No. 5, in the Township of Augusta. Augusta.

The sum of sixty-five pounds, currency, for the purpose of building a School-House therein.

2. That the said sums so to be raised and levied, shall be apportioned on the said property in the said School-Sections, respectively, according to the values assigned to the same by law, and shall be forthwith placed on the Collectors' Rolls by the Clerk of the Peace, and be collected by the respective Collectors of the several Townships, in like manner as any other tax, but shall be paid over by them to the District Superintendent of Common Schools, within the period fixed by law for the payment of rates collected in each year to the Treasurer. *How levied.*

Assessors' duty. 3. That it shall be the duty of the Assessors of the several Townships, to return to the Clerk of the Peace a list of all the rateable property in each of the said School-Sections, with the names of the rateable inhabitants therein, duly attested in the same manner as they are required to make the annual Assessment returns for their respective Townships.

OGLE R. GOWAN, Warden.

[L. S.]

No. CLXI.—BY-LAW

See Con. Stat. U. C., Caps. 54 & 55. *Of the Municipal Council of the Johnstown District to regulate Assessments in the third and sixth Concessions of the Township of Bastard, and other places in said District.*

Preamble. Whereas the inhabitants of the third and sixth concessions of the Township of Bastard, have shown, by the certificate and evidence of a Deputy Provincial Surveyor, that the lots of land they occupy do not contain the usual number of acres, and have by their petition prayed that they might not be obliged to pay rates and assessments for more land than they actually possess; And whereas it is just and reasonable to comply with the prayers of said petition: Be it therefore ordained and enacted, and it is hereby ordained and enacted by the Municipal Council of the District of Johnstown, in Council assembled at the Town of Brockville, in said District, on the third day of February, in the year of our Lord one thousand eight hundred and forty-eight, That from and after this date all and singular, the lots of land contained in the schedule to **How lands to be assessed.** this By-Law annexed, shall be assessed and charged for the number of acres that each is therein specified to contain, and no more, and that a half or a quarter or other part of a lot shall be assessed in proportion, any law or usage to the contrary notwithstanding.

Section 2. And be it enacted by the authority afore- **Where copies of By-laws to be deposited, &c.** said that a copy of this By-Law shall be deposited in the Office of the Treasurer of the District, and in the Office of the Clerk of the Peace and District Clerk, which said copies, instead of the schedule furnished by the Surveyor General or Commissioner of Crown Lands, shall be

sufficient guide and authority for the assessment of all
lots included in the schedule annexed, and shall also be
sufficient guide and authority for the said Treasurer in
charging all wild land assessments or taxes either now due
or to become due on said lots. And also where the
amount of taxes or arrears of taxes on any lot or lots included in said schedule has been computed on a greater
number of acres than it or they are therein specified to
contain, then, in that case, the said Treasurer is hereby
authorised to settle with, and receive from the respective
parties who pay said taxes, a sum as much less in proportion to the whole amount formerly charged as the number
of acres that the lot actually contains (as shewn by said
schedule) *bears* to the number of acres it was formerly
supposed to contain, and by which the said arrears of
taxes have been computed.

SECTION 3. And whereas there may be in the District
lots of land much deficient of the number of acres that
they are marked to contain in the Schedules furnished by
the Surveyor General to the District Treasurer: Be it
therefore enacted by the authority aforesaid, That the
occupant or owner of any such lot, (on proving the fact
and satisfying the Municipal Council of the District that
the said lot contains at least ten acres less than is specified
in the said Treasurer's books) may have said lot so deficient annexed to this schedule, and the owner or occupant
thereof shall then be entitled to all the benefits and
privileges that the owners or occupants of lots now
included in said schedule will be entitled to.

OGLE R. GOWAN, WARDEN

[L. S.]

SCHEDULE.

BASTARD.

3rd concession, each lot 180 acres; 6th concession, from
lot No. 1 to No. 6, inclusive, 190 acres; from No. 7 to No.
12, inclusive, 180 acres; from No. 13 to No. 18, inclusive,
160 acres; and from No. 19 to 29, inclusive, 155 acres.

YONGE.

7th concession, east half of lot No. 16, 53 acres; lot No. 17, 43 acres; lot No. 18, 10 acres. 11th concession lot No. 12, 73 acres.

KITLEY.

1st concession, lot No. 9, 73 acres; lot No. 4, 43 acres. 6th concession, lot No. 4, 81 acres.

SOUTH CROSBY.

2nd concession, north half of lot No. 20, 84 acres; south half of lot No. 21, 86 acres; No. 22, 102 acres; rear half of lot No. 24, 85 acres; rear half of lot No. 25, 90 acres; 3rd concession, south half of lot No. 25, 77 acres; north half of lot No. 25, 30 acres; lot No. 26, 177 acres; 6th concession, lot No. 6, 134 acres; lots Nos. 26 and 27 taken together, 71 acres. 7th concession, lot No. 15, 124 acres. 9th concession, lot No. 22, 142 acres; lot No. 24, 72 acres.

NORTH CROSBY.

3rd concession, lot No. 8, 165 acres. 4th concession, lot No. 1, 172 acres; lot No. 3, front half, east of the lake, 55 acres,; 6th concession, lot No. 8, 125 acres; 7th concession, lot No. 1, 70 acres.

WOLFORD.

A concession, lot No. 4, 180 acres; lot No. 27, 142 acres. B concession, lot No. 29, 91 acres.

ELMSLEY.

1st concession, lot No. 4, 107 acres; lot No. 5, 110 acres. 2nd concession, lot No. 28, 92 acres; lot No. 29, 137 acres.

No. CLXII.—BY-LAW

To establish a Lock-up-House in the unincorporated Village of Gananoque.—Passed February 4, 1848.

Part of sec. No. 3 repealed; see By-law No. 184.

1. Be it enacted by the District Council of the Johnstown District, and it is hereby enacted, That from and after the passing of this By-Law, there shall be established in the unincorporated Village of Gananoque in the said District, a Lock-up-House, pursuant to the Statute in such case made and provided, and that the Justices of the Peace, hereinafter named, shall fix and determine upon the site for the erection of the same within the limits of the said Village of Gananoque.

Justices to fix upon site.

2. That the limits of the said Village of Gananoque for the purposes of this By-Law shall comprise the east half of lot number eight and the whole of lots numbers nine, ten, eleven, twelve, thirteen, fourteen, fifteen, and sixteen, in the first concession of the Township of Leeds, with the broken fronts of said lots.

Limits of Gananoque

3. That for the purpose of defraying the cost of erecting the said Lock-up-House, and purchasing a site for the same, there be levied upon the assessed real and personal property of the inhabitants of the said Village of Gananoque liable to assessment, the sum of fifty pounds currency for the present year, and the further sum of fifty pounds currency for the next year, (clear of charges of assessing, levying and collecting) and that the same shall be imposed, levied, and collected in the same manner and under the same provisions as the other taxes or assessments for the District for local purposes are imposed, levied and collected, under any By-Law of this Council, which said sums of money shall be expended under the direction of Ephraim Webster and James W. Parmenter, Esquires, two of Her Majesty's Justices of the Peace, residing in the said Village of Gananoque, who are hereby required, immediately after the said Lock-up-House shall be completed, to render to this Council a full and detailed account of the expenditure of the said money.

Sums to be levied by a rate.

Expended under direction of Justices.

4. That it shall be the duty of the Assessor of the Townships of Leeds and Lansdowne, in front, for each of the said years, to return to the Clerk of the Peace a list of all the rateable property in the said Village of Gananoque, with the names of the rateable inhabitants

Assessor's duty.

therein, duly attested in the same manner, and at the
same time as he is required to make his annual return for
the Township.

OGLE R. GOWAN, Warden.

[L. S.]

No. CLXIII.—BY-LAW

*To authorize the Assessment and Collection of Rates for
the general purposes of the Johnstown District, for the
year* 1848.—*Passed February* 4, 1848.

(Expired by Limitation.)

No. CLXIV.—BY-LAW

*To Assess the Inhabitants of certain School-Sections in the
Johnstown District.—Passed February* 4, 1848.

1. Be it enacted by the District Council of the District
of Johnstown, That there be raised and levied on the
assessed rateable property of the inhabitants of the School-
Sections hereinafter mentioned in the said District, the
several sums of money required for the said School-
Sections for the following purposes, (clear of all charges
of assessing and collecting) namely :—

In School-Section No. 13, *in the Township of Oxford.*

The sum of thirty pounds, currency, for the purpose of
building a School-House therein.

In School-Section No. 3, *in the Township of Oxford.*

The sum of seventy pounds, currency, for the purpose
of purchasing a site and building a School House therein.

In School-Section No. 16, *in the Township of Edwardsburgh.*

The sum of six pounds, currency, for the purpose of
defraying the expense of erecting a School-house therein.

Sums to be levied in.

Oxford.

Oxford.

Edwardsburgh.

In School-Sections Nos. 5 and 20, in the Townships of Edwardsburgh and Augusta. Edwardsburgh and Augusta.

(Repealed: see By-Law No. 172.)

In School-Section No. 4, in the Township of Oxford. Oxford.

The sum of seventy pounds, currency, for the purpose of building a School-house therein.

In School-Section No. 4, in the Township of North Crosby. North Crosby.

The sum of thirty-five pounds, currency, for the purpose of finishing the School-House therein, which includes the balance of the sum authorized to be raised in said Section under By-law No. 151.

In School-Section No. 1, in the Township of South Gower. South Gower.

The sum of sixty pounds, currency, for the purpose of building a School-House therein.

In School-Section No. 8, in the Township of Augusta. Augusta

The sum of fifty-three pounds, currency, for the purpose of building a School-House therein.

In School-Section No. 20, in the Township of Augusta. Augusta.

The sum of two pounds, eight shillings and three pence, currency, for the purpose of defraying the expense of repairs to School-House therein.

In School-Section No. 20, in the Township of Elizabethtown. Elizabethtown.

The sum of thirty-five pounds, currency for the purpose of building a School-House therein.

In School-Section No. 7, in the Township of Bastard. Bastard.

The sum of seventy-four pounds, currency for the purpose of erecting a School-House therein, which includes the balance of the sum authorized to be raised in said Section under By-Law No. 151.

In School-Section No. 16, in the Township of Wolford. Wolford.

The sum of seventy-five pounds, currency, for the purpose of erecting a School-House therein.

And the said sums so to be raised and levied shall be apportioned on the said property, in the said School Sections, respectively, according to the values assigned to the same by-law, and shall be placed on the Collector's Rolls by the Clerk of Peace.

How apportioned.

2. That the said sums shall be collected by the respective Collectors of the several Townships in which the said School-Sections are situated, in like manner as any other tax for said District, but shall be paid over by them to the District Superintendent of Common Schools, within the period fixed by law for the payment of rates collected in each year to the Treasurer.

How collected.

3. That it shall be the duty of the Assessors of the several Townships in which the said several Sections are respectively situated, to return to the Clerk of the Peace a list of all the rateable property in each of the said School-Sections with the names of rateable inhabitants therein, duly attested in the same manner, and at the same time as they are required to make the annual assessment returns for their respective Townships.

Assessor's duty.

OGLE R. GOWAN, Warden.

[L. S.]

No. CLXV.—BY-LAW

To assess the Inhabitants of the District of Johnstown for the support and maintenance of Common Schools therein for the year 1848.—Passed, February 4, 1848.

(Expired by Limitation.)

No. CLXVI.—BY-LAW

To establish certain Roads in the District of Johnstown.

Preamble.

Whereas Benjamin Warren, Surveyor of Highways in and for the County of Leeds, has been petitioned by twelve freeholders of the said County, to lay out a certain Road in the Township of Escott, and in pursuance of such petition, the said Benjamin Warren has surveyed and laid out the said Road as follows: commencing on the south side of the Queen's Highway leading from Kingston to Brockville, at a post planted on the line between lots numbers twenty-two and twenty-three, in the second concession of Escott, marked centre; from thence on said line a south-south-east course to a post planted forty feet more or less, from the concession line, marked R; from thence angling south-east across the concession line to the allowance for Road between the first and second concessions of said Township; thence on a line of pickets east-south-east on the aforesaid allowance twenty-five rods, more or less, to a post planted on said line, marked R; from thence angling to the south on a line of pickets planted on the west-half of lot number twenty-three in the first concession of said Township of Escott; thence on a line of pickets and blazed trees a south-south east course to the meadow bars; thence on a line of blazed trees following the hay meadow road, known by the name of the La Rue path to and from the meadows, to a post planted on the west side of the present travelled Road leading to La Rue's Mills, where it intersects the aforesaid Road, from the commencement to the concession, the line is the centre of said Road; from thence the monuments and blazes are on the north and north-east side of said Road. which said Road is laid out forty feet in width.

And whereas Benjamin Warren, Surveyor of Highways in and for the County of Leeds, has been petitioned by twelve freeholders of the said County, to lay out a Road in the Township of Escott, and in pursuance of such petition the said Benjamin Warren has surveyed and laid out the said road as follows: commencing in the second Concession of said Township of Escott, in the southern limit of the Queen's Highway, leading to Kingston, and on the line between lots numbers nine and ten, from a post planted on the aforesaid limit; thence a south-south-east course to the front of the second concession forty rods, more or less; from thence angling west-south-west on a line of blazed trees on the rear of the first Concession, fifty rods, more or less; from thence angling south-west on a line of blazed trees, forty rods, more or less, to, at or near the line between lots numbers eight and nine in the first Concession of the aforesaid Township; thence on a line of blazed trees south-south-east, to a post fixed on the south west side of the present travelled Road, called the Holland Road, and west of the School-House, where it intersects the aforesaid travelled Road; the said monuments and blazed trees are on the west side of

K

said Road, and which said Road is laid out forty feet in width.

Whereas James Eaton, Surveyor of Highways in and for the County of Leeds, has been petitioned by twelve freeholders of the said County to lay out a certain Road in the Township of Bastard ; and in pursuance of such petition, the said James Eaton has surveyed and laid out the said Road, as follows : commencing on the New Boyne Road leading to Beverly, where a Cedar post has been planted marked R ; twenty feet from the side line between lots numbers nine and ten in the fourth concession of the Township of Bastard ; thence to the third Concession line, where another Cedar post marked R has been planted, twenty feet from said line, the Road running equally on each of said lots in said fourth Concession ; thence following the third concession line to the centre of lot number nine in said third Concession, where another Cedar post marked R has been planted, twenty feet from the centre line of said lot ; thence following said line until it intersects the Road leading from New Boyne to Portland, where another Cedar post marked R is planted twenty feet from said line,—said Road runs equally on each half of said lot in the said third Concession ; the above posts are all planted on the north-east side of said Road, which Road is laid out forty feet in width.

Description of Road in Bastard.

And whereas Philemon Pennock, Surveyor of Highways in and for the County of Grenville, has been petitioned by twelve freeholders of the said County to lay out a certain Road in the Township of Augusta, and in pursuance to such petition, the said Philemon Pennock has surveyed and laid out the said Road as follows : commencing in rear of the fourth Concession of Augusta aforesaid, at the corner post between lots numbers ten and eleven ; thence on the line between said lots, thirty-two chains seventeen links ; thence south forty degrees, west twenty chains seventy links, across lot number eleven ; thence south twenty degrees, east twenty chains twelve links ; thence south thirty-five degrees west across lot number twelve, twenty chains sixty links to the Road between lots numbers twelve and thirteen ; monuments describing the course of said Road have been placed on the east and south sides thereof which said Road is laid out forty feet in width.

Description of Road in Augusta.

And whereas Hugh Kernahan, Surveyor of Highways in and for the County of Leeds, has been petitioned by twelve freeholders of the said County to lay out a certain Road in the Township of Kitley: and in pursuance of such petition the said Hugh Kernahan has surveyed and laid out the said Road as follows: commencing at the east side of the allowance for a Road between lots numbers twenty-four and twenty-five, at the distance of fifteen rods from the rear of the fourth concession of the Township of Kitley; thence running easterly across lots numbers twenty-four, twenty-three, and twenty-two, to the line between lots numbers twenty-two and twenty-one; thence along said line sixty-seven rods to the rear of said concession; the posts planted on said Road are on the north side thereof,—and which Road is laid out forty feet in width.

Description of Road in Kitley.

And whereas Hugh Kernahan, Surveyor of Highways in and for the County of Leeds has been petitioned by twelve freeholders of the said County, to lay out a Road in the Township of Kitley; and in pursuance of such petition the said Hugh Kernahan has surveyed and laid out the said Road as follows: commencing at the east side of the allowance for a Road between lots numbers twenty-four and twenty-five in the seventh concession of said Township of Kitley, at a distance of eleven chains and fifteen links from the centre of said seventh concession, and on the north side of said centre; thence south seventy-six degrees, east fifteen chains and seven links to a post placed at a distance of twenty feet from the centre of said Concession, and on the north side thereof; thence north fifty-four degrees, east, across the remainder of lots numbers twenty-four, twenty-three, and eight chains and seventy-four links of number twenty-two, to a stone monument placed at the south-west angle of a piece of land belonging to George K. Brennan, twenty feet north of the said centre; thence north fifty-two degrees, east six chains, to a stone monument placed on the west side of the Perth road, at the south-east angle of the said George K. Brennan's lands, thirty-three feet from the said centre; thence north fifty-two degrees and ten minutes, east twenty-eight chains and thirty-eight links to a post placed twenty-five feet north of the said centre; thence north forty-nine degrees and forty minutes, east across the remainder of lots numbers twenty-one, twenty and nineteen, to the allowance for a Road between lots numbers eighteen and nineteen,—the above description applies to the north side of said Road, which Road has been laid out forty feet wide.

Description of Road in Kitley.

Be it therefore ordained and enacted by the District Council of the District of Johnstown, in Council assembled at the Town of Brockville, on the fifth day of February, in the year of our Lord one thousand eight hundred and forty-eight, That the above described Roads be respectively approved of and confirmed as Public Roads and Highways.

Confirmed as Public Roads.

OGLE R. GOWAN, WARDEN.

[L. S.]

No. CLXVII.—BY-LAW

See Con. Stat. U. C., Cap. 64.

To regulate the amount of compensation to be allowed to Assessors and Collectors for extra labor occasioned by any local tax being imposed in any School-Section.— Passed February 5, 1848.

Preamble

Whereas it is necessary to fix the amount of compensation to be allowed to Assessors and Collectors for extra trouble occasioned them when local assessments are imposed on School-Sections : Be it therefore ordained and enacted, and it is hereby ordained and enacted by the District Council of the District of Johnstown, in Council assembled at the Town of Brockville, on the fifth day of February, in the year of our Lord one thousand eight hundred and forty-eight, That the following sums and no more be paid and allowed for said extra labor, that is to say, to Assessors when the local tax is assessed, or might be assessed at the same time with the annual assessment, the sum of ten shillings ; when required by any By-Law to be assessed either before or after the usual time of taking the Township assessment, the sum of one pound, to be paid in all cases by the Trustees of the School-Section so taxed, and out of the funds raised by said tax.

Compensation to Assessors.

SECTION 2. And be it enacted by the authority aforesaid, That it shall and may be lawful for the said Collectors to retain in their hands out of the local tax so imposed, the following sums, and no more, that is to say, when the said tax is collected, or might be collected, at the same time with the annual Township assessment, the sum of ten shillings ; when required by any By-Law to be collected either before or after the Township assessment, the sum of one pound.

Compensation to Collectors.

OGLE R. GOWAN, CHAIRMAN.

[L. S.]

No. CLXVIII.—BY-LAW

To repeal so much of By-Law No. 143 as enacts that the Annual Township Meeting of the Township of Bastard shall be held at the Village of Beverly.

Whereas it would be convenient for the inhabitant Householders and freeholders of the Township of Bastard to assemble to hold their annual Township Meetings at or near the centre of the Township: Therefore be it enacted by the District Council of the District of Johnstown, in Council assembled at the Town of Brockville, on the sixth day of October, in the year of our Lord one thousand eight hundred and forty-eight, That so much of By-Law No, 143, as enacts that the said Township Meetings shall be held at the Village of Beverly, shall be and is hereby repealed. *Preamble.* *Part By-law No. 143 repealed.*

2. And be it further enacted by the authority aforesaid, That the said annual Township Meeting of the Township of Bastard, shall be held at Smyth Mills, on the rear of lot number fifteen, in the fifth Concession of said Township. *Where Meeting to be held.*

OGLE R. GOWAN, Warden.

[L. S.]

No. CLXIX.—BY-LAW

To close a Road in the Township of Elizabethtown.

Whereas William K. Glazier, Surveyor of Highways in and for the County of Leeds, has been petitioned by twelve freeholders of the said County to close a certain Road in the Township of Elizabethtown; and whereas the said William K. Glazier has examined the said Road pursuant to such petition, which Road is as follows: commencing on the line between lots number thirty-three and thirty-four near the rear of the fourth concession of of Elizabethtown aforesaid, at or near a certain stone dam erected across a stream of water running on lot number thirty-three, and from this point southerly and westerly with various windings and anglings, until it strikes the main public highway, leading from Peet Steeley's Saw Mill to Caintown, at or near the line between lot numbers thirty-five and thirty-six, at about the centre of the fourth Concession of said Township of Elizabethtown. *Preamble.* *Description.*

Be it therefore ordained and enacted by the Municipal Council of the District of Johnstown, in Council assembled at the Town of Brockville, on the sixth day of October, in the year of our Lord one thousand eight hundred and forty-eight, That the said above described Road be, and the same is hereby declared closed.

Closed.

OGLE R. GOWAN, Warden.

[L. S.]

No. CLXX.—BY-LAW

To require Township Collectors to pay over all School Monies on or before the third Tuesday in December.— Passed October 6, 1848.

Preamble. Whereas much inconvenience is experienced in consequence of Township Collectors not paying over School Money until the end of the year: Be it therefore enacted, by the District Council of the District of Johnstown, duly assembled at the Town of Brockville, on the sixth day of October, in the year of our Lord one thousand eight hundred and forty-eight, That the Collectors for each and every Township in the District shall, on or before the *To pay District* third Tuesday in December in each and every year, pay *Superintendent.* over to the District Superintendent of Education all School Money collected by them, respectively, and in default of paying said money on or before the said day, it *Collector's per* shall only be lawful for them, the said Collectors, to retain *centage.* at the rate of two-and-half per cent. for their compensation for collecting said Money.

OGLE R. GOWAN, Warden.

[L. S.]

No. CLXXI.—BY-LAW

To Assess the Inhabitants of certain School-Sections in the District of Johnstown.

1. Be it enacted by the District Council of the District of Johnstown, duly assembled at the Town of Brockville, on the sixth day of October, in the year of our Lord one thousand eight hundred and forty-eight, That there be

raised and levied on the assessed rateable property of the Sums to be levied in.
inhabitants of School-Sections hereinafter mentioned in
the said district, the several sums of money required for
the said Sections, for the following purposes, (clear of all
the charges of collecting) namely :—

In School Section No. 20, in the Township of Elizabeth- Elizabethtown.
town.

The sum of forty pounds, currency, for the purpose of
completing a School-house therein, now in the course of
erection.

In School-Section No. 11, in the Township of Bastard. Bastard.

(Repealed: see By-law No. 178.)

In School-Section No. 19, in the Township of Oxford. Oxford.

The sum of twenty-six pounds, currency, for the purpose of purchasing a site for a School-house, and building
a School-house thereon.

In School-Section No. 15, in the said Township of Oxford. Oxford.

The sum of twenty pounds, currency, for purchasing a
site, and erecting a School-house thereon.

In School-Section No. 3, in the Township of Kitley. Kitley.

(Repealed: see By-law No. 194.)

In School-Section No. 8, in the Township of Augusta. Augusta.

The sum of four pounds and ten shillings, currency, for
the purpose of completing a School-house therein.

2. And be it enacted, That the said sums so to be
raised and levied, shall be apportioned on the said pro- How levied, &c.
perty, in the said School Sections respectively, according
to the values assigned to the same by law, and shall be
forthwith placed on the Collectors' Rolls by the Clerk of
the Peace, and be collected by the respective Collectors
of the several Townships, in like manner as any other tax,
but shall be paid over by them to the District Superintendent of Common Schools, within the period fixed by
law for the payment of rates in each year to the District
Treasurer.

Assessor's duty.

3. That it shall be the duty of the Assessors of the several Townships, to return to the Clerk of the Peace a list of all the rateable property in each of the said School-Sections, with the names of the rateable inhabitants therein duly attested, in the same manner as they are required to make the annual Assessment returns for their respective Townships.

OGLE R. GOWAN, Warden.

[L. S.]

No. CLXXII.—BY-LAW

To Assess certain School Sections in the Townships of Edwardsburgh and Augusta.

Preamble.

Whereas by a certain By-law passed by the Municipal Council of the Johnstown District, on the fourth day of February, in the year of our Lord one thousand eight hundred and forty-eight, it is, amongst other things provided, That there shall be raised and levied in School-Sections numbers five and twenty, in the Townships of Edwardsburgh and Augusta, the sum of forty pounds, currency, for the purpose of building a School-House therein; and by By-law CLI., passed in the month of February, in the year 1847, That there be raised and levied on the assessed rateable property of the inhabitants of School-Section number one, in the Township of Augusta, the sum of fifty pounds, for the purpose of erecting a School House therein. And whereas it is necessary to repeal so much of said By-laws as relates to the said tax on the said School Sections numbers five and twenty, in the Townships of Edwardsburgh and Augusta, and School Section number one in the Township of Augusta: Be it therefore ordained and enacted, and it is hereby ordained and enacted by the District Council of the District of Johnstown, duly assembled at the Town of Brockville, on the sixth day of October, in the year of our Lord one thousand eight hundred and forty-eight, That so much of the said By-law as relates to the said tax on said School-Sections numbers five and twenty, in the Townships of Edwardsburgh and Augusta, and School-Section number one, in the Township of Augusta, be repealed, and the same is hereby repealed.

Part By-Laws Nos. 151 and 164 repealed.

153

And whereas it is necessary that School-Sections numbers five and nineteen, in the Townships of Augusta and Edwardsburgh, should be taxed in the sum of fifty pounds, currency, clear of all charges, and that School-Section number one, in the Township of Augusta, should be taxed in the sum of thirty-two pounds, currency, free of all charges; It is hereby ordained and enacted, That there be raised and levied on the assessed rateable property of the inhabitants of said School-Sections numbers five and nineteen, in the Townships of Augusta and Edwardsburgh the sum of fifty pounds, currency, free of all charges, and on said School-Section number one, in the Township of Augusta, the sum of thirty-two pounds, currency, free of all charges, for the purpose of building and finishing School-Houses in said School-Sections.

Sums to be levied in.

Augusta and Edwardsburgh.

And the said sum so to be raised and levied shall be apportioned on the said property, in said School-Sections, respectively, according to the value assigned to the same by law, and shall be placed on the Collectors' Rolls by the Clerk of the Peace.

How levied.

That the said sums shall be collected by the respective Collectors of the several Townships in which the said School-Sections are situated, in like manner as any other tax for said District, but shall be collected immediately upon the receipt of the Roll made out by the Clerk of the Peace for said Section, and shall be paid over by said Collector to the Superintendent of Common Schools for the District, in the month of February, 1849.

How collected.

That it shall be the duty of the Assessors of the several Townships in which the said several Sections are respectively situated, to return to the Clerk of the Peace a list of all the rateable property in each of the said School-Sections, with the names of the rateable inhabitants therein, duly attested in the same manner as they are required to make the annual assessment return for their respective Townships; and that the Assessment Roll for the above mentioned School-Sections be made out immediately on the commencement of the time allowed by law for their assessing property, and returned to the Clerk of the Peace.

Assessor's duty.

OGLE R. GOWAN, Warden.

[L. S.]

No. CLXXIII.—BY-LAW

To establish certain Roads in the District of Johnstown.

Preamble.

Whereas Henry B. Marvin, Surveyor of Highways in and for the County of Leeds, has been petitioned by twelve freeholders of the said County, to lay out a certain Road in the Township of South Crosby; and in pursuance of such petition, the said Henry B. Marvin has surveyed and laid out the said Road as follows: commencing at the south-east corner of lot number nine, in the second Concession of South Crosby, (the corner post of said lot being the centre of the Road;) thence running a south-west course to the creek, the distance of twenty-five rods, where a Maple tree is marked as south side of Road, and a large Hemlock tree is the centre of it; thence angling a little south across the creek and running up the creek close by the Mill-Pond, through the woods where a Maple tree is marked as south side of Road, and thence on a straight line to the four corners at the rear of said lot, where a Cedar post is planted and marked as south side of Road, which Road is laid out forty feet in width.

Description of Road in South Crosby.

And whereas John Robinson, Surveyor of Highways in and for the County of Leeds, has been petitioned by twelve freeholders of the said County, to lay out a certain Road in the Township of Lansdowne, and in pursuance of such petition, the said John Robinson has surveyed and laid out the said Road as follows: commencing at a post marked R (on the north side) on the line between lots numbers twenty-three and twenty-four in the first concession of the Township of Lansdowne; thence easterly across said lot to the Town line to a post planted thereon marked R on the north side, ninety-five rods; thence, same course, sixty-one rods, across the Gore in the front concession or broken front of Escott, to a post planted and marked R (on the north side) until said Road meets with the River Road leading to LaRue's; all of the above mentioned posts are planted on the south side of said Road, which is laid out sixty-six feet wide.

Description of Road in Lansdowne.

And whereas John Robinson, Road Surveyor in and for the County of Leeds, has been petitioned by twelve freeholders of the said County, to lay out a certain Road in the Townships of Escott and Lansdowne, and in pursuance of such petition, he has surveyed and laid out the said Road as follows: commencing at a Beech post planted by

James Brooker, formerly a Road Surveyor, forty feet north from the base of a big hill called Chessey Moore's Hill, on the west side of the now travelled Road that leads up said Hill, called the LaRue Road, eighty feet west from the Town line post marked R, on the east side of the first concession of the Township of Lansdowne; thence running a little east of north on the west side of the Town line to a post marked R, on the east side, one hundred and twenty rods, forty feet west from the corner of Nulty's house; thence running a north-easterly course on the east side of the Town line, sixty-nine rods to a post marked R, on the east side; thence along on the east side of the Town line, forty rods, to a post planted on the Town line and marked R on the east side; thence along on the east side of the Town line, fifty-four rods to a post planted on the west of the Town line marked R, on the east side; thence a north-west course thirty rods to a post marked R on the east side; thence a north-easterly course forty-four rods to a post planted on the concession line between the first and second concessions of Lansdowne, marked R, on the east side; thence, same direction, twenty-seven rods, to a post planted and marked R (on the east side), on the west side of the Town line to the allowance for a Road; thence along the allowance for a Road thirty-nine rods to a post planted and marked R, on the east side; thence a north-west course fifty-four rods to a post planted and marked R, on the east side, on the west side of the allowance for a Road; thence running a north-easterly course fifteen rods round a ledge of rocks, to a post marked R, on the east side, planted on the Town line; thence along on the allowance for a Road on the west side of the Town line, thirty-three rods to a post planted on the west side of the Road marked R, on the east side; thence along on the allowance for a Road, seventy-five rods to a post planted on the corner of Shepherd's clearing, marked R on the east side; thence along the allowance for a Road, sixty-six rods to a post planted on the north corner of Shepherd's clearing and marked R on the east side; thence running a north-easterly direction on the east side of the Town line by a line of marked trees, round a large ledge of rocks, fifty-one rods, to a post planted on the Town line, marked R, on the east side; thence along on the west side of the Town line on the allowance for a Road twenty-eight rods, to a post planted forty feet from the south corner of Henry McIntyre's clearing, to a post planted and marked R, on the east side; from thence along on the allowance for Road two hundred rods more or less, to the Queen's highway in the third concession of the Township of Lansdowne. All the posts and marked trees are on the west side of said Road, which Road is laid out forty feet in width.

Description of Road in Oxford.

And whereas Edward Mix, Surveyor of Highways in and for the County of Grenville, has been petitioned by twelve freeholders of the said County, to lay out a certain Road in the Township of Oxford, and in pursuance of such petition, the said Edward Mix has surveyed and laid out the said Road as follows: commencing at the north end of the bridge over Patterson's Creek, on lot number twenty, in the first Concession of the Township of Oxford, at a Cedar post marked R No. 1, and running in a north-easterly direction to another Cedar post marked R No. 2, planted on the upper side of the lower half of the aforesaid lot number twenty; then a little more northerly to the lower side of said lot to a Cedar post marked R No. 3, planted on the allowance for a Road, between said lots numbers twenty and twenty-one aforesaid, two chains, ninety-three links southerly from the stone monument erected in front of said lot number twenty; then a little more northerly to a Cedar post marked R No. 4, planted on the upper side of lot number twenty-two, seventy-three links south-easterly from the post between lots numbers twenty-one and twenty-two; then in a parallel line with the base line to the lower side of lot number twenty-two aforesaid,—said Road is laid out forty feet in width.

Description of Road in Escott.

And whereas Benjamin Warren, Surveyor of Highways in and for the County of Leeds, has been petitioned by twelve freeholders of the said County, to lay out a certain Road in the Township of Escott, and in pursuance of such petition the said Benjamin Warren has surveyed and laid out the said Road as follows: commencing at or near the centre line of lot number four on the rear of the broken front concession of the Township of Escott, at the Holland Road, from a tree blazed on three sides and marked R; from thence on a line of blazed trees a south-south-west course across the west half of said lot number four; thence on a line of blazed trees and fixed monuments a south-south-west course across lots numbers three, two, and one, to a post planted on the Town line, on the east side of said line, and twelve rods more or less, south of the house formerly occupied by Edward Nulty, where it intersects the present travelled Road running between Escott and Lansdowne. The blazes and fixed monuments are on the south-east side of said Road, which is laid out forty feet wide.

And whereas Simon McGee, Surveyor of Highways in and for the County of Grenville, has been petitioned by twelve freeholders of that County to lay out a certain Road in the Township of Wolford, and in pursuance of such petition, the said Simon McGee has surveyed and laid out the said Road as follows; commencing at a Cedar post planted on the east corner of lot number twenty-one in the eighth concession of the said Township of Wolford, and running east fifty-four degrees, north along a line of blazed trees (in the woods) and stakes planted in the open field one hundred and sixty-seven rods more or less, until it intersects the Road leading from Merricksville to North Augusta,—which Road is laid out fifty feet wide. *Description of Road in Wolford.*

And whereas Stephen Beach, Surveyor of Highways in and for the County of Leeds, has been petitioned by twelve freeholders of the said County, to lay out a new Road in the Township of Elizabethtown, and in pursuance of such petition the said Stephen Beach has surveyed and laid out the said Road as follows: commencing on the north-east side of the said Road on lot number twenty-one in the second concession of the said Township of Elizabethtown, at a tree which has a gate hung on it ; then nearly east about ninety rods more or less, to a stake with stones at the bottom, and marked R with red chalk; thence north easterly about forty-six rods to another stake marked R with red chalk ; thence easterly about fifty rods to an Elm tree standing about two rods north of an Ash tree, mentioned in the Road petition ; thence easterly about twenty-five rods to B. Flint's land, to a Beech tree three feet north of a stake mentioned in the aforesaid Road petition, and marked with red chalk R; thence north-easterly about twenty-five rods to another stake marked R with red chalk, nearly to John Clark's land ; then easterly across the corner of the said John Clark's land to a stake marked R with red chalk, on the south side of the now travelled Road; then easterly along the now travelled Road to the second concession Road. All of the above mentioned trees and stakes are marked R with red chalk, and all stand on the south side of the said Road, and which Road is laid out forty-five feet wide. *Description of Road in Elizabethtown.*

And whereas Edward Mix, Surveyor of Highways in and for the County of Grenville, has been petitioned by twelve freeholders of the said County to lay out a new Road in the Township of Oxford, and in pursuance of such petition, the said Edward Mix has surveyed and laid out the said Road as follows: commencing on the fifth concession line, where it runs into the south branch of the Rideau River on lot number eighteen, at a Cedar tree standing on the bank of said branch and marked R No. 1; thence along the bank of said branch about ten rods more or less, to a Cedar post marked R No. 2, planted on the side line between lots numbers eighteen and seventeen; then south thirty-six degrees, east along said side line about twenty rods more or less, to a stone monument marked R No. 3; thence in about a parallel line with the concession line to the upper side of lot number seventeen, which Road is laid out forty feet in width. That part of the Road between the first and second monuments is taken from the back or south-east side of the monument, and the remainder of the Road is taken equally from each side of the line of survey.

Be it therefore ordained and enacted by the District Council of the District of Johnstown, in Council assembled, at the Town of Brockville, on the sixth day of October, in the year of our Lord one thousand eight hundred and forty-eight, That the above described Roads be respectively approved of and confirmed as Public Roads and Highways.

OGLE R. GOWAN, WARDEN.

Description of Road in Oxford.

Confirmed as Public Roads.

No. CLXXIV.—BY-LAW

To cover the several grants of Money made at this Session of the Council.

Preamble.

Whereas certain petitions for aid, claims for compensation for damages sustained, accounts from the District Officers and others for services rendered, have been presented to this Council; and whereas the said petitions, claims, and accounts have been referred to select committees, appointed by this Council, to enquire into and report upon such petitions, claims, and accounts; and whereas the same have been enquired into and reported upon, by the select Committees to whom they were referred for investigation: Be it therefore ordained and enacted by the District Council of the District of Johnstown, in Council assembled at the Town of Brockville, on the

seventh day of October, in the year of our Lord one
thousand eight hundred and forty-eight, That the following sums be paid by the Treasurer of this District to the
persons whose names are placed before each item respectively, and that this By-Law shall be a sufficient
voucher to that Officer, to pay the said amounts, as
follows:—

No. 1. To Thomas F. McQueen, Surgeon, the sum of £1, *To whom made.*
being for a *post mortem* examination made upon the
body of a deceased person, at the request of a Coroner
and Jury.

No. 2. To *The Statesman* printing-office, the sum of £3 1s. 4d.,
being for Printing and Advertising.

No. 3. To William A. Schofield, Esq., the sum of £2 10s.,
being for his services as Town Clerk for the Township
of Elmsley, for part of the year 1846.

No. 4. To Thomas Gainford, Esq., Surgeon, the sum of £2,
being for services rendered at two inquests held in the
Township of Augusta, at the request of the Coroner
and Juries.

No. 5. To John Morris, Road Surveyor, the sum of 15s., being
for his services in Surveying and laying out a Road in
the Township of Yonge.

No. 6. To Edward Mix, Road Surveyor, the sum of £1 2s. 6d.,
being for his services in the surveying and laying out a
Road in the Township of Oxford.

No. 7. To Simon McGee, Road Surveyor, the sum of £1 6s. 3d.,
being for his services in the surveying and laying out
of a Road in the Township of Wolford.

No. 8. To Benjamin Warren, Road Surveyor, the sum of 15s.,
being for his services in the laying out and surveying
a Road in the Township of Escott.

No. 9. To Stephen Beach, Road Surveyor, the sum of 15s.,
being for his services in surveying and laying out a
Road in the Township of Elizabethtown.

No. 10. To John Robinson, Road Surveyor, the sum of 10s.,
being for his services in the laying out and surveying of
a Road in the Township of Lansdowne.

No. 11. To William Rogers, Enumerator for the Township of
Leeds and Lansdowne, (in front, the sum of £9 0s. 8d.,
being for his services as such Enumerator.

No. 12. To Calvin Struthers, Enumerator for the Township of Leeds and Lansdowne (in rear), the sum of £3 13s. 8d., being for his services as such Enumerator.

No. 13. To James Taylor, Enumerator for the Township of Escott, the sum of £3 5s , being for his services as such Enumerator.

No. 14. To John Purvis, Enumerator for the Township of Yonge the sum of £9 14s. 8d., being for his services as such Enumerator.

No. 15. To Jacob Smith Enumerator for the Township of Elizabethtown, the sum of £14 1s. 4d., being for his services as such Enumerator.

No 16. To Garret Doyle, Enumerator for the Township of Augusta, the sum of £12 13s., being for his services as such Enumerator.

No. 17. To David Snyder, Enumerator for the Township of Edwardsburgh, the sum of £9 5s. 8d., being for his services as such Enumerator.

No. 18. To John Gray, Enumerator for the Township of South Gower, the sum of £2 1s. 8d., being for services as such Enumerator.

No. 19. To Edward Mix, Enumerator for the Township of Oxford, the sum of £11 1s., being for his services as such Enumerator.

No. 20. To John Elliot, Enumerator of the Township of Wolford, the sum of £8 5s., being for his services as such Enumerator.

No. 21. To William Brennan, Enumerator for the Township of Kitley, the sum of £9 2s., being for his services as such Enumerator.

No. 22. To Robert Goodfellow, Enumerator for the Township of Elmsley, the sum of £3 10s., being for his services as such Enumerator.

No. 23. To Alexander Elliott, Enumerator for the Township of Bastard, the sum of £9 1s., being for his services as such Enumerator.

No. 24. To Patrick Wills, Enumerator for the Township of South Burgess, the sum of £1 1s. 4d., being for his services as such Enumerator.

No. 25. To James Kennedy, Enumerator for the Township of South Crosby, the sum of £3 6s., being for his services as such Enumerator.

No. 26. To Walter Whellan, Enumerator for North Crosby, the sum of £4 2s. 4d., being for his services as such Enumerator.

No. 27. To E. H. Burniston, Enumerator for the Town of Brockville, the sum of £3 9s., being for his services as such Enumerator.

No. 28. To Daniel McCarthy, Enumerator for the Town of Prescott, the sum of £2 13s. 10d., being for his services as such Enumerator.

No. 29. To *The Recorder* Printing-Office, the sum of £3 16s. 6d., being for Printing and Advertising.

No. 30. To Christopher Leggo, Gaoler, the sum of £4 16s. 6d., being for White-washing the Gaol and certain repairs to it and to the Court-House.

No. 31. To Amos T. Sweet, Constable, the sum of 10s., being for certain services required by a Coroner's Jury, in the disinterring of a body.

No. 32. To Alfred Poulton, Painter and Glazier, the sum of £3 6s. 9d., being for certain Painting and Glazing done to the Gaol and Court House.

No. 33. To John Lafayette, Tinsmith, the sum of £2 11s., being for certain repairs done at sundry times to the lead work on the outside of the Court-House, and the stove pipes within the building.

No. 34. To Arthur Tilley, the sum of £2 15s. 3d., being for certain repairs done to the Locks and Doors of the Gaol and Court-House.

No. 35. To Francis Bronnel, the sum of £1 1s. 10½d., being for certain work done in one of the corridors of the Gaol.

No. 36, To Aaron Comstock, of the Township of Escott, the sum of £10, being the amount of compensation for land taking from him for a Public Highway.

No. 37. To Peter Munford, of the Township of Escott, the sum of £5, being the amount of compensation allowed him for land taken for a Public Highway.

No. 38. To John Neil, of the Township of Escott, the sum of £5, being the amount of compensation allowed him for land taken for a Public Highway.

No. 39. To Thomas Rogers, of the Township of Bastard, the sum of £7 10s., being the amount of compensation allowed to him for land taken for a Public Highway.

L

No. 40. To John Rodgers, of the Township of Bastard, the sum of £12 10s., being the amount of compensation allowed to him for land taken for a Public Highway.

No. 41. To William Richends, of the Township of Bastard, the sum of £8 5s., being the amount of compensation allowed to him for land taken for a Public Highway.

No. 42. To John Wallace, of the Township of Escott, the sum of £7 10s., being the amount of compensation allowed to him for certain land taken for a Public Highway.

No. 43. To James Eaton, Road Surveyor, the sum of £1 2s. 6d., being for his services in surveying and laying out a Road in the Township of Bastard.

No. 44. To Philemon Pennock, Road Surveyor, the sum of 15s., being for his services in surveying and laying out a Road in the Township of Augusta.

No. 45. To Margaret Jessop, a distressed and destitute female of the Township of Elmsley, the sum of £5, being as part aid toward her support and maintenance.

No. 46. To William Fitzsimmons, Carpenter, the sum of £3 17s. 8d., being for services rendered in putting up a Book-case in the District Clerk's Office, pursuant to the order of this Council.

No. 47. To William Earl, of the Township of Bastard, the sum of £5, to assist in the maintaining of Benjamin Godkin, an insane and destitute person.

No. 48. To Walter Beaty, of the Township of Yonge, the sum of £5, to aid in the sustenance and support of Charlotte McConkey, a distressed and destitute female.

No. 49. To Sophia Stephens, of the Township of Yonge, or order, the sum of £5, to aid in the support of Joseph Palmer, a sick and destitute person.

No. 50. To the order of Thomas Gainford, Esquire, to aid in the maintenance of Benjamin Lane, of Augusta, a destitute and afflicted person, the sum of £5.

No. 51. To James Kincaid, of Brockville, High Constable, the sum of £1 5s., for attending the Council five days this Session.

No. 52. To C. Leggo, of Brockville, Gaoler, the sum of £1 18s. 2d., for fuel, lights, stationery, and other contingencies furnished the Council during this session.

OGLE R. GOWAN, Warden.

[L. S.]

No. CLXXV.—BY-LAW

To make provision for the Completion of the Victoria Road. See By-law No.
Passed February 13, 1849.   231, County
                                             Council.

(Repealed: see By-law No. 4 County Council.)

No. CLXXVI.—BY-LAW

To prevent Nuisances, and to protect the Public Health in the District of Johnstown.

1. Be it enacted by the Municipal Council of the District of Johnstown, in Council assembled at the Town of Brockville, on the thirteenth day of February, in the year of our Lord one thousand eight hundred and forty-nine, That any person or persons having deposited, or who shall hereafter deposit or cause to be deposited in any public Road, Street or Highway within the District of Johnstown, any timber, boards, plank, stone, brick, lime, mortar, or other materials for building, and who shall refuse or neglect to remove the same within twenty-fours after being directed to do so by the Overseer of Highways for the division, or by the District Warden, a Justice of the Peace, or a Town Councillor, shall forfeit and pay a Penalty for, In penalty not exceeding five shillings for every twenty-four Roads, &c. hours thereafter during which the same shall be suffered to remain unmoved: Provided that this regulation shall not extend to any person or persons requiring such materials for immediate use, in order to erect any house or other fixed building, and occupying therewith, not more than half the width of the Road or Street, opposite the site of such intended building for which the same shall be required.

2. Any person who shall deposit in any Road or Public Highway, or in any Church-yard, or Cemetery for the dead, or in any Market-place, Town Hall, or School-yard, Penalty for, In or other Public Grounds, any fire-wood, stone, sleigh, Church-yards, wagon, rubbish, filth or other nuisance, except for the &c. purpose of immediate removal, and shall refuse or neglect forthwith on being directed so to do by the Overseer of Highways for the Division, or by the Warden of the District, or by a Justice of the Peace, or a Township Councillor, shall forfeit and pay a penalty not less than

two shillings and six pence, or more than five shillings for every twenty-four hours which such nuisance shall remain unremoved, after such person shall be so directed to remove the same.

3. Any individual who shall at any time expose his or her person, or conduct himself or herself in an indecent and obscene manner, shall forfeit and pay for every such offence, not less than five shillings or more than ten shillings.

Exposure of person.

4. No person shall leave or cause to be left any dead animal, carrion, putrid meat, or entrails of any animal, or any other matter or substance, dangerous to the public health, or offensive to the public smell, in any public highway, church-yard, or public ground of any kind, under a penalty of not less than five shillings nor more than ten shillings, nor shall any person suffer any such dead animal or other putrid or offensive matter to remain on their lands or on the premises in their care or occupation, without covering the same with earth, when requested so to do by the Warden of the District, or by any Justice of the Peace, or District Councillor, under a penalty of not less than five shillings nor more than ten shillings.

Dead animals, &c.

5. No person shall fish, fowl, or hunt on the Sabbath or Lord's day, within the limits of the District of Johnstown, under a penalty of not less than five shillings nor more than twenty shillings.

Fishing, &c., on Sabbath.

6. All persons, whether travelling on foot or on horseback, in a waggon, sleigh, or other vehicle or carriage, shall take the *right* side on all public Roads and Highways within the District, and all persons refusing or neglecting to do so, when passing any other person, whether on foot or on horseback, or in a waggon, sleigh, cutter, or other carriage, shall forfeit and pay any sum not less than five shillings or more than ten shillings.

Driving &c., on Roads.

7. Any person or persons who shall injure or destroy any tree or trees, planted, growing, or being in any street, highway, public square, market-place, church, school, or Town-hall yard, or other public place, planted or reserved for shade or ornament, or who shall pull down or deface any sign-board, or inscribe or draw any indecent words, figures, or pictures on any building, wall, fence, or other public place, shall forfeit and pay a sum not less than five shillings or more than three pounds.

Destroying Ornamental Trees, &c.

8. Any person who shall be convicted of riding or driving over any bridge or through any street within the limits of any of the Towns following, that is to say :—Lyndhurst, Charleston, Mallorytown, Yonge Mills, Farmersville, Unionville, Addison, New Dublin, Coleman's Corners, Maitland, North Augusta, Johnstown, Spencerville, Kemptville, Merrickville, Brandenburg, Smith's Falls, Beverly, Portland, Vanstondale, faster than a moderate trot, shall forfeit and pay not less than five shillings, or more than twenty shillings. *Driving over Bridges.*

9. The provisions of this By-Law shall and may be enforced, and the penalties recovered upon conviction had before any two Justices of the Peace for the District of Johnstown. *Penalties, how recovered.*

OGLE R. GOWAN, WARDEN.

[L. S.]

No. CLXXVII.—BY-LAW

To appoint Commissioners to superintend the Victoria Road.
Passed February 14, 1849.

See By-law No. 231, County Council.

(Repealed : see By-law No. 4, County Council.)

No. CLXXVIII.—BY-LAW

To repeal part of By-Law No. 171, *and to provide for the Assessment of School-Section No.* 11, *in the Township of Bastard.—Passed February* 14, 1849.

Be it enacted by the Municipal Council of the Johnstown District, That such part of By-Law No. 171, as relates to the taxation of School-Section number eleven, in the Township of Bastard, in the sum of one hundred pounds, for the purpose of building a School-house in said Section, be hereby repealed; and be it furthermore enacted, That the aforementioned School-section number eleven, in the Township of Bastard, be assessed in the sum of one hundred pounds—fifty pounds of which is to be raised in the present year, 1849, and the remaining fifty pounds to be raised in 1850, which sum to be raised and levied as provided for by said By-Law No. 171, and be it furthermore enacted, That no part of the real or personal pro- *Part By-law repealed.* *New Rate.* *How levied.*

perty of William Wiltse or Eli P. Wiltse, living on lot No. 25, in the tenth concession of said Township of Bastard, be included in said assessment.

Certain persons exempted.

OGLE R. GOWAN, Warden.

[L. S.]

No. CLXXIX.—BY-LAW

To provide for the expenditure of certain monies for public Improvements in the District of Johnstown.

Preamble.

Whereas by a certain Resolution of the Municipal Council of the District of Johnstown, the sum of £550 has been set apart for public improvements therein, and whereas it is necessary to divide the sum of £550 among the several Townships in the said District: Be it therefore ordained and enacted by the Municipal Council of the District of Johnstown, in Council assembled at the Town of Brockville, this fourteenth day of February, 1849, and it is hereby ordained and enacted, That the Councillor or Councillors (as the case may be), representing the several and respective Townships in the Municipal Council of the District, are hereby appointed Commissioners to superintend the expenditure of the amount apportioned to their respective Townships, and that their receipt shall be a sufficient voucher to the Treasurer for the payment made to each Township respectively.

Councillors to expend money.

SECTION 2. That the said sum be divided between the several Townships of the District, in accordance with the following scale of apportionment:—

Money, how divided.

Augusta,	£50
Bastard,	50
Burgess, South	10
Crosby, South,	30
Crosby, North,	20
Elizabethtown,	25
Escott,	30
Elmsley,	20
Edwardsburgh,	50
Gower, South,	15
Kitley,	40
Leeds and Lansdowne, (front)	50
Leeds and Lansdowne, (rear)	30
Oxford,	50
Wolford,	50
Yonge,	30

£550

SECTION 3. And whereas from such payment being made out of the common District Fund, there may not remain, or come into the District Treasury, from ordinary sources, during the present year, a sufficient amount of money to meet the current expenses of the District until the usual Assessments for the year shall become available, and it is desirable to provide for such contingency : Be it therefore further ordained and enacted by the authority aforesaid, That the District Treasurer, with the sanction and approbation of the Warden, shall and may, and he is hereby authorized and empowered, if the Warden shall deem it expedient and necessary so to do, to borrow from any person or persons, body Corporate or Bank, willing to loan the same, at a rate of interest or discount, not greater than six per centum per annum in advance from time to time, such sum or sums of money, not exceeding in the whole seven hundred pounds currency, as he may find necessary to meet any deficiency that may occur in the Common District Fund, to pay and discharge the current expenses of the District, including the said sum so appropriated, as before stated for public improvements. *Money to be borrowed.*

SECTION 4. That such money shall be borrowed upon a Promissory Note or Notes, to be made by the District Treasurer and countersigned by the Warden and District Clerk, who shall affix thereto the Seal of the said Council, which Note or Notes shall be made payable at such place and day (not exceeding six calendar months) as the Warden may deem advisable, and such Note or Notes shall be paid and satisfied by the said Treasurer, out of the monies which shall come into his hands applicable to common District purposes. *How borrowed.*

OGLE R. GOWAN, WARDEN.

[L. S.]

No. CLXXX.—BY-LAW

To Repeal so much of By-Law No. 145 as Enacts that the Annual Township Meeting of Burgess shall be held at Coledale, on Lot No. 6, in the Second Concession of Burgess.

Whereas it would be convenient for the inhabitant Householders and freeholders of the Township of Burgess, to assemble to hold their annual Township Meetings at or near the centre of Lot number four, in the second con- *Preamble.*

cession of Burgess : Therefore be it enacted by the District Council of the District of Johnstown, in Council assembled at the Town of Brockville, on the fourteenth day of February, in the year of our Lord one thousand eight hundred and forty-nine, That so much of By-Law No. 143 as enacts that the said Township Meetings shall be held at Coledale, on lot number Six, in the second conces-
Repeal. sion of South Burgess shall be and is hereby repealed.

Where to be held. 2. And be it further enacted by the authority aforesaid, That the said annual Township Meetings of the Township of Burgess shall be held at or near the centre of lot number four, in the second concession of said Township.

OGLE R. GOWAN, Warden.

[L. S.]

No. CLXXXI.—BY-LAW

To Assess the Inhabitants of certain School-Sections in the Johnstown District for the year 1849.—Passed February 15, 1849.

(Expired by Limitation.)

No. CLXXXII.—BY-LAW

To Assess the Inhabitants of the District of Johnstown for the support and maintenance of Common Schools therein, for the year 1849.—Passed February 15, 1849.

£1600 levied.

(Expired by Limitation.)

No. CLXXXIII.—BY-LAW

To Authorise the Assessment and Collection of Rates for the General Purposes of the Johnstown District for the year 1849.—Passed February 15th, 1849.

One Penny in Pound levied.)

(Expired by Limitation.)

·169

No. CLXXXIV.—BY-LAW:

*To appoint Trustees to expend certain monies for the erection
of a Lock-up House in the Village of Gananoque.*

Whereas by the 41st chapter of the Act passed in the Preamble.
10th and 11th years of Her present Majesty's reign,
entitled an Act to establish Lock-up Houses in the unincorporated Towns and Villages in Canada West, power is
conferred on the several Municipal Councils of this
Province to cause Assessments to be levied for the erection
of Lock-up Houses in the several unincorporated Towns
and Villages of Upper Canada; and whereas this Council
did by By-law number 162, passed on the 4th day of
February, 1848, and entitled "*By-law to establish a Lock-
up House in the unincorporated Village of Gananoque*,"
assess the inhabitants of the said Village of Gananoque in
the sum of £100, for the erection of a Lock-up House
therein, and did also by the same By-law appoint Ephraim
Webster and James W. Parmenter, Esquires, residing in
the said Village, to superintend the erection of the said
building, and to expend the said sum of £100, raised and
levied as aforesaid; and whereas it is desirable to appoint
other Trustees in lieu of the said Ephraim Webster and
James W. Parmenter, Esquires, mentioned to carry out
the provisions of the said By-law: Be it therefore ordained
and enacted by the Municipal Council of the District of
Johnstown, assembled at Brockville, this fifteenth day of
February, 1849, and it is hereby ordained and enacted,
That so much of the said By-law No. 162, as appoints Part By-law No.
the said Ephraim Webster and the said James W. Par- 162 repealed.
menter, be, and the same is hereby repealed.

SECTION 2. That in lieu of the said Ephraim Webster
and Jas. W. Parmenter, Ephraim Webster, Hugh B. Cain,
and James Kirker, residents of the Town of Gananoque,
be appointed Trustees to superintend the erection of the New Trustees.
said Lock-up House, and to expend the money raised and
assessed for that purpose, and that the said Ephraim
Webster, Hugh B. Cain, and James Kirker have all the
power and authority vested in the said By-Law in the
Commissioners therein named, and all other powers and
authority which by any Law or Custom of this Province
is vested in and may be exercised by Trustees appointed
for this purpose.

OGLE R. GOWAN, WARDEN.

[L. S.]

No. CLXXXV.—BY-LAW

To establish certain Roads in the District of Johnstown..

Preamble: Whereas James Eaton, Surveyor of Highways in and for the County of Leeds, has been petitioned by twelve freeholders of the said County, to lay out a certain Road in the Township of Burgess, and in pursuance of such petition the said James Eaton has surveyed and laid out the said Road as follows: commencing at the allowance of Road

Description of
Road in Burgess between lots numbers six and seven in the second concession of Burgess, where a Cedar post is planted marked R; thence south-westerly to a post marked R on lot number seven; thence north-westerly upon said lot number seven to the allowance of Road in rear of said second concession, where another Cedar post marked R is planted; thence on said second concession road across the remainder of said lot number seven, the whole of number eight, and part of nine, to where another Cedar post is planted marked R, at a ledge of rocks; thence southerly in the second concession up to the side line between lots numbers nine and ten, where another Cedar post is planted, marked R; thence southerly across the said lot number ten, and from thence upon a ridge called the Hog's Back, the only land fit for a Road across numbers eleven, twelve, and thirteen, to the waters of the Rideau Lake, where another Cedar post is planted: the said intended Road to be on the north-west side of the two first named posts; from thence to the post on concession line to be on the north-east side, and the whole of the said Road after to be on the south-east side of the above named posts, and which said Road is forty feet in width.

And whereas Benjamin Warren, Surveyor of Highways in and for the County of Leeds, has been petitioned by twelve freeholders of the said County, to make a certain alteration in a road in the Township of Escott, and in pursuance of such petition, the said Benjamin Warren has surveyed and made the said alteration as follows: com-

Description of
Road in Escott. mencing at a ledge of rocks eighteen rods more or less from the sixth concession line of Escott; thence on the Town-line laying the Road on the east side of the same to a post planted on the Town-line where it intersects the new line of Road leading to Charleston, which said Road is laid out forty feet in width; and to close up the old Road running an angling course through lot number twenty-six, from where the new Road intersects the aforesaid old Road, forty feet south of a Beach tree, blazed on two sides and marked R; from thence to the Road leading to McIntosh's, or the Ballycanue Road in the fourth concession of Yonge on lot number twenty-six.

And whereas Thomas O. Adkins, Surveyor of Highways in and for the County of Leeds, has been petitioned by twelve freeholders of the said County, to lay out a certain Road in the Township of Lansdowne, and in pursuance of such petition the said Thomas O. Adkins has surveyed and laid out the said Road as follows: commencing at the east corner post of lot number eleven in the third Description of concession of Lansdowne; thence west 5 degrees, north Road in Lans-downe. 30 chains to a post planted and marked R with red chalk, as the north side of Road in the centre of lot number ten in said concession; thence north-west by west thirteen chains forty-four links to a Pine tree on lot number nine, blazed and marked R with red chalk as the north side of said Road; thence west-by-north three chains sixty-six links to a post marked R with red chalk as north side of Road; thence west-south-west five degrees; west twenty-three chains forty-four links to a Beech stump in the concession line on lot number eight, blazed and marked R with red chalk as north side of Road; thence west twenty five chains forty-eight links, following the Concession line to a post marked R with red chalk, intersecting the Kenney Road on lot number seven in said Concession, which said Road is laid out sixty feet in width.

And whereas John Riddle, Surveyor of Highways in and for the County of Leeds, has been petitioned by twelve freeholders of the said County, to lay out a certain Road in the Townships of Kitley and Elmsley; and in pursuance of such petition, the said John Riddle, has surveyed and laid out the said Road as follows: commencing at the line between lots number twenty-one and twenty in Description of the second Concession of Kitley, forty feet east of an Oak Road in Kitley tree said to be standing on or near said line, eight feet and Elmsley. from the water's edge on the east side of the Creek; thence running northerly across lot number twenty and a part of nineteen, passing thirty-three feet west of Mr. John Chalice's frame barn to a stake standing opposite to said Chalice's stable one hundred and eighty-six rods; thence running between said stable and a workshop across nineteen and part of eighteen passing to the east of Mr. William McSpeedin's house, and so on opposite to a blazed Elm stump, eighty rods, said stump standing six feet east of said Road; thence to the Concession line between the first and second Concessions of said Township, supposed to be near the south angle of lot number seventeen in the first concession, and so on till it intersects the allowance for Road in front of the first Concession of Elmsley, forty feet east of a Beech tree marked R, two hundred and eighty-six rods; the line described indicates the eastern boundary of the said Road, which said Road is laid out forty feet in width.

And whereas Benjamin Warren, Surveyor of Highways in and for the County of Leeds, has been petitioned by twelve freeholders of the said County, to make an alteration in a certain Road in the Township of Yonge, and in pursuance of such petition, the said Benjamin Warren. has surveyed and made the said alteration as follows:

Description of Road in Yonge. commencing on the Road running between lots numbers eighteen and nineteen in the first Concession of the Township of Yonge, forty feet south of a ledge of rocks that impede said allowance; thence angling to the east on lot number eighteen, five rods more or less; thence angling to the west to the allowance between said lots; thence along said allowance twenty rods more or less; thence angling to the east sixty feet more or less to said ledge of rocks; thence angling to the west to allowance of said Road; thence along said allowance to the Concession line between the first and second Concessions; from thence on a line of pickets and fixed Monuments a north-north-east course to the bridge over Jones's Mill Pond; thence on the Road now in use to a post fixed on the south side of said Road marked R; thence on a straight course to the allowance for a Road between lots eighteen and nineteen; thence on said allowance eighty rods more or less to a maple stump blazed and marked R; from thence on a line of blazed trees angling to the west of said allowance twenty-five rods more or less to the aforesaid allowance for a Road; thence on said allowance fifteen rods more or less to a stump blazed and marked R; thence angling to the east sixty feet more or less to a hemlock tree blazed and marked R on the north end of the Page clearing where it intersects the present travelled Road leading from Mallorytown to Caintown; the Monuments and blazed trees are on the west and south-west side of said Road, and which is laid out forty feet in width.

And whereas James Bilton, Surveyor of Highways in and for the County of Leeds has been petitioned by twelve freeholders of the said County, to lay out a certain Road in the Township of North Crosby, and in pursuance of such petition the said James Bilton has surveyed and laid out the said Road as follows: commencing at the post between lots numbers nine and ten in the ninth Concession, two Cedar posts are marked and planted on each side of road with red lead; Road runs along said side line to the tenth Concession and from thence along the side line in the tenth concession between lots numbers nine and ten to the Bedford line, two posts are marked and planted on the said Town-line, which said Road is laid out forty feet in width: that is, twenty feet on each side of the line, and is marked and staked on the west side of the Road. Description of Road in North Crosby.

And whereas James Bilton has surveyed and laid out a certain other Road in the said Township of North Crosby as follows: commencing at a post between lots numbers seventeen and eighteen in the seventh concession of the said Township, running along to the concession line to the large swamp; thence along to old line of road a north-west course to lot number twenty-seven in the sixth Concession to the Sherbrooke line, Road marked and blazed on the north side and is laid out forty-five feet in width. Description of Road in North Crosby.

And whereas the said James Bilton has surveyed and laid out a certain other Road in the Township of North Crosby aforesaid, as follows: commencing on lot number twenty-one in the sixth concession, and running an east course through lots numbers twenty-one and twenty-two in said concession to lot number twenty in the third concession to the Perth Road; which said Road is marked and blazed on the south side, and is laid out forty-five feet in width. Description of Road in North Crosby.

And whereas the said James Bilton has surveyed and laid out a certain other Road in the Township of North Crosby aforesaid, as follows: commencing at Mr. B. Lashlay's Mill, on lot number eighteen in the fourth concession, and running on the south-west side of the Mill, and keeping a north course to the bridge on lot number twenty-three in the second concession on the Perth road; which said Road is marked and blazed on the north side, and is laid out sixty feet in width. Description of Road in North Crosby.

And whereas the said James Bilton has surveyed and and laid out a certain other Road in the Township of North Crosby aforesaid, as follows: commencing at a

Description of
Road in North
Crosby. Cedar post marked and planted on the Town line between North Crosby and Burgess, on lot number fourteen in the first Concession of North Crosby, and following the old Road now travelled a south-west course to a Black Oak post on lot number twelve in the sixth Concession on the Perth Road; which said Road is marked and blazed on the north side, and is laid out forty-five feet in width.

And whereas the said James Bilton has surveyed and laid out a certain other Road or Street in the Village of West Port, in the Township of North Crosby aforesaid, Description of
Street in West
Port. as follows: commencing three hundred and sixty-eight feet from the post on the main road leading to Newboro; said street is parallel with the Newboro Road, and is laid out sixty feet in width.

And whereas Simon McGee, Surveyor of Highways in and for the County of Grenville, has been petitioned by twelve freeholders of the said County, to lay out a certain Road in the Township of Wolford, and in pursuance of such petition, the said Simon McGee has surveyed and laid out the said Road as follows: commencing six feet Description of
Road in Wolford. south of a Beech tree, blazed and marked R with red chalk, at the School House on lot number ten in the Township of Wolford, and first Concession, and running on said Concession till it intersects the Town line of the Township of Oxford, which said Road is laid out sixty-six feet in width.

And whereas Benjamin Warren, Surveyor of Highways in and for the County of Leeds, has been petitioned by twelve freeholders of the said County to lay out a certain Road in the Township of Escott, and in pursuance of such petition the said Benjamin Warren has surveyed and laid out the said Road as follows: commencing at the Conces- Description of
Road in Escott. sion line between the broken front and the first Concession of the Township of Escott, from a post planted on the centre of lot number twelve marked centre; from thence on a line of pickets north twenty-four degrees, west ninety rods, more or less; from thence angling to the east of said line nine rods, more or less, to pass a ledge of rocks; from thence angling a south-west course, twelve rods, more or less, to the centre of said lot; thence on said line eighty rods, more or less; thence angling to the east of said line ten rods, more or less, to shun a ledge of rocks; from thence angling a south-west course fifteen rods, more or less, to the centre line of said lot; thence along said

line eighty rods, more or less; thence angling to the west of said line forty feet, more or less, to a post fixed on the east side of the present travelled Road known by the name of the Holland Road where it intersects the same; the Monuments are for the centre of said Road, which is laid out forty feet in width.

And whereas Benjamin Warren, Surveyor of Highways in and for the County of Leeds, has been petitioned by twelve freeholders of the said County, to lay out a certain Road in the Township of Escott, and in pursuance of such petition the said Benjamin Warren has surveyed and laid out the said road as follows: commencing at a post planted on the north side of the Kingston road **Description of Road in Escott.** sixty feet more or less west of the allowance for a Road between lots numbers twelve and thirteen; from thence a north-west course thirteen rods more or less west of the allowance for a Road between lots numbers twelve and thirteen; from thence a north-west course thirteen rods more or less to a Birch tree blazed and marked R; from thence angling to the north-east ten rods more or less to the allowance for a Road between said lots; thence on said allowance thirty rods more or less; from thence angling to the east of said allowance eight rods more or less; from thence angling to the west on a line of blazed trees fifteen rods more or less to the aforesaid allowance; thence on said allowance ninety rods more or less to a tree blazed and marked R; thence angling to the east on a line of blazed trees eight rods more or less; thence angling to the west on a line of blazed trees nine rods more or less; thence angling to the north-west on a line of blazed trees to the line between lots numbers twelve and thirteen; from thence on a line of blazed trees to the concession line between the second and third Concessions of the Township of Escott; from thence on a line of blazed trees to the allowance for a Road between lots numbers twelve and thirteen in the third concession; thence on said allowance to the present travelled Road on the front of the third concession of Escott, where it intersects the same; and which said Road is laid out forty feet in width.

And whereas Henry B. Marvin, Surveyor of Highways in and for the County of Leeds, has been petitioned by twelve freeholders of the said County, to lay out a certain Road in the Township of South Crosby, and in pursuance of such petition the said Henry B. Marvin has surveyed

and laid out the same as follows: commencing at Sand
Beach on the east shore of Sand Lake where a large Pine
tree is marked as north side of Road on lot number six in
the fourth concession of south Crosby, and runs a south-
east course across said lot to the termination of the Road
leading to Jone's Falls, then angles to the east and runs
across lots numbers five, four, and three in the said concession, intersecting the Kingston Road near the Whitefish
Creek where a Pine tree is marked as north side of road,
said road being directly on the old track, and which said
road is laid out forty feet in width.

Be it therefore ordained and enacted by the District
Council of the District of Johnstown, in Council assembled
at the Town of Brockville, on the fifteenth day of
February, in the year of our Lord one thousand eight
hundred and forty-nine, That the above described roads
be respectively approved of and confirmed as public Roads
and Highways.

OGLE R. GOWAN, Warden.

[L. S.]

No. CLXXXVI.—BY-LAW

See By-Laws
Nos. 14, 65, 103,
127 and 148.

*To Regulate the Salaries and Duties of certain District
Officers.*

Whereas it is desirable, in order to prevent future mis-
understanding and collision, to fix, by By-Law for that
purpose, the amount to be paid out of the funds of the
District to the several Officers of the same, and also to
regulate and prescribe certain duties to be by them
performed.

Be it therefore ordained and enacted by the Municipal
Council of the said District of Johnstown, in Council
assembled at Brockville, this fifteenth day of February, in
the year of our Lord 1849, and it is hereby ordained and
enacted:

1. That the following sums, and no more, be paid to
the undermentioned Officers, any By-Law, usage, or
custom to the contrary notwithstanding:

(Repealed: see By-Law No. 71, County Council.)

(Repealed: see By-law No. 26, County Council.) Clerk.

(Partly repealed: see By-Law No. 12, County Council.) Treasurer.

5. To the District Superintendent of Common Schools, Superintendent the sum of one hundred and fifty pounds per annum, to of Schools. be paid out of the School Fund: provided he receives no salary or allowance of any kind from the funds of the District, without the permission of this Council.

(See By-law No. 129, County Council.) District Surveyor.

7. To the District Auditors, the sum of seven pounds Auditors. ten shillings per annum each; provided they receive no further or other salary or allowance of any kind from the funds of the District, without the permission of this Council.

8. That the said several salaries and allowances shall be payable quarterly, that is to say, on the first day of the months of January, April, July and October, in each When payable. and every year upon the certificate of the Clerk, countersigned by the Warden, and that such certificate, when receipted by the party in whose favor it may be given, or by his authorized agent, shall be sufficient voucher to the Treasurer, for every such payment.

9. That the respective Offices of Clerk of the District and Treasurer of the District, shall be kept open for the Office hours. transaction of Public business, from the hour of Ten o'clock in the forenoon, to Four o'clock in the afternoon, on each and every day,—every Sunday, Good Friday, and Christmas Day alone excepted, or except with the permission of the Warden.

10. That the District Surveyor shall not be allowed to charge against the District as a day actually employed on Public business, except he shall previously report to the Surveyor to report. Clerk or to the Warden, the business upon which he is about to enter and the expense of which he intends to charge against the funds of the District.

11. That the District Clerk shall hereafter make out and Clerk to make extend the Assessment Rolls in all cases where a tax is or Assessm'nt Rolls. may be imposed for any purpose by any By-Law of this Council.

12. That all Letters, Returns, Assessments, and all Other duties. other matters and things connected with this Council, or

M

TOWNSHIP OF SOUTH CDSBY.

No. 1 composed of lots 1, 2, 3, 4, 5, 6 7, and 8 in the 1, 2, 3, 4, 5, 6, 7, 8, 9 and 10th Concessins, and the Meeting for said ward be held in the Schoc House, on Lot No. 7 in the 3rd Concession, Charles Rcd to be Returning Officer for said Ward.

No. 2 composed of Lots 9, 10, 11, 12 nd 13 in the 1, 2, 3, 4, 5, 6, 7, 8, 9 and 10th Concession and the Meeting for said Ward be held in the School, Hose, on Lot No. 12 in 2nd Concession, Henry Lashly be Returning Officer for said Ward.

No. 3 composed of Lots 14, 15, 16 al 17 in the 1, 2, 3, 4, 5, 6, 7, 8, 9 and 10th Concessions, and the Meeting for said Ward to be held in the School ouse, on Lot No. 17 in the 1st Concession, Horace Kilbor to be Returning Officer for said Ward.

No. 4 composed of Lots 18, 19, 20 an 21 in the 1, 2, 3, 4, 5, 6, 7, 8, 9 and 10th Concessions, and also Lots 22, 23, 24, 25, 26 and 27 from the 7th Conosion to the 10th Concession inclusive, and the Meeting fr said Ward to be held in the School House, on Lot 19 in the 6th Concession, John Leggett, Esq., to be Retning Officer for said Ward.

No. 5 composed of Lots 22, 23, 24, 2 26, and 27 in the 1, 2, 3, 4, 5, and 6th Concessions, ad the Meeting for said Ward to be held in the School Hbe, on Lot No. 22 in the 2nd concession, John N. Pool to be Returning Officer for said Ward.

TOWNSHIP OF YONE.

The first Ward to include all that pt of the Township in front of the fourth Concession, om the eastern boundary to the division line between Tts No. 15 and 16, and the election to be held at th School House, near the stone Church, near Peter Purs, being on Lot No 8 in the 2nd Concession, Christoher Leggo the younger, to be Returning Officer.

The Second Ward to include the rmaining of said Township west of said division lir, the of the fourth Concession from the divion lin

Registered a good and sufficient Deed of the School-site in said School-Section, to be approved of by the Clerk of this Council,

OGLE R. GOWAN, WARDEN.

[L. S.]

No. CXC.—BY-LAW

See 12 Vic. Cap. 81.
Sec 14 Vic., Cap. 109.
See Con. Stat. U. C., Cap. 54.

To Divide certain Townships in the Johnstown District, into Rural Wards.

Preambles.

Whereas by an Act passed in the 12th year of the reign of Her Majesty Queen Victoria, entitled "*An Act to repeal the Acts in force in Upper Canada relative to the establishment of Local and Municipal Authorities, and other matters of a like nature,*" it is amongst other things enacted, That it shall and may be lawful for every Municipal Council, if they shall deem it expedient so to do, in and by a By-Law, to divide each of the Townships in each County into Rural Wards, for the election of Township Councillors for such Townships:

And whereas the Municipal Council of the District of Johnstown, in Council assembled at the Court House in the Town of Brockville, in the said District, on the thirtieth day of October, in the year of our Lord one thousand eight hundred and forty-nine, have deemed it expedient, for the better accommodation and convenience of the inhabitants, freeholders and Householders of the said District, to divide certain Townships within the limits of

Certain Townships divided into Wards.

the said District into Rural Wards, pursuant to the said Act: Be it therefore ordained and enacted, and it is hereby ordained and enacted by the Municipal Council of the District of Johnstown, in Council assembled at the Town of Brockville, in the said District, this thirtieth day of October, in the year last aforesaid, That the following Townships be divided; and they are hereby divided into Rural Wards pursuant to Law, and the limits and description of the said Rural Wards shall be as follows: that is to say,

Wolford.

TOWNSHIP OF WOLFORD.

(Repealed; see By-law No. 11 County Council.)

TOWNSHIP OF SOUTH CROSBY.

No. 1 composed of lots 1, 2, 3, 4, 5, 6, 7, and 8 in the 1, 2, 3, 4, 5, 6, 7, 8, 9 and 10th Concessions, and the Meeting for said ward be held in the School House, on Lot No. 7 in the 3rd Concession, Charles Read to be Returning Officer for said Ward.

No. 2 composed of Lots 9, 10, 11, 12 and 13 in the 1, 2, 3, 4, 5, 6, 7, 8, 9 and 10th Concessions, and the Meeting for said Ward be held in the School House, on Lot No. 12 in 2nd Concession, Henry Lashly to be Returning Officer for said Ward.

No. 3 composed of Lots 14, 15, 16 and 17 in the 1, 2, 3, 4, 5, 6, 7, 8, 9 and 10th Concessions, and the Meeting for said Ward to be held in the School House, on Lot No. 17 in the 1st Concession, Horace Kilborn to be Returning Officer for said Ward.

No. 4 composed of Lots 18, 19, 20 and 21 in the 1, 2, 3, 4, 5, 6, 7, 8, 9 and 10th Concessions, and also Lots 22, 23, 24, 25, 26 and 27 from the 7th Concession to the 10th Concession inclusive, and the Meeting for said Ward to be held in the School House, on Lot 19 in the 6th Concession, John Leggett, Esq., to be Returning Officer for said Ward.

No. 5 composed of Lots 22, 23, 24, 25, 26, and 27 in the 1, 2, 3, 4, 5, and 6th Concessions, and the Meeting for said Ward to be held in the School House, on Lot No. 22 in the 2nd concession, John N. Poole, to be Returning Officer for said Ward.

TOWNSHIP OF YONGE.

The first Ward to include all that part of the Township in front of the fourth Concession, from the eastern boundary to the division line between Lots No. 15 and 16, and the election to be held at the School House, near the stone Church, near Peter Purvis', being on Lot No 8 in the 2nd Concession, Christopher Leggo the younger, to be Returning Officer.

The Second Ward to include the remaining part of said Township west of said division line, the front half of the fourth Concession from the division line, between fifteen and sixteen, and the election to be held, at T. P. Kenyon's, being on Lot No. 21 in first Concession, Frederick Lee to be Returning Officer.

The Third Ward to include the remaining part of the fourth Concession not included in the second Ward, the whole of the fifth and sixth Concessions and the front half of the seventh Concession, and the election to be held at M'Intosh's Mill, being on Lot No. 15 in the fifth Concession, John M'Intosh to be Returning Officer.

The Fourth Ward to include the rear half of the seventh Concession from Lot No. 12, and all the Concessions in rear to the northern boundary of the said Township, and that Farmersville be the place for holding the election, being on Lot No. 12 in the ninth Concession, William H. Giles to be Returning Officer.

The Fifth Ward to include the rear half of the seventh Concession from the eastern boundary of said Township to the division line between Lots No. 12 and 13 and all the Concessions in rear to the northern boundary of said Township, and that the election be held at the School House near Bellamy's Mills, being on Lot No. 3 in the eighth Concession, Daniel Philips to be Returning Officer.

Elmsley.

TOWNSHIP OF ELMSLEY.

(Repealed: see By-law No. 11, County Council.)

South Gower.

TOWNSHIP OF SOUTH GOWER.

(Repealed; see By-law No. 11, County Council.)

Bastard & Burgess.

TOWNSHIPS OF BASTARD AND BURGESS.

That Ward No. 1 be composed of all that part of Burgess to the east of lot No. 15, including that lot, and the first and second Concessions of Bastard, from No. one to fifteen inclusive, and that the first meeting for the election of a Township Councillor be held at the School House on lot number four in the second Concession of Burgess, and that Joseph Polk be Returning Officer.

That Ward No. 2 shall include the 3, 4, 5, and 6th Concessions of Bastard, from lots No. 1 to 15, both lots included, and the place of meeting for the election of Township Councillor be at the School-House on lot No. 5 in the 3rd Concession, and that Samuel Robb be appointed to hold said first election.

That Ward No. 3 shall include the 7, 8, 9, and 10th Concessions of Bastard, from lots No. 1 to No. 15, both included, and that the first meeting for the election of a Township Councillor be held at the School-House on lot No. seven in the 7th Concession, and that Wm. V. Shorman be appointed to hold the first election for Township Councillor.

Ward No. 4 shall consist of all that part of Burgess West of lot No. 16, including that lot, and the 1, 2, 3, 4, and 5th Concessions of Bastard from lot No. 16 to South Crosby, including that lot, and that the first meeting for the election of a Township Councillor be held at the Stone School-House near Richard Hale's, and that Edward Oates be appointed to hold the first Election,

Ward No. 5 be composed of the 6, 7, 8, 9, and 10th Concessions of Bastard, from lot No. 16 to South Crosby, including that lot, and that the first election for Township Councillor be held at Beverly, and that John Warren be appointed to hold the said first Election.

OGLE R. GOWAN, Warden.

[L. S.]

No. CXCI.—BY-LAW

To apportion the sum of Six Hundred Pounds for Mac- See By-Law No. *adamized, Plank, or Gravel Roads in the District* 231, County Council. *of Johnstown.—Passed October 30, 1849.*

(Repealed: see By-Law No. 4, County Council.)

No. CXCII.—BY-LAW

To Close Certain Roads in the District of Johnstown.

Whereas Benjamin Warren, Surveyor of Highways Preamble. in and for the County of Leeds, has been petitioned by twelve freeholders of the said County, to close a certain

Road in the Gore of the Township of Escott, as unnecessary for public use.   And whereas the said Benjamin Warren has examined the said Road and recommends that the same be closed as follows, to wit: from the west line of lot No. twenty-two, in the first Concession of Lansdowne, to the line between the Gore or letter A and lot No. one, in the broken front Concession of the Township of Escott, to where the new Road intersects the old one.

Description of Road in Escott.

And whereas Edward Mix, Surveyor of Highways in and for the County of Grenville, has been petitioned by twelve freeholders of the said County to close a certain Road in the Township of Oxford, as unnecessary for public use.   And whereas the said Edward Mix has examined the said Road and recommends it to be closed as follows: commencing on the side line between lots Nos. 24 and 25, in the third Concession of Oxford aforesaid, at the top of the Hill commonly called Hurd's Hill, about the middle of said Concession; running from thence west 14 degrees, south across lots Nos. 24, 23, and about two-thirds of 22; from thence across the remainder of 22 and a part of 21, west 17 degrees, north to its junction with the Concession Road in front of the third Concession, about 32 rods south of the post between 21 and 22 aforesaid.

Description of Road in Oxford.

Be it therefore ordained and enacted by the Municipal Council of the District of Johnstown, in Council assembled at the Town of Brockville, on the thirtieth day of October, in the year of our Lord one thousand eight hundred and forty-nine, That the said above described Roads be, and the same are hereby declared closed.

Declared closed.

OGLE R. GOWAN, Warden.

[L. S.]

No. CXCIII.—BY-LAW

To establish certain Roads in the District of Johnstown.

Preamble.

Whereas John Byce, Surveyor of Highways in and for the County of Grenville, has been petitioned by twelve freeholders of the said County, to lay out a certain Road in the Township of South Gower, and in pursuance of such petition, the said John Byce has surveyed and laid out the said Road as follows: commencing on the east side of Lot No. 14 in the eighth concession of South Gower at a black Ash tree blazed on the sides marked A with a red pencil; thence, a south-westerly course by blazed trees till it intersects the south branch of the River Rideau where is planted a black Ash post on an open ground marked B, about four rods from the banks' edge; thence nearly a south course to Oxford line is planted a Cedar post in open ground marked C; thence a south-westerly course across No. 30 in the first concession of Oxford to the concession line between the first and second concessions to a Hemlock post in bush ground marked E, thence on 29 in the second concession nearly the same course till it intersects the concession line between the second and third concessions of Oxford; thence nearly a south course on 29 in the third to a Cedar post marked F, standing on open ground about fifteen rods from south branch at the big bend; thence to the water's edge where the bridge is to be built; the said road to come off the west side of said line, and to be forty feet in width. *Description of Road in South Gower.*

And whereas Benjamin Chapman, Surveyor of Highways in and for the County of Leeds, has been petitioned by twelve freeholders of the said County to lay out a certain Road in the Township of Elizabethtown, and in pursuance of such petition the said Benjamin Chapman has surveyed and laid out the said Road, as follows: commencing one hundred and twenty rods from the rear of Lots 30 and 31 in the 10th concession of the Township of Elizabethtown, commencing at a Maple tree marked R, thence running across Lots 31 and 32 to the centre of 32 and 33, thence running down the side line till it intersects the concession road, the said road is laid out on the west side of the Maple tree marked R, and running down the centre of the line between Lots 32 and 33 till it intersects the concession Road, the said Road to be forty feet in width. *Description of Road in Elizabethtown.*

And whereas Benjamin Chapman, Surveyor of Highways in and for the County of Leeds, has been petitioned by twelve freeholders of said County to lay out a certain Road in the Township of Elizabethtown, and in pursuance of such petition the said Benjamin Chapman has surveyed and laid out the said Road as follows: commencing at a post marked A, on the side line between Lot A, and Lot No. 1 in the sixth concession of the Township of Elizabethtown, forty-one chains and sixty-four links from the centre of what is called Walker's Creek, thence down *Description of Road in Elizabethtown.*

the side line between the above named Lot A, and Lot No. 1 the distance of sixteen chains to a post marked B, thence along the present travelled road which leads to Brockville seven chains and five links to a post marked C, in an easterly direction till it strikes the West Common in the sixth concession of the Township of Augusta; to be forty feet in width, and the posts are on the south side of said Road.

Description of Road in Elizabethtown.

And whereas Benjamin Chapman, Surveyor of Highways in and for the County of Leeds, has been petitioned by twelve freeholders of said County, to lay out a certain Road in the Township of Elizabethtown, and in pursuance of such petition the said Benjamin Chapman has surveyed and laid out the said Road as follows: commencing at a post marked A with red chalk at the Four Corners, near the residence of John Golden, in the fourth concession of the Township of Elizabethtown, on the line of old road past the residence of Noah Holiday, until it comes opposite the house of Sylvester Wright, Esq., till it strikes the side line between the said Sylvester Wright and Billa Flint's at a post marked C, with red chalk; thence across a piece of land which belongs to Billa Flint, Esq., the distance of eleven rods and eight links to a post marked D with red chalk on the Macadamized Road, opposite the residence of Sylvester Wright, Esq.; to be forty feet in width, and the posts are on the south-east side of said road.

Description of Road in Edwardsburgh.

And whereas Allan Hunter, Surveyor of Highways in and for the County of Grenville, has been petitioned by twelve freeholders of said County, to lay out a certain Road in the Township of Edwardsburgh, and in pursuance of such petition, the said Allan Hunter has surveyed and laid out the said Road as follows; commencing at a post at the front of the fifth concession marked 34 and 35, said post is in the centre of the Road, thence to the front of the sixth concession to a post also in the centre of the Road, thence west fourteen chains to a stake planted in the open field, thence seven chains north by west to the end of the Bridge across the Nation River; and the said Road is laid out forty feet in width.

And whereas Philemon Pennock, Surveyor of Highways in and for the County of Grenville, has been petitioned by twelve freeholders of the said County to lay out a certain Road in the Township of Augusta, and in pursuance of

such petition, the said Philemon Pennock has surveyed and
laid out the said Road as follows: commencing on the
east side of lot No. 37 in the fifth concession of the said Description of
Road in Augusta.
Township of Augusta, eighty-five chains in rear of the
front of the said concession; thence east ten degrees, north
17 chains to a post marked R; thence east 25 degrees,
north 20 chains to the line between lots Nos. 36 and 35
to a post marked R; thence in the same direction across
part of Lot No. 35, five chains and forty-one links to the
travelled Road leading from North Augusta to Brockville;
and said Road is laid out 40 feet in width, and monuments are placed at the intermediate points on the south
side of the Road.

And whereas Matthew Morrison, Surveyor of Highways
in and for the County of Leeds, has been petitioned by
twelve freeholders of said County, to lay out a certain
Road in the Township of Bastard, and in pursuance of
such petition, the said Matthew Morrison has surveyed and
laid out the said Road as follows: commencing upon the
new line of road leading to Smith's Falls, where is planted a Description of
Road in Bastard.
Cedar post marked R, on the centre line of said lot; thence
running along the side line to an Elm tree marked R;
thence running along the side line to the new travelled
Road leading to the Perth Road, where is planted another
Cedar post marked R,—the said Road to be on the south-
westerly side of the said posts, and to be forty feet in width.

And whereas Matthew Morrison, Surveyor of Highways
in and for the County of Leeds, has been petitioned by
twelve freeholders of said County, to lay out a certain
Road in the Township of Burgess; and in pursuance of
such petition, the said Matthew Morrison has surveyed and
laid out the said Road as follows: commencing at the
Town-line of Elmsley, where is planted a Cedar post Description of
Road in Burgess.
marked R; thence north-easterly across an angle of Lot
No. 30 and the whole of 29 in the second concession of
said Township, where is marked the letter R on a large
Maple tree; thence north-westerly across lot 28 in said
concession of said Township, where it intersects the
Smith's Falls Road, and where is planted another Cedar
post marked R, the said Road is laid out on the north-east
side of the two first named posts: from thence to the post
on the Smith's Falls Road on the north-west side, and
forty feet in width.

And whereas Benjamin Chapman, Surveyor of Highways in and for the County of Leeds has been petitioned
by twelve freeholders of said County, to lay out a

certain Road in the Township of Elizabethtown; and in pursuance of such petition the said Benjamin Chapman has surveyed and laid out the said Road as follows: commencing on the side line between lots Nos. 24 and 25 in the 4th concession of Elizabethtown, at a post marked A with red chalk, the said post is 25 chains 38 links from the rear of said lot No. 24; thence in a straight course with the Road that leads from the Macadamized Road to Archibald Fletcher's (or parallel with the concession Road) till it intersects the side line between Lots 27 and 28; thence along said line till it intersects the concession Road in rear of the fourth concession; thence along the said concession to the main Road that leads from Coleman's Corners to Unionville, at a post marked B, with red chalk: the said Road is marked out by stakes planted in the open ground and blazes on trees, and which are on the north side of said Road, and said Road is laid out forty feet in width.

Description of Road in Elizabethtown.

And whereas Thomas O. Adkins, Surveyor of Highways in and for the County of Leeds, has been petitioned by twelve freeholders of said County, to lay out a certain Road in the Township of Leeds and Lansdowne,— And in pursuance of such petition, the said Thomas O. Adkins has surveyed and laid out the said Road as follows: commencing in rear of said Concession at the west corner post of Lot No. 24, thence south 27 chains and 50 links along the side line between Lots Nos. 23 and 24 to a post planted and marked R, with red chalk; thence south 17 degrees 30 Minutes west 5 chains and 25 links to a post planted and marked R, with red chalk on the north side of the Queen's Highway, and said Road is laid out forty feet in width.

Description of Road in Leeds and Lansdowne.

And whereas Matthew Morrison, Junr., Surveyor of Highways in and for the County of Leeds, has been petitioned by twelve freeholders of the said County to lay out a certain Road in the Township of South Burgess —And in pursuance of such petition, the said Matthew Morrison has surveyed and laid out the said Road as follows: commencing at the Road leading to New Boyne, where is planted a Cedar post marked R, on part of Lot No. 4 in the first Concession of South Burgess, thence crossing part of Lot No. 4 and the whole of Nos. 3, 2, and 1 in said Concession, in said Township; thence to the Town line of Elmsley on Lot No. 1, where is planted a cedar post marked R; the said Road is laid out on the north-east side of said posts, and to be forty feet in width.

Description of Road in South Burgess.

And whereas Matthew Morrison, Junr., Surveyor of Highways in and for the County of Leeds, has been petitioned by twelve freeholders of said County, to lay out a certain Road in the Township of South Burgess—And in pursuance of such petition the said Matthew Morrison, Junr., has surveyed and laid out the said Road as follows: commencing upon the south-east angle of Lot No. 29 in the fourth Concession of the Township of Elmsley, where is planted a Cedar post marked R, intersecting the Perth Road, thence running a south-westerly course across Lot No. 30 in said Concession of said Township, thence crossing the Town line of Elmsley across Lots Nos. 1, 2 and 3 to a large Maple tree marked R, thence crossing Lots 4 and 5 to the new established road leading to Clemmons's wharf where is planted another post marked R; the said road is laid out on the north-west side of said posts, and forty feet in width.

Description of Road in South Burgess and Elmsley.

And whereas John Morris, Surveyor of Highways in and for the County of Leeds, has been petitioned by twelve Freeholders of the said County to lay out a certain Road in the Township of Lansdowne—And in pursuance of such petition the said John Morris has surveyed and laid out the said Road as follows: commencing at the Furnace Waters, where a bridge is part built on Lot No. 7 in the eighth concession of Lansdowne, from thence on the east side of said waters to the side line between Nos. 6 and 7 in the said concession, where a post is now planted marked R, from thence along the present travelled Road between Lots Nos. 6 and 7 in the said Concession of Lansdowne to a post marked R, from thence bearing south-east along the present travelled Road to Lot No. 10 in the seventh Concession, where a post is planted by the garden fence of Samuel Slack marked R; from thence across the clearing on the west side of Slack's barn to a Maple tree on Lot No. 11 in the said Concession marked Road, from thence following said Road to a post marked R; from thence along said Road to the outlet of the Wiltse Lake, where a bridge is built and there intersects what is called the Kidd Road leading from the front of Lansdowne. And in pursuance of the said petition the said John Morris has surveyed and laid out a branch Road from the said Road as follows: commencing on Lot No. 11 in the seventh Concession of Lansdowne at a Maple tree marked Road; from thence east to a pair of bars on the west side of Lot No. 12, where a post is marked R; from thence through the fields to another pair of bars, where a post is marked R; from

Description of Road in Lansdowne.

thence following a Road that is now travelled across Lots Nos. 13 and 14 to west side of No. 15; from thence across No. 15 to a post marked R, in the open field, and on the side line between Nos. 15 and 16; from thence through the open fields on No. 16 in said Concesison to a bay of the Wiltse Lake, where a post is now planted marked R, and south of David Reed's house; the said Roads are laid out on the north side of said monuments, and fifty feet in width.

Description of Road in Edwardsburgh.

And whereas Allan Hunter, Surveyor of Highways in and for the County of Grenville, has been petitioned by twelve freeholders of the said County, to lay out a certain Road in the Township of Edwardsburgh, and in pursuance of such petition, the said Allan Hunter has surveyed and laid out the said Road as follows: commencing at a post on the north side of the Road leading down through the sixth concession, on Lot No. 15, thence to the front of the seventh concession to a post in the centre of Lot No. 15, thence along the centre of said Lot to a post at the front of the eighth concession, thence across the Nation River to the side line between Lots 15 and 16, and along said line till the Road intersects the present Road leading through the eighth concession, and the said Road is laid out forty feet in width.

Description of Road in Edwardsburgh.

And whereas Allan Hunter, Surveyor of Highways in and for the County of Grenville has been petitioned by twelve freeholders of said County, to lay out a certain Road in the Township of Edwardsburgh, and in pursuance of such petition the said Allan Hunter has surveyed and laid out the said Road as follows: commencing at a post in front of the seventh concession, marked 28 and 29, the post being on the west side of said Road, thence to the rear of said seventh concession to a post also on the west side of the road; the west side of said Road is marked through by stakes, and the said Road is laid out forty feet in width.

Description of Road in North Crosby.

And whereas James Bilton, Surveyor of Highways in and for the County of Leeds, has been petitioned by twelve freeholders of said County, to lay out a certain Road in the Township of North Crosby, and in pursuance of such petition, the said James Bilton has surveyed and laid out the said Road as follows: commencing at a Cedar post marked and planted fifteen rods and eighteen links from the allowance of Road between the first and second Concessions of North Crosby, and running a north-west course across lots numbers one, two, three, four and five in the first Concession of said Township, to the Narrows on the Rideau Lake, and said Road is laid out sixty feet in width.

And whereas James Bilton, Surveyor of Highways in and for the County of Leeds, has been petitioned by twelve freeholders of the said County, to lay out a certain Road in the Township of North Crosby, and in pursuance of such petition the said James Bilton has surveyed and laid out the said Road as follows: commencing at a post marked and planted at the angle of the Road leading from Bedford, on Mr. B. D. Rorison's farm, and running along the old Road a north course to a post marked and planted on the Road side leading from Mr. James Rorison's mill across said Road, the same course to the Creek, thence across the Creek to a pine tree marked as a post on the north side of said Creek, and from thence along the high bank of said Creek an easterly course to the Perth Road at Mr. Stephen M'Eathron's corner post, the line of posts is on the west side of said Road, and marked with red chalk; the said Road is laid out forty feet in width. *Description of Road in North Crosby.*

And whereas John Ross, Surveyor of Highways in and for the County of Grenville, has been petitioned by twelve freeholders of said County, to lay out a certain Road in the Township of Oxford, and in pursuance of such petition, the said John Ross has surveyed and laid out the said Road as follows: commencing at a stone monument placed in or near the centre of the eighth concession of the Township of Oxford, in the centre of the established Road between lots numbers fourteen and fifteen in said concession; thence in a line parallel with the concession line across lots numbers fourteen, thirteen and twelve, to a cedar post marked R on the line between lots numbers eleven and twelve; thence west across the east half of lot number eleven to a cedar post marked R; thence west by south-half-west, thirteen and one-fourth rods to a Cedar post marked R; thence south-west to a Cedar post marked R on the side line between lots numbers ten and eleven; thence south-by-east forty-one and one-fourth rods to a Cedar post marked R; thence south-west fifty-five and one-half rods to a Cedar post marked R; thence west-by-north half-west twenty-eight and one-fourth rods to a Cedar post marked R at the south bank of the south branch of the Rideau River; thence across the south branch north-north-west, to a Cedar post marked R, on the north bank; thence north-west seventeen and one-half rods to a Cedar post marked *Description of Road in Oxford.*

R; thence west-south-west to a Cedar post marked R, where it intersects the Road between lots numbers eight and nine in the said eighth Concession; the half width of the Road to be taken from each side of the line or posts above described, and which said Road is laid out forty feet in width.

Be it therefore ordained and enacted by the District Council of the District of Johnstown, in Council assembled at the Town of Brockville, on the thirteenth day of October, in the year of our Lord one thousand eight hundred and forty-nine, That the above described Roads be respectively approved of and confirmed as Public Roads and Highways.

Confirmed as Public Roads.

OGLE R. GOWAN, WARDEN.

[L. S.]

No. CXCIV.—BY-LAW

Amended: See By-law No. 14 County Council.

Preamble.

Whereas it is necessary to repeal part of By-law No. 171, so far as relates to the Assessment of School Section No. 3, of the Township of Kitley, in the District of Johnstown, passed in the month of February, one thousand eight hundred and forty-eight: Be it therefore enacted by the District Council of the District of Johnstown duly assembled at the Town of Brockville, on Wednesday, the thirtieth day of October, one thousand eight hundred and forty-nine, That so much of the said By-law be repealed, that relates to the Assessment of School Section No. 3, of the Township of Kitley, directing the sum of seventy pounds to be levied on the said Section for the purpose of building and completing a School House therein, and it is hereby repealed.

Part By-law No. 171 repealed.

SEC. 2. Be it therefore ordained and enacted by the Municipal Council of the District of Johnstown, in Council assembled in the Town of Brockville, on the thirtieth day of October, 1849, That the aforesaid Section No. 3, in the Township of Kitley, in the District of Johnstown, be assessed in the sum of fifty pounds, for the purpose of defraying all expenses incurred in erecting a School House in the School Section aforesaid, previous to the passing of this By-law, and that the same be placed on the Assessment Roll of the Township of Kitley, by the Clerk of the District Council, to be collected forthwith.

£50 to be levied.

OGLE R. GOWAN, WARDEN.

[L. S.]

STANDING RULES

OF THE

COUNTY COUNCIL.

(See By-Law No. 253.)

N

BY-LAWS

OF THE

COUNTY COUNCIL.

No. I—BY-LAW

To assess the Inhabitants of the United Counties of Leeds and Grenville.—Passed 31st January, 1850.

1. Be it enacted by the Municipal Council of the United Counties of Leeds and Grenville, that for the purpose of meeting the past, current and future expenses of the said United Counties, there be raised and levied upon the assessed real and personal property therein, the sum of one penny in the pound on the assessed value thereof, according to the rates established by law. Rate 1 d. in £ for current expenses.

2. That the further sum of one-eighth of a penny in the pound be also raised and levied, as aforesaid, for the erection, maintenance and support of the Provincial Lunatic Asylum, according to the statute in such case made and provided. Lunatic Asylum.

3. That the said sums or rates be levied and collected How levied. by the Collectors of the several Townships or United Townships within the said United Counties, and by them paid to the Treasurer of the said United Counties, in the manner and at the time provided by law; Provided, however, that nothing herein contained shall be so construed Proviso. as to authorize or require any part of the said sums or rates to be raised and levied as aforesaid, to be apportioned or rated upon the real or personal property liable to assessment within the limits of the Incorporated Towns of Brockville and Prescott.

OGLE R. GOWAN, Chairman.

[L. S.]

JAMES JESSUP, County Clerk.

No. II—BY-LAW

See By-Law No. 142. District Council.
See By-law No. 86, County Council.

To Compensate Councillors for their attendance at the Meetings of the Municipal Council of the United Counties of Leeds and Grenville.

Be it ordained and enacted by the Municipal Council of the United Counties of Leeds and Grenville, in Council assembled, at the Town of Brockville, on the thirty-first day of January, in the year of our Lord one thousand eight hundred and fifty, that at this present Session of the Council, and at every subsequent Session hereafter to be held, the County Clerk shall duly enter the names of each and every Councillor, for each and every day he shall actually sit in Council, and shall certify the same at the end of the Session, which certificate shall be countersigned by the Warden or Chairman for the time being, and shall be deemed and taken to be a true statement of the number of days the Councillor receiving the same had actually sat in Council, at any such Session as aforesaid.

Clerk to enter names and grant certificates.

2. That for each and every day so certified as aforesaid, the Councillor in whose favour it shall be given, shall be entitled to receive from the Treasurer of the District the sum of seven shillings and six pence for each and every day so certified, and the Treasurer of the said Counties is hereby authorized and required to pay to the Councillor or to his authorized agent producing the same, the sum of seven shillings and six pence for each and every day it shall appear by such certificate that he sat in Council, and that such certificate shall be taken as a proper voucher from such Treasurer, and be allowed and credited to that officer in his accounts with the said Counties.

Sum allowed per day.

OGLE R. GOWAN, Warden.

[L. S.]

JAMES JESSUP, County Clerk.

No. III.—BY-LAW

To authorize the raising of a certain sum of Money for the ordinary expenses of the Counties during the current year.

(Repealed: see By-Law No. 228.)

No. IV.—BY-LAW

To Repeal certain By-laws therein mentioned, and to make further provisions than are at present by Law made, for the construction of Four Toll Roads in the United Counties of Leeds and Grenville.—Passed 14th March, 1850.

(Repealed : see By-Law No. 231.)

No. V.—BY-LAW

To Authorize the Issue of Debentures.

See Con. Stat. Cap. 54.

Whereas it is desirable that power should be given to the Warden of the United Counties of Leeds and Grenville, to anticipate the revenue, income, and assessments of the said Counties, by the issue of Debentures for certain purposes, and under certain restrictions: Be it therefore ordained and enacted by the Municipal Council of the said Counties, assembled at Brockville, this fourteenth day of March, in the year of our Lord one thousand eight hundred and fifty, and it is hereby ordained and enacted, That whenever any grant or grants of money shall be made by the Municipal Council of the said Counties, for the erection of any Bridge, or for the making, repairing, or constructing of any Road or Public Highway, or for any other Public Work or Works, which said grant or grants, shall not be less in amount than the sum of £25, Provincial currency, it shall and may be lawful for the Warden of the said United Counties, in conjunction with the Clerk and Treasurer of the same, to cause a Debenture or Debentures to be issued, for the amount or amounts so granted, and that said Debenture or Debentures shall be made payable at such time or times as shall appear to the said Warden, and to the said Clerk and Treasurer, there shall be funds in the Treasury applicable to the payment of such order or orders as aforesaid.

Preamble.

How issued and paid.

SECTION 2. That the Treasurer be authorized to procure a plate for such debentures, and to defray from the general revenues of the said United Counties the costs attending the same, and that the form of the said plate, together with the words and devices to be engraved thereon, be approved by the Warden and Clerk.

Plate for Debentures.

Treasurer to enter orders for grants of money. SECTION 3. That the Treasurer shall enter in a book to be kept for that purpose, all orders which may be passed by the Municipal Council as aforesaid, which entries shall be made in regular numerical progression, from number one upwards, and that in all cases, when demanded by the party or parties legally authorized to receive the same, a Debenture or Debentures shall issue, according to the priority in date, of the passing of the grant or grants, for which such Debenture or Debentures may be demanded.

Book to be kept, and duty of Treasurer. SECTION 4. That in the Book so to be kept by the Treasurer as aforesaid, he shall also enter the number of all Debentures issued; the amount of each Debenture respectively; the date when issued; the period when payable; the person to whom delivered; and under the authority of what By-Law, or order granted; and that the said Book, so to be kept as aforesaid, shall be open, at all seasonable and proper hours, to the examination and inspection of any and every member of the Municipal Council of the said Counties, who may demand or desire to examine or inspect the same.

OGLE R. GOWAN, WARDEN.

[L. S.]

JAMES JESSUP, COUNTY CLERK.

No. VI.—BY-LAW

To Authorize the Borrowing of a certain Sum of Money.

(Repealed: see By-Law No. 228.)

No. VII.—BY-LAW

To Authorize the Collection of an Assessment on the Inhabitants of the Township of Oxford, for the support of Common Schools.

Preamble. Whereas the Municipal Council of the Township of Oxford, on the thirteenth day of August last, passed a By-Law providing amongst other things, that an additional rate or sum of money equal to the Government appropria-

tion for Common Schools in the said Township, should Sum to be levied.
be raised, levied, and collected on the rateable or assessed
property of the inhabitants of the said Township for the
present year, for the support of Common Schools therein;
And whereas at the time of the passing of the said By-Law
the present Common School law was in full force and
effect, and which provides that the said Assessment should
be raised by the County Council: Be it therefore ordained
and enacted, and it is hereby ordained and enacted by the
Municipal Council of the United Counties of Leeds and
Grenville, duly assembled at the Town of Brockville, on
the tenth day of October, in the year of our Lord one
thousand eight hundred and fifty, That there be raised
and levied for the support and maintenance of Common
Schools in the said Township of Oxford, for the present
year, on rateable assessed property of the inhabitants of
the said Township returned on the Township Roll for the
said year, an additional rate or sum of one hundred and
sixteen pounds eight shillings and one penny half-penny
currency (clear of all charges of collection), being the
amount of the Legislative grant for the said Township,
and that the County Clerk be authorized to apportion the
said rate on the said property, according to the values
assessed to the same by law, and to place the same forthwith on the Collector's Roll of the said Township.

Section 2. That the said rate or sum of money, when
so apportioned and placed on the said Roll as aforesaid,
shall be levied by the Collector of the said Township in How levied.
the same manner as is now provided by law for the collection of any other rate, and shall be paid by the said
Collector to the Township Treasurer on or before the sixteenth day of December next.

OGLE R. GOWAN, Warden.
[L. S.]
JAMES JESSUP, County Clerk.

No. VIII.—BY-LAW

*To Amend By-Laws Nos. 4 and 5, passed on the 14th day
of March, 1850.—Passed 10th October, 1850.*

(Repealed: see By-Law No. 231.)

No. IX.—BY-LAW

To divide the United Counties of Leeds. and Grenville into School Circuits, and for other purposes therein mentioned.

Be it ordained and enacted by the Municipal Council of the United Counties of Leeds and Grenville, duly assembled at the Town of Brockville, on the twelfth day of October, in the year of our Lord one thousand eight hundred and fifty, and it is hereby ordained and enacted, that the several and respective Townships or union of **Townships constituted Circuits.** Townships, shall be and are hereby constituted separate and District School Circuits, pursuant to the provisions of the 27th Section of the Common School Act, 13 and 14 Victoria, Chap. 48.

Township Treasurers to be Sub-Treasurers. 2. That the Treasurers of the several Townships in the said Counties shall be, and they are hereby appointed Sub-Treasurers of School moneys for their respective Townships.

3. That the following persons be, and they are hereby appointed Superintendents of Schools for the following School Circuits respectively, commencing the first day of January, 1851:—

Superintendents.

Rev. Matthew Connor,	Bastard & Burgess.
" Matthew Connor,	North Crosby.
" Matthew Connor,	South Crosby.
" James Geggie,	Edwardsburgh.
" Harvey M'Alpine,	Oxford.
" Wm. J. M'Dowall,	South Gower.
" Joshua Johnson,	Yonge.
James Clapperton,	Augusta.
Jacob A Brown,	Elizabethtown.
Edward F. Weeks,	Elmsley, (Repealed : see By-Law No. 18.)
Samuel Graham,	Kitley.
Henry P. Washburn,	Leeds & Lansdowne (rear.)
Thomas Vanston, Esq.,	Leeds & Lansdowne (front.)
Thomas Vanston, Esq.,	Escott.

Sub-Treasurers to give security. 4. That before any Sub-Treasurer shall receive any School moneys, he shall enter into a bond with at least two good and sufficient sureties, himself in double the amount of the Government appropriation for the Schools of his Township for the present year, and each of his sureties in a sum at least equal to such appropriation, for the faithful performance of his duties as Sub-Treasurer, and the Reeves of the several Townships of these United Counties, are hereby authorized and required in behalf of this Council to attend to the execution of said bonds, which bonds, after being properly executed and duly attested, shall be deposited with the Clerk of this Council, and his certificate of such deposit shall be the County Treasurer's warrant for paying to any Sub-Treasurer the amount of School money in the County Treasury, and payable for the benefit of the Schools of the Township to which such Sub-Treasurer belongs.

OGLE R. GOWAN, Warden.

[L. S.]

JAMES JESSUP, County Clerk.

No. X.—BY-LAW.

To provide for the collection of Rates.

See Con. Stat. U. C., Cap. 65.

1. Be it ordained and enacted by the Municipal Council of the United Counties of Leeds and Grenville duly assembled at the Town of Brockville on the twelfth day of October in the year of our Lord one thousand eight hundred and fifty, and it is hereby ordained and enacted that if any person whose name is inserted upon the assessment Roll of any Township in the said Counties, shall neglect or refuse to pay the sum or rate for which he or she stands rated thereon, for the space of fourteen days after the demand duly made of the same by the Collector of such Township or his Agent duly appointed, the said Collector, upon oath before any of her Majesty's Justices of the Peace in and for the said United Counties, of such demand and refusal or neglect of payment, as aforesaid, shall be entitled to demand an execution for the amount of rate or rates, which execution of said Justice is hereby authorized to grant; and upon receipt of the same the said Collector shall, and is hereby authorized and required to levy the same, by distress and sale of the goods and chattels of the person so neglecting or refusing to pay, giving eight days previous notice of such sale in three public places in the Township, and render the overplus (if any there be) to the owner thereof, after deducting the amount of the rates assessed, and the legal charges of the distress and sale.

How enforced after demand.

2. That the Collector or Constable to whom such execution may be directed, authorized to be issued as aforesaid, shall be entitled to the following fees and no more Fees on Warrant. for executing such execution, namely; four pence per mile for every mile he may have to travel to execute the same, which travel must be verified upon oath, if required ; and for levying, advertising, selling, and making returns, two shillings and sixpence.

OGLE R. GOWAN, Warden.

[L. S.]

JAMES JESSUP, County Clerk.

No. XI.—BY-LAW

To Repeal part of By-Law No. 190, Passed on the thirtieth day of October, 1849.

Be it ordained and enacted by the Municipal Council of the United Counties of Leeds and Grenville, duly assembled at the Town of Brockville, on the twelfth day of October, in the year of our Lord one thousand eight hundred and fifty, and it is hereby ordained and enacted, that so much of a certain By-Law passed by the Municipal Council of the late District of Johnstown on the thirtieth day of October, 1849, and entitled, " By-Law to divide certain Townships in the Johnstown District into Rural Wards," as ordains and enacts that the Townships of Wolford, Elmsley, and South Gower be divided into Rural Wards pursuant to Law and the limits and descriptions of the said Rural Wards as relates to the said Townships of Wolford, Elmsley and South Gower therein contained and expressed, be, and the same is hereby repealed.

Part as to Wolford, Elmsley & South Gower repealed.

OGLE R. GOWAN, Warden.

[L. S.]

JAMES JESSUP, County Clerk.

No. XII.—BY-LAW

To Repeal part of By-Law No. 186, Passed by the late District Council on the fifteenth day of February, 1849. ^{See By-Law No. 6, C. C.}

Be it ordained and enacted by the Municipal Council of the United Counties of Leeds and Grenville, duly assembled at the Town of Brockville, on the twelfth day of October in the year of our Lord one thousand eight hundred and fifty and it is hereby ordained and enacted, that so much of the fourth section of a certain By-Law, passed by the Municipal Council of the District of Johnstown on the fifteenth day of February, 1849, and entitled, "By-Law to regulate the Salaries and Duties of certain District Officers, as provides that the percentage of the Treasurer of these United Counties shall in no case exceed the sum of one hundred and fifty pounds per annum, shall be repealed, and the same is hereby repealed. ^{Part as to Treasurer's per centage repealed.}

OGLE R. GOWAN, Warden.

[L. S.]

JAMES JESSUP, County Clerk.

No. XIII.—BY-LAW

To Cover certain Grants of Money.

Be it ordained and enacted by the Municipal Council of the United Counties of Leeds and Grenville, duly assembled at the Town of Brockville, on the twelfth day of October in the year of our Lord one thousand eight hundred and fifty, and it is hereby ordained and enacted, that the sum of one hundred and fifty pounds be granted and paid to the Municipal Council of the Townships of Leeds and Lansdowne in rear, in the manner hereinafter provided, to aid in the construction of a new bridge at the Village of Lyndhurst, in the Township of Lansdowne; provided a like sum shall be appropriated and expended by the Municipality of the said Townships for the same purpose. ^{Lyndhurst Bridge. See By-Law No. 23.}

SECTION 2. And be it further ordained and enacted, that the sum of one hundred pounds be granted and paid to the Municipal Council of the Township of Oxford, in

Burritt's Rapids Bridge, £100.

the manner hereinafter provided, to aid in the construction of a new bridge at Burritt's Rapids in the said Township : provided the Municipal Council of the County of Carlton shall appropriate and expend a like sum for that object.

SECTION 3. And be it further ordained and enacted, that the sum of twenty-five pounds be granted and paid to the Municipal Council of the Township of Wolford, Kilmarnock Bridge, £25. in the manner hereinafter provided, to aid in the construction of a new bridge at the Village of Kilmarnock in the said Township ; provided the Municipal Council of the United Counties of Lanark and Renfrew, shall appropriate and expend a sum at least equal to that amount for the same purpose.

SECTION 4. And be it further ordained and enacted, that the sum of twenty-seven pounds be granted and paid to the Municipal Council of the Township of Escott, and the sum of ninety-five pounds to the Municipal Council of the Townships of Leeds and Lansdowne in front, in the manner hereinafter provided, and that the said sums shall be taken and received by the said Council, respectively, as an equivalent for the sum to be raised by assessment and expended in the construction of the Four Toll Roads authorized to be made and constructed by this Council pursuant to the provisions of By-Laws Nos. 4 and 5, Escott and Leeds and Lansdowne (front.) See By-law No. 43, sec. 10. passed on the fourteenth day of March last entitled "By-Law to repeal certain By-Laws therein mentioned and to make further provisions than are at present by law made, for the construction of Four Toll Roads in the United Counties of Leeds and Grenville," and of a certain other By-Law passed by this Council on the tenth day of October instant, entitled, "By-Law to amend By-Laws Nos. 4 and 5, passed on the fourteenth day of March, 1850," and that the said sums shall be expended by the Municipal Councils of the said Townships respectively in the making or repairing of the Roads and Bridges, or in the construction of any new Road or Bridge therein, as to them shall seem expedient.

SECTION 5. And be it further ordained and enacted, that the sum of twenty-five pounds be granted and paid to the Municipal Council of the United Townships of Bastard and Burgess, in the manner hereinafter provid-Sheldon Creek Bridge. ed, to aid in the erection of a new Bridge over Sheldon Creek, in the first Concession of the Township of Bastard.

SECTION 6. And be it further ordained and enacted, that the Municipal Council of the Township of Oxford be authorized and empowered to treat with the Municipal Council of the County of Carlton, and to do all things that may be necessary for the construction of the said Bridge at Burritt's Rapids, and that the Council of the Township of Wolford be also authorized to treat with the Municipal Council of the United Counties of Lanark and Renfrew, as to what may be necessary for the construction of the said Bridge at the Village of Kilmarnock. *Under whose direction Bridges at Burritt's Rapids and Kilmarnock to be built.*

SECTION 7. And be it further ordained and enacted, that the Warden, upon the requisition of the Municipal Councils of the said Townships respectively, to which the grants of money aforesaid are hereby made, shall cause Debentures to be issued for the same pursuant to the provisions of By-Law No. 5, passed on the fourteenth day of March last, and entitled "By-Law to authorize the issue of Debentures." *Debentures for certain grants. See Con. Stat. U. C., Cap. 64.*

SECTION 8. And be it further ordained and enacted, that the following sums be granted and paid by the County Treasurer to the person or persons whose names are placed before each item, respectively, and that the By-Law shall be a sufficient voucher to that officer for the payment of the said sums :— *Sums granted to certain persons.*

No. 1. To Thomas Reynolds, M. D., the sum of one pound five shillings, for attending at the the Inquest and making a post mortem examination on the body of John Cranstoun, by request of the Coroner and Jury.

No. 2. To David Wylie, the sum of eighteen pounds thirteen shillings and nine-pence, for printing and advertising.

No. 3. To Stephen B. Merrill, the sum of four pounds seven shillings, for printing and advertising.

No. 4. To Alfred Poulton, the sum of thirteen shillings and one penny half-penny, for glazing windows in the Gaol and Court House.

No. 5. To the Canada Gazette Office, the sum of five pounds and fifteen shillings, for advertising.

No. 6. To Stephen B. Merrill, the sum of fourteen pounds seventeen shillings and five pence for advertising.

No. 7. To the Statesman Printing Office, the sum of sixty-four pounds one shilling and eleven pence, for printing and advertising.

No. 8. To J. W. Huddleston, the sum of one pound nineteen shillings and ten pence half-penny, for repairs and for pipes furnished to stoves in the Court House.

No. 9. To Benjamin Hopkins, the sum of seven shillings and six pence, for repairs to the roof of the Court House.

No. 10. To William Buell, the sum of five pounds fourteen shillings and four pence, for stationery furnished to the clerk's office.

No. 11. To Adam Anderson, the sum of one pound six shillings, for ruled paper for Assessment Rolls.

No. 12. To James Jessup, the sum of three pounds ten shillings, being the amount paid by him to the Hon. John H. Cameron for his opinion on the Wild Land Tax Act.

No. 13. To the Canada Gazette, the sum of twenty-two pounds two shillings and eight pence, for advertising Wild Lands in arrear for taxes.

No. 14. To Municipal Council of the Township of Wolford, the sum of five pounds, for building a bridge over the middle branch of the Rideau, agreeably to a Resolution passed at the present Session.

No. 15. To Municipal Council of the Township of Leeds and Lansdowne, in front, the sum of fifteen pounds, to aid in the erection of the Bridge at Marble Rock.

No. 16. To Christy Ruttan, the sum of fourteen shillings, for an over assessment in 1849.

No. 17. To Stephen B. Phillips, the sum of one pound five shillings, for serving notices relating to the division of certain Townships into Rural Wards.

No. 18. To Wellington W. Mott, the sum of fifteen shillings for similar service as performed by Stephen B. Phillips.

No. 19. To Alfred Poulton, the sum of one pound seven shillings, for glazing windows in the Court House and Gaol.

No. 20. To James Kincaid, the sum of one pound five shillings, for attending the Council during this Session.

No. 21. To Christopher Leggo, the sum of three pounds two shillings and six pence half-penny, for preparing Room for the sitting of the Council, and furnishing stationery and fuel.

No. 22. To D. Wylie, the sum of two pounds ten shillings, for reporting and publishing the proceedings of the Council this Session.

OGLE R. GOWAN, Warden.

[L. S.]

JAMES JESSUP, County Clerk.

No. XIV.—BY-LAW

To amend By-Law No. 194, passed by the late District Council. See By-Law No. 171, District Council.

Whereas by a certain By-Law passed by the Municipal Council of the late District of Johnstown, on the thirtieth day of October, in the year of our Lord one thousand eight hundred and forty-nine, and No. 194, it was intended to repeal so much of a certain other By-Law, passed by the said Council on the sixth day of October, in the year one thousand eight hundred and forty-eight, entitled, "By-Law to assess the inhabitants of certain School-Sections in the District of Johnstown," and numbered 171, as relates to the assessment of School-Section number three in the Township of Kitley, and to make other provisions for the assessment of the said Section. And whereas the time of the passing of the said first mentioned By-Law was erroneously recited in the said last mentioned By-Law, and it is expedient and right to correct the same, by authorizing the collection of the assessment imposed on the said Section: Be it therefore ordained and enacted by the Municipal Council of the United Counties of Leeds and Grenville, assembled at the Town of Brockville, on the first day of February, in the year of our Lord one thousand eight hundred and fifty-one, and it is hereby ordained and enacted, That the Collector of Rates of the said Township of Kitley, be required, and he is hereby required to proceed forthwith to collect the rates imposed on the inhabitants of the said School-Section number three, in the Township of Kitley aforesaid, as apportioned and placed on the Collector's Roll of the said Township of Kitley for the last year by the County Clerk, under the authority of the said last mentioned By-Law, and that the said Collector pay over the same to the Treasurer of the said Township of Kitley, when collected.

Collector required to collect rates in Section No. 2, Kitley.

GEORGE SHERWOOD, WARDEN,

United Counties of Leeds and Grenville.

[L.S.]

JAMES JESSUP, COUNTY CLERK.

No. XV.—BY-LAW

To define the Jurisdiction of Local Superintendents of Schools, in certain cases.

Be it ordained and enacted by the Municipal Council of the United Counties of Leeds and Grenville, duly assembled at the Town of Brockville, on the first day of February, in the year of our Lord one thousand eight hundred and fifty-one, and it is hereby ordained and enacted, That the local divisions of the several Townships and union of Townships in the said United Counties into School-Sections, shall remain and continue as now established, for the present year, and that in every part Section formed from portions of two or more Townships, the Local Superintendent of the Township, where the School-House may be erected for any such part section, shall have the sole Superintendence of the School therein for the above mentioned period so far as relates to the examination of such School and delivery of Lectures therein, any other usage or custom to the contrary notwithstanding.

Sections to remain as established.

Superintendents to have sole direction in certain cases.

GEORGE SHERWOOD, WARDEN,

United Counties of Leeds and Grenville.

[L. S.]

JAMES JESSUP, COUNTY CLERK.

No. XVI.—BY-LAW

To Repeal part of By-Law No. 9, and for other purposes therein mentioned.

1. Be it ordained and enacted by the Municipal Council of the United Counties of Leeds and Grenville, assembled at the Town of Brockville, on the first day of February, in the year of our Lord one thousand eight hundred and fifty-one, and it is hereby ordained and enacted, That so much of the third section of a certain By-Law passed on the twelfth day of October, in the year of our Lord one thousand eight hundred and fifty, entitled, "By-Law to divide the United Counties of Leeds and Grenville into School-Circuits, and for other purposes therein mentioned," and numbered 9, as provides for the appointment of Edward F. Weeks as Superintendent of Schools for the Township of Elmsley, be repealed, and the same is hereby repealed, and that the Reverend William Atkin be appointed Superintendent of Schools of the said Township of Elmsley, for the present year. *Part repealed.* *Rev. Wm. Atkin appointed instead.*

2. And be it further enacted, That Thomas Graffe be appointed Superintendent of Schools of the Township of Wolford for the present year. *Thomas Graffe for Wolford.*

GEORGE SHERWOOD, WARDEN,
United Counties of Leeds and Grenville.

[L. S.]

JAMES JESSUP, COUNTY CLERK.

No. XVII.—BY-LAW

To appoint a Commissioner for the Road therein mentioned.
Passed 1st February, 1851.

(Repealed: see By-law No. 231.)

No. XVIII.—BY-LAW

To cover certain Grants of Money.

1. Be it ordained and enacted by the Municipal Council of the United Counties of Leeds and Grenville, duly assembled at the Town of Brockville, on the first day of

O

February, in the year of our Lord one thousand eight hundred and fifty-one, and it is hereby ordained and enacted, That the sums following be granted and paid by the County Treasurer, to the person or persons whose names are placed before each item, respectively, and that this By-Law shall be a sufficient voucher to that officer, for the payment of the said sums:—

Sums granted to certain persons.

No. 1. To the County Board of Public Instruction, the sum of three pounds five shillings and five pence, to defray certain expenses incurred by the Board, as detailed in the Report of the Committee on Education.

No. 2. To James Jessup, the sum of one pound one shilling and seven-pence, being the amount of his account, for charges paid by him on boxes from the Education office, and disbursements for postages.

No. 3. To the Council of the Township of Escott, the sum of seven pounds ten shillings, granted for building the Bridge over the Creek on Lot No. 12, in the 2nd Concession of the said Township.

No. 4. To David B. O. Ford, Esq., President of the Agricultural Society of these Counties, the sum of two hundred pounds granted by this Council, for the Provincial Agricultural Exhibition, to be held at the Town of Brockville, during this present year

No. 5. To B. Hopkins, the sum of fifteen shillings and nine pence, for articles furnished the County Clerk's office.

No. 6. Messrs. Tilly & Hopkins, the sum of three pounds fifteen shillings, for certain repairs to the Gaol and Court House.

No. 7. That the several sums allowed to the Enumerators in the year 1848, from the funds of these Counties, for their services as such Enumerators, be paid to the respective Township Treasurers, to remunerate the Enumerators of 1850, for similar services rendered by them.

No. 8. To Christopher Leggo, the sum of two pounds seventeen shillings and ten pence, for stationery and other contingencies furnished the Council, during its present Session.

No. 9 To James Kincaid, the sum of one pound five shillings, for services as messenger of the Council during this Session.

GEORGE SHERWOOD, Warden,
United Counties of Leeds and Grenville.

[L. S.]

JAMES JESSUP, County Clerk.

No. XIX.—BY-LAW

To Amend By-Law No. 4, passed on the 14th March. 1850.—Passed 10th April, 1851.

(Repealed ; see By-law No. 231.)

No. XX.—BY-LAW

To repeal a certain By-law of the late District Council therein mentioned.

Be it ordained and enacted by the Municipal Council of the United Counties of Leeds and Grenville, duly assembled at the Town of Brockville, on the tenth day of April, in the year of our Lord one thousand eight hundred and fifty-one, and it is hereby ordained and enacted, That the By-Law of the late District Council, entitled, "By-law to provide for the custody of certain Books the property of the District shall be repealed, and the same is hereby repealed. *By-Law No. 157 repealed as to custody of books.*

2. That the County Clerk shall, immediately after the passing of this By-law, call upon any party or parties having any of the said books in their possession, to return the same into his office without delay, and that hereafter the said books shall be kept by him in his office, for the use of the Criminal Courts held in these Counties, and for no other purpose. *Duty of Clerk.*

GEORGE SHERWOOD, Warden,
United Counties of Leeds and Grenville.

[L. S.]

JAMES JESSUP, County Clerk.

No. XXI.—BY-LAW

To authorize the borrowing of a certain Sum of Money for the purposes therein mentioned.—Passed 10th April, 1851.

(Repealed : see By-law No. 228.)

No. XXII.—BY-LAW

To explain the Third Section of By-Law No. 4.—Passed 18th June, 1851.

(Repealed : See By-law No. 231.)

No. XXIII.—BY-LAW

To authorize the Issue of Debentures for the Lyndhurst Bridge.

Be it ordained and enacted by the Municipal Council of the United Counties of Leeds and Grenville, assembled at the Town of Brockville on the twentieth day of June, in the year of our Lord one thousand eight hundred and fifty-one, and it is hereby ordained and enacted that the Warden of these Counties, on the requisition of the Municipal Council of the Township of Leeds and Lansdowne in rear, be authorized to issue debentures to the amount of seventy-five pounds on account of the grant made by this Council to aid in the construction of the Bridge at the Village of Lyndhurst ; Provided a certificate be produced from the County Surveyor stating that the progress of the work will justify the advance of the said sum ; and provided also that such Debentures shall be taken in part payment of the sum of one hundred and fifty pounds granted by the first Section of By-Law No. 13, passed on the twelfth day of October, 1850, and entitled, "By-Law to cover certain grants of money."

How issued. See Con. Stat. U. C., Cap. 54.

Proviso.

Proviso.

See By-Law No. 13, sec. 1.

GEORGE SHERWOOD, WARDEN,
United Counties of Leeds and Grenville.

[L. S.]
JAMES JESSUP, COUNTY CLERK.

No. XXIV.—BY-LAW

To repeal the Eighth and Ninth Sections of By-Law No. 4.
—Passed 21st June, 1851.

(Repealed; see By-law No. 231.)

No. XXV.—BY-LAW

To Assess the United Counties of Leeds and Grenville.

Be it ordained and enacted by the Municipal Council of
the United Counties of Leeds and Grenville, assembled at
the Town of Brockville, on the twenty-first day of June,
in the year of our Lord one thousand eight hundred and
fifty-one, and it is hereby ordained and enacted, that there
shall be raised and levied on all the taxable real and personal property in the said Counties for the present year,
the sum of £1799 18s. 6d., currency, (free and clear of all
charges and percentages for assessing, collecting and paying over the same) for common County purposes and for
the support and maintenance of Common Schools in the
said Counties, and that the said sum of £1799 18s. 6d.
shall be divided and apportioned on the several Township
Municipalities of the said Counties in the following manner,
that is to say, on Oxford the sum of £148 5s. 7d.; on
Bastard and Burgess the sum of £138 1s. 3d.; on North Sums raised in
Crosby the sum of £53 9s. 7d.; on Yonge the sum of each Township.
£194 2s. 3d.; on Kitley the sum of £121 19s. 11d.; on
Leeds and Lansdowne (in Rear) the sum of £65 14s. 8d.;
on Elmsley the sum of £48 18s. 2d.; on Escott the sum
of £48 2s. 10d.; on Edwardsburgh the sum of £130 16s.
3d.; on Elizabethtown the sum of £333 9s. 0d.; on South
Gower the sum of £52 2s. 5d.; on Leeds and Lansdowne
(in front) the sum of £85 8s. 10d.; on Augusta the sum
of £212 5s. 8d.; on Wolford the sum of £105 10s. 2d.;
and on South Crosby the sum of £61 11s. 11d.; and the
Township Clerks are hereby required to place the said
several sums on the Collectors' Rolls of their respective
Townships for the present year, by apportioning the same
rateably on all the taxable real and personal property of
such Municipalities respectively.

2. That there shall also be raised and levied on all the
taxable real and personal property in each and every of the

said Township Municipalities, the sum of sixpence in the
hundred pounds, and so in proportion on any less sum for
Lunatic Asylum the Lunatic Asylum as required by the second section of
the Act 13 and 14 Victoria, chapter 68, and that the Town
Clerk of every such Municipality is hereby required to
place the said rate on the Collectors' Roll of his Township
for the present year.

County Toll Roads' rate. 3. That there shall also be raised and levied on the said
taxable property in every such Township Municipality,
the sum of three-eighths of a penny in the pound, on the
assessed value of the said property, as provided for by the
eighth section of By-law No. 8, passed by this Council on
the tenth day of October, in the year of our Lord one
thousand eight hundred and fifty, and entitled "By-law to
amend By-laws Nos. 4 and 5 passed on the fourteenth day
of March, 1850," and that the Township Clerk of every
such Municipality is hereby required to place the said
rate on the Collector's Roll of his Township for the
present year.

Collector's duty. 4. That the Township Collector shall collect the rates
hereby imposed on their respective Township Municipali-
ties, and shall pay over the same to the Township
Treasurers respectively, and finally close their respective
accounts with those officers, on or before the fifteenth day
of December next.

To be paid to County Treasurer. 5. That the said Township Treasurers respectively shall
pay over the said rates to the County Treasurer on or
before the thirty-first day of September next.

GEORGE SHERWOOD, WARDEN,

United Counties of Leeds and Grenville.

[L. S.]

JAMES JESSUP, COUNTY CLERK.

No. XXVI.—BY-LAW

To Amend By-Law No. 186 of late District of Council.

Be it ordained and enacted by the Municipal Council
of the United Counties of Leeds and Grenville, assembled
at the Town of Brockville, on the twenty-first day of June,

in the year of our Lord one thousand eight hundred and
fifty-one, and it is hereby ordained and enacted, That the
third section of a certain By-law passed by the late District
Council on the fifteenth day of February, in the year of
our Lord one thousand eight hundred and forty-nine, and
entitled "By-Law to regulate the salaries and duties of
certain District Officers," be, and the same is hereby
repealed, and that hereafter the salary of the County Clerk
shall be one hundred and fifty pounds currency, payable
quarterly, that is to say, on the first day of January, April,
July and October in each year, on the certificate of the
Warden.

See By-Laws Nos. 90 and 196

3rd Section repealed.

Clerk's Salary.

GEORGE SHERWOOD, WARDEN,
United Counties of Leeds and Grenville.

[L. S.]

JAMES JESSUP, COUNTY CLERK.

No. XXVII.—BY-LAW

To Cover certain Grants of Money.

Be it ordained and enacted by the Municipal Council
of the United Counties of Leeds and Grenville, assembled
at theTown of Brockville, on the twenty-first day of June,
in the year of our Lord one thousand eight hundred and
fifty-one, and it is hereby ordained and enacted, That the
sum of one hundred pounds be granted and paid to the
Municipal Council of the Township of Wolford, in Debentures to be issued by the Warden upon the requisition of
the said Council of Wolford, under the provisions of By-Law No. five, passed on the fourteenth day of March,
1850, and entitled "By-Law to authorize the issue of
Debentures," to aid in the construction of a new Bridge
across Irish Creek, in the Township of Wolford aforesaid;
provided a like sum shall be appropriated and expended
by the said Council of Wolford.

Irish Creek Bridge. See By law No. 86.

2. That the Treasurer be authorized to pay to Pierce
Acheson and Richard Osburn the amount which may be
due them for keeping in repair the Victoria Macadamized
Road leading from Brockville to Addison, upon their producing to him a requisition from a majority of the Commissioners of the said Road, stating the amount which

Acheson and Osburn.

under the circumstances of the case they consider in justice due them for the said repairs.

3. That the following sums be granted and paid by the County Treasurer to the parties to whom they are respectively granted, and that this By-Law shall be a sufficient voucher to that officer for the payment of the said sums :—

No. 1. To the Statesman Printing Office, the sum of £19 4s. 2d., for advertising.

No. 2. To David Wylie, the sum of £24 11s. 8d., for printing and advertising.

No. 3. To Stephen B. Merrill, the sum of £18 6s. 8d., for advertising.

No. 4. To the County Clerk, the sum of £0 19s. 4½d., for postages and charges on Collector's Rolls.

No. 5. To the Statesman Printing Office, the sum of £0 19s. 0d., for advertising.

No. 6. To D. Wylie, the sum of £1 9s. 2d., for advertising.

No. 7. To Hugh Scobie, Esq., the sum of £8 0s. 0d., currency, for Collectors' Forms.

No. 8. To James Gallena, the sum of £8 1s. 3d., for repairs to the Gaol.

No. 9. To Thomas S. Shenston, Esq., the sum of £20 0s. 0d., for twenty-four packages of the County Warden.

No. 10. To C. Leggo, the sum of £6 18s. 1d., for attendance and materials furnished for the Court Room.

No. 11. To James Kincaid, the sum of £1 5s. 0d., for attending the Council this Session.

GEORGE SHERWOOD, Warden,
United Counties of Leeds and Grenville.

[L. S.]

JAMES JESSUP, County Clerk.

No. XXVIII.—BY-LAW

To Appoint a Superintendent of Common Schools for the See By-Law No. 9.
Township of Oxford.

Be it ordained and enacted by the Municipal Council of
the United Counties of Leeds and Grenville, duly assembled
at the Town of Brockville, on the fifteenth day of October,
in the year of our Lord one thousand eight hundred and
fifty-one, and it is hereby enacted, That the Rev. William Rev. Wm. J. Mc-
J. M'Dowell, of the Township of Oxford aforesaid, be and Dowell appoint-
he is hereby appointed Superintendent of Common ed.
Schools for the said Township of Oxford, for the residue
of the present year, in the place and stead of the Rev.
Harvey M'Alpin, who has left the said Township of Oxford.

GEORGE SHERWOOD, Warden,
United Counties of Leeds and Grenville.
[L. S.]
JAMES JESSUP, County Clerk.

No. XXIX.—BY-LAW

To grant further aid to the Toll Roads therein mentioned.
—Passed October 17, 1851.

(Repealed: see By-Law No. 35.)

No. XXX.—BY-LAW

To Authorize the Payment of the Superintendents of See Con. Stat. U.
Common Schools. C., Cap. 64, sec. 83.

Be it ordained and enacted by the Municipal Council
of the United Counties of Leeds and Grenville, assembled
at the Town of Brockville, on the seventeenth day of
October, in the year of our Lord one thousand eight
hundred and fifty-one, and it is hereby ordained and
enacted, That the County Treasurer be authorized, and he
is hereby directed to pay to the Local Superintendents of
Common Schools appointed by the Council, the sum pro- Sum to be paid.
vided by the thirtieth section of the School Act, on their

218

presenting to him a certificate from the Reeve and Clerk
of their respective Townships, stating the number of
Schools in actual operation during the time for which
they are entitled to receive payment.

GEORGE SHERWOOD, Warden,
United Counties of Leeds and Grenville.

[L. S.]

JAMES JESSUP, County Clerk.

No. XXXI.—BY-LAW

See By-Law No. 33.

*To Appoint Superintendent of Common Schools for the
year* 1852.

Be it ordained and enacted by the Municipal Council of
the United Counties of Leeds and Grenville, duly assembled
at the Town of Brockville, on the seventeenth day of
October, in the year of our Lord one thousand eight
hundred and fifty-one, and it is hereby ordained and
enacted, That the following persons be, and they are
hereby appointed Superintendents of Schools for the following School Circuits respectively, commencing the first
day of January, 1852 :—

Persons appoint-
ed.

Augusta..............................James Clapperton.
Oxford...............................Rev. W. J. M'Dowell.
Escott...............................Thomas Vanston, Esq.
Front Leeds and Lansdowne......Thomas Vanston, Esq.
Yonge..............................Rev. Joshua Johnson,
Elizabethtown......................Jacob A. Brown,
Edwardsburgh......................Rev. James Geggie.
South Gower.......................Rev. J. Anderson.
Wolford............................Thomas Graffe.
Kitley.............................Samuel Graham.
Elmsley ....Rev. Wm. Aitkin,—
[See By-law No. 33.]
Bastard and Burgess...............Lewis Chipman.
South Crosby......................Rev. Matthew Connor.
North Crosby ....Rev. Matthew Connor.
Leeds and Lansdowne (rear).....Henry P. Washburn.

GEORGE SHERWOOD, Warden,
United Counties of Leeds and Grenville.

[L. S.]

JAMES JESSUP, County Clerk.

No. XXXII.—BY-LAW

To Cover certain Grants of Money.

Section 1. Be it ordained and enacted by the Municipal Council of the United Counties of Leeds and Grenville, assembled at the Town of Brockville, on the seventeenth day of October, in the year of our Lord one thousand eight hundred and fifty-one, and, it is hereby ordained and enacted, That the sum of twenty-five pounds be paid to Hiram Fulford, Contractor, for the erection of Grant's Bridge, on the Kingston Road, in the Township of Elizazethtown, so soon as the Reeve of that Township shall certify that the work is done and performed agreeable to contract and specification. Grant's Bridge.

Section 2. That the sum of fifty pounds be granted for the purpose of building a Bridge and making a Road between lots numbers six and seven, through the eighth and part of the ninth concessions of the Township of Elizabethtown, to be paid so soon as the Municipal Council of the said Township shall certify that the said Bridge and Road have been completed, and that an outlay of one hundred and fifty pounds has been made thereon, and approved and certified by the Council of said Township. Bridge in Elizabethtown.

Section 3. That the sum of ten pounds be granted for the purpose of opening the allowance for Road on the line between the Townships between South Crosby and Leeds, so soon as the Reeves for the said Townships shall certify that the said Roads shall be opened. Road in South Crosby & Leeds.

Section 4. That the sum of twelve pounds ten shillings be granted for the opening and repairs of the Town line between Crosby, Bastard and Burgess, so soon as the Reeves for Bastard and North and South Crosby shall certify that a like amount has been expended on the said Road by the Municipalities through which the said Road passes. Road in North Crosby, Bastard and Burgess.

Section 5. That the sum of fifty pounds be granted to the Municipal Council of the Township of Elmsley, for the erection of a Bridge across Otter Creek, pursuant to the prayer of the petition of John Ward, Edward Miles, and others, so soon as the Township Council, or the inhabitants, or both, shall expend a like sum for the same purpose. Otter Creek Bridge.

SECTION 6. That the sum of twenty-five pounds be granted to the Municipal Council of the Township of Augusta, to be expended in the erection of a Bridge on the Road laid out on lot No. 24, in the fourth Concession of said Township, or on such parts of said Road as the said Township Council, through their Town Reeve or Clerk, may direct from time to time, payable in a Debenture to be issued under the authority of By-Law No. 5, passed on the fourth day of March, 1850, on the certificate of the said Township Council, stating that the said Bridge has been completed : Provided that the Council of the said Township or the inhabitants, or both, shall appropriate and expend a like sum for that purpose.

Road in Augusta.

SECTION 7. That the following sums be granted and paid to the parties, respectively :—

Sums to certain parties.

No. 1. To E. Lawless, the sum of six shillings and six pence, for candles furnished this Council.

No. 2. To B. Kilborn, the sum of seven shillings and six-pence, for articles furnished for the use of the Council.

No. 3. To Thomas Hume, the sum of three pounds, for services as County Surveyor.

No. 4. To John Goodall, the sum of four pounds, for whitewashing cells in the Gaol.

No. 5. To James Kincaid, the sum of nineteen shillings and ten pence, for stationery furnished the Council.

No. 6. To Henry Bradfield, Esq., the sum of seventy-three pounds five shillings and five pence, for materials furnished and work done to the Cells of the Gaol.

No. 7. To J. W. Huddleston, the sum of two pounds nine shillings and seven-pence half-penny, for stove pipes furnished and work done in the Court House and Gaol.

No. 8. To Alfred Poulton, the sum of five pounds for glass and materials furnished, and glazing the windows of Court House.

No. 9. To D. Wylie, the sum of one pound nineteen shillings and two pence, for advertising and printing.

No. 10. To Gardiner Wing, the sum of five shillings and two pence, for an over assessment.

No. 11. To Richard F. Steele, Esq., the sum of two pounds ten shillings, for a retaining fee in the defence of James Elliot, Collector of Rates for the Township of Kitley.

No. 12. To the County Clerk, the sum of eleven shillings and six-pence, for postages disbursed by him since the last meeting.

SECTION 8. That the said several grants of money in the first, second, fifth and sixth sections of this By-Law, shall be paid in debentures to be issued under the provisions of By-Law No. 5, upon the requisition of the Councils of the Townships respectively, for which such grants have been made. *Certain grants to be paid in Debentures.*

SECTION 9. That the County Treasurer be authorized to pay the Township Treasurer of Escott the sum of two pounds, the same being a balance due that Township, granted by virtue of By-Law No. 13. *Balance to Escott.*

SECTION 10. That the Warden in his discretion may direct the Treasurer to pay all or any of the above sums that amount to twenty-five pounds or upwards, instead of issuing a Debenture or Debentures therefor, if it appear to him that there is money in the Treasurer's hands that may be properly applied to that purpose. *Warden may direct money to be paid instead of Debentures.*

SECTION 11. That the sum of one hundred pounds currency be granted to aid in the survey and exploration of the route of Railway from the Georgian Bay to the St. Lawrence at Brockville and Prescott, pursuant to the petition of George Crawford, Esq., and that the same be paid to the Receiver of the St. Lawrence and Lake Huron Railway Committee. *Surveying Georgian Bay & St. Lawrence Railway.*

SECTION 12. That the sum of one pound five shillings be paid to James Kincaid for attending the Council this Session. *James Kincaid.*

GEORGE SHERWOOD, WARDEN,
United Counties of Leeds and Grenville.

[L. S.]

JAMES JESSUP, COUNTY CLERK.

No. XXXIII.—BY-LAW

See By-Law No. 31. *To Appoint a Superintendent of Common Schools for the Township of Elmsley.*

Be it enacted by the Municipal Council of the United Counties of Leeds and Grenville, duly assembled at the Town of Brockville, on the twenty-eighth day of January, in the year of our Lord one thousand eight hundred and fifty-two, and it is hereby enacted, That Elisha Landon, Esquire, be, and he is hereby appointed Superintendent of Common Schools for the Township of Elmsley, for the residue of the present year, in the place and stead of the Rev. William Aitkin, who has resigned.

Elisha Landon, Esq., appointed in place of Rev. Wm. Atkins, resigned.

ROBERT. PEDEN, Warden.

[L. S.]

JAMES JESSUP, County Clerk.

No. XXXIV.—BY-LAW

To Divide the United Counties of Leeds and Grenville into School-Circuits.—Passed 30th January, 1852.

(Repealed: see By-law No. 192.)

No. XXXV.—BY-LAW

To Repeal By-Law Number twenty-nine.—Passed 31st January, 1852.

(Repealed; see By-Law No. 231.)

No. XXXVI.—BY-LAW

See By-Law No. 27, sec. 1. *To Cover certain Grants of Money.*

Be it enacted by the Municipal Council of the United Counties of Leeds and Grenville, duly assembled at the Town of Brockville, on the thirty-first day of January, in the year of our Lord one thousand eight hundred and

fifty-two, and it is hereby enacted, That the sum of one
hundred pounds granted by By-Law number twenty-seven,
passed on the twenty-first day of June last, to aid in the
construction of a new Bridge across Irish Creek in the
Township of Wolford, be paid out of the County funds by
the Treasurer, instead of debentures, as provided in the
said By-Law, and that the same be paid to the Municipality
of Wolford aforesaid : Provided a like sum shall be appropriated and expended by the said Municipality, or the
inhabitants thereof, in the construction and completion of
the said Bridge.

Irish Creek Bridge.
How paid.
Proviso.

2. That the sum of fifty pounds be granted to the
Municipal Council of the Township of Leeds and Lansdowne (front), to be laid out on such Roads in the Municipality as the Council thereof may think fit.

Leeds and Lans-downe (front).

3. That the sum of one hundred pounds currency be
granted to aid in the survey and exploration of the route
of Railway from Georgian Bay to the St. Lawrence at
Brockville and Prescott, pursuant to the petition of the
Executive Committee of the said Railroad, and that the
same be paid to the Receiver of the said Committee.

Survey Georgian Bay & St. Law-rence Railway.

4. That the following sums shall be granted and paid
to the parties, respectively, viz :—

Sums to certain parties.

To James Jessup, the sum of five shillings and nine pence,
for charges on maps and postages disbursed.

To the Board of Public Instruction, the sum of eleven
shillings and nine pence, for stationery, lights, &c.

To the Commissioners of the Bridge at Burritt's Rapids,
the sum of twenty-seven pounds ten shillings, to make
up deficiency by discount on Debentures.

To William Buell, the sum of three pounds seven shillings
and six pence, for stationery furnished.

To the Queen's Printer, the sum of seven pounds and six
pence, for Books furnished the Registry office of the
County of Leeds.

To James Kincaid, the sum of one pound ten shillings and
ten pence, for attending at the present Session as
messenger.

To Christopher Leggo, the sum of two pounds eight shillings, for fuel and keeping Council chamber in order.

To David Wylie, the sum of two pounds nineteen shillings for printing By-Laws and advertising.

ROBERT PEDEN, Warden.

[L.S.]

JAMES JESSUP, County Clerk.

No. XXXVII.—BY-LAW

To Close certain Old Roads on the Line of the Victoria Macadamized Road.

Preamble.

Whereas, a thoroughfare has been established, and in greater part completed, between the Town of Brockville in the County of Leeds, and the Village of Smith's Falls, in the County of Lanark, and which thoroughfare is known and called by the name of the Victoria Macadamized Road; And whereas in consequence of the opening and making of the said Victoria Macadamized Road, certain other Roads, or part of Roads, formerly opened and travelled, have been rendered unnecessary for public travel and convenience, and it is desirable and necessary that such old Roads, or parts of old Roads, should be closed, and whereas due public notice has been given, pursuant to Law, of the intention of this Council, to close certain parts or portions of the said old or formerly travelled Road, hereinafter described. Be it therefore enacted and ordained by the Municipal Council of the United Counties of Leeds and Grenville, in Council assembled, that all that part of the said old or formerly travelled Road leading from Brockville to Smith's Falls, passing through or over Lot No. 34, in the eighth Concession of Elizabethtown, at present occupied by Peter Davis, Esq., and Mr. Jacob Gallinger, is unnecessary for public use, travel, or convenience, and the same should be, and hereby is, declared closed as a public Road and Highway.

Road on Lot 34, 8th Con. Elizabethtown closed.

2. That all that part of the said old or formerly travelled Road leading from Brockville to Smith's Falls, passing through or over Lot No. 21, in the tenth Concession of Kitley at present occupied by Nelson Leahy; and also all

that part of the said old or formerly travelled Road leading from Brockville to Smith's Falls, passing through or over Lot No. 21, in the ninth Concession of Kitley, at present occupied by Thomas Newson and William Smith, Esquires, and also Lot No. 20 in the 9th concession of Kitley, occupied by Mr. Ruben L. Hamblin, and also Lot No. 21, in the ninth concession of Kitley, occupied by Mr. James Kilborn, are unnecessary for public use, travel or convenience, and the same should be, and hereby is, declared closed as a public Road and Highway. *Road in Kitley closed.*

3. That the Commissioners of the said Victoria Macadamized Road be authorized to treat with the parties interested in the said old or formerly travelled Road, for the sale or transfer thereof, according to the Statute, and report the result of their negotiations at the next meeting of this Council. *Commissioners to treat for sale of old roads.*

4. That the said Commissioners be empowered, and they are hereby authorized and empowered, to negotiate for the purchase of a side road leading from the residence of Reuben L. Hamblin, hereinbefore named, to the public Highway or Victoria Road in the Township of Kitley aforesaid. *To negotiate a purchase for side road.*

ROBERT PEDEN, Warden.

[L. S.]

JAMES JESSUP, County Clerk.

No. XXXVIII.—BY-LAW

To authorize the Payment of the sum therein mentioned for Repairs to the Macadamized Road.

Whereas, at a final settlement, made between the Commissioners of the Victoria Macadamized Road and Richard Osborne and Pierce Acheson, contractors thereon, it was agreed that the sum of one hundred and fifty-three pounds, eighteen shillings and two pence should be paid to the said Richard Osborne and Pierce Acheson, in full compensation for keeping the said Road in repair up to the first day of January, 1852, under the terms of their contract upon condition only of their surrendering their contract and releasing all further claims thereunder, and of de- *Preamble.* *Claim of Acheson & Osborne, of £153 18s. 2d.*

P

livering over to the said Commissioners all stone, broken and unbroken, now on the line of the said Road, and placed there by the said Richard Osborne and Pierce Acheson; and whereas it is expedient to carry into effect the said settlement, and to provide for the payment of the said sum of one hundred and fifty-three pounds, eighteen shillings and two pence. Be it therefore enacted by the Municipal Council of the United Counties of Leeds and Grenville, and it is hereby enacted that the County Treasurer be authorized and directed to pay the said sum of one hundred and fifty-three pounds, eighteen shillings and two pence, to the said Richard Osborne and Pierce Acheson, out of the County Toll Roads Fund, and that this By-law and the receipt of the said Richard Osborne and Pierce Acheson, shall be, to the said County Treasurer, sufficient authority for such payment.

ROBERT PEDEN, Warden.

[L. S.]

JAMES JESSUP, County Clerk.

No. XXXIX.—BY-LAW

To authorize the Contraction of a Loan for certain Public Works.—Passed 7th May, 1852.

(Expired and Debentures paid.)

No. XL.—BY-LAW

To regulate the Printing of the Council.—Passed May 7, 1852.

(Repealed; see By-Law No. 119.)

No. XLI.—BY-LAW

To Regulate the Performance of Statute Labor on the See By-Law No
County Toll Road in Bastard and North and South 281.
Crosby.—Passed May 8, 1852.

Whereas it is expedient and desirable to place the Preamble.
Statute Labor, within the limit hereinafter mentioned, on
that part of the County Toll Road from West Port to
Farmersville, which is within the Townships of Bastard
and North Crosby and South Crosby; under the control of
the Municipal Councils thereof. Be it therefore enacted
by the Municipal Council of the United Counties of Leeds
and Grenville, and it is hereby enacted, That the Statute
Labor within a half mile on either side of the said County
Toll Road, in the Townships of Bastard and North Crosby
and South Crosby, aforesaid, and all commutation money
accruing from the same or any part thereof shall be and is
hereby placed, so far as this Council can legally do so,
under the control and direction of the Municipal Councils To be under con-
of the said Townships respectively, to be expended by trol of Township
them in the immediate vicinity of the said Toll Road, on Councils.
the lateral Roads leading into or intersecting the same, and
that the said Municipal Councils shall have all the powers
and authority to make such orders, rules and regulations
for the performance of such Statute Labor, and for the
collecting and enforcing payment of such commutation
money as this Council could legally exercise for that
purpose.

      ROBERT PEDEN, Warden.

[L. S.]

JAMES JESSUP, County Clerk.

No. XLII.—BY-LAW.

To Assess the United Counties of Leeds and Grenville, for
the year 1852.—Passed May 8, 1852.

1. Be it enacted by the Municipal Council of the United
Counties of Leeds and Grenville, and it is hereby enacted,
That there be raised and levied upon the whole rateable Sum for County
property in the said United Counties, for the present year, purposes, £1799
the sum of £1799 18s. 6d. to defray the current and or- 18s. 6d.
dinary expenses thereof, and the further sum of £1049 Common Schools
£1049 18s 6d.

18s. 6d. for the payment of the salaries of legally qualified Common School Teachers, and the support of
Common Schools therein, and that the said sums shall be
so raised and levied in addition to all other rates and
assessments, and be apportioned to the several Township
Municipalities in the said Counties in the following
manner, viz :

Municipalities.	County Rate.			Common Schools.		
Elizabethtown	£333	9	0	£117	18	0
Augusta	212	5	8	124	4	0
Yonge	194	2	3	84	16	6
Oxford	148	5	7	104	17	0
Kitley	121	19	11	97	10	0
Edwardsburgh	130	16	3	98	6	6
Bastard & Burgess	138	1	3	80	17	0
Wolford	105	10	2	83	15	6
Front of Leeds & Lansdowne	85	8	10	71	2	0
Escott	48	2	10	29	12	6
South Gower	52	2	5	17	5	0
Rear of Leeds & Lansdowne	65	14	8	36	9	0
South Crosby	61	11	11	35	12	6
Elmsley	48	18	2	35	9	6
North Crosby	53	9	7	32	3	6
	£1799	18	6	£1049	18	6

2. And be it further enacted, That there be raised and
levied upon the said property in the said Township Municipalities respectively, the sum of six pence in the hundred
pounds, and so in proportion on any less sum, in addition
Lunatic Asylum. to all other rates and Assessments, for the Lunatic Asylum
as required by the second Section of the Act 13 and 14
Victoria, Chapter 68.

3. And be it further enacted, That there be raised and
levied upon the said property in the said Township Municipalities respectively, the sum of one half-penny in the
pound, in addition to all other rates and assessments,
County Toll pursuant to the provisions of By-Law number eight, passed
Roads. on the tenth day of October, 1850, entitled, "By-Law to
amend By-Laws Nos. 4 and 5, passed on the fourteenth
day of March, 1850, and By-Law No. 39, passed on the
seventh day of May, 1852, entitled "By-Law to authorize
the construction of a Loan for certain Public Works.

4. And be it further enacted that the said several sums
hereinbefore directed to be raised and levied in the Muni-

cipalities respectively, shall be placed on the Collector's Rolls by the Clerks thereof, in separate columns, and collected in like manner as all other rates and assessments are by Law directed to be collected, and shall be paid over to the County Treasurer on or before the fourteenth day of December next, by the said Township Municipalities respectively. *How collected and paid.*

5. And be it further enacted, that the said Township Municipalities respectively, shall, immediately after the completion of the Collector's Rolls, cause a statement of the total of each of the said rates hereby directed to be raised, levied, and collected, to be furnished to the County Treasurer as the same shall appear upon such Collector's Rolls respectively. *Statement to be furnish'd County Treasurer.*

6. And be it further enacted, that each and every Collector shall, on or before the fourteenth day of December next, return his Collector's Roll to the Treasurer of his Municipality and pay over to such Treasurer the sums directed by this By-Law to be raised, levied and collected thereon, and shall also, on or before the day last mentioned, deliver to the County Treasurer an account of the Taxes remaining due on his Roll, as required by the 42nd Section of the Act 13th and 14th Victoria, Chapter 67. *When Collector to make return.*

7. That this By-law shall come into force and take effect upon, from and after the day of the passing hereof. *When to take effect.*

ROBERT PEDEN, Warden.

[L. S.]

JAMES JESSUP, County Clerk.

No. XLIII—BY-LAW

To Cover certain Grants of Money.—Passed May 8, 1852.

Be it enacted by the Municipal Council of the United Counties of Leeds and Grenville, and it is hereby enacted that the sums following shall be paid to the parties respectively, viz:— *Sums to certain persons.*

To Alpine Grant, for an over assessment, the sum of two pounds one shilling and eight pence. *Alpine Grant.*

S. B. Merrill.	To S. B. Merrill, for Printing and Advertising, the sum of eleven pounds, fourteen shillings and eleven pence.
County Clerk.	To the County Clerk, for Postages, disbursed the sum of eight shillings and eight pence.
Thomas Hume.	To Thomas Hume, County Surveyor, for services as such Surveyor, the sum of one pound.
Hugh Scoble.	To Hugh Scobie, Esquire, for blank Assessment Forms, the sum of twenty-eight pounds, fifteen shillings and seven pence half-penny.
Board of Public Instruction.	To the Chairman of the Board of Public Instruction, for expenses incurred by the Board, the sum of eight shillings and nine pence.
Statesman printing office.	To the Statesman Printing Office, for Advertising and Printing, the sum of twenty-six pounds, ten shillings and three pence.
William Fitzsimmons.	To William Fitzsimmons, for work to the Court House, the sum of one pound eight shillings and nine pence.
D. Wylie.	To David Wylie, for Printing and Advertising, the sum of thirteen pounds, three shillings and ten pence.
Thomas Hume.	To Thomas Hume, the sum of four pounds, for services as County Surveyor, to be equally paid by the Commissioners of the Merrickville and Maitland, and Kemptville and Prescott Toll Roads.
Christopher Leggo.	To Christopher Leggo, the sum of one pound two shillings and four pence, for articles furnished the Council.
James Kincaid.	To James Kincaid, the sum of one pound ten shillings for attendance at this Session as Messenger.
	2. That the sums granted in this Section be paid out of the County Toll Roads' Funds, viz,—
James Finlay.	To James Finlay, for work on the Victoria Macadamized Road, discount on Debentures and loss on Tolls, the sum of forty-six pounds six shillings and ten pence half-penny.
J. Dennison.	To J. Denison, for services in surveying the Victoria Macadamized Road, and the West Port and Farmersville Toll Road, the sum of thirty pounds.

3. That the sum of ten pounds be granted to be expended on the Road in the Town Line between Kitley and Elizabethtown, provided the Councils of Kitley and Elizabethtown shall each appropriate and expend the sum of five pounds on the said Road. — *Road in Kitley and Elizabethtown.*

4. That the sum of seven pounds ten shillings be granted to be expended on the Road between Lots Nos. 6 and 7 from the front of the third concession to the rear of the fourth concession, in the Township of Edwardsburgh; Provided the Council of Edwardsburgh shall appropriate and expend a like sum on the said Road. — *Road in Edwardsburgh.*

5. That the sum of fifteen pounds be granted to aid in erecting a Bridge over the Middle Branch, and also another Bridge over the Beaver Meadow, both on the Road leading from the Merrickville Macadamized Road to Prescott, provided the Council of Wolford shall appropriate and expend a like sum on the said Bridges. — *Bridge over Middle Branch, &c.*

6. That the sum of ten pounds twelve shillings be granted to aid in the erection of a Bridge over the Creek at Charleston Mills in the Township of Yonge, provided the Council of Yonge shall appropriate and expend a like sum on the said Bridge. — *Bri'ge at Charleston Mills. See By-law No. 48, sec. 6.*

7. (Repealed: see By-law No. 122.) — *Smith's Falls Bridge.*

8. That the sum of twenty-five pounds be granted as the portion of these Counties for erecting the Kilmarnock Bridge in the Township of Wolford. — *Kilmarnock Bridge.*

9. That the said several grants of money in the third, fourth, fifth, sixth, seventh and eighth sections of this By-Law shall be paid by the County Treasurer upon the requisition of the Councils of the Townships respectively, for which such grants have been made. — *How certain grants to be paid.*

10. That the sum of twenty pounds granted by the resolution of this Council on the 14th of October, 1851, being the balance due the Township of Front of Leeds and Lansdowne of the ninety-five pounds granted by By-L 7 No. 13, as an equivalent for the construction of the Four County Toll Roads, and that the said sum of tw...y pounds be paid by the County Treasurer to the Co ...il of the Front of Leeds and Lansdowne. — *Balance due Front Leeds and Lansdowne. See By-Law No. 13, sec. 4.*

ROBERT PEDEN, Warden.

[L. S.]

JAMES JESSUP, County Clerk.

No. XLIV.—BY-LAW

To Cover certain Grants of Money.—Passed June 17, 1852.

1. Be it enacted by the Municipal Council of the United Counties of Leeds and Grenville, and it is hereby enacted,

Sums to certain persons. That the sums in this section mentioned shall be paid to the parties respectively, viz:—

Adam Anderson. To Adam Anderson, the sum of £1 11s. 10½d., for covers for the Collectors' Rolls.

Messrs. Derbyshire and Desbarats. To Messrs. Derbyshire & Desbarats, the sum of fourteen shillings, for advertising.

D. Wylie. To D. Wylie, the sum of four pounds, for Collectors' rolls.

James Kincaid. To James Kincaid, the sum of £1 10s., being the amount of his account for attendance as Messenger and for Stationery furnished.

Bridge over Big Creek, South Gower. 2. That the sum of twelve pounds ten shillings be granted to aid in the erection of a Bridge across the big Creek in the Township of South Gower; Provided a like sum be

Proviso. appropriated and expended by the Council or the inhabitants of the said Township.

Johnstown Bridge. 3. That the sum of twelve pounds ten shillings, be granted to aid in the repair of the Bridge in Johnstown on the Main Road; Provided a like sum be appropriated and

Proviso. expended by the Council or the inhabitants of the Township of Edwardsburgh.

How certain grants to be paid. 4. That the said grants of money in the second and third sections of this By-law shall be paid by the County Treasurer on the requisition of the Councils of the Townships respectively, for which such grants have been made.

John Burchill. 5. That the sum of twenty-four pounds sixteen shillings and sixpence be paid to John Burchill out of the County Toll Funds by the County Treasurer, being the amount of his account for the Survey and Plans of the Kemptville and Prescott County Toll Road.

ROBERT PEDAN, Warden.

[L. S.]

JAMES JESSUP, County Clerk.

No. XLV.—BY-LAW

To appoint Superintendents of Common Schools for the See By-Law No. 49.
year 1853.—Passed October 15, 1852.

1. Be it enacted by the Municipal Council of the United Counties of Leeds and Grenville, and it is hereby enacted, That the following persons be and they are hereby appointed Superintendents of Schools for the respective Townships hereinafer mentioned, such appointment to commence on the first day of January, one thousand eight hundred and fifty-three:

Augusta .... James Clapperton.   Appointments.
Oxford................. Andrew Holmes.
Escott .... Thomas Vanston.
Front of Leeds & Lansdowne Thomas Vanston.
Yonge........ ..... Rev. James Cooper.
Elizabethtown.......... Jacob A. Brown.
Edwardsburgh........... Rev. James Geggie.
South Gower.. .... Rev. Joseph Anderson.
Wolford............... Thomas Graffe.
Kitley.... .... Samuel Graham.
Elmsley.... .... Elisha Landon, (Repealed: see By-Law No. 49.)
Bastard and Burgess. . .. Lewis Chipman.
South Crosby........... Rev. Matthew Connor.
North Crosby .... Rev. Matthew Connor.
Rear Leeds & Lansdowne... Henry P. Washburn.

2. Whereas the Rev, Joshua Johnson has tendered his resignation of the office of Superintendent of Schools for the Township of Yonge, such resignation to take effect on the first day of November next; Be it therefore further enacted, That the Reverend James Cooper be and is hereby appointed Superintendent of Schools for the said Township of Yonge, for residue of the present year, in the place of the Reverend Joshua Johnston aforesaid,— such appointment to take effect on the said first day of November next, and not before.

Rev. Jas. Cooper for residue of 1852, in place of Rev. Joshua Johnson, resigned.

ROBERT PEDEN, Warden.

[L. S.]

JAMES JESSUP, County Clerk.

No. XLVI.—BY-LAW

See Com. School Act, U. C.

To provide for Auditing the Accounts of Officers entrusted with School Monies.—Passed October 16, 1852.

When to be audited.

1. Be it enacted by the Municipal Council of the United Counties of Leeds and Grenville, and it is hereby enacted, That from and after the passing of this By-Law, it shall be the duty of the Auditors appointed, or that may be hereafter appointed, in pursuance of the fifth sub-section of the twenty-seventh section of the Act passed in the thirteenth and fourteenth years of Her Majesty's reign, chapter forty-eight, to audit the accounts of all officers to whom School monies shall be entrusted, on or before the fourth Monday of the month of January, in each and every year, and to report such audit to the said Council during the first meeting thereafter, in such form as the Chief Superintendent of Education for Upper Canada shall from time to time direct and appoint.

Accounts to be furnished by Sub-Treasurers.

2. And be it further enacted, That for the purpose of enabling the said Auditors to audit the said Accounts as hereinbefore required, it shall be the duty of the sub-Treasurers of School-monies now appointed, or that may be hereafter appointed, for the several Municipalities in the said United Counties, and of all other officers entrusted with such monies, to lay before such Auditors annually, at the County Treasurer's Office, at any time before the third Monday in January, in each year, a true and correct account in detail of the receipts and expenditure of all School monies entrusted to them respectively during the year immediately preceding the second Monday in January, together with all receipts and other vouchers appertaining to the expenditure of such monies.

Penalty for neglect.

3. And be it further enacted, That if any such Sub-Treasurer, or other officer, shall neglect or refuse to comply with any or all the requirements contained in the second section of this By-law, he shall forfeit and pay a fine of not less than five shillings, nor more than twenty shillings, with costs, to be recovered before any Justice of the Peace for the said United Counties, and in default of payment at such time as the said Justice shall limit and appoint to be levied by distress and sale of the offenders' goods and chattels under the warrant of the said Justice.

4. And be it further enacted, That all fines collected

under this By-law, shall be paid by such Justice of the Application of Peace to the Treasurer of the Township for the public uses Fines. thereof.

ROBERT PEDEN, Warden.

[L. S.]

JAMES JESSUP, County Clerk.

No. XLVII.—BY-LAW

To Establish, Assume, and open the County Toll Roads therein mentioned.—Passed October 16, 1852.

(Repealed: see By-law No. 231.)

No. XLVIII.—BY-LAW

To cover certain Grants of Money.—Passed October 16, 1852.

1. Be it enacted by the Municipal Council of the United Counties of Leeds and Grenville, and it is hereby enacted, That the County Treasurer be authorized to pay to the Commissioners of the County Toll Road from Kemptville to Prescott, the sum of one hundred and fifty-seven pounds ten shillings, being the balance due Ambrose Clothier on his contract on that part of the said Road between Christie's Corners and Kemptville, and that said sum be paid out of the County Tolls fund, pursuant to a Resolution passed by this Council at its last meeting, any other By-Law to the contrary notwithstanding. *[marginal note: Commissioners of Kemptville & Road.]*

2. And be it further enacted, That the County Treasurer be authorized and directed to pay to the Commissioners of the Victoria Macadamized Road, any balance which they may find to be due to Thomas Newsom, John Wood or Holmes P. Clow, so soon as their respective contracts shall have been completed to the satisfaction of the said Commissioners, and the works respectively approved of and accepted by them, to be paid out of the County Tolls Fund, any other By-Law to the contrary notwithstanding. *[marginal note: Balance to Thos. Newsom and others.]*

Section 3. (Repealed: see By-Law No. 64.)

4. And be it further enacted, That the County Treasurer be authorized to pay the Commissioners of the Kemptville and Prescott Toll Road, the sum of seventy-five pounds to pay for the Toll House erected on the said Road near Kemptville, the said sum to be paid out of the County Tolls Fund, any other By-Law to the contrary notwithstanding.

Commissioners of Kemptville & Prescott Road.

5. And be it further enacted, That the sum of twelve pounds ten shillings be paid to John Burchill out of the County Tolls Fund by the County Treasurer, being the amount of his account for the survey and plans of the Merrickville and North Augusta County Toll Road.

John Burchill.

6. That the sum of ten pounds ten shillings be paid to the Municipal Council of Yonge to assist to pay for building a Bridge at Charleston Mills, in Yonge, as provided by the sixth Section of By-Law No. 43.

Bri'geat Charleston Mills, grant £12 10s. See By-Law No. 43.

7. That the sum of fifty pounds be granted to the Council of Escott, to be applied in constructing a Road from the main Road leading from Brockville to Kingston to the St. Lawrence River, on Lot No. 7, on the broken front; Provided the said Council of Escott shall appropriate a like sum, and expend the same, together with the amount hereby granted on the said Road.

Council of Escott to make a road.

8. That the sum of twelve pounds ten shillings be granted to the Council of Yonge, to be applied on the repair of the Bridge at Yonge Mills; Provided the said Council of Yonge, or the inhabitants thereof, shall appropriate a like sum, and expend the same, together with the amount hereby granted for the said Road.

Bridge at Yonge Mills.

9. That the sum of seventeen pounds ten shillings be granted to the Council of Augusta, to be applied to complete a Bridge near Heck's Mills; Provided the said Council of Augusta shall appropriate a like sum, and expend the same, together with the amount hereby granted for the said Bridge.

Bridge near Heck's Mills, Augusta.

10. That the sum of thirty-five pounds be granted to the Council of Kitley, to be applied to erect a Bridge across Irish Creek in Kitley; Provided the said Council of Kitley, or the inhabitants of that Township, shall appropriate a like sum, and expend the same, together with the amount hereby granted for the said Bridge.

Bridge over Irish Creek.

11. That the County Treasurer be authorized to pay to the Commissioners of the Victoria Macadamized Road, such sum of money which they may agree to be paid to William Smith, for damages by the construction of the said Road over his land in Kitley, (not exceeding the sum of thirty-seven pounds ten shillings), such sum of money to be paid out of the County Tolls fund, any other By-Law to the contrary notwithstanding. *Commissioners of Victoria Road to pay W. Smith.*

12. And be it further enacted, That the sums in this Section mentioned shall be paid to the parties, respectively, viz:— *Sums to certain parties.*

To Thomas Hume, the sum of two pounds five shillings, for services as County Surveyor. *Thomas Hume.*

To Alfred Poulton, the sum of five pounds, for repairs to the Court House. *Alfred Poulton.*

To David Wylie, the sum of one pound four shillings and eight pence, for printing. *D. Wylie.*

To County Clerk, the sum of one pound five shillings and eight pence half-penny, for postages and other disbursements. *County Clerk.*

To S. B. Merrill, the sum of fifteen shillings and four pence, for printing. *S. B. Merrill.*

To J. W. Huddleston, the sum of five pounds six shillings and six pence, for Pipes and work to Court House and Gaol. *J. W. Huddleston.*

To John Shepherd, the sum of twenty-four pounds eighteen shillings and seven pence half-penny, for repairs to the Gaol. *John Shepherd.*

To Harvey Miller, the sum of four pounds eight shillings and nine pence, for repairs to the Gaol. *Harvey Miller.*

To Christopher Leggo, the sum of two pounds fifteen shillings and ten pence, for articles furnished for Court House. *Chris. Leggo*

To Edward Robertson, the sum of three pounds, for putting notices on Toll Roads. *Edward Robertson.*

To Jacob A. Brown, the sum of two pounds five shillings, for putting up notices on Toll Roads. *Jacob A. Brown.*

Statesman printing office.

To the Statesman Printing Office, the sum of four pounds seventeen shillings and seven pence, for Printing and Advertising.

Richard F. Steele, Esq.

To Richard F. Steele, Esquire, the sum of two pounds ten shillings, for legal advice.

James Kincaid.

To James Kincaid, the sum of one pound eight shillings and eleven pence half-penny, for services as Messenger, and articles furnished the Council.

How certain grants to be paid.

13. And be it further enacted, That the said Grants of Money in the third, sixth, seventh, eighth, ninth, and tenth Sections of this By-Law, shall be paid by the County Treasurer, on the requisition of the Councils of the Townships respectively, for which such grants have been made.

ROBERT PEDEN, Warden.

[L. S.]

JAMES JESSUP, County Clerk.

No. XLIX.—BY-LAW

To repeal part of By-Law Number Forty-five. — Passed January 28, 1853.

Be it enacted by the Municipal Council of the United Counties of Leeds and Grenville, and it is hereby enacted, that so much of By-Law No. 45, passed on the fifteenth day of October, in the year of our Lord one thousand eight hundred and fifty-two, and entituled "By-Law to appoint Superintendents of Common Schools for the year 1853," as provides or relates to the appointment of Elisha Landon,

Appointment of Elisha Landon repealed.

as Superintendent of Schools for the Township of Elmsley, be repealed, and the same is hereby repealed.

Edward F. Weeks appointed instead.

2. And be it further enacted, that Edward F. Weeks be appointed Superintendent of Schools for the said Township of Elmsley for the residue of the present year, and the said Edward F. Weeks is hereby appointed such Superintendent for the said Township.

ROBERT PEDEN, Warden.

[L. S.]

JAMES JESSUP, County Clerk.

No. L.—BY-LAW

*To authorize the removal of Toll House and Gate, and for
other purposes therein mentioned.—Passed January
28, 1853.*

(Repealed : see By-Law No. 231.)

No. LI.—BY-LAW

*To Repeal part of the fifth section of By-Law number
Four, and for other purposes therein mentioned.—
Passed January 29, 1853.*

(Repealed : see By-Law No. 231.)

No. LII.—BY-LAW

*To apply the Tolls collected on each of the Four County Toll
Roads to its completion.—Passed January 29, 1853.*

(Repealed : see By-Law No. 231.)

No. LIII.—BY-LAW.

*To prevent certain Nuisances in the Public Highways of
the United Counties of Leeds and Grenville.— Passed
January 29, 1853.*

Be it enacted by the Municipal Council of the United
Counties of Leeds and Grenville, and it is hereby enacted,
That from and after the passing hereof, if any person or
persons shall race or otherwise immoderately ride or drive
any horse or horses, in any of the public highways in the
said United Counties, whether the same be Township or
County Roads, such person or persons so offending, and
being thereof convicted before any one or more Justices of
the Peace, having jurisdiction within the locality in which
the offence shall be resident, or within that in which the
offender was committed, shall forfeit and pay a fine not
exceeding fifty shillings, or less than ten shillings.

Fine for racing,
&c., on.

2. And be it further enacted, That if any person or persons shall ride or drive any horse or horses, or other cattle, carriage, sleigh or other vehicle, on or over any County Bridge erected or to be erected, under the authority of the Municipal Council of the said United Counties, faster than a walk, such person or persons so offending, and being thereof convicted before any such Justice or Justices, shall forfeit and pay a fine not exceeding ten shillings, or less than five shillings.

Fine for driving, &c., over Bridge faster than a walk.

3. And be it further enacted, That if any person or persons shall put, place or deposit any wood, timber, stone or other material in and upon any of the said County Highways or Bridges, or shall in any way wilfully injure or damage the same, or any part thereof, or shall obstruct, hinder or molest any person or persons riding or driving thereon, so as to prevent the free and uninterrupted use of the said Highways or Bridges, such person or persons so offending, in any or either of the said cases, and being thereof convicted before any such Justice or Justices, shall forfeit and pay a fine not exceeding twenty shillings, or less than five shillings.

Fine for depositing wood, &c. on.

4. And be it further enacted, That all such fines shall be paid with costs forthwith, or at the time limited by such Justice or Justices, and in default thereof to be levied by distress and sale of the offender's goods and chattels, under the warrant of such Justice or Justices, according to the provisions of the Statute in that behalf.

To be paid with costs.

5. And be it further enacted, That all fines collected under this By-Law shall be paid over by such Justice or Justices to the County Treasurer, to be applied by him to the common uses of the said United Counties.

Application of fines.

ROBERT PEDEN, WARDEN.

[L. S.]

JAMES JESSUP, COUNTY CLERK.

No. LIV.—BY-LAW

To cover certain Grants of Money.—Passed 29th January, 1853.

Be it enacted by the Municipal Council of the United Counties of Leeds and Grenville, and it is hereby enacted, that the several sums hereinafter mentioned shall be paid by the County Treasurer to the parties respectively, viz :— *Sums to certain parties.*

1. To Richard F. Steele the sum of two pounds and ten shillings, being the amount of his account rendered. *Richard F. Steele.*

2. To William Buell the sum of three pounds sixteen shillings and eleven pence half-penny, being the amount of his account rendered against the Council. *William Buell.*

3. To Arthur Tilly the sum of one pound six shillings and three pence, being the amount of his account against the Council. *Arthur Tilly.*

4. To Billings Kilborn the sum of four pounds four shillings and six pence, being the amount of his account against the Council. *Billings Kilborn.*

5. To Thomas Newsom, the sum of sixty-eight pounds, awarded to him for damages done to Lot No. 21, in the ninth concession of Kitley. *Thomas Newsom.*

6. To Justus Lockwood, the sum of twelve pounds ten shillings, awarded to him for damages done to Lot No. 21, in the tenth concession of Kitley. *Justus Lockwood.*

7. To Gideon Leahey, the sum of forty-two pounds, awarded to him for damages done to Lot No. 21, in the tenth concession of Kitley. *Gideon Lehey.*

8. To James Connors, the sum of ten pounds twelve shillings and six pence, being the amount awarded him for damages to Lot No. 2, in the fifth concession of Augusta. *James Connors.*

9. To Charles Spencer, the sum of twenty-one pounds five shillings, awarded him for damages done to Lot No. 29, in the sixth concession of Edwardsburgh. *Charles Spencer.*

10. To the County Clerk, the sum of sixteen shillings and six-pence, for disbursements made by him on account of the County. *County Clerk.*

Q

11. **John Young, Thomas Boyd & John Holmes.** To John Young, the sum of one pound ten shillings. To Thomas Boyd, the sum of one pound, and to John Holmes the sum of ten shillings, to indemnify them for acting as arbitrators on the claim of Thomas Newsom, for damages by construction of the Victoria Macadamized Road.

12. **Joseph Goff, Jno. Young and William Goff.** To Joseph Goff and John Young, the sum of one pound each, and to William Goff the sum of ten shillings, to indemnify them for acting as arbitrators on the claim of Justus Lockwood, for damages by the construction of the Victoria Macadamized Road.

13. **John Young and John Keeler.** To John Young and John Keeler, the sum of two pounds ten shillings, to indemnify them for acting as arbitrators on the claim of Gideon Leahey, for damages by the construction of the said Road.

14. **Alex. McMillan, Joseph Cook and Daniel Laferty.** To Alexander M'Millan, Joseph Cook, and Daniel Laferty, the sum of three pounds and five shillings, being the expense of the arbitration on the claim of James Connors, for damages by the construction of the County Toll Road from Kemptville to Prescott.

15. **Chris. Leggo.** To Christopher Leggo, the sum of one pound twelve shillings and six-pence, being the amount of his account against the Council.

16. **James Kincaid.** To James Kincaid, the sum of one pound ten shillings and six-pence, being the amount of his account against the Council.

17. **Thomas Robertson and W. B. Butland.** To Thomas Robertson and W. B. Bullard, the sum of one pound to indemnify them as arbitrators on the claim of Charles Spencer, for damages by the construction of the Kemptville and Prescott County Toll Road.

18. **Francis Wright.** To Frances Wright, the sum of twelve pounds and ten shillings, being the amount due him for advances for the erection of a School House in Section No. 3 in the Township of Kitley.

ROBERT PEDEN, Warden.

[L. S.]

JAMES JESSUP, County Clerk.

No. LV.—BY-LAW

To provide for regular Meetings of the Municipal Council Amended: (See
of the United Counties of Leeds and Grenville.— By-Law Nos. 160
Passed 21st June, 1853. and 199.

Whereas it is expedient that the times for the regular Preamble.
meetings of this Council should be fixed at stated periods in order that the public may be duly advised
thereof; be it therefore enacted by the Municipal Council of the United Counties of Leeds and Grenville, and
it is hereby enacted, that the regular Sessions of this
Council shall be held in the Court House in the Town of Times and places
Brockville, on the fourth Monday in January, the third of holding Meet-
Monday in June, and the second Monday in October in ings.
each and every year; provided always that nothing herein Proviso for call-
contained shall prevent the Warden from calling special ing special meet-
meetings of this Council at such other times as he may ings.
deem expedient.

2. And be it further enacted, that in calling such special
meeting the Warden shall give six days public notice Notice to be
thereof, and state the purpose for which the same are so given.
called, and no other business shall be transacted at any
such special meetings except that mentioned in such
notice, unless it be respecting matters connected with the
internal management of this Council or its officers.

3. And be it further enacted, that this By-law shall When to take
come into force and take effect upon, from, and after the effect.
thirtieth day of June, 1853.

ROBERT PEDEN, Warden.
[L. S.]
JAMES JESSUP, County Clerk.

No. LVI.—BY-LAW

To extend the time for receiving Tenders for Printing for the present year.—Passed 24th June, 1853.

(Expired by Limitation.)

No. LVII.—BY-LAW

To Repeal part of the First Section of By-Law No. 51, and for other purposes therein mentioned.—Passed 24th June, 1853.

(Repealed : See By-law No. 231.)

No. LVIII.—BY-LAW

To Assess the United Counties of Leeds and Grenville, for the year 1853.—Passed June 25, 1853.

Sums to be levied.

1. Be it enacted by the Municipal Council of the United Counties of Leeds and Grenville, and it is hereby enacted, That there be raised and levied upon the whole rateable property in the said United Counties for the present year, the sum of £1970 4s. 11d., to defray the current and ordinary expenses thereof, and the further sum of £1091 4s. 2d., for the payment of the salaries of legally qualified Common School Teachers and the support of Common Schools therein, and the further sum of £3743 0s. 0½d. as a special rate authorized to be raised and levied upon the said property, pursuant to the provisions of By-Laws Nos. 8 and 39, passed respectively on the 10th day of October, 1850, and on the 7th day of May, 1852, and that the said several sums shall be so raised and levied, in addition to all other rates and assessments, and be apportioned to the several Municipalities in the said Counties, in the following manner, viz :—

Municipalities.	For General Rate.			For Common Schools			Special Rate for County Toll Roads.			
	£	s.	D.	£	s.	D.	£	s.	D.	
Elizabethtown,. ...	347	17	10	124	15	6	508	1	1	How appor-
Augusta,..........	218	18	4	123	9	7	320	6	8½	tioned.
Yonge,........ ...	193	3	6	87	14	2	286	6	10½	
Oxford,..........	189	2	7	107	2	10	266	0	8¼	
Kitley,..	133	9	6	84	9	0	194	18	11	
Edwardsburgh,....	141	18	6	113	18	5	207	6	4½	
Bastard & Burgess,.	139	1	3	89	4	5	203	10	0	
Wolford,..........	116	5	11	78	1	7	169	16	8½	
Front Leeds & Lans-										
downe,..	153	0	6	76	9	6	223	9	7½	
Escott,......	46	10	10	33	10	4	67	19	5½	
South Gower......	53	6	11	20	13	6	77	17	3½	
Rear Leeds & Lans-										
downe,...........	57	19	4	36	13	1	84	13	7	
South Crosby, ...	76	19	2	37	16	1	112	8	3	
Elmsley,.........	51	7	7	34	10	11	75	0	5	
North Crosby, ...	51	3	2	42	15	3	74	14	8	
Town of Brockville,	...			...			590	14	2	
Town of Prescott,..	...			...			279	15	2	
	£1970	4	11	1091	4	2	3743	0	0½	

2. And be it further enacted, That there be raised and levied upon the said property in the said Township Municipalities respectively, the sum of six pence in the hundred pounds and so in proportion on any less sum, in addition to all other Rates and Assessments for the Lunatic Asylum as required by the second Section of the Act 13 and 14 Victoria, Chapter 68.

Six-pence in £100 for Lunatic Asy - lum.

3. And be it further enacted, That the said several sums hereinbefore directed to be raised and levied in the said Municipalities respectively, shall be placed on the Collector's Rolls by the Clerks thereof, in separate columns, and collected in like manner as all other rates and Assessments are by law directed to be collected, and shall be paid over to the County Treasurer on or before the fourteenth day of December next, by the said Municipalities respectively.

How to be placed on Collector's Roll, &c.

4. And be it further enacted, That the said Municipalities respectively shall, immediately after the completion of the Collectors' Rolls, cause a statement of the total of

Statement to be furnish'd County Treasurer. each of the said rates hereby directed to be raised, levied, and collected, to be furnished to the County Treasurer, as the same shall appear upon such Collector's Rolls respectively.

5. And be it further enacted, That each and every Collector shall, on or before the fourteenth day of December When Rolls to be returned. next, return his Roll to the Treasurer of his Municipality and pay over to him the sums directed by this By-Law to be raised, levied, and collected, and shall also, on or before the day last mentioned, deliver to the County Treasurer an account of the Taxes remaining due on his Roll according to the Statute in that behalf.

6. And be it further enacted, That this By-Law shall When By-Law to take effect. come into force and take effect upon, from and after the day of the passing thereof.

ROBERT PEDEN, WARDEN.

[L. S.]

JAMES JESSUP, COUNTY CLERK.

No. LIX.—BY-LAW

To Cover certain Grants of Money.—Passed 25th June, 1853.

1. Be it enacted by the Municipal Council of the United Counties of Leeds and Grenville, and it is hereby enacted, Grant of £10 for Road in Leeds. That the sum of ten pounds be granted to aid in the cutting down of two hills in the sixth concession of Leeds, known as the Baxter and Gainford Hills, as soon as the Municipal Council of that Township shall appropriate and expend a like sum for that purpose, to be paid on the requisition of the Township Council of the Rear of Leeds and Lansdowne.

2. That the several sums in this Section mentioned be Sums granted to. granted and paid by the County Treasurer to the parties, respectively, viz:—

Receiver-General. To the Receiver General the sum of four pounds eighteen shillings, for books furnished the Register of the County of Grenville.

To Adam Anderson, the sum of two pounds eighteen Adam Anderson.
shillings and four pence, for book binding.

To the County Clerk, the sum of seventeen shillings and County Clerk.
six-pence, for postage paid by him for the Counties.

To Christopher Leggo, the sum of sixteen shillings and one Chris. Leggo.
penny, for expenses incurred in cleansing the Gaol.

To David Wylie, the sum of twenty-seven pounds twelve D. Wylie.
shillings and one penny, for printing.

To C. Fields, the sum of fifteen shillings, for a table for C. Fields.
the use of the Council.

To the Statesman Printing Office, the sum of twenty-two Statesman print-
pounds fourteen shillings and six pence, for Printing. ing office.

To Arthur Tilly, the sum of one pound, for balance of his Arthur Tilly.
account rendered at the last Session.

To John Burchill, the sum of thirty pounds, being the John Burchill.
amount of his account for surveying the Merrickville
and Maitland Road.

To John Woods, the sum of one hundred and forty-four John Woods.
pounds, for work done by him on the Kemptville
and Prescott Macadamized Road.

To James Kincaid, the sum of two pounds two shillings James Kincaid.
and eleven pence, for articles furnished, and attendance as Messenger during this Session.

ROBERT PEDEN, Warden.
[L. S.]
JAMES JESSUP, County Clerk.

No. LX.—BY-LAW

To Regulate the Salary of the County Treasurer.—Passed See By-Laws
12th October, 1853. Nos. 86 and 147.

Be it enacted by the Municipal Council of the United
Counties of Leeds and Grenville, and it is hereby enacted,
That By-Law No. 12, passed on the twelfth day of October,
in the year of our Lord one thousand eight hundred and

By-Law No. 12 repealed.

4th sec. By-Law No. 186 District Council repeal'd.

fifty, and entituled, " By-Law to repeal part of By-Law No. 186, passed by the late District Council on the 15th day of February, 1849," and also the fourth section of By-Law No. 186 of the late District Council, passed on the 15th day of February, in the year last aforesaid, and entitled " By-Law to regulate the salaries and duties of certain District Officers," and also any other By-Law or part of a By-Law of the late District Council, or of this Council relating to the salary, percentage or allowance to the County Treasurer, be, and the same are hereby repealed.

2. And be it further enacted, that upon, from and after the passing of this By-Law, the sum of two hundred and twenty-five pounds, be fixed as the Salary of the said Treasurer in lieu of all fees, percentages or demands for services as such Treasurer, and that the same shall be payable quarterly, that is to say, on the first day of January, April, July and October in each year, on the certificate of the Warden.

Salary.

ROBERT. PEDEN, Warden.

[L. S.]

JAMES JESSUP, County Clerk.

No. LXI.—BY-LAW

To repeal part of the fifth section of By-Law No. 4, and for other purposes therein mentioned.—Passed October 12, 1853.

(Repealed: see By-law No. 231.)

No. LXII.—BY-LAW

To appropriate certain Tolls for the completion of the Kemptville and Prescott County Toll Road.—Passed 13th October, 1853.

(Repealed; see By-Law No. 231.)

No. LXIII.—BY-LAW

To regulate the management of the County Roads, and to establish a uniform rate of Tolls.—Passed 14th October, 1853.

(Repealed: see By-law No. 231.)

No. LXIV.—BY-LAW

To Repeal part of By-Law number Forty-eight.—Passed October 14, 1853.

Be it enacted by the Municipal Council of the United Counties of Leeds and Grenville, and it is hereby enacted, That the third section of By-Law number Forty-eight, passed on the sixteenth day of October, in the year of our Lord one thousand eight hundred and fifty-two, and entitled, "By-Law to cover certain grants of money," be, and the same is hereby repealed, and that the sum of fifty pounds, granted by the said Section, be transferred to the Municipal Council of the front of Leeds and Lansdowne, to be expended in repairing the Bridge across the River at Gananoque, and that the County Treasurer be authorized to pay the same to the Treasurer of the said Council of the Front of Leeds and Lansdowne, for the purpose of making such repairs immediately. *(3rd section repealed. £50 granted for Gananoque Bridge.)*

ROBERT PEDEN, WARDEN.

[L. S.]

JAMES JESSUP, COUNTY CLERK.

No. LXV.—BY-LAW

To Cover certain Grants of Money.—Passed October 15, 1853.

Be it enacted that the Municipal Council of the United Counties of Leeds and Grenville, and it is hereby enacted, That the sum of five pounds be paid to the Township Council of the Township of Edwardsburgh, for opening and *(£5 for survey of Road between Edwardsburgh & Matilda.)*

surveying the Road between that Township and Matilda, pursuant to the Resolution of the Council passed on the twelfth day of October, 1850.

£250 to contractor on West Port and Farmersville Road.

2. That the sum of two hundred and fifty pounds be paid out of the County funds to the Commissioners of the West Port and Farmersville County Toll Road to enable them to liquidate the debt due the Contractors on the said Road.

£50 to Council of Rear of Leeds & Lansdowne.

3. That the sum of fifty pounds be granted to the Municipal Council of the Rear of Leeds and Lansdowne, to be expended as follows, that is to say: the sum of twenty-five pounds, part thereof, on the Beverly and Kingston Road; the sum of twelve pounds ten shillings, other part thereof, on the White Fish Road, and the sum of twelve pounds ten shillings, the residue, on the two Roads leading to Gananoque.

Sums granted to,

4. That the several sums in this Section mentioned be granted and paid by the County Treasurer to the parties respectively, viz:—

D. Wylie.

To David Wylie, the sum of one pound four shillings and three pence, for printing.

S. B. Merrill.

To Stephen B. Merrill, the sum of twelve shillings and three pence, for printing.

Alfred Poulton.

To Alfred Poulton, the sum of five pounds, for repairs to Gaol and Court House.

William Buell.

To William Buell, the sum of three pounds and nine shillings, for stationery.

Henry Lillie.

To Henry Lillie, the sum of twenty-five pounds, for surveying the West Port and Famersville Road.

Harvey Miller.

To Harvey Millar, the sum of one pound and sixpence, for work to the Gaol.

County Clerk.

To the County Clerk, the sum of fourteen shillings, for postages disbursed by him for the Counties.

James Kincaid.

To James Kincaid, the sum of two pounds and tenpence half-penny, for stationery furnished and attendance as Messenger of the Council.

To Henry Lillie, the sum of three pounds five shillings, for *Henry Lillie.* surveying Roads in Bastard and South Crosby.

To Christopher Leggo, the sum of nineteen shillings, for *Chris. Leggo.* fuel, and cleaning the Court House.

To James Kincaid, the sum of five shillings, for one day's *James Kincaid.* additional attendance as Messenger.

5. That a sum not exceeding the sum of twenty-five *£25 granted to* pounds be granted for the purpose of lighting the Court *light Court House* House with Gas, and that the Warden be authorized to *with gas.* arrange for such lighting.

6. That the sum of fifteen pounds be granted to repair *£15 to repair* the West Port and Farmersville County Road, and paid by *West Port & Far-* the County Treasurer to the Commissioners of that Road. *mersville Road.*

7. That the sum of one hundred and ninety-five pounds *£195 for lot and* be granted for the purpose of purchasing a Lot in the *Registry Office in* Town of Prescott, and for the erection of a suitable build- *Grenville.* ing thereon for a Registry Office for the County of Gren- ville, and that the Warden for the time being, William H. Brouse, and William Garvey be appointed Commissioners to purchase the said lot and to erect or cause to be erect- ed the said building for a Registry Office as aforesaid, and that the Treasurer be authorized and required to pay the said sum of one hundred and ninety-five pounds at such times and in such sums as the said Commissioners, or a majority of them, shall require.

8. That the sum of twenty-five pounds be granted to *£25 to repair* the Commissioners of the Victoria Macadamized Road out *Victoria Road.* of the County funds for repairing the said Road.

ROBERT PEDEN, WARDEN.

[L. S.]

JAMES JESSUP, COUNTY CLERK.

No. LXVI.—BY-LAW

To Assume, Open and Establish the County Toll Roads therein mentioned.—Passed December 7th, 1853.

(Repealed; see By-law No. 231.)

No. LXVII.—BY-LAW

*To Impose a Duty on Hawkers, Pedlars, &c., trading
within the United Counties of Leeds and Grenville.—
Passed December 8, 1853.*

Be it enacted by the Municipal Council of the United
Council of Leeds and Grenville, and it is hereby enacted,
That there shall be raised, collected, and paid to the
Treasurer of the said United Counties, to and for the public uses of the said United Counties, the several and
Duties to be paid for licenses issued. respective duties herein mentioned, for and upon the
respective licenses to be taken out in the manner and by
the persons hereinafter mentioned, that is to say, from
and after the first day of January next, in that and every
ensuing year, during the continuance of this By-Law,
there shall be taken out a License by every Hawker, Pedlar,
and petty Chapman, and any trading person or persons,
such persons going from Town to Town, or to other men's
houses, either on foot, or with a horse, or horses, mule or
mules, or other beast, bearing or drawing burthen; boat or
boats, decked vessels or other craft, or otherwise, within
these Counties, carrying to sell or exposing to sale, any
goods, wares, and merchandize; for which License there
shall be paid the following sums at the time of such
License being taken out:—

For every man travelling on foot, £1, of the current money
money of this Province.

For every horse, ass, or mule, or other beast, bearing burthen, an additional sum of £2.

For every man sailing with a decked vessel, trading and
exposing for sale, goods, wares and merchandize, on
board or from the same, the sum of £12 10s. 0d.

For every man trading with a boat or other craft, and exposing for sale, goods, wares and merchandize, for
each boat and craft the sum of £5.

Not to prohibit real makers of goods, &c., from selling by retail or otherwise. 2. And be it further enacted, That nothing herein contained shall extend or be constructed to extend to prohibit
any person or persons who are the real makers of any
goods, wares, and merchandize of the manufacture of this
Province, or his, her, or their agents from selling such
goods, wares, and merchandize, by retail or otherwise.

3. And be it further enacted, That it shall be lawful
for any Justice of the Peace, Constable, or Peace Officer,

to seize and detain any such Hawker, Pedlar, or Petty Chapman, or other trading person as aforesaid, who shall be found trading without a License, contrary to this By-Law, or being found trading, shall refuse or neglect to produce a License according to this By-Law, after being required so to do, in order to his or her being carried, and they are hereby required to carry such persons so seized, unless he or she shall produce their respective Licenses, before one or more Justices of the Peace, the nearest to the place where such offence or offences shall be committed, which said Justice or Justices are hereby required and authorized, either upon the confession of the party offending, or due proof by witness or witnesses, other than the informer upon oath ; which oath he or they are hereby authorized to administer, that the person or persons so brought before him or them, had traded as aforesaid, without a License, and in case no such License shall be produced by such offender or offenders before such Justice or Justices, the said Justice or Justices by warrant under his or their hands and seals, directed to a Constable or other Peace Officer shall cause a sum not exceeding £10 with reasonable costs, to be forthwith levied by distress and sale of the goods, wares and merchandize of such offender or offenders, or of the goods with which such offender or offenders shall be found trading as aforesaid, rendering the overplus, if any there be, to the owners thereof, after deducting the reasonable charges for taking the said distress, and for want of sufficient distress the offender or offenders shall be sent to the Common Gaol for a space not exceeding one calendar month, as such Justice or Justices of the Peace shall think most proper.

Justices, &c., to seize persons selling without a license.

How offenders to be proceeded against.

Fines.

To whom duties and fines to be paid,

4. And be it further enacted, that the duties imposed by this By-Law, and the pecuniary penalty imposed thereby shall be paid to the Treasurer of the said United Counties, for the general uses of the same, and the said Treasurer is hereby authorized to issue such license, which shall be in force until the first day of January, in the year following that in which such license shall be issued.

Treasurer to issue License.

Duration of License.

5. And be it further enacted, that this By-Law shall be in force from and after the first day of January next and not until then, any thing to the contrary herein notwithstanding.

When By-Law to take effect.

ROBERT PEDEN, WARDEN.

[L. S.]

JAMES JESSUP, COUNTY CLERK.

No. LXVIII.—BY-LAW

To Cover certain Grants of Money.—Passed 8th December,
1853.

Sums granted to. Be it enacted by the Municipal Council of the United
Counties of Leeds and Grenville, and it is hereby enacted,
that the several sums hereinafter mentioned shall be paid
by the County Treasurer to the parties, respectively, viz:—

County Clerk. 1. To the County Clerk, the sum of nine shillings and six-
pence, for disbursements made by him for the Counties.

County Clerk. 2. To the County Clerk the sum of fifty pounds for revis-
ing the By-Laws of the late District Council, and of
these Counties.

John Burchill. 3. To John Burchill, the sum of ten pounds and ten
shillings, for surveying a part of the Victoria Macadamized Road, namely, from Irish Creek to Washburn's Bridge.

J. W. Huddle-
ston. 4. To J. W. Huddleston the sum of one pound seven
shillings and seven pence, for pipes furnished the
Counties.

Walter Finlay. 5. To Walter Finlay, the sum of fifteen pounds, as a
remuneration to him for services rendered in the
investigation of the Treasurer's Accounts.

James Kincaid. 6. To James Kincaid, the sum of one pound one shilling,
for his attendance at the present Session of the
Council, and for lights furnished.

ROBERT PEDEN, Warden.

[L. S.]

JAMES JESSUP, County Clerk.

No. LXIX.—BY-LAW

To assume, open and establish the County Toll Roads
therein mentioned.—Passed 25th January, 1854.

(Repealed; see By-law No. 231.)

No. LXX.—BY-LAW

To Appoint Superintendents of Common Schools in the United Counties of Leeds and Grenville.—Passed 25th January, 1854.

Be it enacted by the Municipal Council of the United Counties of Leeds and Grenville, and it is hereby enacted, that the following persons be and they are hereby appointed Superintendents of Schools, for the respective Townships hereinafter mentioned, such appointments to commence on the first day of April, 1854, and not before:

Augusta..........................James Clapperton.   *Appointments.*
Oxford...........................Andrew Holmes.
Front of Yonge and Escott.......Rev. James Cooper.
Front of Leeds and Lansdowne...Thomas Vanston.
Rear of Yonge and Escott........Rev. James Cooper.
Elizabethtown....................Jacob A. Brown.
Edwardsburgh....................Rev. James Geggie.
South Gower.....................Rev. Joseph Anderson.
Wolford..........................Thomas Graffe.
Kitley...........................Robert Ferguson.
Elmsley..........................Edward F. Weeks.
Bastard and Burgess.............Lewis Chipman.
South Crosby....................Rev. Matthew Connor.
North Crosby ....Rev. Matthew Connor.
Rear of Leeds and Lansdowne...Henry P. Washburn.

E. H. WHITMARSH, Warden.

[L. S.]

JAMES JESSUP, County Clerk.

No. LXXI—BY-LAW

To amend By-Law No. 186, passed by the late District Council.

1. Be it enacted by the Municipal Council of the United Counties of Leeds and Grenville, duly assembled at the Town of Brockville, on the twenty-fifth day of January, in the year of our Lord one thousand eight hundred and fifty-four, and it is hereby enacted, that the second section of a certain By-law passed by the late District Council on the

fifteenth day of February, in the year of our Lord one
thousand eight hundred and forty-nine, end entitled By-
law to regulate the salaries of certain District Officers, be
and the same is hereby repealed.

2nd Section repealed.

2. And be it further ordained and enacted, that the Warden of these United Counties, for the time being, shall
from and after the passing of this By-law be paid the sum
of twenty shillings per day, for each and every day he may
be actually and necessarily employed in the performance
of any duty as Warden out of Council.

Warden allowed 20s. per day instead of salary.

E. H. WHITMARSH, Warden.

[L. S.]

JAMES JESSUP, County Clerk.

No. LXXII.—BY-LAW

*To stop up and close a certain Road in the Township of
Kitley.—Passed 25th January, 1854.*

Preamble.

Whereas, in consequence of the opening and making of
the County Toll Road, known as the Victoria Macadamized
Road, the old road passing through lots numbers fourteen
and fifteen, in the fifth concession of the Township of
Kitley, as hereinafter described, has been rendered unnecessary for public use and travel: And whereas public
notice has been given according to the statute in that behalf, that a By-law would be passed at the present meeting
of the Municipal Council of the United Counties of Leeds
and Grenville, to stop up and close the said old road,
which has been surveyed, described and reported by John
Burchill, Provincial Land Surveyor, substantially and to
the effect as follows, that is to say: "commencing at the
distance of twenty-nine chains ninety links, (on the new
line of road) from the front of the sixth concession of
Kitley; thence on the course north seventeen degrees, west
magnetically eight chains seventy links; thence on the
course north nineteen degrees thirty minutes, east eight
chains five links; thence on the same course north sixteen
degrees thirty minutes, east twenty-one chains to the intersection of the new line of road, which makes the whole
length of said old road *thirty-seven chains* seventy-five
links." Be it therefore enacted by the Municipal Council

Notice.

Description of old road closed.

of the said United Counties, and it is hereby enacted, that
the said old road as hereinbefore described, be and the same Closed as a public road.
is hereby stopped up and closed, as unnecessary for a
public road and highway.

E. H. WHITMARSH, Warden.

[L. S.]

JAMES JESSUP, County Clerk.

No. LXXIII.—BY-LAW.

*To appoint Trustees for each of the County Grammar
Schools in the United Counties of Leeds and Grenville.—Passed January 26, 1854.*

Whereas, by the ninth section of a certain Act of the Preamble.
Legislature of this Province, passed in the 16th year of
the reign of Her Majesty Queen Victoria, and entitled
"An Act to amend the law relating to Grammar Schools
in Upper Canada," it is amongst other things provided,
that the several County Municipalities in Upper Canada,
at their first sittings, to be held after the first day of
January, in the year of our Lord one thousand eight hundred and fifty-four, shall select and appoint three fit and
proper persons to be Trustees for each of the Grammar
Schools within their Counties or union of Counties, and
shall also decide the order in which the said persons so
chosen by them, as Trustees, shall retire from the Board,
of which they shall be such Trustees; Be it therefore
enacted by the Municipal Council of the United Counties
of Leeds and Grenville, and it is hereby enacted, that the
persons hereinafter mentioned, shall be, and they are
hereby selected, and appointed Trustees of the County Appointment of Trustees.
Grammar Schools in the said United Counties as they are
respectively assigned for each of the said Schools, that is
to say:—

For the County Grammar School established in the Brockville School.
Town of Brockville:

1. Rev. Oliver Kelly.
2. Richard F. Steele.
3. Rev. J. T. Lewis.

R

Kemptville
School.

For the County Grammar School, established in the
Village of Kemptville:

    1. Ambrose Clothier.
    2. Joseph Leeming.
    3. Robert Leslie.

Prescott School.

For the County Grammar School established in the
Town of Prescott:

    1. Hamilton D. Jessup.
    2. Alpheus Jones.
    3. William J. Scott.

Gananoque
School.

For the County Grammar School established in the
village of Gananoque:

    1. Thomas Richmond.
    2. Thomas Vanston.
    3. Robert McCrum.

How Trustees to
retire from office.

2. And be it further enacted, that on the thirty-first
day of January, in the year of our Lord one thousand
eight hundred and fifty-five, and on the same day in the next
two succeeding years, one of the said Trustees for each of
the said Grammar Schools hereinbefore appointed, shall
go out of office in the order in which they are so
appointed, and thenceforward in all future years, those
persons who shall be hereafter chosen by the said Council,
shall also annually retire in the same order as the said
Trustees hereby appointed, Provided that no such Trustees shall remain in office, unless re-appointed, for a longer
period than three years.

Certificate of re-
tirement of old
Trustees.

3. And be it further enacted, that the chairman and
Secretary of each Board of Trustees, shall certify to the
Clerk of the said Council the names of the Trustees, not
appointed by the said Council, and the order in which
such persons shall retire from office, as soon as the same
shall be decided according to the Statute in that behalf.

                  E. H. WHITMARSH, WARDEN.

[L. S.]

JAMES JESSUP, COUNTY CLERK.

No. LXXIV.—BY-LAW

To Cover certain Grants of Money.—Passed 26th January, 1854.

Be it enacted by the Municipal Council of the United Counties of Leeds and Grenville, and it is hereby enacted, that the several sums of money hereinafter mentioned, shall be paid by the County Treasurer to the parties respectively, viz :— Sums paid to.

To Edward Robinson, County Surveyor, the sum of three pounds ten shillings, for seven days' service in putting up notices on the Victoria and Westport and Farmerville Roads. Edward Robinson.

To Stephen B. Merrill, the sum of eleven pounds six shillings and four pence, for advertising in the *Prescott Telegraph.* S. B. Merrill.

To William Humphries, the sum of one pound fourteen shillings and ten pence for moneys advanced by him to Toll Gate Keeper at North Augusta. William Humphries.

To David Wylie, the sum of one hundred and twenty-five pounds seven shillings and eleven pence for printing By-Laws and advertising. D. Wylie.

To James Jessup, the sum of one pound two shillings, for disbursements made by him for the Counties. James Jessup.

To William Humphries, the sum of seven pounds, seventeen shillings and one penny, for building a stable at the North Augusta Toll Gate. William Humphries.

To Henry Lillie, the sum of seven pounds, being the balance of his account for the survey of the Westport and Farmersville County Road. Henry Lillie.

To Eugene Brown the sum of eight pounds eighteen shillings and seven pence for disbursements at the North Augusta Toll House and Gate. Eugene Brown.

To William Fitzsimmons, the sum of fourteen shillings for work done to the Court House. William Fitzsimmons.

To Christopher Leggo, the sum of two pounds seven shillings and six pence for fuel and other contingencies for the Council. Chris. Leggo.

James Kincaid. To James Kincaid, the sum of one pound for his attendance as Messenger of the Council.

E. H. WHITMARSH, Warden.

[L. S.]

JAMES JESSUP, County Clerk.

No. LXXV.—BY-LAW

To stop up and close certain parts of the old Road, between Beverly and Newboro'.—Passed 21st June, 1854.

Preamble.

Whereas, in consequence of the opening and making of a certain portion of the County Toll Road, known as the Westport and Farmersville Road, those parts of the old or formerly travelled Road passing through part of Lot number twenty-four, in the fifth Concession, of the Township of Bastard, and part of Lot number twenty-six, in the third Concession, of the Township of South Crosby, have become unnecessary for Public use and travel. And

Notice.

whereas, public notice has been given according to the statute in that behalf, that a By-law would be passed at the present meeting of the Municipal Council, of the United Counties of Leeds and Grenville, to stop up and close the same, and which have been surveyed, described, and reported, by Henry Lilley, Provincial Land Surveyor, substantially and to the effect as follows: that is to say,

Description of old road closed.

"commencing at a stone boundary, planted in the north-erly limit of the allowance of Road, between the 5th and 6th Concessions of the Township of Bastard, distant on the course north fifty-four degrees, east along the rear of the fifth Concession aforesaid, nine chains sixty links from the south west angle of said Lot No. 24: thence north fifty-four degrees twenty-two minutes, west twenty-five chains seventy-two links: thence north thirty-seven degrees forty minutes, west twelve chains twenty links: thence north forty degrees eighteen minutes, west seven chains, more or less to a stone boundary planted in the south westerly limit of the new Macadamized Road, leading from Beverly to Newboro': thence south easterly along the said south westerly limit three chains fourteen links to a stone boundary: thence south forty degrees eighteen minutes, east five chains fifty-eight links: thence south thirty-seven degrees forty minutes, east twelve chains twenty links: thence south fifty-four degrees twenty-two minutes, east twenty-five chains seventy-two links, more or less to the rear of the 5th Concession aforesaid : thence south fifty-four degrees west along the rear of the said 5th Concession, forty feet to the place of beginning, containing by admeasurement one acre and fifty-four square rods be the same more or less," and also commencing at a post marked A, planted in the westerly limit of the allowance of road, between the 2nd and 3rd Concessions of the said Township of South Crosby, distant on the course north thirty-six, west along the front of the third Concession aforesaid eight chains ten links from the south east angle lot No. 26: thence south sixty-five degrees seven minutes, west ten chains : thence south sixty degrees fifteen minutes, west four chains sixty-one links : thence south sixty-seven degrees twenty-three minutes, west five chains twenty-five links ; thence south seventy-two degrees forty-three minutes, west eleven chains thirty links ; thence south eighty-three degrees fifty-one minutes west five chains, eighty links, more or less to a post marked "B," planted in the northerly limit of the Macadamized Road leading to the village of Newboro' : thence westerly along the northerly limit aforesaid six chains ninety-eight links, to a post marked "C": thence north eighty degrees twenty-one minutes, east four chains thirty-seven links : thence north eighty-three degrees fifty one minutes, east eight chains thirty-five links : thence north seventy-two degrees forty-three minutes, east eleven chains thirty links : thence north sixty-seven degrees twenty-three minutes, east five chains twenty-five links : thence north sixty degrees fifteen minutes, east four chains sixty-one links : thence north sixty-five degrees seven minutes, east ten chains, more or less to a post marked "D," planted at the front of the 3rd Concession aforesaid : thence south thirty-six degrees, east forty feet to the place of beginning, containing by admeasurement one acre and thirty-five sq. rods, be the same more or less. Be it therefore enacted by the Municipal Council of the said United Counties, and it is hereby enacted, that those parts of the said old or formerly travelled road as herein before described, be and the same are hereby stopped up and closed as unnecessary for public use and travel.

Closed as a Public Road.

(Signed,)   E. H. WHITMARSH, Warden.

   [L. S.]

JAMES JESSUP, County Clerk.

No. LXXVI.—BY-LAW

To appoint Local Superintendents in Yonge and Escott.—Passed 22nd June, 1854.

Thomas Vanston for front of Yonge and Escott.

Rev. J. Betts for rear of Yonge & Escott, in place of James Cooper, resigned.

Be it enacted by the Municipal Council of the United Counties of Leeds and Grenville, and it is hereby enacted, that Thomas Vanston be, and is hereby appointed Superintendent of Common Schools for the front of Yonge and Escott, and the Rev. George I. Betts, for the Rear of Yonge and Escott, in place of the Rev. James Cooper resigned.

(Signed,) E. H. WHITMARSH, Warden.

[L. S.]

JAMES JESSUP, County Clerk.

No. LXXVII.—BY-LAW

To assume the Bridge in the Village of Gananoque, as County work.—Passed 22nd June, 1854.

(Repealed : see By-Law No. 243.)

No. LXXVIII.—BY-LAW

To authorize a temporary Loan until the Assessments for the present year become available .—Passed 23rd June, 1854.

(Repealed : see By-Law No. 228, sec. 4.)

No. LXXIX.—BY-LAW.

To Assess the United Counties of Leeds and Grenville, for the year 1854.—Passed June 23, 1854.

Be it enacted by the Municipal Council of the United Counties of Leeds and Grenville, and it is hereby enacted, That there be raised and levied upon the whole rateable property in the said United Counties, for the present year, the sum of £3612 14s. 7d., to defray the past and current expenses thereof, and the further sum of £1313 14s. 2d. for the payment of the salaries of legally qualified Common School Teachers and the support of Common Schools therein, and the further sum of £3673 17s. 11d., as a special rate authorized to be raised and levied upon the said property under the provisions of By-Laws No. 8 and 39 passed respectively on the tenth day of October, 1850, and on the seventh day of May, 1852, and that the said several sums shall be raised and levied, in addition to all other rates and assessments, and be apportioned to the several Municipalities in the said Counties in the following manner, viz.

County rate, £3612 14s. 7d.

Common Schools £1313 14s. 2d.

Special rate, £3673 17s. 11d., under By-Laws 8 and 39.

How apportion'd to Municipalities.

MUNICIPALITIES.	For General Rate.			For Common Schools.			Special rate for County Roads.		
	£.	s.	D.	£.	s.	D.	£.	s.	D.
Elizabethtown.	512	6	3	150	14	8	571	13	11
Augusta.	327	9	1	148	13	6	346	15	5
Bastard and Burgess.	202	11	9	107	11	3	206	14	7
Rear of Yonge and Escott.	170	2	9	68	13	5	170	2	10
Front of Yonge and Escott.	194	5	4	76	16		194	5	3
South Gower.	240	8	11	92	0	5	242	19	8
Front of Leeds and Lansdowne.	76	4	11	24	16	3	82	5	2
Edwardsburgh.	212	14	6	137	4	1	229	1	1
Oxford.	266	7	6	129	1	5	223	15	6
North Crosby.	77	9	9	51	8	10	77	1	
Elmsley.	89	6	7	41	9		64	6	7
Wolford.	169	18	6	94	3	11	186	11	2
Rear of Leeds and Lansdowne.	88	19	3	43	19	9	89	7	2
Kitley.	188	10	7	101	11	10	193	7	
South Crosby.	106	4	4	45	9	10	106	5	4
Town of Brockville.	448	3	4				448	3	4
Town of Prescott.	241	1	3				241	1	3
Total.	£3612	14	7	£1313	14	2	£3673	17	11

2. And be it further enacted, that there be raised and levied upon the said property in the said Township Municipalities, respectively the sum of six pence in the hundred pounds, and so in proportion on any less sum, in addition to all other rates and assessments for the Lunatic Asylum as required by the second section of the Act 13 and 14 Vic. chap. 68.

Lunatic Asylum tax.

3. And be it further enacted, that the said several sums hereinbefore directed to be raised and levied in the said Municipalities respectively, shall be placed on the Collect- or's Roll by the Clerk thereof, in separate columns, and collected in like manner as all other rates and assessments are by the law directed to be collected, and shall be paid over to the County Treasurer on or before the fourteenth day of December next, by the said Municipalities respec- tively.

How to be col- lected.

4. And be it further enacted, that the said Municipalities respectively shall immediately on the completion of the Collectors' Roll, cause a statement of the total of each of the said rates hereby imposed, to be furnished to the County Treasurer as the same shall appear upon such Collectors' Rolls respectively.

Statement to be furnished Treas- urer.

5. And be it further enacted, that every Collector shall on or before the fourteenth day of December next, return his Roll to the Treasurer of the Municipality, and pay over to him the sums hereby directed to be raised, levied and collected, and shall also deliver to the County Treasurer an account of those taxes remaining due on the Roll on the last day aforesaid.

When Roll to be returned.

6. And be it further enacted, that this By-law shall come into force and take effect upon, from and after the day of passing thereof.

When By-Law to take effect.

(Signed,) PHILO HICOCK, CHAIRMAN.

　[L. S.]

JAMES JESSUP, COUNTY CLERK.

No. LXXX.—BY-LAW

To Cover certain Grants of Money, and for other purposes.
—Passed June 23, 1854.

1. Be it enacted by the Municipal Council of the United Counties of Leeds and Grenville, and it is hereby enacted, that the several sums of money hereinafter in this section mentioned, shall be paid by the County Treasurer to the parties respectively, viz :

Sums paid to.

Robert Kernahan & Ambrose Clothier. To Robert Kernahan and Ambrose Clothier the sum of six pounds eleven shillings and one penny half penny, being amount expended by them on Roads in Oxford.

Walter Findlay. To Walter Findlay the sum of ten pounds, being the balance of his claim for examining Treasurer's books and accounts.

D. Wylie. To David Wylie the sum of one hundred and twenty three pounds two shillings and nine pence, for advertising and printing.

Edward Robertson. To Edward Robinson the sum of two pounds five shillings for services as County Surveyor.

Adam Anderson. To Adam Anderson the sum of seven pounds eighteen shillings and one penny half-penny, for binding books.

S. B. Merrill. To Stephen B. Merrill the sum of six pounds ten shillings and nine pence, for printing and advertising.

Andrew Smail. To Andrew Smail the sum of thirty-eight pounds ten shillings being amount awarded for damages to land on the line of the Kemptville and Prescott County Road, and for the costs of Arbitration.

Leeds and Grenville printing Co. To the Leeds and Grenville printing and publishing Company, the sum of eight pounds nineteen shillings and four pence for publishing Treasurer's accounts.

Commissioners Victoria Road. To the Commissioners of the Victoria Macadamized Road, the sum of seventy-five pounds, to be set apart for the purpose of keeping the said Road in a proper state of repair.

Jos. Pritchard. To Joseph Pritchard the sum of forty-eight pounds two shillings and eight pence for work done on the Kemptville and Prescott Road.

To Robert Mitchell the sum of thirty-six pounds nine Robt. Mitchell. shillings and eleven pence half-penny, being balance due for putting up fixtures and to light the Court House with gas.

To Christopher Leggo the sum of four pounds six shillings Chris. Leggo. and three pence for disbursements, for white-washing Gaol, &c.

To the County Clerk the sum of £1 15s. 6d. for dis- County Clerk. bursements.

To James Kincaid the sum of £1 11s. 10¼d., for services James Kincaid. as Messenger.

To Andrew Gay the sum of three shillings and six-pence Andrew Gay. for mending a chair.

2. And be it further enacted, that the sum of one Clerk's Salary. hundred pounds be added annually to the salary of the See By-Law No. County Clerk and paid by the County Treasurer in the 26. same manner and at the times provided in By-law No. 26 for his present salary, and that such addition shall take effect from the first day of the year.

3. And be it further enacted, that the sum of two hundred and fifty pounds be appropriated to build a Registry office for the County of Leeds, and that a further grant of the Registry offices, sum of seventy-five pounds be made to build a Registry Leeds and Gren- office in Prescott for the County of Grenville, and that ville. the said sums be paid to the Commissioners appointed to build the said Registry office.

PHILO HICOCK, Chairman.

[L. S.]

JAMES JESSUP, County Clerk.

No. LXXXI.—BY-LAW

To appoint a Local Superintendent of Common Schools for the Rear of Yonge and Escott.—Passed October 11, 1854.

Be it enacted by the Municipal Council of the United Counties of Leeds and Grenville, and it is hereby enacted, that so much of By-law numbered seventy-six, passed on

Part By-Law No.
75 repealed.

Philip Wing,
Esq., appointed
in place of Rev.
G. J. Betts.

the twenty-second day of June last, as appoints the Rev. George J. Betts, Local Superintendent for the Rear of Yonge and Escott in the place of the Rev. James Cooper resigned, be repealed, and the same is hereby repealed, and that Philip Wing, Esq., be and he is hereby appointed such Superintendent in the place of the said Rev. G. J. Betts and one Morgan C. Gould, temporary appointed by the Warden, who have both removed from the said Municipality.

E. H. WHITMARSH, WARDEN.

[L. S.]
JAMES JESSUP, COUNTY CLERK.

No. LXXXII.—BY-LAW

To authorize the Commissioners of the Victoria Macadamized County Road to remove Toll Gate No. 4 on the said Road.—Passed 12th October, 1854.

(Repealed: see By-law No. 231.)

No. LXXXIII.—BY-LAW

To cover certain Grants of Money.—Passed October 12, 1854.

ums paid to.

1. Be it enacted by the Municipal Council of the United Counties of Leeds and Grenville, and it is hereby enacted, that the several sums of money hereinafter mentioned shall be paid by the County Treasurer to the parties respectively, viz:—

J. W. Huddle-
ston.

To J. W. Huddleston the sum of three pounds one shilling and three pence for work in Court House, fixing stoves and pipes.

William Buell.

To William Buell the sum of one pound eighteen shillings and ten pence half-penny for stationery.

William Fitzsim-
mons.

To William Fitzsimmons the sum of four pounds six shillings and six pence half-penny, for work done to the Court House and Gaol.

To David Wylie the sum of one pound and three pence David Wylie.
for Advertising.

To Philip Vankonghnet, Esq., the sum of seven pounds Philip Vankoughnet.
ten shillings for legal services rendered.

To Messrs. Sherwood and Steele the sum of five pounds Sherwood & Steele.
for legal services rendered.

To A. Poulton the sum of five pounds for work done to Alfred Poulton.
the Gaol and Court House.

To the County Clerk the sum of one pound and nine County Clerk.
pence for disbursements for the County.

To Robert S. Ennis the sum of fifteen pounds, for plans, Robert S. Ennis.
specifications, &c., for the Gananoque Bridge.

To D. Wylie the sum of six shillings and eight pence for D. Wylie.
Advertising.

To the Monitor Printing Office the sum of one pound eight *Monitor* printing office.
shillings and one penny for advertising.

To Hugh Kernahan the sum of thirty-nine pounds ten Hugh Kernahan.
shillings, being the amount allowed by the Arbitrators
for damages done to his property in Kitley, by the
construction of the Victoria Macadamized Road and
for the costs of the Arbitrators.

To the Warden the sum of ten pounds for his services out The Warden:
of Council for the current year.

To James Kincaid the sum of one pound and seven pence James Kincaid.
half-penny for services as Messenger and for stationery.

2. That the additional sum of one hundred and fifty James Elliott, for work on West pounds be paid to James Elliott for alterations made and Port & Farmersville County work performed on nine miles of the Westport and Far- Road.
mersville County Road.

3. That the sum of twenty pounds be granted to build Bridges in South Gower. bridges referred to in the petition of the Rev. Joseph
Anderson and others, and that the Municipal Council of
the Township of South Gower be authorized to expend
the same for the purpose aforesaid.

4. That the sum of twenty-five pounds be granted to be Covel Road, Augusta. laid out on the road commonly called the Covel Road, run-

ning between Augusta and Edwardsburgh (being in lieu of the Town Line Road), and that the said sum be paid William H. Flynn, Stephen Covell and Duncan Christie, Commissioners hereby appointed for expending the same, provided the different amounts subscribed by the inhabitants, be paid into the hands of the said Commissioners, to be by them expended thereon as the money now granted by this Council.

Proviso.

5. That the sum of ten pounds be remitted from the rent of Elizabeth Bird for her losses and services at Toll Gate No. 1, on the Westport and Farmersville County Road in the months of February and March last, in consequence of persons crossing the ice on the Rideau Lake, thereby evading the said Toll Gate, and the Treasurer give her credit for the same.

Remission of rent to Elizabeth Bird.

6. That the sum of three hundred pounds be granted and set apart out of the County Funds for the purpose of relieving the parties who have suffered by the late destructive fires which prevailed in several of the Townships of which these United Counties are composed, and that Messrs. Peden, Lothrop, Parish, Shanks and the Warden, be a Committee to distribute the same amongst the sufferers as they may in their discretion deem best.

Relief of sufferers by fires.

E. H. WHITMARSH, Warden.

[L. S.]

JAMES JESSUP, County Clerk.

No. LXXXIV —BY-LAW

To extend to the Brockville and North Augusta Plank Road Company further time to complete their road.— Passed 12th October, 1854.

Preamble.

Whereas the said Company have made application to the Municipal Council of the United Counties of Leeds and Grenville for further time to complete their road from Brockville to North Augusta, and it is expedient and proper to comply therewith; Be it therefore enacted by the said Council, and it is hereby enacted, that in pursuance of the power vested in the said Council by the twenty-seventh section of the Act sixteen Victoria, chapter 180, further

time be granted to the said Company to complete the said
road, and that such further time be extended to the first
day of October, in the year of our Lord one thousand Extended to 1st October, 1855.
eight hundred and fifty-five, and no longer.

E. H. WHITMARSH, Warden.

[L. S.]

JAMES JESSUP, County Clerk.

No. LXXXV.—BY-LAW

To amend By-Law numbered seventy-seven.—Passed 13th October, 1854.

(Repealed : see By-Law No. 243.)

No. LXXXVI.—BY-LAW

To provide for the payment of certain sums of money and for other purposes.—Passed 13th October, 1854.

Be it enacted by the Municipal Council of the United
Counties of Leeds and Grenville, and it is hereby enacted,
that the several sums of money hereinafter mentioned Sums paid to.
shall be paid by the County Treasurer to the parties
respectively, viz:

To James Kincaid the sum of five shillings for one day's James Kincaid.
attendance as Messenger.

To John McMullen the sum of ten pounds three shillings John McMullen.
and ten pence for printing.

To David Wylie the sum of five pounds ten shillings and David Wylie.
eleven pence for advertising.

To James Kincaid the sum of twelve shillings and six James Kincaid.
pence for increased pay as Messenger.

2. That the sum of fifty pounds be added to the salary Addition to Treasurer's salary. See By-Laws Nos. 60 & 147.
of the County Treasurer, to be paid in the same manner
and at the times provided for his present salary, and that
such addition shall take effect from the first day of October
instant.

Additi'n to Coun-
cillor's pay. See
By-Law No. 2,
sec. 2. 3. That an additional sum of two shillings and six pence per day be allowed to each member for attending the sittings of this Council during the present and future sessions thereof.

E. H. WHITMARSH, Warden.

[L. S.]

JAMES JESSUP, County Clerk.

No. LXXXVII.—BY-LAW

To appoint Superintendents of Common Schools in the United Counties of Leeds and Grenville.— Passed January 25, 1855.

Be it enacted by the Municipal Council of the United Counties of Leeds and Grenville, and it is hereby enacted, That the following persons be, and they are hereby appointed, Local Superintendents of Schools for the several and respective Townships hereinafter mentioned, such appointments to commence on the first day of April, 1855, and not before, viz. :—

Appointments.

Augusta	James Clapperton.
Oxford	Andrew Holmes.
Front of Yonge and Escott.	Thomas Vanston.
Front of Leeds & Lansdowne	Thomas Vanston.
Rear of Yonge and Yonge.	Rev. James Coopor.
Elizabethtown	Jacob A. Brown.
Edwardsburgh	Rev. James Geggie.
South Gower	Rev. Joseph Anderson.
Wolford	Thomas J. Graffe.
Kitley	Robert W. Ferguson.
Elmsley	Edward F. Weeks.
Bastard and Burgess.	Lewis Chipman.
South Crosby	William Robert Taylor.
North Crosby	William Robert Taylor.
Rear Leeds & Lansdowne	Henry P. Washburn.

Proviso.

Provided always, nevertheless, that the said William Robert Taylor be, and is hereby appointed, Local Superintendent for the said Townships of South Crosby and

North Crosby for the residue of the current year, for which the Rev. Matthew Connor, who has resigned, was appointed.

E. H. WHITMARSH, Warden.

[L. S.]

JAMES JESSUP, County Clerk.

No. LXXXVIII.—BY-LAW

To appoint Trustees of each of the County Grammar Schools in the place of those who shall retire from office on the 31st January, 1855.—Passed January 25, 1855.

Be it enacted by the Municipal Council of the United Counties of Leeds and Grenville, and it is hereby enacted, That the persons hereinafter mentioned are selected and appointed Trustees of the County Grammar Schools in the said United Counties, as they are respectively assigned for each of the said Schools, that is to say : **Appointment**

For the County Grammar School, established in the Town of Brockville, Dr. Robert Edmondson, in the place of the Rev. William Smart, and Robert Peden, Esq., in place of the Rev. Oliver Kelly, who retires from office. **Brockville School.**

For the County Grammar School established in the Village of Kemptville, Ambrose Clothier, re-elected, and Robert Kernahan in the place of the person who shall retire by lot. **Kemptville School.**

For the County Grammar School established in the Town of Prescott, Hamilton D. Jessup, re-elected, and Chancey H. Peck in the place of the Rev. Edward P. Roche, who retires from office. **Prescott School.**

For the County Grammar School established in the Village of Gananoque, Rev. John Carroll in the place of Thomas Richmond, who retires, and the Rev. Henry Gordon, re-elected. **Gananoque School.**

E. H. WHITMARSH, Warden.

[L. S.]

JAMES JESSUP, County Clerk.

S

No. LXXXIX.—BY-LAW

*To amend By-Law number sixty-one and for other purposes.
—Passed January 26, 1855.*

(Repealed : See By-law No. 231.)

———

No. XC.—BY-LAW

*To authorize a temporary Loan until the Assessments for
the present year become available.—Passed January
26, 1855.*

(Repealed : see By-law No. 231.)

———

No. XCI.—BY-LAW

*To cover certain Grants of Money.—Passed 26th January,
1855.*

Be it enacted by the Municipal Council of the United
Counties of Leeds and Grenville, and it is hereby enacted,
that the several sums of money hereinafter in this section
mentioned shall be paid by the County Treasurer to the
parties respectively, viz :—

Sums paid to.

William Fitzsimmons. To William Fitzsimmons the sum of four pounds three
shillings and six pence, for work done on Court
House.

D. Wylie. To David Wylie the sum of ten pounds seventeen shillings
and nine pence, for printing and advertising.

S. B. Merrill. To Stephen B. Merrill the sum of six pounds fifteen
shillings and four pence for printing and advertising.

William Garvey. To William Garvey the sum of five pounds twelve shillings
and six pence, for cloth furnished to cover the tables
in the court room.

**Commissioners
Prescott and
Kemptville Toll
Road.** To the Commissioners for the Prescott and Kemptville
Toll Road the sum of one hundred and fifty-eight
pounds two shillings and six pence, being balance
due by Lessees of the Toll Gates Nos. one and two

on said road for last year, the said sum to be charged
to the account of the Prescott and Kemptville Toll
Road.

The Municipal Council of the Township of Elmsley the Council of Elms-
sum of twenty-nine pounds thirteen shillings and four ley.
pence, being for over assessment, in consequence of
the island property at Smith's Falls having been
separated from the said Township of Elmsley.

To John McMullen the sum of twenty-eight pounds eight John McMullen.
shillings and six pence for printing and stationery.

To William Garvey the sum of five pounds, for services William Garvey.
rendered by him for the Council.

To E. H. Whitmarsh the sum of twelve pounds ten shillings E. H. Whitmarsh.
for services rendered by him for the Council.

To County Clerk the sum of one pound eight shillings County Clerk.
and ten pence, for disbursements made by him for the
Council.

To William Caffrey the sum of five pounds four shillings William Caffrey.
and five pence for printing and advertising.

To the Reeves of the Municipalities of the Townships of Reeves of Rear
Rear of Leeds and Landsdowne and of South Crosby, Leeds and Lans-
the sum of twenty-five pounds, for the purpose of Crosby.
opening the town line between the Townships of
Leeds and South Crosby.

To the Gas Company of Brockville the sum of ten shillings Gas Company.
and six pence, for gas furnished.

To Christopher Leggo the sum of one pound fifteen Chris. Leggo.
shillings, for keeping court room in order during the
sitting of the Council, and fire-wood furnished.

To James Kincaid the sum of one pound eighteen shillings James Kincaid.
and one penny half-penny, for attendance as messenger
and for ink furnished.

2. That the sum of two hundred and fifty pounds be Patriotic Fund
granted to aid the widows and orphans of all the noble for Widows and
and patriotic Britons who have fallen or may yet fall in Orphans of Bri-
fighting the battles of liberty and of their country, during tish Soldiers.
the present European war, and that the Treasurer be

authorized and empowered to pay and transmit the same
to the proper authority at the Seat of Government for receiving contributions to the Patriotic Fund.

(Signed,)   E. H. WHITMARSH, WARDEN.

[L. S.]

(Signed,)   JAMES JESSUP, COUNTY CLERK.

No. XCII.—BY-LAW

*To appoint additional Commissioners for re-building the
Gananoque Bridge.—Passed January 27, 1855.*

(Repealed; see By-law No. 243.)

No. XCIII.—BY-LAW

*To appoint Local Superintendents for the Townships of
Wolford and Edwardsburgh,—Passed June 21, 1855.*

Appointments.

Be it enacted by the Municipal Council of the United
Counties of Leeds and Grenville, and it is hereby enacted,
That the following persons be and they are hereby ap-
pointed Local Superintendents of Common Schools for
the residue of the current year, ending on the first day of
April next, viz:

**Wolford, Rev.
Ebenezer Morris.
Edwardsburgh,
William B. Im-
rie.**

For the Township of Wolford, the Reverend Ebenezer
Morris, in the place of Thomas Graffe, resigned; and for
the Township of Edwardsburgh, William B. Imrie, in the
place of the Reverend James Geggie, resigned.

(Signed,)   E. H. WHITMARSH, WARDEN.

[L. S.]

(Signed,)   JAMES JESSUP, COUNTY CLERK.

No. XCIV.—BY-LAW

To transfer that portion of the old Road, leading from Brockville to Smith's Falls, on lot number thirty-four in the eighth Concession of Elizabethtown, to Jacob Gallinger.—Passed June 22, 1855.

1. Be it enacted by the Municipal Council of the United Counties of Leeds and Grenville, and it is hereby enacted, that that part of the old or formerly travelled road leading from Brockville to Smith's Falls, which passes over or through lot number thirty-four, in the eighth Concession of the Township of Elizabethtown, be and the same is hereby granted and assigned, so far as this Council has the right to make such an assignment, to Jacob Gallinger, the proprietor of the said lot at the time of the construction of the Victoria Macadamized Toll Road, in lieu of and as a compensation for the land taken on the said lot from the said Jacob Gallinger for the said Victoria Macadamized Toll Road, and that the resolutions passed by this Council, ordering a deed to be given to Ira Lewis, be and the same are hereby rescinded.

Old road granted as compensation for land for Victoria Road.

(Signed,) E. H. WHITMARSH, Warden.
[L. S.]
(Signed,) JAMES JESSUP, County Clerk.

No. XCV.—BY-LAW

To regulate the management of the County Toll Roads.—Passed June 22, 1855.

(Repealed: see By-Law No. 231.)

No. XCVI.—BY-LAW

To Cover certain Grants of Money.—Passed 22nd June, 1855.

Be it enacted by the Municipal Council of the United Counties of Leeds and Grenville, and it is hereby enacted, that the several sums of money hereinafter mentioned shall be paid by the County Treasurer to the parties respectively, viz :—

Sums paid to.

Arza Parish — To Arza Parish, Esquire, the sum of two pounds ten shillings, for two days' attendance in settling claims against Brockville and Prescott.

S. B. Merrill. — To Stephen B. Merrill, the sum of twenty-nine pounds thirteen shillings and fourpence, for advertising.

Kemptville Progressionist. — To the Proprietor of the Kemptville *Progressionist* newspaper the sum of seven pounds eleven shillings and nine pence for advertising.

David Wylie. — To David Wylie the sum of fifty-three pounds ten shillings and eight pence, for advertising and printing.

Billings Kilborn. — To Billings Kilborn the sum of five shillings for repairing water pipe in Court House.

William Caffrey. — To William Caffrey the sum of twenty-eight pounds nineteen shillings for advertising and printing.

County Clerk. — To the County Clerk, the sum of seventeen shillings and eightpence, for postages disbursed for the Counties.

Gas Company. — To the Brockville Gas Company, the sum of three pounds fifteen shillings, for lighting the Court House.

Adam Anderson. — To Adam Anderson, the sum of six pounds eight shillings, for assessment covers, &c.

John L. Read. — To John L. Read, the sum of eight pounds, for services rendered as arbitrator on behalf of this Council.

Wm. P. Welton. — To William P. Welton, the sum of two pounds, for services rendered as arbitrator on behalf of this Council.

Michael Kelly. — To Michael Kelly, the sum of three pounds fifteen shillings, for putting up notices for the establishment of County Roads.

Harvey Miller. — To Harvey Miller, the sum of nine pounds seven shillings and sixpence, for work done in the Gaol.

Council of Rear Leeds and Lansdowne for Lyndhurst Bridge. — To the Municipal Council of the Rear of Leeds and Lansdowne, the sum of one hundred pounds, for the purpose of repairing the Bridge at Lyndhurst.

Jos. Pritchard. — To Joseph Pritchard, the sum of forty pounds fifteen shillings and four pence, for repairing the Kemptville and Prescott County Toll Road, provided his account be certified by the Commissioners of said Road to be correct.

To the Treasurer of the Board of Public Instruction at Kemptville, the sum of five pounds, for the expenses of the Board, as recommended by the first report of the Committee on Education, on the 23rd January last, and adopted by the Council. Kemptville Board Public Instruction.

To the Treasurer of the County Grammar School at Brockville, the sum of six pounds five shillings, for procuring apparatus as recommended by the Committee on Education, on the 12th October last, and adopted by the Council. Brockville Gram'ar School.

To the Municipal Council of Edwardsburgh, the sum of one hundred pounds, to aid in repairing Bridges on the front road in said Township. Council of Edwardsburgh.

To the Committee for the Registry Office of the County of Leeds, the sum of three hundred and fifty pounds, to be applied in building the said Office. Registry Office of Leeds.

To Christopher Leggo, the sum of one pound four shillings, for repairs to the Court House. Chris: Leggo.

To John McMullen, the sum of fourteen pounds eight shillings and six pence, for printing and stationery. John McMullen.

To the Reeve of North and South Crosby, the sum of thirty pounds, for the improvement of the Road on the Town Line between Burgess and Bastard, North Crosby and South Crosby. Reeves of North & South Crosby.

2. And be it further enacted, that the several sums in this section shall be paid to the parties respectively, viz. :— Sums paid to.

To George Weir, the sum of twenty-two pounds ten shillings, being the award of Arbitrators on his claim for damages to Lot number thirty-five in the Sixth Concession of the Township of Edwardsburgh, by running the Kemptville and Prescott County Toll Road through the said Lot. George Weir.

To John Crawford, the sum of eighteen pounds fifteen shillings, being the award of Arbitrators on his claim for damages to the north-east quarter of Lot John Crawford.

number nineteen in the ninth Concession of the Township of Edwardsburgh, by running the Kemptville and Prescott County Toll Road through that part of said Lot.

Thomas King. To Thomas King, the sum of thirty-five pounds, being the award of arbitrators on his claim for damages to Lot number twenty-three in the Eighth Concession of the Township of Edwardsburgh, by running the Kemptville and Prescott County Toll Road through the said Lot.

Hugh Ross. To Hugh Ross, the sum of nine pounds, being the award of Arbitrators on his claim for damages to the east half of Lot number thirteen, in the third Concession of the Township of Kitley, by running the Victoria Macadamized Road through a part of said Lot.

William Mara. To William Mara, the sum of nine pounds, being the award of Arbitrators on his claim for damages done on the north-west corner of Lot number twelve in the fourth Concession of the Township of Kitley, by running the Victoria Macadamized Road through a part of said Lot.

Ephraim Earl. To Ephraim Earl, the sum of ten pounds, being the award of Arbitrators on his claim for damages to Lot number twenty-nine, in the fifth Concession of the Township of Augusta, by running the Merrickville and Maitland County Toll Road through said Lot., in case the land shall be required for the said Road.

James Bryan. To James Bryan, the sum of three pounds, being the award of Arbitrators on his claim for damages to Lot number nineteen, in the seventh Concession of the Township of Wolford, by running the Merrickville and Maitland County Toll Road through or over said Lot.

Proviso. Provided always, nevertheless, that the said Treasurer shall not pay the said sums of money in this section mentioned, or any or either of them, until the parties respectively shall, at their own expense, furnish to this Municipality a good and sufficient title in law for the land taken from them respectively for the said Roads, subject to the approval of the County Clerk.

3. And be it further enacted, That the following sums Sums paid to. shall be paid by the said Treasurer to the parties respectively, viz. :—

To Levi Adams, the sum of one pound, for services as Levi Adams. Arbitrator on the claim of George Weir.

To John L. Read the sum of four pounds for services as John L Read. Arbitrator on the claims of John Crawford and Ephraim Earl.

To John M'Neil the sum of one pound for services as John McNeil. Arbitrator on the claim of John Crawford.

To Robert Smail the sum of one pound ten shillings, and Robert Smail. to William Stitt the sum of one pound, for services as Arbitrators on the claim of Thomas King.

To Hugh Kernahan the sum of two pounds, for services as Hugh Kernahan. Arbitrator on the claims of Hugh Ross and William Mara.

To Daniel Collins the sum of one pound, for services as Daniel Collins. Arbitrator on the claim of Ephraim Earl.

To John Hill and William P. Welton the sum of one John Hill and W. pound each, for services as Arbitrators on the claim P. Pelton. of James Bryan.

To the Committee for the Registry Office of the County Registry Office of of Grenville the sum of one hundred and seventy-five Grenville. pounds, to be applied in building the said Office.

To James Kincaid the sum of two pounds thirteen shillings James Kincaid. and one penny, for services as messenger and stationery furnished.

(Signed,) E. H. WHITMARSH, WARDEN.

[L. S.]

(Signed,) JAMES JESSUP, COUNTY CLERK.

No. XCVII.—BY-LAW

To provide for the Inspection of the County Toll Roads and for other purposes therein mentioned.—Passed 23rd June, 1855.

(Repealed; see By-law No. 231.)

No. XCVIII.—BY-LAW

To assess the United Counties of Leeds and Grenville for the year 1855.—Passed 23rd June, 1855.

Sums to be
levied.

Be it enacted by the Municipal Council of the United Counties of Leeds and Grenville, and it is hereby enacted, That there be raised and levied upon the whole rateable property in the said United Counties for the present year County rate. the sum of £5,997 5s 1d to defray the current expenses thereof, and the further sum of £1,181 4s 6d for the pay- Com'on Schools. ment of the salaries of legally qualified Common School Teachers, and the further sum of £3,813 17s 8d as a special Special Rate. rate, authorized to be raised and levied upon the said pro- perty, under the provisions of By-Laws numbers eight and thirty-nine, passed respectively on the tenth day of Octo- ber 1850, and the seventh day of May, 1852, and that the said several sums shall be raised and levied in addition to all other rates and assessments, and be apportioned to the several Municipalities of the said United Counties in the following manner, viz :—

Municipalities.	County Rate.			Common Schools.			Special Rate for County Roads.		
	£	s.	D.	£	s.	D.	£	s.	D.
Elizabethtown,	896	0	10	115	15	3	571	5	8
Bastard & Burgess,	325	2	5	109	18	0	206	13	3
Rear of Yonge and Escott	268	9	0	58	12	6	170	12	10
Front of Yonge and Escott	323	16	3	70	0	0	205	16	8
Front of Leeds and Lansdowne	383	5	1	94	3	0	243	12	4
Rear of Leeds and Lansdowne	161	12	1	40	8	6	102	14	6
North Crosby,	121	4	3	43	8	0	77	1	0
Elmsley,	95	7	5	32	0	6	60	12	5
Kitley,	312	4	8	92	12	9	198	9	5
South Crosby,	167	3	0	31	18	9	106	5	0
Town of Brockville.	740	2	7	....			470	9	4
Augusta,	549	7	6	115	4	9	349	4	3
Edwardsburgh,	376	0	2	119	3	6	239	0	3
Oxford,	421	12	8	147	0	0	268	0	3
South Gower.	129	10	11	22	8	0	82	6	11
Wolford,	298	6	6	88	11	0	189	12	7
Town of Prescott,	427	19	0	....			272	1	0
	£5997	5	1	1181	4	6	3813	17	8

How apportion'd to Municipalit's.

2. That the said several sums hereinbefore directed to be raised and levied in the said Municipalities respectively shall be placed on the Collector's Roll by the Clerks thereof, in separate columns, and collected in like manner as all other rates and assessments are by law directed to be collected, and that every Collector shall, on or before the fourteenth day of December next, return his Roll to the Treasurer of the Municipality, and pay over to him the sums hereby directed to be raised, levied and collected therein.

How levied and collected.

3. That the said Municipalities respectively shall, on the completion of the Collector's Roll, cause a statement of the total of each of the said rates hereby imposed to be furnished to the County Treasurer as the same shall appear upon such Rolls respectively.

Statement for Treasurer.

(Signed,) E. H. WHITMARSH, WARDEN.

[L. S.]

(Signed,) JAMES JESSUP, COUNTY CLERK.

No. XCIX.—BY-LAW

To authorise the Erection of a Registry Office in the County of Leeds.—Passed October 9, 1855.

Whereas this Council have granted and appropriated the sum of six hundred pounds of lawful money of Canada to provide a safe and proper fire-proof Office for the keeping of all Books, Records, and other papers belonging to the Office of Register of the County of Leeds, in pursuance of the 19th section of the Act 9th Victoria, chapter 34, and did also on the twenty-third day of June, in the year of our Lord one thousand eight hundred and fifty-four, in and by a certain resolution then passed, nominate and appoint William Garvey, Fordyce Lawton Lothrop, and Robert Peden, all of the Town of Brockville, Merchants, a Building Committee for the erection of the said Registry Office, but did not define the duties and powers of the said Committee; And whereas the said Committee have selected and fixed upon that piece or parcel of land being the south west angle of the Court House and Gaol block, at the intersection of Church and William Streets, in the Town of Brockville, for the Site of the Registry Office

Preamble.

aforesaid, and have for and on behalf of this Council entered into a Contract with Henry Bradfield, the younger, of the Township of Elizabethtown, Gentleman, for the erection of the said Registry Office on the said Site, according to the plans, elevations and specifications procured and approved by the said Committee, and which are annexed to the said Contract. And whereas it is necessary to confirm the acts of the said Committee in this respect :

Site, &c., confirmed. Be it therefore enacted by the Municipal Council of the United Counties of Leeds and Grenville, and it is hereby enacted, That the selection of the said Site for the said Registry Office by the said Committee, and all and every their other proceedings and acts for and in respect of the said Registry Office, shall be and they are hereby approved and confirmed, as having been done and executed for and on behalf of and by this Corporation, in pursuance of the said in part recited Act.

2. That as soon as the said Registry Office shall be erected and completely finished, according to the said contract, and to the entire satisfaction of the said Committee, who are hereby authorized and empowered to *When complet'd, declared to be Registry Office of the County of Leeds.* accept and receive the same for and on behalf of this Corporation, and from and after the day it shall be so accepted and received it is hereby declared to be the Registry Office of the County of Leeds, erected in pursuance of the 19th section of the said in part recited Act.

3. That in case the said Committee shall accept and receive the said Registry Office, as provided in the second section of this By-Law, they shall thereupon endorse on *Certificate to be endorsed on Contract.* the said contract a certificate to that effect, and that the said contract so certified shall be kept by the Clerk among the records of the said Corporation as evidence of such acceptance.

(Signed,)　E. H. WHITMARSH, Warden.

[L. S.]

(Signed,)　JAMES JESSUP, Clerk.

No. C.—BY-LAW

To authorize the erection of a Registry Office in the County of Leeds.—Passed 9th October, 1855.

Whereas this Council have granted and appropriated the sum of four hundred and forty-five pounds of lawful money of Canada to purchase a lot in the Town of Prescott, for and to provide a safe and proper fire-proof Office for the keeping of all books, records and other papers belonging to the Office of Register of the County of Grenville, in pursuance of the 19th section of the Act 9th Victoria, chapter 34, and did nominate and appoint the Warden, for the time being, William H. Brouse and Chauncey H. Peck, a Building Committee for the erection of the said Registry Office, but did not fully define the duties and powers of the said Committee. And whereas this Council did, on the twenty-sixth day of October, in the year of our Lord one thousand eight hundred and fifty-three, purchase of and from Hamilton D. Jessup, of the Town of Prescott aforesaid, Esquire, the west half of Town Lot number twenty-six, fronting on the north side of Henry Street, as laid down on the additional plan of the survey of the Town Plot of Prescott aforesaid, for the site of the said Registry Office, which said half lot is more particularly described in the deed or conveyance from the said Hamilton D. Jessup to the said Council, reference thereto will more fully and at large appear; And whereas it is considered advisable by the said Committee to sell the said half lot so purchased of the said Hamilton D. Jessup, and to purchase another site in the said Town of Prescott for the said Registry Office; And whereas the said Committee have agreed and bargained with William Patrick, of the Town of Prescott aforesaid, Esquire, to purchase the front part of the east half of Town Lot number eighteen on the north side of Henry Street aforesaid, extending back from the said street fifty feet and of uniform width, as a site for the said Registry Office, and have for and on behalf of the said Council entered into a contract with Thomas S. Fox, of the Town of Prescott aforesaid, builder, for the erection of the said Registry Office on the said last mentioned lot or site, according to the plans, elevations and specifications procured and approved by the said Committee, and accompanying the said contract; And whereas it is expedient and necessary to confirm the acts of the said Committee in reference

Preamble.

Site purchased of H. D. Jessup.

Warden to convey the same. Exchanged for that bought of Wm. Patrick.

Contractor, T. S. Fox.

thereto; Be it therefore enacted by the Municipal Council of the United Counties of Leeds and Grenville, and it is hereby enacted, That the selection of the said lot so purchased of the said William Patrick, as a site for the said Registry Office, and all and every the other proceedings and acts of the said Committee, for and in respect to the erection of the said Registry Office shall be and they are hereby approved and confirmed as having been done

Approval of site. and executed for and on behalf of and by this Corporation, in pursuance of the said in part recited Act.

2. That the Warden be and he is hereby authorized and

Warden to convey lot purchas'd of H. D. Jessup to Wm. Patrick empowered to convey to the said William Patrick the said half lot so purchased of the said Hamilton D. Jessup, as part of the consideration for the said lot sold by him to the said Council, and to take, accept and receive of and

To take deed from W. Patrick. from the said William Patrick a good and sufficient deed in law, in the corporate name of the said Council, conveying a fee simple estate in the said lot so purchased of him by the said Committee as the site for the said Registry Office, and containing the requisite release of dower and covenants of title.

3. That as soon as the said Registry Office shall be

When complet'd, declared to be Registry Office of the County of Grenville. erected and completely finished, according to the said contract, and to the entire satisfaction of the said Committee, who are hereby authorized and empowered to accept and receive the same for and on behalf of this Corporation, and from and after the day it shall be so accepted and received it is hereby declared to be the Registry Office of the County of Grenville, erected in pursuance of the 19th section of the said in part recited Act.

4. That in case the said Committee shall accept and receive the said Registry Office, as provided in the next preceding section of this By-Law, they shall thereupon

Certificate to be endorsed on contract. endorse on the said contract a certificate to that effect, and that the said contract so certified shall be kept by the Clerk, together with the plans, elevations and specifications among the records of the said Corporation, as evidence of such acceptance.

(Signed,)   E. H. WHITMARSH, Warden.

[L. S.]

(Signed,)   JAMES JESSUP, Clerk.

No. CI.—BY-LAW

To provide for Macadamizing the Roads therein mentioned.
—Passed 11th October, 1855.

(Repealed : see By-Law No. 231.)

No. CII.—BY-LAW

To cover certain grants of money.—Passed October 11, 1855.

Be it enacted by the Municipal Council of the United Counties of Leeds and Grenville, and it is hereby enacted, Sums paid to. That the several sums of money hereinafter in this section mentioned, shall be paid by the County Treasurer to the parties respectively, viz:—

To the County Clerk, the sum of two pounds seven County Clerk. shillings and two pence, for disbursements made by him for the Counties.

To William Fitzsimmons, the sum of one pound eighteen William Fitzsimmons. shillings and three pence, for work done on the Court House and Gaol.

To Alfred Poulton, the sum of five pounds, for work Alfred Poulton. done in Court House and Gaol according to contract.

To David Wylie, the sum of seventeen pounds seven- David Wylie. teen shillings and eight pence, for printing and advertising.

To Thomas Robertson, the sum of ten pounds, for super- Thos. Robertson. intending work on the County Road from Spencerville to Christie's Corners.

To Michael Kelly, the sum of twelve pounds, for services Michael Kelly. as County Surveyor.

To Harvey Miller, the sum of three pounds, for work Harvey Miller. done on the Court House and Jail.

The David Wylie, the sum of five pounds, for ten days D. Wylie. attendance to report the proceedings of the Council at the June and present meeting.

To William Caffrey, the sum of two pounds ten shillings, William Caffrey. for reporting in June and at the present meeting.

Council of South Gower. To the Municipal Council of the Township of South Gower, the sum of ten pounds, to aid that Municipality in repairing certain bridges therein; provided the said Council of South Gower provide and expend an equal amount.

James Keeler. To James Keeler, Esquire, the sum of twenty-eight pounds five shillings, being balance due him on settlement with the Warden.

James Kincaid. To James Kincaid, the sum of two pounds and three pence, for services as messenger and stationery furnished.

Chris. Leggo. To Christopher Leggo, the sum of one pound two shillings and six pence, for fuel and cleaning Council Room.

Taxes due by Prescott granted for repair of road to Kemptville. 2. That the sum of two hundred and thirty-two pounds two shillings and six pence, being the amount of balance of taxes due by the Town of Prescott to this Council, be granted for the purpose of repairing the Macadamized Road leading through the said Town to the termination of the Kemptville and Prescott Toll Road, and that the money, when paid over to the County Treasurer, shall be **How to be expended.** subject to the orders of and be expended by the Commissioners of the County Toll Roads.

(Signed,)   E. H. WHITMARSH, Warden.

[L. S.]

(Signed,)   JAMES JESSUP, Clerk.

No. CIII.—BY-LAW

To authorize the Board of Commissioners for the County Toll Roads to execute the Contract with Robert Peden, Esquire, for the completion of the said Roads.—Passed October 12th, 1855.

(Repealed: see By-law No. 231.)

No. CIV.—BY-LAW

To provide for the payment of Jurors.—Passed October 12, 1855.

Whereas it is expedient and necessary to comply with the provisions of the Act 14 and 15 Vic., chap. 14, entituled, "An Act to provide for the payment of Jurors in Upper Canada," and to make provision for that purpose in the United Counties of Leeds and Grenville: Be it therefore enacted by the Municipal Council of the said United Counties, and it is hereby enacted, That every Grand and Petit Juryman, actually attending any of the Courts of Assize and Nisi Prius, Oyer and Terminer, General Gaol Delivery, General Quarter Sessions of the Peace or County Court, held in the said United Counties, shall be paid the sum of five shillings per day for every day he shall attend such Court, and the sum of six pence for every mile he shall necessary travel from his place of residence to the Court House in the Town of Brockville, subject always to the provisions contained in the first, fourth and sixth sections of the said in part recited Act. *Preamble.* *To be paid five shillings per day, and six-pence per mile.*

2. That the sum of five hundred pounds annually be appropriated for the payment of Jurors out of the County Funds and which sum, with all fines and penalties imposed and levied in the said Counties, not payable to the Receiver General, and all fines upon Jurors for non-attendance levied in the said Counties, and all fees and sums of money applicable under the said Act, shall form a fund for the payment of Jurors in the said United Counties. *£500 appropriated, besides fines, &c.*

3. That the Sheriff be paid the sum of ten shillings for every Jury List, and five shillings per day for checking the same at the opening of the Court, to be paid by the County Treasurer on the affidavit of the Sheriff or his Deputy that the same is correct, such affidavit to be taken by any Justice of the Peace of the said United Counties which shall be sufficient voucher to the said Treasurer for such payment in the audit of his accounts. *Fees to Sheriff.*

4. That this By-Law shall come into force and take effect, upon, from and after the first day of January, in the year of our Lord one thousand eight hundred and fifty-six, and not before. *By-Law to take effect 1st January, 1856.*

(Signed,)   E. H. WHITMARSH, Warden.
[L. S.]
(Signed,)   JAMES JESSUP, Clerk.

T

No. CV.—BY-LAW

To provide for the payment of certain grants of Money.—
Passed 12th October, 1855.

Be it enacted by the Municipal Council of the United Counties of Leeds and Grenville, and it is hereby enacted, That the further sum of one hundred pounds be granted to the Municipal Council of the Rear of Leeds and Lansdowne, for the purpose of erecting a new Bridge over the Gananoque waters at the village of Lyndhurst, and that the said sum be paid by the County Treasurer on the certificate or order of the Reeve of that Municipality.

Grant for Lyndhurst Bridge.

2. That the sum of ten pounds be granted to the Municipal Council of the Township of Elmsley, to be expended on the Road leading from the Town Line of Kitley to Oliver's Ferry, provided the Municipality of Elmsley expend a like sum on the said Road.

Council of Elmsley.

2. That the sum of three pounds three shillings be paid to Wm. Buell, Esquire, for stationery furnished.

William Buell.

(Signed,)   E. H. WHITMARSH, Warden.

[L. S.]

(Signed,)   JAMES JESSUP, Clerk.

No. CVI.—BY-LAW

To appoint Local Superintendents of Common Schools in the United Counties of Leeds and Grenville.—Passed January 30, 1856.

Be it enacted by the Municipal Council of the United Counties of Leeds and Grenville, and it is hereby enacted, that the following persons be and they are hereby appointed Local Superintendents of Schools, for the respective Municipalities hereinafter mentioned, such appointments to commence on the first day of April next, and not before, viz:—

Appointments.

Augusta...........................James Clapperton.
Oxford...........................Andrew Holmes.
Front of Yonge and Escott.......Thomas Vanston.
Front of Leeds and Lansdowne...Thomas Vanston.

Rear of Yonge and Escott................Arza Parish.
Elizabethtown......................Jacob A. Brown.
Edwardsburgh...................William B. Imrie.
South Gower.....................Rev. Joseph Anderson.
Wolford.........................Rev. Ebenezer Morris.
Kitley..........................Robert W. Ferguson.
Elmsley.........................Edward F. Weeks.
Bastard and Burgess.............Lewis Chipman.
South Crosby....................Wm. Robert Taylor.
North Crosby....................Wm. Robert Taylor.
Rear of Leeds and Lansdowne.....Henry P. Washburn.

     (Signed,)   E. H. WHITMARSH, Warden.
  [L. S.]
(Signed,)   JAMES JESSUP, Clerk.

No. CVII.—BY-LAW.

*To appoint Trustees for each of the County Grammar
Schools, in the places of those retiring from office on the
31st day of January, 1856.—Passed January 30, 1856.*

Be it enacted by the Municipal Council of the United
Counties of Leeds and Grenville, and it is hereby enacted,
that the persons hereinafter mentioned are selected and
appointed Trustees of the County Grammar Schools in the <small>Appointments.</small>
said United Counties, as they are respectively assigned to
each of the said Schools, that is to say:

For the County Grammar School at Brockville, Richard <small>Brockville Sch'l.</small>
Farmer Steele, re-elected, and the Rev. Edmund John
Senkler, in the place of the Rev. John McMurray.

For the County Grammar School at Kemptville, Rev. <small>Kemptville Sch'l.</small>
Daniel Farley, re-elected, and Joseph Bower in the place
of Joseph Leeming.

For the County Grammar School at Prescott, Alpheus <small>Prescott School.</small>
Jones, re-elected, and John Patton, re-elected.

For the County Grammar School at Gananoque, Hon. <small>Gananoque Sch'l</small>
John McDonald, re-elected, and Thomas Vanston, re-
elected.

     (Signed,)   E. H. WHITMARSH, Warden.
  [L. S.]
(Signed,)   JAMES JESSUP, Clerk.

No. CVIII.—BY-LAW.

To authorize a temporary Loan until the Assessments for the present year become available.—Passed February 2, 1856.

(Repealed : see By-Law No. 228, sec. 4.)

———

No. CIX.—BY-LAW

To cover certain Grants of Money.—Passed February 2, 1856.

Be it enacted by the Municipal Council of the United Counties of Leeds and Grenville, and it is hereby enacted,

Sums paid to. That the several sums of money hereinafter in this section mentioned, shall be paid by the County Treasurer to the parties respectively, viz :—

County Clerk. To the County Clerk, the sum of one pound five shillings and one penny, for postages and charges on journals and school registers, disbursed by him for the Counties.

S. B. Merrill. To S. B. Merrill, the sum of three pounds twelve shillings and two pence, for printing and advertising.

David Wylie. To David Wylie, the sum of twenty pounds eighteen shillings and eight pence, for printing and advertising.

William Caffrey. To William Caffrey, the sum of six pounds five shillings and five pence, for printing and advertising.

Philo Hicock. To Philo Hicock, the sum of five pounds, for services as Commissioner of the Gananoque Bridge.

Edward Green. To Edward Green, the sum of four pounds, for services as Commissioner of the Gananoque Bridge.

James Kirker. To James Kirker, the sum of four pounds fifteen shillings, for services as Commissioner of the Gananoque Bridge, and for disbursements.

Snooks & Cole. To Snooks and Cole, the sum of four pounds two shillings and six pence, for making and fitting up hot-air case in the Gaol, and for Iron elbow.

To Harvey Miller, the sum of two pounds seventeen shil- Harvey Miller.
lings and six pence, for Iron work in the Gaol.

To Hugh Kernahan, the sum of two pounds and five shil- Hugh Kernahan.
lings, in full of his claims for services as Arbitrator
in certain Road cases.

To John McMullen, the sum of two pounds, for stationery John McMullen.
furnished.

To James Edgar, the sum of twenty pounds; to Robert James Edgar.
Hunt, the sum of five pounds; to Robert Bruce, the Robert Hunt.
sum of ten pounds, and to Francis Scott, the sum of Francis Scott.
three pounds fifteen shillings, for damages awarded
to them respectively, for lands taken for the construction of the Victoria Macadamized Road, provided
that the said parties first execute a sufficient deed of
conveyance to this Council of the lands taken from
them respectively for the said road, and also sign
receipts in full for the said damages, such deeds to
be subject to the approval of the County Clerk.

To W. B. M'Clean, the sum of one pound ten shillings, W. B. McClean.
for drawing leases of Toll Gates in 1854.

To C. H. Ganesby, the sum of ten pounds for surveying C. H. Ganesby.
road from Gananoque to the Pittsburgh line.

To the Commissioners for the Gananoque Bridge, the sum Commissioners
of fifty-five pounds nineteen shillings, to meet the Gan'oque Bridge
payment of disbursements attached to their report,
remaining unpaid, the said sum to be paid out of the
fund for the said bridge.

To Ambrose Clothier, the sum of one hundred pounds in Ambrose
full of all claims against this Council, for and in Clothier.
respect to his Contracts on the Kemptville and Prescott County Toll Road.

To John Crawford, the sum of four pounds, for services John Crawford.
as Arbitrator.

To Henry Freeland, the sum of two pounds five shillings, Henry Freeland.
for services as Arbitrator.

To David Jones, the sum of ten shillings, for searches in David Jones.
the Registry Office.

Gas Company   To the Brockville Gas Company, the sum of three pounds seventeen shillings and six-pence, for Gas furnished in Court House.

Wm. Gilmour.   To William Gilmour, the sum of two pounds two shillings, for cast iron chambers for the use of prisoners in Gaol.

Henry Bull.   To Henry Bull, the sum of two pounds ten shillings, for painting and lettering Toll Boards for the Prescott and Kemptville Toll Road Gates.

Edward Green   To Edward Green, the sum of twenty-three pounds, for services as Commissioner of County Toll Roads.

Allan Hunter.   To Allan Hunter, the sum of fifteen pounds, for services as Commissioner of County Toll Roads.

E. H. Whitmarsh.   To E. H. Whitmarsh, the sum of four pounds, for services as Commissioner of County Toll Roads.

A. N. Richards.   To Albert N. Richards, the sum of five pounds in full, for drawing contracts for the Gananoque Bridge.

James Agnew.   To James Agnew, the sum of two pounds ten shillings, for drawing agreement including specifications for Gananoque Bridge.

James Kincaid.   To James Kincaid, the sum of three pounds three shillings and six pence, for services as messenger and stationery furnished.

David Wylie.   To David Wylie, the sum of three pounds for six days reporting during this session.

William Caffrey.   To William Caffrey, the sum of three pounds, for six days reporting during this session.

Chris. Leggo.   To Christopher Leggo, the sum of one pound nineteen shillings, for fuel, &c., furnished during this session.

(Signed,)   E. H. WHITMARSH, WARDEN.

[L. S.]

(Signed,)   JAMES JESSUP, CLERK.

No, CX.—BY-LAW

To authorize a temporary loan until the Assessments for the present year become available.—Passed 5th March, 1856.

(Repealed : See By-law No. 228, Sec. 4.)

No, CXI.—BY-LAW

To Cover certain Grants of Money—Passed 6th March, 1856.

Be it enacted by the Municipal Council of the United Counties of Leeds and Grenville, and it is hereby enacted, that the several sums of money hereinafter mentioned, shall be paid by the County Treasurer to the parties respectively, viz. :— Sums paid to.

To Adam Anderson, the sum of three pounds sixteen shillings, for portfolios for assessment rolls. Adam Anderson.

To Allan Hunter, the sum of three pounds ten shillings, for attendance as one of the Commissioners of the County Toll Roads, at the Council in January, five days, and in March 1856, two days. Allan Hunter.

To R. W. Kelly, the sum of five pounds fifteen shillings, for advertising county matters to 19th December, 1855, in the Kemptville *Progressionist.* R. W. Kelly.

To John Davidson, the sum of one pound ten shillings, for services as Arbitrator. John Davidson.

To William Fitzsimmons, the sum of five pounds ten shillings, for work in the Court House, and the further sum of one pound ten shillings for work in the said Court House. William Fitzsimmons.

To David Wylie, the sum of twenty-three pounds, for Assessment and Collectors blanks furnished to Council. D. Wylie.

To James Kincaid, the sum of one pound ten shillings, for services as Messenger at the present meeting. James Kincaid.

D. Wylie.

To David Wylie, the sum of two pounds, and to William Caffrey, the sum of two pounds, for four days reporting at the present meeting.

(Signed,)   E. H. WHITMARSH, WARDEN.

[L. S.]

(Signed,)   JAMES JESSUP, CLERK.

No. CXII.—BY-LAW

To repeal a part of the third section of By-law numbered sixty-three.—Passed 7th March, 1856.

(Repealed: see By-Law No. 231.)

No. CXIII.—BY-LAW

To authorize the execution of the new contract between Robert Peden, Esq., and this Council, for the completion and keeping in repair the four County Toll Roads.—Passed 7th March, 1856.

Warden to execute contract.

Be it enacted by the Municipal Council of the United Counties of Leeds and Grenville, and it is hereby enacted, That the Warden of the said United Counties be, and is hereby authorized and empowered to sign and fully execute the new contract between Robert Peden, Esq., and the Municipal Council of the said United Counties, for the completion and keeping in repair of the County Toll Roads therein mentioned, (such contract having been accepted and approved of by said Council,) and that the Warden at the time of such execution, do affix the Seal of the Corporation thereto.

(Signed,)   E. H. WHITMARSH, WARDEN.

[L. S.]

(Signed,)   JAMES JESSUP, CLERK.

No. CXIV.—BY-LAW

To establish Toll Gates and Toll Houses on the four County
Toll Roads.—Passed 7th March, 1856.

(Repealed; see By-Law No. 231.)

No. CXV—BY-LAW

To amend By-law numbered ninety-seven.—Passed 7th
March, 1856.

(Repealed ; see By-law No. 231.)

No. CXVI.—BY-LAW

To amend part of the tenth Section of By-Law numbered
forty-seven.—Passed 19th June, 1856.

(Repealed : see By-Law No. 231.)

No. CXVII.—BY-LAW

To assess the United Counties of Leeds and Grenville
—Passed 19th June, 1856.

Be it enacted by the Municipal Council of the United
Counties of Leeds and Grenville, and it is hereby enacted, **Sums to be levied.**
That there be raised and levied upon the whole rateable
property in the said United Counties for the present year
the sum of £5,000 to defray the current expenses there- **County rate.**
of, and the further sum of £1,322. 1s. 1d. for the pay-
ment of the salaries of legally qualified Common School **Com'on Schools.**
Teachers, and the further sum of £3,813 17s 8d as a special
rate, authorized to be raised and levied upon the said pro- **Special Rate for**
perty, under the provisions of By-Laws numbered eight and **County Roads.**
thirty-nine, passed respectively on the tenth day of Octo-
ter 1850, and the seventh day of May, 1852, and that the
said several sums shall be raised and levied in addition to

all other rates and assessments, and be apportioned to the several Municipalities of the said United Counties in the following manner, viz:—

Municipalities.	County Rate.			Common Schools.			Special Rate for County Roads.		
	£	s.	D.	£	s.	D.	£	s.	D.
Elizabethtown,. ...748		19	1	148	3	8	571	5	8
Bastard & Burgess,. .270		18	8	120	16	0	206	13	3
Rear of Yonge and Escott............223		14	3	53	13	0	170	12	10
Front of Yonge and Escott.... 269		16	10	79	18	5	205	16	8
Front of Leeds and Lansdowne 319		7	9	102	13	6	243	12	4
Rear of Leeds and Lansdowne.....134		13	5	50	6	5	102	14	6
Kitley,. 260		4	0	109	17	9	198	9	5
North Crosby, ...101		0	2	49	2	4	77	1	0
South Crosby, ...139		5	10	40	12	2	106	5	0
Elmsley,. 79		9	7	27	13	2	60	12	5
Brockville 616		15	7	....			470	9	4
Augusta,..........457		16	3	156	12	1	349	4	3
Edwardsburgh,....313		6	10	121	1	8	239	0	3
Oxford,.........351		7	4	148	0	0	268	0	3
Wolford,.........248		12	2	90	11	1	189	12	7
South Gower.....107		19	2	23	0	8	82	6	11
Prescott, ...356		13	1	....			272	1	0
Totals.....£5000		0	0	1322	1	11	3813	17	8

How apportion'd to Municipalti's.

2. That the said several sums hereinbefore directed to be raised and levied in the said Municipalities respectively shall be placed on the Collector's Roll by the Clerk thereof, in separate columns, and collected in like manner as all other rates and assessments are by law directed to be collected, and that every Collector shall, on or before the fourteenth day of December next, return his Roll to the Treasurer of the Municipality, for which he is appointed and pay over to him the sums hereby directed to be raised, levied and collected therein.

How levied and collected.

3. That the said Municipalities respectively shall, on the completion of the Collector's Roll, cause a statement of the total of each of the said rates hereby imposed to be

Statement] for Treasurer.

furnished to the County Treasurer as the same shall appear upon such Rolls respectively.

(Signed,)   E. H. WHITMARSH, Warden.

[L. S.]

(Signed,) JAMES JESSUP, Clerk.

No. CXVIII.—BY-LAW

*To provide for the payment of certain Grants of Money.—
Passed 20th June, 1856.*

Be it enacted by the Municipal Council of the United Counties of Leeds and Grenville, and it is hereby enacted, That the several sums of money hereinafter mentioned in this section, shall be paid by the County Treasurer to the parties respectively, viz:— Sums paid to.

To David Wylie, the sum of forty eight pounds fourteen shillings and ten pence for printing and advertising. David Wylie.

To Harvey Miller, the sum of seven pounds fourteen shillings and three pence, for work done to the Court House and Gaol. Harvey Miller.

To Stephen B. Merrill, the sum of six pounds one shilling and two pence, for printing and advertising. Stephen B. Merrill.

To William Caffrey, the sum of one pound fourteen shillings and three pence, for printing and advertising. William Caffrey.

To the Chairman of the Board of Commissioners of the County Toll Roads, the sum of twenty-seven pounds, for services as Commissioner. Commissioners County Roads.

To Messrs. Landon and Hill, the sum of four pounds ten shillings for services on Special Committee relating to Roads and repairing Bridge on Merickville and Maitland Road. Messrs. Landon and Hill.

To the Commissioners of the Registry Office, for the County of Grenville, the sum of one hundred pounds, to complete the said office. Grenville Registry Office.

John McMullen. To John M'Mullen, the sum of twenty-seven pounds twelve shillings and three pence, for printing and advertising, to be received by him as in full payment of his account.

Adam Anderson. To Adam Anderson, the sum of one pound fourteen shillings, for covers for Collector's Rolls.

Edward Green. To Edward Green, the sum of fourteen pounds ten shillings, for services as Commissioner of the County Roads.

County Clerk. To the County Clerk, the sum of eighteen shillings, for postages disbursed for the Counties.

R. W. Kelly. To R. W. Kelley, the sum of ten pounds eighteen shillings and eight pence, for printing and advertising.

Chris. Leggo. To Christopher Leggo, the sum of two pounds two shillings and nine pence, for fuel for Council, and cleaning Court Room.

Gas Company. To Brockville Gas Light Company, the sum of four pounds two shillings and six pence, for Gas furnished the Counties.

James Kincaid. To James Kincaid, the sum of two pounds eight shillings and three pence, for stationery furnished, and services as messenger of the Council.

(Signed,)   E. H. WHITMARSH, Warden.
[L. S.]
(Signed,)   JAMES JESSUP, Clerk.

No. CXIX,—BY-LAW

To repeal By-Law numbered forty.—Passed 20th June, 1856.

Repeal. Be it enacted by the Municipal Council of the United Counties of Leeds and Grenville, and it is hereby enacted, That By-Law numbered forty, passed on the 7th day of May, 1852, and entituled "By-Law to regulate the Printing of the Council," be repealed, and the same is hereby repealed.

(Signed,)   E. H. WHITMARSH, Warden.
[L. S.]
(Signed,)   JAMES JESSUP, Clerk.

No. CXX.—BY-LAW

*To authorize the negotiation of a Loan of money by the issue
of Debentures to pay the debt and other liabilities therein
mentioned.—Passed 13th October, 1856.*

Whereas it is necessary to raise, by way of loan, on the Preamble.
securities hereinafter mentioned, the sum of seven thousand
five hundred pounds, of lawful money of Canada, to pay off
the debt of the United Counties of Leeds and Grenville
to the Commercial Bank of the Midland District, and
other liabilities thereof; and whereas it will be necessary to
raise the sum of £1,076 annually, as a special rate for the
payment of the said loan and the interest thereon, at the
several days and times herein limited for the payment
thereof; and whereas the valuation of the whole rateable
property of the said United Counties for the year 1855
was £1,786,869 0s 10d; and whereas the annual rate in
the pound upon such property required as a special rate
for the payment of the interest and the creation of a sinking fund for the payment of the principal of a loan of £7,500
is one-seventh of a penny in the pound:

Be it therefore enacted by the Municipal Council of the
United Counties of Leeds and Grenville, in Council assembled, and it is hereby enacted as follows:

1. That it shall and may be lawful for the Warden of
the said United Counties for the time being, to raise, by
way of Loan, from any person or persons, body, corporate
or politic, who may be willing to advance the same upon
the credit of the Debentures hereinafter mentioned, and
the special rate hereinafter imposed, a sum not exceeding Loan £7,500.
in the whole the sum of seven thousand five hundred
pounds, of lawful money of Canada, and to cause the same
to be paid into the hands of the Treasurer of the said
United Counties, for the time being, to be by him employed in the payment of the said debt to the Commercial
Bank aforesaid, and the remainder in such manner as the
said Council shall from time to time direct.

2. That it shall and may be lawful for the Warden to
cause or direct any number of Debentures to be made out Warden to issue
for such sum or sums of money, not exceeding in the debentures.
whole the sum of seven thousand five hundred pounds, as
any person or persons, body, corporate or politic, shall
agree to advance on the credit of such Debentures; the

Rate of interest. said Debentures to bear interest at the rate of six per centum per annum, and to be signed by the Warden, Treasurer and Clerk, and made out in such manner and form as they or a majority of them shall think fit.

How interest and principal to be paid. 3. That the interest on the said Debentures shall be payable half-yearly, at the County Treasurer's Office, in the Town of Brockville, and the principal of the said loan shall be payable at the said Treasurer's Office in ten years from the date of the Debentures.

Special Rate. 4. That a special rate of one-seventh of a penny in the pound upon the assessed value of the whole rateable property in the United Counties, over and above and in addition to all other rates whatsoever, shall be levied annually for ten years from the time this By-law shall take effect and come into operation, for the payment of the interest, and the creation of a sinking fund for the payment of the principal of the said Debentures to be issued under this By-law.

Sinking Fund. 5. That it shall be the duty of the said Treasurer to invest all sums of money raised by special rate for the sinking fund, provided in this By-law, in any Government Debentures of this Province, or in such other manner as directed by the one hundred and seventy-seventh section of the Municipal Corporations Act of Upper Canada.

When By-Law to take effect. 6. That this By-law shall take effect and come into force upon, from and after the thirteenth day of October, in the year of our Lord one thousand eight hundred and fifty-six.

(Signed,) E. H. WHITMARSH, Warden.

[L. S.]

(Signed,) JAMES JESSUP, Clerk.

No. CXXI.—BY-LAW

To Cover certain Grants of Money.—Passed October 14, 1856.

Be it enacted, by the Municipal Council of the United Counties of Leeds and Grenville, and it is hereby enacted, Sums paid to. That the several sums of money hereinafter mentioned, shall be paid by the County Treasurer to the parties respectively, viz:

To John Watson, the sum of nine pounds twelve shillings **John Watson.**
and six pence ; Samuel Armstrong, the sum of fifteen **Sam. Armstrong.**
pounds ; Bazail Thrasher, the sum of fourteen pounds **Bazail Thrasher.**
ten shillings ; George Adams, the sum of twenty- **George Adams.**
three pounds fifteen shillings; James Graham, the sum **James Graham.**
of seventeen pounds ten shillings, and John Edgar, the **John Edgar.**
sum of two pounds fourteen shillings—being the
amounts allowed to them respectively in the awards of
the Arbitrators appointed to ascertain the damages
done to their respective properties by the construction
of the County Toll Roads, provided that the said parties do give good and sufficient deeds, free of expense,
to this Municipality, for the lands for which the above
awards have been made, such deeds to be subject to
the approval of the Clerk.

To Thomas Newson, the sum of one pound ten shillings; **Thos. Newson.**
Hugh Kernahan, the sum of one pound ten shillings; **Hugh Kernahan.**
Robert Pedan, the sum of two pounds five shillings ; **Robert Peden.**
James Gibson the sum of one pound ten shillings; **James Gibson.**
Daniel McGaudy, the sum of fifteen shillings; Henry **Daniel McGaudy**
Bradshaw the sum of fifteen shillings William B. **Harry Bradshaw.**
Imrie, the sum of two pounds five shillings; and **W. B Imrie.**
John Crawford, the sum of six pounds fifteen shill- **John Crawford.**
ings, for services as Arbitrators in the foregoing cases.

To the County Clerk, the sum of one pound eighteen **County Clerk.**
shillings and five pence, for disbursements for the
Counties.

To the Warden, the sum of twenty-five pounds, in full for **Warden.**
his services out of Council for the current year, in
lieu of the sum of one pound per day, as fixed by
By-Law.

To James Kincaid, the sum of eighteen shillings and three **James Kincaid.**
pence, for stationery furnished and services as Messen-
ger of the Council.

To David Wylie, the sum of one pound, for reporting the **David Wylie.**
proceedings of this Council at the present Session,
and also the sum of two pounds ten shillings, for
reporting the proceedings of the June Session.

To John McMullen, the sum of two pounds ten shillings, **John McMullen.**
for reporting the proceedings of the June Session of
the Council.

Edward Green. To Edward Green, the sum of eighteen pounds, for services as Commissioner for the County Roads.

Alfred Poulton. To Alfred Poulton, the sum of three pounds, for repairing windows in the Court House and Gaol for the past year.

Harvey Miller. To Harvey Miller, the sum of six pounds seven shillings and three pence, for work done to the Gaol.

Henry Bradfield. To Henry Bradfield, the younger, the sum of thirteen pounds five shillings and six pence half penny, being balance due to him for building the Registry Office for the County of Leeds, and that the same be received by him in full satisfaction for all claims on this Council in respect to the building of such Office.

(Signed,) E. H. WHITMARSH, Warden.

[L. S.]

(Signed,) JAMES JESSUP, Clerk.

———

No. CXXII.—BY-LAW

To repeal the seventh section of By-Law numbered forty-three.—Passed 28th January, 1857.

Repeal. Be it enacted, by the Municipal Council of the United Counties of Leeds and Grenville, and it is hereby enacted, That from and after the passing hereof, the seventh section of By-law numbered forty-three, past on the eighth day of May, in the year of our Lord one thousand eight hundred and fifty-two, and intituled "By-Law to cover certain grants of money," be and the same is hereby repealed.

(Signed,) H. D. JESSUP, Warden.

[L. S.]

(Signed,) JAMES JESSUP, County Clerk.

No. CXXIII.—BY-LAW

To appoint Trustees for each of the County Grammar Schools in the place of those retiring from office on the 31st January, 1857.—Passed January 29, 1857.

See 29 Vic. Cap. 23.

Be it enacted by the Municipal Council of the United Counties of Leeds and Grenville, and it is hereby enacted, That the persons hereinafter mentioned be selected and appointed Trustees of the County Grammar Schools in the said United Counties, as they are respectively assigned for each of the said Schools, that is to say :

Trustees appointed.

For the County Grammar School at Brockville :

Brockville School.

Rev. J. T. Lewis and John Ross, re-appointed.

For the County Grammar School at Kemptville :

Kemptville School.

Rev. Joseph Anderson re-appointed, and Rev. Richard Lewis, in place of Robert Leslie, who retires.

For the County Grammar School at Prescott :

Prescott School.

John Easton and William Ellis, in place of William J. Scott and Rev. Robert Boyd, who retire.

For the County Grammar School at Gananoque :

Gananoque School.

Robert McCrum and William S. McDonald, re-appointed.

(Signed,)   H. D. JESSUP, Warden.

[L. S.]

(Signed,)   JAMES JESSUP, Clerk.

No. CXXIV.—BY-LAW

To appoint Local Superintendents of Common Schools in the United Counties of Leeds and Grenville.—Passed 29th January, 1857.

Be it enacted by the Municipal Council of the United Counties of Leeds and Grenville, and it is hereby enacted, That the following persons be, and they are hereby appointed Local Superintendents of Schools for the respective Municipalities hereinafter mentioned, that is to say :—

U

Elizabethtown	Jacob A. Brown.
Augusta.....................	Francis Blakeley.
Edwardsburgh	William B. Imrie.
Oxford	Rev. Richard Lewis.
Front of Leeds and Lansdowne..	Thomas Vanston.
Front of Yonge and Escott......	Thomas Vanston.
Rear of Yonge and Escott..	Seabury Scovill.
Wolford...............	John Burchill.
Kitley ....,...	Robert W. Ferguson.
South Gower ....,......	Daniel B. Pelton.
Bastard and Burgess...........	Lewis Chipman.
Rear of Leeds and Lansdowne ..	Henry P. Washburn.
South Crosby..........	Wm. R. Taylor.
North Crosby.......................	Wm. R. Taylor.
Elmsley.................	Elisha Landon.

And that the said appointments shall commence and take effect on the first day of April next, and not before, except the appointment of John Burchill, for the Municipality of Wolford, which shall commence on the passing of this By-Law.

(Signed,)   H. D. JESSUP, Warden.

[L. S.]

(Signed,)   JAMES JESSUP, Clerk.

No. CXXV.—BY-LAW

See By-Laws Nos 136, 169 and 200.

To regulate the uses to which the Court Room and certain other Apartments in the Court House of these Counties may be applied.—Passed 29th January, 1857.

Be it enacted by the Municipal Council of the United Counties of Leeds and Grenville, and it is hereby enacted, That the Court Room and Grand Jury Room, shall be used hereafter for the following purposes only in this **For what purpose to be used.** section mentioned, that is to say : For the holding of the Superior and Inferior Courts of Record, including the Division Court, and the Meetings of the County Council, and that all orders and resolutions heretofore passed by this Council or the late Council of the District of Johnstown, allowing them to be used for any other purpose, shall be and they are hereby repealed, from the passing of this By-

Law; Provided that the Mechanics' Institute of Brockville
be allowed to hold their lectures in the Court Room.

2. That a Committee be appointed to take charge of
the Court Room, Grand Jury Room, and other apartments
in the Court House not occupied by the Gaoler, and that
the said Committee consist of Messrs. James Jessup, James
L. Schofield and Thomas Webster.

Committee to take charge of Court House.

(Signed,) H. D. JESSUP, WARDEN.

[L. S.]

(Signed,) JAMES JESSUP, CLERK.

No. CXXVI.—BY-LAW

To cover certain grants of money.—Passed January 30, 1857.

Be it enacted by the Municipal Council of the United
Counties of Leeds and Grenville, and it is hereby enacted,
That the several sums of money hereinafter mentioned, be
paid by the County Treasurer to the parties respectively,
viz:—

Sums paid to.

To John Crawford, Esquire, the sum of five pounds five
shillings, for services as Arbitrator.

John Crawford, Esq.

To the Brockville Gas Company the sum of eight pounds
fifteen shillings, for Gas furnished to the 31st December, 1856.

Gas Company.

To A. N. Richards, Esq., the sum of five pounds, for
written opinion given to Committee on Mr. Peden's
contract.

A. N. Richards, Esq.

To John Hill, Esq., the sum of four pounds sixteen shillings
and four pence, for materials and labor furnished for
rebuilding the Bridge at North Augusta, on the
County Road.

John Hill, Esq.

To David Wylie, the sum of three pounds ten shillings,
for printing blank Leases and Bonds for Toll Gates.

David Wylie.

To Messrs Snook and Cole, the sum of six pounds ten
shillings and two pence, for Pump furnished and for
work in the Gaol.

Messrs. Snooks & Cole.

David Wylie.

To David Wylie, the sum of thirty pounds, as an advance upon his contract with the Council, for Printing and Advertising.

James Keeler.

To James Keeler, the sum of one pound ten shillings, for services as Arbitrator.

William Fitzsimmons.

To William Fitzsimmons, the sum of seventeen pounds sixteen shillings and seven pence, for Furniture provided for the Registry Office, and repairs to the Court House and Gaol.

John Moran.
James Caldwell.
Duncan Christie.

To John Moran, the sum of three pounds five shillings; to James Caldwell the sum of seven pounds ten shillings; and to Duncan Christie the sum of thirteen pounds five shillings, being the amounts allowed to them respectively in the awards of the Arbitrators appointed to ascertain the damages done to their respective properties by the construction of the County Toll Road, called the Kemptville and Prescott County Toll Road, provided the said parties do give good and sufficient deeds, free of expense, to the Municipality, for the lands taken of them respectively for the said Road; such deeds to be subject to the approval of the Clerk.

Chris. Leggo.

To Christopher Leggo, the sum of two pounds seven shillings and six pence, for cleaning the Court Room and Fuel furnished.

James Kincaid.

To James Kincaid, the sum of one pound eighteen shillings and one penny half-penny, for attendance as Messenger and for Stationery furnished.

(Signed,)   H. D. JESSUP, Warden.

[L. S.]

(Signed,)   JAMES JESSUP, Clerk.

No. CXXVII.—BY-LAW

To appoint Local Superintendents for the Municipalities therein mentioned.—Passed June 17, 1857.

Preamble.

Whereas, since the last meeting of the Council, vacancies occurred in the Office of Local Superintendent of Common Schools, for the Municipalities hereafter mentioned; and by virtue of the statute in that case made and provided, the Warden appointed Dr. Robert McCrum for the Front of Leeds and Lansdowne, William B. Gowan, Esq., for the Front of Yonge and Escott, and the Rev. Joseph Anderson for Oxford, to supply such vacancies respectively until the present meeting. Be it therefore enacted by the Municipal Council of the United Counties of Leeds and Grenville, and it is hereby enacted, That the said Robert McCrum, William B. Gowan, and Joseph Anderson, be appointed and continued in office as such Local Superintendents for the said Municipalities respectively, until the first day of April, in the Year of Our Lord One Thousand Eight Hundred and Fifty-Eight.

Robert McCrum, Wm. B. Gowan & Joseph Anderson appointed.

(Signed,)   H. D. JESSUP, Warden.

[L. S.]

(Signed,)   JAMES JESSUP, Clerk.

No. CXXVIII.—BY-LAW

To Assess the United Counties of Leeds and Grenville, for the year 1857.—*Passed June* 19, 1857.

Be it enacted by the Municipal Council of the United Counties of Leeds and Grenville, and it is hereby enacted, That there be raised and levied upon the whole rateable property in the said United Counties for the present year, the sum of £5,450 to defray the ordinary and current expenses thereof, and the further sum of £1,429 6s. for the payment of the salaries of legally qualified Common School Teachers, and the further sum of £3,743 6s. 8d. as a special rate, authorized to be raised and levied upon the said property, under the provisions of By-laws numbered eight and thirty-nine, passed respectively on the 10th day of October, 1850, and the seventh day of May, 1852, and the further sum of £1,073 16s. as a special rate, authorized to be raised and levied upon the said property, under the provisions of By-law numbered one hundred and twenty, passed on the thirteenth day of October, 1856, and intituled " By-Law to authorize the negotiation of a Loan of Money, by the issue of Debentures, to pay the debt and other liabilities therein mentioned," and that the said several sums shall be raised and levied in addition to all other rate and assessments, and be apportioned to the several Municipalities of the said United Counties in the following manner, viz. :—

Sums to be levied.

County Rate.

Com'on Schools.

Special rate for County Roads.

Special rate for loan.

How apportioned to Municipalities.

MUNICIPALITIES.	County Rate.			Common Schools.			Special Rate for County Roads.			Special Rate of Loan To pay Debt.		
	£	s.	D.	£	s.	D.	£	s.	D.	£	s.	D.
Elizabethtown	807	17	6	160	4	0	569	19	3	162	16	11
Bastard and Burgess	188	18	8	130	12	0	185	8	2	52	19	6
Rear of Yonge and Escott	241	3	11	58	0	0	163	11	3	46	14	8
Front of Yonge and Escott	289	6	5	86	8	0	192	11	11	55	0	6
Front of Leeds and Lansdowne	345	9	8	111	0	0	246	3	-1	70	6	7
Rear of Leeds and Lansdowne	145	9	11	54	8	0	103	9	2	29	11	2
Kitley	278	0	5	118	16	0	161	16	1	46	4	7
North Crosby	108	14	4	53	2	0	70	16	10	20	4	9
South Crosby	148	16	10	43	18	0	95	7	1	27	4	10
Elmsley	87	6	6	29	18	0	62	2	7	17	15	1
Brockville	711	14	6	00	0	0	511	12	11	146	3	8
Augusta	489	12	10	169	6	0	339	3	10	96	18	3
Edwardsburgh	336	10	4	130	18	0	230	1	4	65	17	6
Oxford	310	13	9	160	0	0	221	6	5	66	1	10
Wolford	265	19	7	97	18	0	189	15	7	54	4	6
South Gower	114	17	3	24	18	0	79	11	5	24	3	3
Prescott	382	1	4	00	0	0	250	9	3	71	11	2
Kemptville	97	10	3	00	0	0	69	10	6	19	17	3
Totals	5,450	0	0	1,429	6	0	3,743	6	8	1,073	16	0

2. That the said several sums hereinbefore directed to *How levied and collected.* be raised and levied in the said Municipalities respectively, shall be placed on the Collector's Roll by the Clerk thereof in separate columns, and collected in like manner as all other rates and assessments are by law directed to be collected, and that every Collector shall, on or before the fourteenth day of December next, return his roll to the Treasurer of the Municipality for which he is appointed, and pay over to him the sums hereby directed to be raised, levied and collected therein.

3. That the said Municipalities respectively shall, on the completion of the Collector's Roll, cause a statement *Statement for Treasurer.* of the total of each of the said rates hereby imposed to be furnished to the County Treasurer, as the same shall appear upon such rolls respectively.

(Signed,)   H. D. JESSUP, Warden.

[L. S.]

(Signed,)   JAMES JESSUP, Clerk.

No. CXXIX.—BY-LAW

To appoint a County Engineer.—Passed June 19, 1857.

Whereas great inconvenience has been experienced by *Preamble.* the inhabitants of these Counties from the want of a County Engineer : Be it Therefore enacted, by the Municipalities' Council of the United Counties of Leeds and Grenville, and it is hereby enacted, That John Burchell, of *John Burchell appointed.* Mirickville, be appointed County Engineer for said United Counties, and that he receives the sum of one pound per *To be paid £1 per day.* day when actually engaged in the duties of his office as such County Engineer.

(Signed,)   H. D. JESSUP, Warden.

[L. S.]

(Signed,)   JAMES JESSUP, Clerk.

No. CXXX.—BY-LAW

To cover certain Grants of Money.—Passed June 19, 1857.

Be it enacted by the Municipal Council of the United Counties of Leeds and Grenville, and it is hereby enacted,

Sums to be paid to. that the several sums of money hereinafter mentioned shall be paid by the Treasurer to the parties respectively, out of money in his hands applicable to such purposes, viz:—

Grenville Registry Office. To the Commissioners for building Registry Office in Grenville, the sum of £12 10s., being balance due the Contractor.

Samuel Keefer. To Samuel Keefer, Esq., Civil Engineer, the sum of £10, for inspecting and reporting to the Judge of the County Court the state of certain portions of the Toll Roads.

Allan Hunter. To Allan Hunter, Esq., the sum of £13 10s., for services as Commissioner of the County Toll Roads.

E. H. Whitmarsh. To E. H. Whitmarsh, Esq., the sum of £23, for services as Commissioner of the County Toll Roads.

Edward Green. To Edward Green, Esq., the sum of £22 10s., for services as Commissioner of County Toll Roads.

David Jones. To David Jones, Esq., the sum of £30, for certain statements of titles registered in his office, of lands lying in the County of Grenville.

David Wylie. To David Wylie, the sum of £37 10s., for printing and advertising.

Adam Anderson. To Adam Anderson, the sum of £6 18s., for Assessors' and Collectors' Port Folios, and binding Minutes.

John Patton. To John Patton, Esq., the sum of £26 17s. 2d., for furniture and fitting up of Registry Office in Prescott.

County Clerk. To County Clerk, the sum of £1 15s., for postages disbursed, and charges on boxes from Toronto.

Harvey Miller. To Harvey Miller, the sum of £5 9s. 9d., for work in the Gaol.

William Fitzsimmons. To William Fitzsimmons, the sum of £66 8s. 7d., for fitting up the Registry Office, and alterations in the Clerk's Office, and carpeting Court Room.

To Messrs. Thompson & Co., the sum of £2 14s. 2d., for Messrs. Thompson & Co.
advertising County Debentures.

To James Kincaid, the sum of £1 19s. 9d., for services as James Kincaid.
Messenger, and stationery furnished.

2. That the several sums in this section shall be paid to Sums to be paid to.
the parties respectively:

To J. Gillet, the sum of £27 10s., for damages to Lot No. J. Gillet.
33, in the 8th Concession of the Township of Augusta, and for fences, by the construction of the Mirickville and Maitland County toll road.

To Edward Bissel, sen., the sum of £30, for damages to Edward Bissell, Senr.
Lot No. 33, in the 7th concession of the township of Augusta, and for fences, by the construction of the Mirickville and Maitland County toll road.

To Stewart Herron, the sum of £64, for damages to the Stewart Herron.
North-half of Lot No. 33, in the 6th concession of the township of Augusta, and for land taken, and fences to be made by him, by the construction of the Mirickville and Maitland County toll road.

To Edward Bissell, jun., the sum of £8 15s., for damages Edward Bissell, Junr.
to his farm by the construction of the Mirickville and Maitland County toll road.

To B. Throop, the sum of £12 10s., for damages and B. Throop.
making new fences on his farm, by the construction of the Mirickville and Maitland County toll road; Provided that the said parties first execute a sufficient Proviso.
deed of conveyance to the Council of the land taken from them respectively for the said road, and also give receipts in full for the said damages, such deed to be subject to the approval of the County Clerk.

(Signed,)   H. D. JESSUP, WARDEN.

[L. S.]

(Signed,)   JAMES JESSUP, CLERK.

No. CXXXI.—BY-LAW

See By-Law No. 140. *To repeal the Third Section of By-law No. 95.—Passed June 19, 1857.*

(Repealed: see By-law No. 231.)

No. CXXXII.—BY-LAW

To appoint a Local Superintendent for the Townships of North and South Crosby.- Passed 14th October, 1857.

James Bilton appointed.

Be it enacted by the Municipal Council of the United Counties of Leeds and Grenville, and it is hereby enacted, That James Bilton, Esq., be appointed Local Superintendent of Common Schools for the Townships of North Crosby and South Crosby until the first day of April next, in the place and stead of William Taylor, resigned.

(Signed,) H. D. JESSUP, WARDEN.

[L. S.]

(Signed,) JAMES JESSUP, CLERK.

No. CXXXIII.—BY-LAW

To appoint a Local Superintendent of Common Schools, for the Township of Augusta, in the place of Francis Blakely.—Passed 16th October, 1857.

William Dowling appointed.

Be it enacted by the Municipal Council of the United Counties of Leeds and Grenville, and it is hereby enacted, That Francis Blakely, Local Superintendent of Common Schools for the Township of Augusta, be removed from office for neglect of duty as such Local Superintendent, and he is hereby removed from the said office, and that William Dowling of the said Township of Augusta, be appointed such Local Superintendent in the place and stead of the said Thomas Blakely, so removed as aforesaid, until the first day of April, in the year of our Lord one thousand eight hundred and fifty-eight.

(Signed,) H. D. JESSUP, WARDEN.

[L. S.]

(Signed,) JAMES JESSUP, CLERK.

No. CXXXIV.—BY-LAW

To cover certain Grants of Money—Passed 16th *October,*
1857.

Be it enacted by the Municipal Council of the United
Counties of Leeds and Grenville, and it is hereby enacted,
that the several sums of money hereinafter mentioned Sums to be paid to.
shall be paid by the Treasurer to the parties respectively,
out of any monies in his hands applicable to such purpose,
viz :—

To Alfred Poulton, the sum of £11 0s. 5½d., for glazing Alfred Poulton.
and repairing windows in Court-house and Gaol,
and painting in County Clerk's office.

To John McMullen, the sum of £9 6s. 4½d., for advertis- John McMullen.
ing and stationery furnished for Clerk's office.

To Stephen B. Merrill, the sum of £2 2s. 1d., for adver- S. B. Merrill.
tising.

To David Jones, the sum of 18s. 1½d., for work at Registry David Jones.
office.

To County Clerk, the sum of £2 12s. 3d., for disburse- County Clerk.
ments for postages and charges on boxes of statutes
and Journals.

To Harvey Miller, the sum of £2 17s., for work done in Harvey Miller.
the Gaol.

To William Fitzsimmons, the sum of £95 7s. 9d., for work William Fitzsim-
done and materials furnished in the Gaol and Trea- mons.
surer's Office.

To John Burchill, the sum of £2, for services as County John Burchill.
Engineer.

To Jacob Snooks, the sum of £8 11s. 9d., for work in Jacob Snooks.
Goal.

To James Kincaid, the sum of £1 13s. 3d., for services as James Kincaid.
messenger and stationery furnished.

To the Arbitrators in the case of Hiram H. Bellamy, the Arbitrators in the case of Hiram H. Bellamy.
sum of £6, for the expenses of the Arbitration.

Hiram H. Bellamy.

To Hiram H. Bellamy, the sum of £140, being the amount of the award of Arbitrators on his claim for damages for land taken on Lot No. 34, in the eighth concession of the township of Augusta, for the Mirickville and Maitland County Toll Roads ; Provided that the said Hiram B. Bellamy, first execute a sufficient deed of conveyance to the Council of the land so taken from him for the said road; and also give a receipt in full discharge of the said damages, such deed to be subject to the approval of the County Clerk.

(Signed,)   H. D. JESSUP, Warden.

[L. S.]

(Signed,)   JAMES JESSUP, Clerk.

No. CXXXV.—BY-LAW

To cover certain Grants of Money.—Passed 18th November, 1857.

Be it enacted by the Municipal Council of the United Counties of Leeds and Grenville, and it is hereby enacted, That the several sums of money hereinafter mentioned, Sums to be paid to. shall be paid by the Treasurer to the parties respectively, out of any moneys in his hands applicable to such purposes, viz. :

Arbitrators. To the Arbitrators on the claim of Hiram B. Bellamy, the sum of 15s., being balance of their account.

Mirickville Chronicle. To the Mirickville *Chronicle*, the sum of £1 15s. 7d., for advertising.

Edward Green. To Edward Green, the sum of £20, for services as Commissioner for the County Toll Roads.

John Miller. To John Miller, the sum of £5, for services as Commissioner for the County Toll Roads.

Wm. Humphries. To William Humphries, the sum of £12, for services as Commissioner for the County Toll Roads.

Alfred Poulton. To Alfred Poulton, the sum of 8s. 9d., for glazing the Gaol.

James Kincaid. To James Kincaid, the sum of £1 2s. 6d., for services as messenger.

To the Warden, the sum of £25 in full for his services *The Warden:*
out of Council for the current year, in lieu of the
sum of £1 per day, as fixed by By-law.

To Edward Green, Esq., the sum of £3, granted to him *Edward Green.*
for land taken of Northrop Curtis, for the Westport
and Farmersville County Road.

To David Wylie, the sum of £25, in part payment of his *David Wylie.*
contract for printing and advertising.

      (Signed,)   H. D. JESSUP, WARDEN.

[L. S.]

(Signed,)   JAMES JESSUP, CLERK.

No. CXXXVI.—BY-LAW

To allow the Town Council of the Town of Brockville and See By-Law No.
the Mayor of the said Town, to use the Court Room. 125.
—Passed 27th January, 1858.

Be it enacted by the Municipal Council of the United
Counties of Leeds and Grenville, and it is hereby enacted,
That the Town Council of the Town Brockville may hold
their meetings in the Court Room of the Court House of
the said United Counties, and that the Mayor of the said *Mayor's Court,*
town may also hold his Court in the said Court Room, *&c., may be held in room.*
until further notice to the contrary from this Council.

      (Signed,)   WM. SMITH, WARDEN.

[L. S.]

(Signed,)   JAMES JESSUP, CLERK.

No. CXXXVII.—BY-LAW

To appoint Trustees for each of the County Grammar See 29 Vic., cap
Schools and Local Superintendents in the United 23.
Counties of Leeds and Grenville.—Passed 27th January, 1858.

Be it enacted by the Municipal Council of the United
Counties of Leeds and Grenville, and it is hereby enacted,
That the persons hereinafter in this section mentioned, be

Trustees appointed.
elected and appointed trustees of the County Grammar Schools in the said United Counties, as they are respectively assigned to each of the said schools, that is to say :

Brockv'leSchool. For the Grammar School at Brockville, David Robertson and Robert Fitzsimmons, jun., in place of Robert Edmondson and Robert Peden, who retire.

Prescott School. For the Grammar School of Prescott, Hamilton D. Jessup and Chauncey H. Peck re-appointed.

Gananoque School. For the Grammar School at Gananoque, Rev. John Carroll and Rev. Henry Gordon re-appointed, and Thos. Richmond in place of the late Thomas Vanston.

Kemptville School. For the Grammar School at Kemptville, Ambrose Clothier and Robert Kernahan re-appointed, and Robt. Leslie in place of the Rev. D. Farley, who has removed from this part of the province.

Local Superintendents.
2. That the persons hereinafter mentioned be, and they are hereby appointed Local Superintendents of Schools for the respective municipalities in this section mentioned, that is to say :

Augusta............................James Clapperton.
Oxford..............................Rev. Joseph Anderson.
Front of Leeds and Lansdowne..Robert McCrum.
Rear of Leeds and Lansdowne...Henry P. Washburn.
Front of Yonge and Escott.. ..Rev. W. A. Sills.
Rear of Yonge and Escott........George Wite.
Elizabethtown.....................Jacob A. Brown.
Edwardsburgh.....................William B. Imrie.
South Gower.......................Daniel B. Pelton.
Wolford............................John Burchill.
Kitley........ ....Robert W. Ferguson.
Elmsley ....Elisha Landon.
Bastard and Burgess.....·......Lewis Chipman.
South Crosby...................James Bilton.
North Crosby..:.............. ....   do.   do.

And that the said appointments of Local Superintendents shall commence and take effect on the first day of April next, and not before.

(Signed,)   WILLIAM SMITH, Warden.
[L. S.]
(Signed,)   JAMES JESSUP, Clerk.

No. CXXXVIII.—BY-LAW

To cover certain Grants of Money.—Passed 29th January, 1858.

Be it enacted by the Municipal Council of the United Counties of Leeds and Grenville, and it is hereby enacted, That the several sums of money hereinafter mentioned shall be paid by the Treasurer to the parties respectively, out of any monies in his hands applicable to such purposes, viz. : Sums to be paid to.

To R. W. Kelly, the sum of £2 8s. for advertising in the Kemptville *Progressionist.* R. W. Kelly.

To Joseph Adams, the sum of £2 for services as arbitrator on the claims of Duncan Christie and Jas. Caldwell. Joseph Adams.

To William Fitzsimmons, the sum of £167 5s. 7d., for work and repairs done and performed in the gaol, and locks and materials furnished. William Fitzsimmons.

To Harvey Miller, the sum of £2 11s. 10d., for work done in the gaol. Harvey Miller.

To Thomas Bell, the sum of £1 for services in arranging the amount of taxes the town of Brockville should pay to the United Counties. Thomas Bell.

To James Kincaid, the sum of £3 4s. 5d., for attendance as messenger, and stationery furnished. James Kincaid.

    (Ssigned,)   WILLIAM SMITH, Warden.

[L. S.]

    (Signed,)   JAMES JESSUP, Clerk.

———

No. CXXXIX.—BY-LAW

To authorize a loan of two thousand pounds to Robert Peden, Esquire.—Passed 30th January 1858.

[Repealed: see By-law No. 231.

No. CXL.—BY-LAW

To repeal By-Law No. 131, passed on the 19th day of June, 1857, and intituled " By-Law to repeal the third section of By-Law No. 95."—Passed 30th January, 1858.

(Repealed : See By-law No. 231.)

No. CXLI.—BY-LAW

Granting £2,000 to repair and finish the County Toll Roads.—Passed 18th March, 1858.

(Repealed : see By-Law No. 231.)

No. CXLII.—BY-LAW

To assess the United Counties of Leeds and Grenville for the year 1858.—Passed 24th June 1858.

Be it enacted by the Municipal Council of the United Counties of Leeds and Grenville, and it is hereby enacted, That there be raised and levied upon the whole Rateable Property in the said United Counties for the present year, the sum of £5,750, to defray the ordinary and current expenses thereof, and the further sum of £1,378 15s. 0d., to pay the salaries of legally qualified common school Teachers, and the further sum of £3,700 4s. 10d., as a special rate, authorized to be raised and levied upon the said property, under the provisions of By-laws numbered eight and thirty-nine, passed respectively on the tenth day of October, 1850, and the seventh day of May, 1852, and the further sum of £1057 5s. 3d., as a special rate, authorized to be raised and levied upon the said property, under the provisions of By-law numbered one hundred and twenty, passed on the thirteenth day of October, 1856, and intituled "By-Law to authorize the negotiation of a loan of money, by the issue of Debentures, to pay the debt and other liabilities therein mentioned." And that the said several sums shall be raised and levied in addition to all other rates and assessments, and be apportioned to the several Municipalities of the said United Counties, in the following manner, viz:

Sums to be levied.

County rate.

Com'on Schools.

Special Rate for County Roads.

Special rate for loan.

How apportioned to Municipalities.

MUNICIPALITIES.	County Rate.			Common Schools.			Special rate for County Roads.			Special rate for Loan.		
	£.	s.	D.	£.	s.	D.	£.	s.	D.	£.	s.	D.
Elizabethtown	826	6	9	160	0	0	529	13	0	151	7	7
Bastard and Burgess	276	15	8	130	10	0	201	9	3	57	11	3
Rear of Yonge and Escott	260	19	4	58	0	0	167	11	2	47	17	6
Front of Yonge and Escott	306	16	0	86	5	0	130	17	7	37	7	11
Front of Leeds and Lansdowne	366	7	7	111	0	0	232	4	5½	66	6	11½
Rear of Leeds and Lansdowne	156	16	2	54	5	0	105	6	3½	30	0	8
Kitley	294	15	11	118	15	0	195	6	3½	55	16	1
North Crosby	120	3	10	53	0	0	71	16	4½	20	10	5
South Crosby	157	11	5	43	15	0	99	16	9	28	10	6
Elmsley	96	1	7	29	15	0	64	6	7½	18	7	8
Brockville	790	14	3	0	0	0	537	9	0	153	11	1
Augusta	520	11	0	169	5	0	348	19	1½	99	14	0½
Edwardsburgh	356	19	9	130	15	0	233	11	3½	66	14	8
Oxford	329	10	4	111	0	0	215	8	10½	61	11	1
Wolford	292	10	9	97	15	0	188	13	8	53	18	2
South Gower	122	0	3	24	15	0	79	13	1½	22	15	2
Prescott	381	7	10	0	0	0	248	14	8	71	1	4
Kemptville	103	11	7	0	0	0	49	11	2½	14	3	2
Totals	£5750	0	0	£1378	15	0	£3700	4	10	£1057	5	3

w

2. That the said several sums hereinbefore directed to be raised and levied in the said Municipalities respectively, shall be placed on the Collector's Roll by the Clerk thereof in separate columns, and collected in like manner as all other rates and assessments are by law directed to be collected, and that every Collector shall, on or before the fourteenth day of December next, return his roll to the Treasurer of the Municipality for which he is appointed, and pay over to him the sums hereby directed to be raised, levied and collected therein.

How levied and collected.

3. That the said Municipalities respectively shall, on the completion of the Collector's Roll, cause a statement of the total of each of the said rates hereby imposed to be furnished to the County Treasurer, as the same shall appear upon such rolls respectively.

Statement for Treasurer.

(Signed,)   WILLIAM SMITH, WARDEN.

[L. S.]

(Signed,)   JAMES JESSUP, CLERK.

No. CXLIII.—BY-LAW

To authorize a temporary Loan until the Assessments for the present year become available.—Passed 24th June, 1858.

(Repealed : see By-Law No. 231.)

No. CXLIV.—BY-LAW

To Cover certain Grants of Money.—Passed 24th June, 1858.

Be it enacted by the Municipal Council of the United Counties of Leeds and Grenville, and it is hereby enacted, That the several sums of money hereinafter mentioned shall be paid by the Treasurer to the parties respectively, out any moneys in his hands applicable to such purposes, VIZ :—

Sums to be paid to.

To William Fitzsimmons, the sum of four pounds twelve William Fitzsim-
shillings and eight pence, for repairs to Gaol and mons.
Court House.

To the County Clerk, the sum of two pounds nine shillings County Clerk.
and one penny for disbursements for postages and
charges on books.

To Adam Anderson, the sum of five pounds sixteen shil- Adam Anderson.
lings for Port-folios for Collectors' and Assessors' Rolls.

To Stephen B. Merrill, the sum of two pounds seven S. B. Merrill.
shillings for advertising.

To David Wylie, the sum of twenty-five pounds twelve David Wylie.
shillings and six pence for printing and advertising,
as per contract.

To Adiel Sherwood, the sum of two pounds fourteen shil- Adiel Sherwood.
lings and three pence, for carpeting furnished for
Court House.

To John Millar, the sum of one pound, for services as John Millar.
Commissioner of County Roads.

To John McMullen, the sum of five pounds seven shillings John McMullen.
and eight pence, for advertising and stationery.

To John Burchill, the sum of eight pounds fifteen shillings, John Burchill.
. for services on County Toll Roads, in full to this date.

To James Kincaid the sum of two pounds eight shillings James Kincaid.
and one penny, for services as Messenger.

(Signed,)   WILLIAM SMITH, Warden.
[L. S.]
(Signed,)   JAMES JESSUP, Clerk.

No. CXLV.—BY-LAW

*To appoint a Local Superintendent of Schools for the Town-
ship of South Crosby.—Passed 14th October, 1858.*

Be it enacted by the Municipal Council of the United
Counties of Leeds and Grenville, and it is hereby enacted, Henry Laishley
That Henry Laishley be appointed Local Superintendent appointed.

of Common Schools for the Township of South Crosby, in
the place of James Belton, such appointment to be held
by the said Henry Laishley until the first day of April
next.

(Signed,) WILLIAM SMITH, Warden.

[L. S.]

Signed,) JAMES JESSUP, Clerk.

No. CXLVI.—BY-LAW

*To change the location of Toll Houses and Gates therein
mentioned, and to provide for a more satisfactory
method of leasing the Toll Houses and Gates upon the
four County Toll Roads.—Passed 14th October, 1858.*

(Repealed: see By-law No. 231.)

No. CXLVII.—BY-LAW

See By-laws Nos. 12, 60 and 86. *Relating to the Treasurer's Salary.—Passed 14th October,
1858.*

Be it enacted by the Municipal Council of the United
Counties of Leeds and Grenville, and it is hereby enacted,
£25 added to salary. That the sum of twenty-five pounds be added to the salary
of the County Treasurer, from the first day of November
next, and paid in the same manner and at the times provided for the payment of his present salary.

(Signed,) WILLIAM SMITH, Warden.

[L. S.]

(Signed,) JAMES JESSUP, Clerk.

No. CXLVIII.—BY-LAW

To cover certain Grants of Money.—Passed 14*th October,*
1858.

Be it enacted by the Municipal Council of the United
Counties of Leeds and Grenville, and it is hereby enacted,
That the several sums of money hereinafter mentioned Sums paid to.
shall be paid by the Treasurer to the parties respectively,
out of any moneys in his hands applicable to such purposes, viz. :

To John Burchill, the sum of nineteen pounds twelve shil- John Burchill.
lings and six pence, for services as County Engineer.

To David Miller, the sum of two pounds five shillings, for David Miller.
three days' services as Arbitrator.

To Alfred Poulton, the sum of five pounds, for materials Alfred Poulton.
furnished and work done to the Court House, accord-
ing to contract.

To William Humphries, the sum of twenty-four pounds, Wm. Humphries,
for services as Commissioner of County Roads.

To William Young, the sum of eleven pounds ten shillings, William Young.
for services as Commissioner of County Roads.

To Thomas Bell, the sum of thirteen pounds, for services Thomas Bell.
as Commissioner of County Roads.

To J. Snooks, the sum of two pounds eighteen shillings J. Snooks.
and seven pence, for repairs, &c., done to Court
House.

To Edward Green, the sum of four pounds for services as Edward Green.
Commissioner of County Roads in 1857 and 1858.

To the County Clerk, the sum of one pound three shillings County Clerk.
and nine pence, for postages disbursed for the Coun-
ties.

To Thomas Bell, the sum of two pounds five shillings for Thomas Bell.
services on repairs of Court House.

To William Garvey, the sum of two pounds five shillings, William Garvey.
for services on repairs of Court House.

The Warden. To the Warden, the sum of twenty-five pounds in full, for his services out of Council for the current year, in lieu of the sum of £1 per day as per By-Law.

J. H. Brooks. To J. H. Brooks, the sum of fifteen shillings for estimate, measuring and report on Court House Roof.

William Fitzsimmons. To William Fitzsimmons, the sum of seven pounds seven shillings and eleven pence half-penny, for work done in the Court House and Gaol.

David Black. To David Black, the sum of seven shillings and nine pence, for work done in the Gaol.

James Kincaid. To James Kincaid, the sum of one pound eleven shillings and ten pence, for services as Messenger and stationery furnished.

(Signed,) WILLIAM SMITH, WARDEN.

[L. S.]

(Signed,) JAMES JESSUP, CLERK.

No. CXLIX.—BY-LAW

To appoint Trustees for each of the County Grammar Schools, and Local Superintendents in the United Counties of Leeds and Grenville.—Passed 27th January, 1859.

Trustees appointed. Be it enacted by the Municipal Council of the United Counties of Leeds and Grenville, and it is hereby enacted, That the persons hereinafter in this section mentioned, be elected and appointed Trustees of the County Grammar Schools in the said United Counties, as they are respectively assigned to each of the said schools, that is to say :

Brockville School. *For the Grammar School at Brockville.*

Richard F. Steel and Rev. Edmund J. Senkler, re-appointed.

Kemptville School. *For the Grammar School at Kemptville.*

Joseph Bower and Robert Leslie, re-appointed.

For the Grammar School at Prescott Prescott School.

William Hillyard, in place of Alpheus Jones and John Patton, re-appointed.

For the Grammar School at Gananoque. Gananoque School.

Honorable John Macdonald and Thomas Richmond, re-appointed, and that the said appointments are to commence on the thirty-first day of January instant.

2. That the persons hereinafter mentioned, be, and they are hereby appointed Local Superintendents of Schools for the Municipalities respectively in the section mentioned, that is to say:

Local Superintendents.

Augusta.	James Clapperton.
Oxford.	Rev. Joseph Anderson.
Front of Leeds & Lansdowne	Robert McCrum.
Rear of Leeds & Lansdowne.	Henry P. Washburn.
Rear of Yonge and Escott.	Asher A. Chamberlain.
Front of Yonge and Escott.	Charles N. Hagerman.
Elizabethtown	Jacob A. Brown.
Edwardsburg	Rev. Andrew Melville.
South Gower	Rev. Joseph Anderson.
Wolford	Rev. T. R. Parnell.
Kitley.	Rev. D. Evans.
Elmsley	Elisha Landon.
Bastard and Burgess	Lewis Chipman.
South Crosby	Rev. John Davidson.
North Crosby	James Bilton.

And that the said appointments of Local Superintendents shall commence and take effect on the first day of April next, and not before.

(Signed,) H. D. JESSUP, WARDEN.
[L. S.]
(Signed,) JAMES JESSUP, CLERK.

No. CL.—BY-LAW

To assume a certain alteration in a part of the line of the County Toll Road from Merrickville to Maitland.— —Passed 27th January, 1859.

(Repealed: see By-Law No. 231.)

No. CLI.—BY-LAW

To prevent the sale or gift of intoxicating drink to a child
or apprentice, without the consent of parent, master or
legal protector.—Passed 29th January, 1859.

Be it enacted by the Municipal Council of the United
Counties of Leeds and Grenville, and it is hereby enacted,
as follows :—

Fine.

1. That if any person or persons, shall sell or give any
intoxicating drink to any child or apprentice within the
said United Counties, without the consent of the parent,
master or legal protector of such child or apprentice, such
person or persons so offending, and being thereof convicted
before one or more Justices of the Peace having jurisdiction within the said United Counties, shall forfeit and pay
a fine or penalty not exceeding ten dollars.

How fines, &o ,
collected.

2. That all fines and penalties imposed under this By-
Law shall be paid with costs at the time limited by such
Justice or Justices, and in default thereof, to be levied by
distress and sale of the goods and chattels of the offender,
and in case there being no distress found, out of which
such fine or penalty can be levied, then every such offender shall be imprisoned with or without hard labor in the
County Gaol of the said United Counties for any period
not exceeding twenty-one days.

To be paid to
Treasurer of
Municipality.

3. That all fines and penalties collected under this By-
Law, shall be paid over by such Justice or Justices to the
Treasurer of the Municipality in which any such conviction shall take place, to be applied by him to the common
uses of the Municipality.

Not to apply to
Brockville and
Prescott.

4. That this By-Law shall not apply to the incorporated
Towns of Brockville and Prescott.

(Signed,)   H. D. JESSUP, Warden.

[L. S.]

(Signed,)   JAMES JESSUP, Clerk.

No. CLII.—BY-LAW

To confirm a By-Law of the Municipal Council of the
Township of Rear of Leeds and Lansdowne.—Passed
2nd February, 1859.

Whereas it is expedient and necessary to confirm a cer- Preamble.
tain By-Law passed by the Municipal Council of the Township of the Rear of Leeds and Lansdowne, vesting in
James Brown a certain allowance for road in the Township of Leeds : Be it therefore enacted by the Municipal
Council of the United Counties of Leeds and Grenville,
and it is hereby enacted, that By-Law No. 5, passed on
the 7th day of August, 1858, by the said Municipal Council of the Township of the Rear of Leeds and Lansdowne,
and entitled, " By-Law to vest in James Brown a certain By-Law No. 5
allowance for road in the Township of Leeds," be and the confirmed.
same is hereby confirmed.

(Signed,)　　H. D. JESSUP, Warden.
[L. S.]
(Signed,)　JAMES JESSUP, Clerk.

No. CLIII.—BY-LAW.

To confirm a By-Law of the Municipal Council of the
Township of the Rear of Leeds and Lansdowne.—
Passed 2nd February, 1859.

Whereas it is expedient and necessary to confirm a cer- Preamble.
tain By-Law passed by the Municipal Council of the Township of the Rear of Leeds and Lansdowne, vesting in John
Summerville a certain allowance for road in the Township
of Leeds : Be it therefore enacted by the Municipal Council of the United Counties of Leeds and Grenville, and
it is hereby enacted, that By-Law No. 6, passed on the
seventh day of August 1858, by the said Municipal Council of the Township of the Rear of Leeds and Lansdowne,
and entitled, " By-Law to vest in John Summerville a cer- By-Law No. 6
tain allowance for road in the Township of Leeds," be and confirmed.
the same is hereby confirmed.

(Signed,)　　H. D. JESSUP, Warden.
[L. S.]
(Signed,)　JAMES JESSUP, Clerk.

No. CLIV.—BY-LAW

To License Auctioneers.—Passed 3rd February, 1859.

Be it enacted by the Municipal Council of the United Counties of Leeds and Grenville, and it is hereby enacted, as follows :—

Not to sell without License.

1. That no person or persons shall sell or put up for sale within the said United Counties, goods, wares, merchandize or effects by Public Auction, without having first obtained a license as hereinafter provided.

How granted.

2. That Licenses may be granted for the whole Counties, or for any Township, Town or Village therein, and shall be signed by the County Treasurer, who is hereby required to provide the Township, Town and Village Clerks with Licenses for sale to parties applying for the same.

Sum to be paid for License.

3. That there shall be raised, collected and paid for each and every License to be taken out by every Auctioneer, the sum of Forty Dollars, when such License shall be for the whole Counties, and the sum of Four Dollars when for any Township, and the sum of Fifteen Dollars when for any Town, and the sum of Five Dollars when for any Village, and shall be paid to the Treasurer of the Municipality for which any such License may issue, to form part of the funds thereof.

To be issued on Certificate of Treasurer.

4. That the said Clerk shall not issue any such License except on the production of a certificate from the Treasurer of the Municipality, that the duty or sum hereby imposed for every such License, has been paid to him by the party applying for the same, which certificate shall be filed and kept among the papers of his office.

Penalty for selling without License.

5. That if any person or persons shall sell or put up for sale within the said United Counties, goods, wares, merchandize or effects by public Auction, without having first obtained a License under this By-Law, such person or persons so offending, and being thereof convicted before any one or more Justices of the Peace having jurisdiction within the said United Counties, shall forfeit and pay a fine or penalty not exceeding twenty dollars, nor less than twelve dollars.

6. That all fines and penalties imposed under this By-Law, shall be paid with costs at the time limited by such

Justice or Justices, and in default thereof, to be levied by
distress and sale of the goods and chattels of the offender,
and in case of there being no distress found out of which
such fine or penalty can be levied, then every such offender shall be imprisoned, with or without hard labor in the
common gaol of the said United Counties, for any period
not exceeding twenty-one days. *How fines collected.*

7. That every such License shall be in force until the
first day of January, in the year following that in which
such License shall be issued. *How long in force.*

8. That all fines and penalties collected under this By-
Law, shall be paid over by such Justice or Justices to the
Treasurer of the Township, Town or Village in which any
such conviction shall take place for the common uses of
the Municipality. *To whom fines to be paid.*

(Signed,)   H. D. JESSUP, Warden.

[L. S.]

(Signed,)   JAMES JESSUP, Clerk.

No. CLV.—BY-LAW

*To confirm a By-Law of the Municipal Council of the
Township of the Rear of Young and Escott.—Passed
3rd February, 1859.*

Whereas it is expedient and necessary to confirm a certain By-Law passed by the Municipal Council of the
Township of the Rear of Yonge and Escott, stopping up
and vesting in Harmonious Alguire, Esquire, a certain part
of an allowance for Road, in the Township of Yonge: Be
it therefore enacted by the Municipal Council of the United
Counties of Leeds and Grenville, and it is hereby enacted,
That By-Law No. 74, passed on the eighth day of May,
1858, by the said Municipal Council of the Township of
the Rear of Yonge and Escott, and entitled, "By-Law
No. 74, to stop up the front of the allowance for Road between Lots Nos. 12 and 13 in the 10th concession, and to
vest the same in Harmonious Alguire, Esquire," be and
the same is hereby confirmed. *Preamble.* *By-Law No. 74 confirmed.*

(Signed,)   H. D. JESSUP, Warden.

[L. S.]

(Signed,)   JAMES JESSUP, Clerk.

No. CLVI.—BY-LAW

To authorize an arrangement for the resumption of the County Toll Roads on the terms therein mentioned.— Passed 5th February, 1859.

(Repealed: see By-Law No. 231.)

No. CLVII.—BY-LAW

To cover certain Grants of Money—Passed 5th February, 1859.

Be it enacted by the Municipal Council of the United Counties of Leeds and Grenville, and it is hereby enacted, Sums to be paid that the several sums of money hereinafter mentioned, to. shall be paid by the Treasurer to the parties respectively out of any moneys in his hands applicable to such purposes, viz. :—

A. Sherwood and Dr. Reynolds. To Adiel Sherwood, Esq., and Dr. Thomas Reynolds, the sum of Ten Pounds, to aid them in purchasing a Library for the use of the Prisoners confined in the Gaol of these Counties.

County Clerk. To the County Clerk, the sum of One Pound Two Shillings and Nine Pence, for postages and other disbursements for the Counties.

J. G. Elwood. To J. G. Elwood, the sum of One Pound Five Shillings and Nine Pence, for keeping Council Room in order, and articles furnished as per account.

John Burchill. To John Burchill, the sum of Two Pounds, for survey of Road between Lansdowne and Escott.

W. H. Campbell. To W. H. Campbell, the sum of Seven Pounds Ten Shillings, for putting up pigeon holes in the office of the Clerk of the County Court.

C. J. Hynes. To C. J. Hynes, the sum of Seven Pounds Five Shillings and Six Pence, for advertising.

R. W. Kelly. To R. W. Kelly, the sum of one Pound Eighteen Shillings, for advertising Toll Gates.

To William Garvey, the sum of Fifteen Shillings, for one days' services in attending to Court House matters.

William Garvey.

To Thomas Bell, the sum of Fifteen Shillings, for one days' services in attending to Court House matters.

Thomas Bell.

To A. B. Dana, the sum of Three Pounds, for seven days' services in attending to Court House matters.

A. B. Dana.

To A. Poulton, the sum of Twelve Pounds Two Shillings and Two Pence, for work on Court House roof and materials furnished.

A. Poulton.

To J. H. Brooks, the sum of Fourteen Pounds Seven Shillings and Four Pence, for work on Court House and materials furnished.

J. H. Brooks.

To John McMullen, the sum of Twenty-five Pounds, on account of contract for printing and advertising.

John McMullen.

To William Clarke, the sum of Twelve Shillings and Six Pence, for services in assisting County Engineer on the Mirrickville and Maitland Road.

William Clark.

To C. E. Buell, the sum of Five Pounds, for services rendered in arresting and procuring testimony in the case of Simpson, convicted of the murder of Fell.

C. E. Buell.

To Messrs. Desbarats and Derbyshire, the sum of Fifty-three Pounds Fourteen Shillings, for publishing in the Canada Gazette, return of Debentures issued by this Municipality.

Messrs Desbarats & Derbyshire.

To Holmes P. Clow, the sum of Twenty Pounds and Three Shillings, balance of his account for work as a contractor on the County Roads.

Holmes P. Clow.

To James Kincaid, the sum of Three Pounds Eighteen Shillings and Five Pence, for services as messenger and stationery furnished.

James Kincaid.

To Dargavel and McCracken, the sum of Fifteen Shillings, for measuring and making estimate of the cost of fence on the Court Ground.

Dargaval & McCracken.

2. That there be granted to the Municipal Council of the Township of the Front of Leeds and Lansdowne, the sum of Two Hundred Pounds, to aid in the construction

Front of Leeds and Lansdowne.

of a Bridge at the South Lake outlet, such sum to be provided for in the annual estimate of this year, and paid out of the assessment to be collected for that purpose,

(Signed,) H. D. JESSUP, Warden.

[L. S.]

(Signed,) JAMES JESSUP, Clerk.

No. CLVIII.—BY-LAW

To authorize the execution of the contract therein mentioned.
Passed 5th February, 1859.

(Repealed: see By-law No. 231.)

No. CLIX.—BY-LAW

To appoint Commissioners for the County Toll Roads.—
Passed 5th February, 1859.

(Repealed: see By-law No. 231.)

No. CLX.—BY-LAW

To Regulate and Govern the proceedings of the Council.—
Passed June 20, 1859.

(Repealed: see By-law No. 253.)

No. CLXI.—BY-LAW

To establish a Lock-up House in the unincorporated Village
of Farmersville.—Passed June 21, 1859.

Preamble.   Whereas it is expedient and necessary to establish a Lock-up House in the said Village of Farmersville; and whereas a certain room in the Town Hall of the Municipality of the Township of Rear of Yonge and Escott has been set apart and fitted up by the Council of the said Municipality for that purpose :—

Be it therefore enacted by the Municipal Council of the Corporation of the United Counties of Leeds and Grenville, and it is hereby enacted, That the said Room, being in the North angle of the said Town Hall, on the first floor thereof, be and the same is hereby declared and established as a Lock-up House in the said United Counties. *Lock-up estab-lished.*

                [Signed,]   H. D. JESSUP, WARDEN.
        [L. S.]   .
[Signed,]   JAMES JESSUP. CLERK.

No. CLXII.—BY-LAW

To establish a Lock-up House in the unincorporated Village of Mirrickville.—Passed June 21, 1859.

Whereas it is expedient and necessary to establish a Lock-up House in the said Village of Mirrickville ; and whereas two certain Rooms in the Town Hall of the Municipality of the Township of Wolford have been set apart and fitted up by the Council of the said Municipality for that purpose— *Preamble.*

Be it therefore enacted by the Municipal Council of the Corporation of the United Counties of Leeds and Grenville, and it is hereby enacted, That the said Rooms, being in the north-east and north-west angles of the said Town Hall, on the first floor thereof, be and the same are hereby declared and established as a Lock-up House in the said United Counties. *Lock-up estab-lished.*

                [Signed,]   H. D. JESSUP, WARDEN.
        [L. S.]
[Signed,]   JAMES JESSUP. CLERK.

No. CLXIII.—BY-LAW

*To appoint an Arbitrator for the purpose therein mentioned.
—Passed June, 21, 1859.*

Preamble.

Whereas the Council of the Town of Brockville has passed a By-law to withdraw the said Town from the jurisdiction of the Council of the United Counties of Leeds and Grenville, pursuant to the twenty-sixth section of the Act passed in the 22nd year of Her Majesty's Reign, and intituled "An Act respecting the Municipal Institutions of Upper Canada."

Preamble.

And whereas the Council of the said Town of Brockville and the Council of the said United Counties, have not been able mutually to agree upon the terms of such withdrawal.

William Garvey appointed.

Be it therefore enacted by the Municipal Council of the Corporation of the United Counties of Leeds and Grenville, and it is hereby enacted, That William Garvey, of the Township of Augusta, Esquire, be, and he is hereby appointed Arbitrator on behalf of the Corporation of the said United Counties, pursuant to the Statute in such case made and provided, and that the Clerk do give notice of the said appointment to the Mayor of the said Town of Brockville, as required by the first sub-section of the 336th section of the said in part recited Statute.

(Signed,)   H. D. JESSUP, Warden.

[L. S.]

(Signed,)   JAMES JESSUP, Clerk.

No. CLXIV.—BY-LAW

To authorize a temporary loan until the Assessments for the present year become available.—Passed June 23, 1859.

(Repealed : see By-Law No. 228, sec. 4.)

No. CLXV.—BY-LAW

To Authorize the Execution of certain Deeds therein men- See By Law No.
tioned.—Passed June 23, 1859. 231.

Whereas the Council, in and by two certain Resolutions Preamble.
passed on the fourteenth day of October, in the year of
our Lord one thousand eight hundred and fifty-seven,
agreed to sell to the parties entitled to purchase the same,
certain parts or portions of the Old Road in the Township
of Kitley, closed up by the second section of By-law No.
37, passed on the sixth day of May, in the year of our
Lord one thousand eight hundred and fifty-two, at the
rate of Five Pounds Currency per acre,—

Be it therefore enacted by the Municipal Council of the
Corporation of the United Counties of Leeds and Grenville,
and it is hereby enacted, That the Warden be authorized, on
the receipt of the price or sum per acre above mentioned,
to convey to the several parties mentioned in the Report Deeds to parties
of the Survey of the County Engineer hereto annexed, in Engineer's re-
except Mr. Newsom, to whom a deed has already been port.
given, the part or portion of the said Old Road described
to them respectively in the said Report, and to cause the
seal of the Corporation to be affixed to the Deeds conveying the same, and that the Clerk do countersign such
Deeds.

2. That the money received by the Warden for the Warden to pay
said lands so conveyed, shall be paid over by him to the money to Treas-
Treasurer, and form part of the County funds. urer.

3. That in case William Smith, Esquire, shall produce Old Road to Wil-
satisfactory proof to the Warden, that in the arrangement liam Smith.
made by him with the Commissioners, he was to have the
Old Road as part of the compensation for the land conveyed by him for the Victoria Road, the Warden is
authorized to convey the portion of the Old Road to which
he would be entitled, without requiring the payment of
the price above fixed.

(Signed,) H. D. JESSUP Warden.

[L. S.]

(Signed,) JAMES JESSUP, Clerk.

X

Description of Mr. Newsom's part.

A certain parcel or tract of land situate, lying and being part of Lot No. 21, in the 9th Concession of the Township of Kitley, being part of an Old Road, butted and bounded as follows, that is to say : commencing where a post has been planted on the side line between said Lot and Lot No. 20, at the centre of said concession ; thence south-westerly on said centre line 48 links, to the west side of said old road ; thence on the west side of said road, north 36 degrees, west 21 chains 92 links ; thence north 72 degrees 20 minutes, west 14 chains 86 links, more or less, to the south side of Queen Street in the Village of Frankville ; thence on the south side of said street north-easterly 78 links ; thence south 72 degrees 20 minutes, east 14 chains 58 links, more or less, to the side line between Lots Nos. 20 and 21 aforesaid ; thence on the said side line, south 36 degrees, east 22 chains 8 links, to the place of beginning, containing by admeasurement one acre three roods and thirty-two and one-half perches, be the same more or less.

Description of Mr. Robinson's Part.

A certain parcel or tract of land situate, lying and being part of Lot No. 20, in the 9th concession of the Township of Kitley, being part of an Old Road, butted and bounded as follows, that is to say : commencing on the side line between said Lot and Lot No. 21, at the distance of 12 chains 74 links northerly, from a post planted between said Lots at the centre of said concession ; thence north 36 degrees, west 9 chains ; thence north 54 degrees, east 13 links, more or less, to the east side of said old road, thence on the east side of said old road south 36 degrees, east 9 chains ; thence south 54 degrees, west 13 links, more or less, to the place of beginning, containing by admeasurement nineteen square perches, be the same more or less.

Description of Mr. Southworth's Part.

A certain parcel or tract of land situate, lying and being part of Lot No. 20, in the 9th concession of the Township of Kitley, being part of an Old Road, butted and bounded as follows, that is to say : commencing at the side line

between said Lot and Lot No. 21, in rear of said concession; thence north thirty-six degrees, west 51 chains 75
links; thence north 54 degrees, east 13 links, more or less,
to the east side of said Old Road; thence south 36
degrees, east 51 chains 75 links, more or less, to the rear
of said concession; thence on the rear of said concession
south 54 degrees, west 13 links, more or less, to the place
of beginning, containing by admeasurement three roods and
twenty-seven and one-half perches, be the same more or less,

Description of Mr. Smith's Part.

A certain parcel or tract of land situate, lying and being
part of Lot No. 21, in the 9th concession of the Township
of Kitley, being part of an Old Road, butted and bounded
as follows, that is to say: commencing where a post has
been planted on the side line between said Lot and Lot
No. 20, at the centre of said concession; thence south 36
degrees, east 24 chains 14 links; thence south 54 degrees,
west 48 links, more or less, to the west side of said Old
Road; thence on the west side of said road, north 36 degrees, west twenty-four chains fourteen links, more or less,
to the said centre line of said concession; thence north 54
degrees, east 48 links, more or less, to the place of beginning, saving and excepting out of said portion that part of
a road which intersects said Old Road, containing by
admeasurement one acre and twenty and three-fourth
perches, be the same more or less.

Description of Mr. Kilburn's Part.

A certain parcel or tract of land situate, lying and being
part of Lot No. 21, in the 9th concession of the Township
of Kitley, being part of an Old Road, butted and bounded
as follows, that is to say: commencing at the side line
between said Lot and Lot No. 20, in rear of said concession; thence north 36 degrees, west 14 chains 87 links,
more or less, to a stone post planted on said side line;
thence south 54 degrees, west 48 links, more or less, to the
west side of said Old Road; thence on the west side of said
road, south 36 degrees, east 14 chains 87 links, more or
less, to the rear of said concession; thence north 54
degrees, east 48 links, more or less, to the place of beginning, containing by admeasurement two roods and thirty-
four perches, be the same more or less.

(Signed,)   JOHN BURCHILL,
Co. Engineer L. & G.

Mirickville, 30th September, 1858.

No. CLXVI.—BY-LAW

To establish a Road between the Townships of Lansdowne and Escott.—Passed June 23rd, 1859.

Preamble.

Description of Road.

Whereas by order of this Council, the County Engineer was directed to survey the road hereinafter mentioned, which survey the said Engineer has performed, and described in his reports substantially, and to the effect as follows: That is to say, commencing on that part of the Town line between Lansdowne and Escott, lying between the main road and the River St. Lawrence, at Mr. Darling's wharf near the water's edge of said river, 8 links east of said Town line, thence on the course, north 12 degrees, 45 minutes, west two chains 68 links; thence north 27 degrees, 45 minutes, east 1 chain 17 links to the Town line between Lansdowne and Escott; thence on the same course 2 chains 22 links; thence north 46 degrees, 55 minutes, east 4 chains 27 links; thence north 17 degrees, 45 minutes, east 3 chains 28 links; thence north 16 degrees west, 1 chain 66 links; thence north 32 degrees west, 8 chains 60 links to the Town line aforesaid, laying out the road on the road allowance, and on Lot No. A in Escott; thence north 34 minutes, west 12 chains 38 links; thence north 29 degrees, 29 minutes, west 2 chains 70 links; thence north 29 degrees 54 minutes, east 2 chains 89 links; thence north 28 degrees, 19 minutes, west 2 chains 28 links; thence north 3 degrees, 10 minutes, east 13 chains 21 links; laying out the road, on the road allowance, and on Lot No. 24 in Lansdowne, and No. A in Escott; thence north 28 minutes, east 20 chains 30 links; thence north 3 degrees, 20 minutes, west 27 chains 63 links; thence north 1 degree 44 minutes, east 13 chains 14 links, laying out the road on the road allowance on No. A and No. 1 in Escott, and on No. 24 in Lansdowne; thence on the road allowance north 20 minutes, west 8 chains 45 links, thence north 30 degrees 30 minutes, west 4 chains 66 links; thence north 27 degrees 48 minutes, east 1 chain 80 links to the front of the second concession of Lansdowne; thence north 27 degrees 48 minutes, east 5 chains 10 links, laying out the road on the road allowance, and on Lot No. 24 in the first and second concessions of Lansdowne; thence north on the road allowance, north 6 minutes, east 12 chains 48 links; thence north 10 degrees, 33 minutes, west 6 chains 13 links; thence north 18 degrees 27 minutes, east 3 chains 60 links, laying out the road on the road allowance, and on Lot No. 24 in the said second concession; thence north 5 degrees 43 minutes, east 6 chains 13 links; thence north 2 degrees 58 minutes, west 11 chains 20 links, laying out the road on the road allowance and on Lot No. 2 in Escott; thence north 18 degrees, 37 minutes, west 2 chains 39 links; thence north 21 degrees, 23 minutes, east 2 chains, 11 links, laying out the road on the road allowance, and on Lot No, 24, in said second concession; thence on the road allowance north 34 minutes; east 12 chains 8 links; thence north 3 degrees 37 minutes, east 16 chains; thence north 30 degrees, 42 minutes, east 6 chains 50 links; thence north 28 degrees 8 minutes, west 2 chains 18 links; thence north 59 degrees 20 minutes, west 2 chains 44 links; thence north 6 degrees, 37 minutes, east 6 chains 23 links: thence on the road allowance north 1 degree 6 minutes, east 18 chains 74 links, to the front of the third concession of Lansdowne; thence on the road allowance north 45 minutes, west 42 chains 5 links to the travelled road leading from Kingston to Brockville, which makes the whole distance from the said River St. Lawrence to the said road three miles and a half and 6 chains and 87 links, laying out all the courses and distances 40 feet in width, except the first, which is laid out but 30 feet wide as by the said report and plans will fully appear: And whereas it is Preamble. expedient and necessary to establish the said survey; And Preamble. whereas public notice has been given according to the statute in such case made and provided, that this Council would at its present meeting pass a By-law to establish the said survey, and open the same as a Public Highway: Be it therefore enacted by the Municipal Council of the Corporation of the United Counties of Leeds and Grenville, and it is hereby enacted that the said road so surveyed, described, and reported as aforesaid, be and the same is Road estab- hereby established and opened as a Public Road and lished. Highway.

(Signed,)   H. D. JESSUP, Warden.

[L. S.]

(Signed,)   JAMES JESSUP, Clerk.

No. CLXVII.—BY-LAW

To Assess the United Counties of Leeds and Grenville, for the year 1859.—Passed June 25, 1859.

Be it enacted by the Municipal Council of the Corporation of the United Counties of Leeds and Grenville, and it is hereby enacted, That there be raised and levied upon the whole Rateable Property in the said United Counties for the present year, the sum of £4,250, to defray the ordinary and current expenses thereof, and the further sum of £1,527 5s., to pay the salaries of legally qualified common school Teachers, and the further sum of £3,502 16s. 9d., as a special rate, authorized to be raised and levied upon the said property, under the provisions of By-laws numbered eight and thirty-nine, passed respectively on the tenth day of October, 1850, and the seventh day of May, 1852, and the further sum of £1057 16s. 5d., as a special rate, authorized to be raised and levied upon the said property, under the provisions of By-law numbered one hundred and twenty, passed on the thirteenth day of October, 1856, and intituled "By-Law to authorize the negotiation of a loan of money, by the issue of Debentures, to pay the debt and other liabilities therein mentioned." And that the said several sums shall be raised and levied in addition to all other rates and assessments, and be apportioned to the several Municipalities of the said United Counties, in the following manner, viz:

Marginal notes:

Sums to be levied.

County Rate.

Com'on Schools.

Special rate for County Roads.

Special rate for loan.

How apportioned to Municipalities.

MUNICIPALITIES.	County Rates.			Common Schools.			Special Rate for County Roads.			Special rate for Loans.		
	£	s.	D.	£	s.	D.	£	s.	D.	£	s.	D.
Elizabethtown............	604	8	4	175	5	0	496	8	8	141	16	9
Bastard and Burgess.....	219	7	7	130	15	0	199	14	2	57	1	2
Yonge and Escott, Rear...	190	17	4	57	15	0	166	1	6	47	8	11
Yonge and Escott, Front...	294	8	3	91	0	0	177	0	2	50	11	7
Leeds and Lansdowne, Front...	268	4	8	125	5	0	229	2	2	65	9	2
Leeds and Lansdowne, Rear...	114	14	0	67	10	0	112	17	5	32	4	11
Kitley	215	14	6	127	5	0	198	4	3	56	12	7
North Crosby............	87	18	4	65	15	0	69	7	8	19	6	6
South Crosby............	115	5	1	57	15	0	101	16	6	29	1	10
Elmsley.................	70	7	1	51	0	0	63	12	5	18	3	6
Brockville	585	3	9	....	....	....	550	5	5	157	4	5
Augusta	380	15	0	184	15	0	356	2	5	101	14	10
Edwardsburgh...........	261	2	5	132	10	0	242	0	7	69	3	0
Oxford..................	241	0	3	130	15	0	222	8	5	63	10	11
Wolford.................	226	17	4	98	15	0	196	16	2	53	7	6
South Gower............	89	4	11	31	5	0	79	11	1	22	14	7
Prescott	278	18	0	....	....	....	208	6	8	59	10	5
Kemptville.............	75	15	2	....	....	....	43	16	6	12	5	10
Totals.................	4,250	0	0	1,527	5	0	3,502	16	9	1,057	16	5

2. That the said several sums hereinbefore directed to be raised and levied in the said Municipalities respectively, shall be placed on the Collector's Roll by the Clerk thereof in separate columns, and collected in like manner as all other rates and assessments are by law directed to be collected, and that every Collector shall, on or before the fourteenth day of December next, return his roll to the Treasurer of the Municipality for which he is appointed, and pay over to him the sums hereby directed to be raised, levied and collected therein.

How levied and collected.

3. That the said Municipalities respectively shall, on the completion of the Collector's Roll, cause a statement of the total of each of the said rates hereby imposed to be furnished to the County Treasurer, as the same appear upon such rolls respectively.

Statement for Treasurer.

(Signed.)   H. D. JESSUP, WARDEN.

[L. S.]

(Signed.)   JAMES JESSUP, CLERK.

No. CLXVIII.—BY-LAW

To cover certain Grants of Money.—Passed June 25, 1859.

Be it enacted by the Municipal Council of the Corporation of the United Counties of Leeds and Grenville, and it is hereby enacted, That the several sums of money hereinafter mentioned shall be paid by the Treasurer to the parties respectively, out of any moneys in his hands applicable to such purposes, viz:

Sums to be paid to.

To the County Clerk the sum of one pound, eighteen shillings and six pence, for postages and other disbursements.

County Clerk.

To Ephraim Earl the sum of ten pounds; Joseph Briggs, the sum of twelve pounds and ten shillings; and ——— Cole, the sum of four pounds, for land taken from them for the Merrickville and Maitland County Road, provided they shall respectively give a good and sufficient Deed of the said land, to be approved by the Clerk.

Ephraim Earl.

To John Burchill the sum of two pounds and ten shillings, John Burchill.
for examining that part of the Victoria County Road
lying between Smith's Falls and Whitson's Bridge,
and reporting thereon, by order of the County Judge.

To Adam Anderson the sum of five pounds and sixteen Adam Anderson.
shillings, for making Assessors' and Collectors' Port
Folios.

To Messrs. Thompson & Co., the sum of three pounds, for Messrs. Thompson & Co.
six Manuals.

To J. G. Elwood the sum of fifteen shillings, for keeping J. G. Elwood.
Court Room in order during January and February
meeting.

To William Buell the sum of four shillings and three pence, William Buell.
for Wrapping Paper and Twine.

To Messrs. Maclear & Co., the sum of one pound, for two Messrs. Maclear & Co.
Manuals.

To Thomas Woods the sum of one hundred and twelve Thomas Woods.
pounds, twelve shillings and six pence, being one
quarter's contract price for keeping the County Toll
Roads in repair, to the 10th instant.

To William Smith the sum of two pounds, for attending William Smith.
Special Committee to effect an arrangement with the
Town of Brockville.

To Richey Waugh the sum of one pound and ten shillings Richey Waugh.
for the same purpose.

To William H. Fredenburgh the sum of one pound and Wm. H. Fredenburgh.
ten shillings for the same purpose.

To David Wylie the sum of eleven shillings and nine D. Wylie.
pence, for Printing.

To John McMullen the sum of thirty-two pounds three John McMullen.
shillings and four pence, for Stationery and balance
on Contract for Printing and Advertising.

To the County Attorney the sum of nine pounds seven County Attorn'y.
shillings and six pence, for Stove, Pipes and Cases for
Papers in the Crown Office.

William Fitzsimmons. To William Fitzsimmons the sum of ten pounds and one shilling, for work done to the Court House and Gaol.

James Kincaid. To James Kincaid the sum of two pounds and seven shillings, for services as Messenger and Stationery furnished.

J. G. Elwood. To James G. Elwood the sum of fifteen shillings, for keeping Council Room in order during this Session.

John Meikle, Jr. To John Meikle, Jr., the sum of seventeen pounds and ten shillings, to repair the Bridge over the Rideau at Burritt's Rapids, provided the County of Carlton grant a similar sum.

Commissioners of Merrickville & Maitland Road. To the Commissioner of the Merrickville and Maitland County Road the sum of two pounds and ten shillings to repair the Bridge at North Augusta.

(Signed,)   H. D. JESSUP, WARDEN.
[L. S.]
(Signed,)   JAMES JESSUP, CLERK.

No. CLXIX.—BYLAW

See By-laws Nos. 125, 136 and 200. To appoint a Keeper of the Court House.—Passed 13th October, 1859.

(Repealed: see By-Law No. 200.)

No. CLXX.—BY-LAW

To authorize the Warden to give to the contractor for keeping the County Toll Roads in repair, orders on the Treasurer for the quarterly payments under the contract.—Passed 13th October, 1859.

(Repealed: See By-law No. 231.)

No. CLXXI.—BY-LAW

To authorize the execution of the Deed therein mentioned.
Passed 13th October, 1859.

Be it enacted by the Municipal Council of the Corporation of the United Counties of Leeds and Grenville, and it is hereby enacted, that the Warden be authorized to convey to "the Trustees of School Section No. 6, in the Township of Rear of Yonge and Escott, in the County of Leeds," that piece or parcel of land heretofore conveyed by Joshua Bates, of Farmersville, in the District of Johnstown, Esquire, to the District Council of the District of Johnstown, by a certain Indenture, made the fourteenth day of October, in the year of our Lord one thousand eight hundred and forty-six, which said piece or parcel of land is situate in the village of Farmersville, aforesaid, and composed of a part of Lot No. 13 in the eighth concession of Yonge, as particularly described in the said Indenture; and to cause the seal of the Corporation to be affixed to the Deed so conveying the said piece or parcel of land, and that the Clerk do countersign the same.

Deed to Trustees of School Section No. 6, Rear of Yonge & Escott.

(Signed,)   H. D. JESSUP, WARDEN.

[L. S.]

(Signed,)   JAMES JESSUP, CLERK.

No. CLXXII.—BY-LAW

To confirm a By-law of the Municipal Council of the Township of Elizabethtown to sell a certain Road allowance to Joseph A. Pritchard.—Passed 13th October, 1859.

Whereas it is expedient and necessary to confirm a certain By-law passed by the Municipal Council of the Township of Elizabethtown, to sell a certain Government allowance for Road in the said Township of Elizabethtown, to Joseph A. Pritchard; Be it therefore enacted by the Municipal Council of the Corporation of the United Counties of Leeds and Grenville, and it is hereby enacted, that a certain By-law, passed by the said Council of Elizabethtown, on the fourth day of July, in the year of our Lord one thousand eight hundred and fifty-nine, and

Preamble.

348

By-law confirmed. intituled, "By-law to sell a certain Government allowance for a Road in the Township of Elizabethtown, to Joseph A. Pritchard," be, and the same is hereby enacted.

(Signed,) H. D. JESSUP, WARDEN.

[L. S.]

(Signed,) JAMES JESSUP, CLERK.

No. CLXXIII.—BY-LAW

To Cover certain Grants of Money.—Passed October 14, 1859.

Be it therefore enacted by the Municipal Council of the Corporation of the United Counties of Leeds and Grenville, and it is hereby enacted, that the several sums **Sums to be paid to.** of money hereinafter mentioned shall be paid by the Treasurer to the parties respectively, out of any moneys in his hands applicable to such purposes, viz:

David Wylie. To David Wylie, the sum of twenty-five pounds, on account of his contract for printing and advertising for the Council.

County Clerk. To the County Clerk, the sum of two pounds one shilling and nine pence, for postage and other disbursements for the Counties.

Messrs. Sherwood & Steele. To Messrs. Sherwood and Steele, the sum of twenty-seven pounds ten shillings, being the amount of their account for attending the arbitration between the Counties and the Town of Brockville as the Solicitors of the Council, and drawing the award of the Arbitrators.

William Garvey. To William Garvey, Esquire, the sum of thirty-seven pounds ten shillings, being the amount of his account as the Arbitrator of this Council on the withdrawal of Brockville from the jurisdiction of the Council.

Council of Edwardsburgh. To the Municipal Council of the Township of Edwardsburgh, the sum of twelve pounds ten shillings, to aid in opening out the Town Line between Edwardsburgh and Matilda, in the County of Dundas, provided the Council of the United Counties of Dundas, Stormont and Glengarry, grant and expend a like sum for the same purpose.

To the Municipal Council of the Township of Rear of Leeds and Lansdowne, the sum of twenty-five pounds, to aid in building a new bridge over the Furnace Falls waters, at the Black Rapids, in the Township of Lansdowne, provided the Municipal Council of the Township of Rear of Leeds and Lansdowne grant and expend a like sum for the same purpose. *Council of Rear of Leeds & Lansdowne.*

To E. H. Whitmarsh and William Garvey, Esquires, the sum of fifty pounds, to finish the County Toll Road from North Augusta to Maitland, according to the prayer of the petition of John Wright and others. *Messrs. Whitmarsh & Garvey.*

To Alfred Poulton, the sum of five pounds, for repairing windows, in Gaol and Court House, from the first day of October, 1858, to the first day of October, 1859. *Alfred Poulton.*

To C. J. Hynes, the sum of one pound ten shillings for printing and advertising notice to Teachers in the Prescott *Messenger*. *C. J. Hynes.*

To the Municipal Council of the Township of South Crosby, the sum of twenty-five pounds, to aid in opening out the Road between the Township of North and South Crosby, and Bastard and Burgess, provided the Councils of the said Townships grant and expend a like sum for the same purpose. *Council of South Crosby.*

To William H. Fredenburgh the sum of two pounds ten shillings, for one day's attendance at Brockville on County business, at the request of the Warden. *Wm. H. Fredenburgh.*

To Richey Waugh, the sum of two pounds ten shillings, for one day's attendance at Brockville on County business, at the request of the Warden. *Richey Waugh.*

To William Smith, the sum of five pounds, for one day's attendance at Brockville on County business, at the request of the Warden, and for one day at the request of the Arbitrators. *William Smith.*

To David Jones, the sum of four pounds ten shillings, for registering By-laws and returns under the Debentures Registration Act, and for repairs to office. *David Jones.*

To the Commissioner of the Victoria Macadamized Road, the sum of six pounds, to repair the toll houses on the said Road. *Commissioner Victoria Road.*

Commissioner Merrickville and Maitland Road. To the Commissioner of the Merrickville and Maitland County Toll Road, the sum of twelve pounds, to repair the toll houses on said road.

Commissioner West Port & Farmersville Road. To the Commissioner of the Westport and Farmersville County Toll Road, the sum of three pounds, to repair the toll houses on said road.

J. G. Elwood. To J. G. Elwood, the sum of one pound ten shillings, for making fires and keeping Court House in order, during the sitting of the Council.

Council Front Yonge & Escott. To the Municipal Council of the Front of Yonge and Escott, the sum of fifty pounds, to aid in opening the Road between Lansdowne and Escott, lying between the Kingston Road and the River St. Lawrence, provided the Councils of the said Townships grant and expend a like sum on the said road, and that Thomas Darling, Esq., be appointed to superintend such expenditure.

The Warden. To the Warden, the sum of twenty-five pounds, in full for his services out of Council for the current year, in lieu of the sum of £1 per day as per By-Law.

James Kincaid. To James Kincaid, the sum of one pound eighteen shillings and three pence, being the amount of his account for services as messenger and stationery furnished.

James Kincaid. That James Kincaid be directed to procure a stove pan for the office of Deputy Clerk of the Crown, and to give an order on the Treasurer for the expense of the same.

(Signed,)   H. D. JESSUP, Warden.

[L. S.]

(Signed,)   JAMES JESSUP, Clerk.

No CLXXIV.—BY-LAW

To appoint Auditors for the current year.—Passsd January 25th, 1850.

Be it enacted by the Municipal Council of the Corporation of the United Counties of Leeds and Grenville, and it is hereby enacted as follows:

1. That Jacob A. Brown, of the Township of Elizabeth- Jacob A. Brown. town, having been nominated by the Warden, be appointed Auditor for the current year.

2. That Chaney H. Peck, of the Town of Prescott, be Chaney H. Peck. also appointed Auditor for the same period.

3. That the said Jacob A. Brown, and Chaney H. Peck, School Auditors. be also appointed School Auditors for the current year, under the 5th sub-section of the 27th section of the Act, 13th and 14th Vic., chap. 48.

(Signed,)　　WM. GARVEY, Warden.
[L. S.]
(Signed,)　　JAMES JESSUP, Clerk.

No. CLXXV.—BY-LAW

To appoint Trustees for each of the County Grammar Schools and Local Superintendents of Common Schools in the United Counties of Leeds and Grenville.— Passed 26th January, 1860.

Be it enacted by the Municipal Council of [the Corporation of the United Counties of Leeds and Grenville, and it is hereby enacted as follows:

1. That the persons hereinafter in this section mentioned, be elected and appointed trustees of the County Grammar Trustees ap- Schools in the said United [Counties, as they are respec- pointed. tively assigned to each of the said schools, that is to say:

For the Grammar School at Brockville, Rev. J. T. Lewis Brockv'leSchool. and John Ross, re-appointed.

Kemptville Sch'l For the Grammar School at Kemptville, Rev. Joseph Anderson, re-appointed, Samuel Christie in place of Rev. J. Lewis, and Rev. John Charles Quin in place of Joseph Bower, re-appointed.

Prescott School. For the Grammar School at Prescott, John Easton and William Ellis, re-appointed.

Gananoque School. For the Grammar School at Gananoque, William S. McDonald, re-appointed, and James Kirker in place of Robert McCrum.

And that the said appointments are to commence on the 31st day of January, instant.

2. That the persons hereinafter mentioned be, and they are hereby appointed Local Superintendents of Common Schools for the Municipalities respectively in this section mentioned, that is to say :

Local Superintendents.

Augusta.............................James Clapperton.
Oxford...............................Rev. Joseph Anderson.
Front of Leeds and Lansdowne..Robert McCrum.
Rear of Leeds and Lansdowne...Rev. John Davison.
Rear of Yonge and Escott.......Asher A. Chamberlain.
Front of Yonge....................Rev. J. C. Pomeroy.
Front of Escott. ....Charles N. Hagerman,
Elizabethtown......................Jacob A. Brown.
Edwardsburgh......................Rev. Andrew Melville.
South Gower.......................Rev. Joseph Anderson.
Wolford............................Rev. T. N. Parnell.
Kitley.............................Rev. Thos. Campbell.
Elmsley............................John Ferguson.
Bastard and Burgess............Lewis Chipman.
South Crosby.....................Rev. John Davison.
North Crosby....................James Bilton.

And that the said appointments of Local Superintendents shall commence and take effect on the first day of April next, and not before.

(Signed,)   WM. GARVEY, Warden.

[L. S.]

(Signed,)   JAMES JESSUP, Clerk.

No. CLXXVI.—BY-LAW·

To appoint a Surgeon to the Gaol.—Passed January 26th,
1860.

Be it enacted by the Municipal Council of the Corporation of the United Counties of Leeds and Grenville, and it is hereby enacted as follows:

1. That John H. Morden be, and is hereby appointed Dr. John H. Surgeon to the Gaol of these Counties, according to the Morden. Statutes in that behalf.

2. That the salary of the said Surgeon be £25 currency Salary. per annum.

. (Signed,) WM. GARVEY, Warden.

[L. S.]

(Signed,) JAMES JESSUP, Clerk.

No. CLXXVII.—BY-LAW

To appoint a Special Committee for the purpose therein mentioned.—Passed January 27th, 1860.

Be it enacted by the Municipal Council of the Corporation of the United Counties of Leeds and Grenville, and it is hereby enacted,

That a Special Committee be appointed to confer with the Inspectors of Prisons, appointed under the first section To confer with of the Act, 22 Vic., cap. 110 of the Consolidated Statutes Inspectors of Prisons, &c. of Canada, and that the said Special Committee consist of Wm. Garvey, Warden of the said United Counties, and Messrs. Kirker, Smith, White and Waugh, members of this Council, such Committee being appointed in conformity with the 18th section of the said Act.

(Signed,) WM. GARVEY, Warden.

[L. S.]

(Signed,) JAMES JESSUP, Clerk.

Y

No. CLXXVIII.—BY-LAW

To define the powers to be exercised over the Road therein mentioned.—Passed 27th January, 1860.

Preamble. Whereas by a certain By-Law, passed on the 23rd day of June, in the year one thousand eight hundred and fifty-nine, and intituled, "By-Law to establish a road between the Townships of Lansdowne and Escott," the powers intended to be exercised by the Council over the said road are not expressed therein ; and for remedy thereof, be it therefore enacted by the Municipal Corporation of the United Counties of Leeds and Grenville, and it is hereby enacted and declared :

Powers to be exercised. That the powers intended to be exercised by this Council over the said road, as described and established in and by the said in part recited By-law, are those only which, in its discretion, it might of right exercise, if the said road were wholly on the Town line or original allowance for road between the said Townships of Lansdowne and Escott.

Warden to appoint Arbitrator. 2. And be it further enacted, That it shall be the duty of the Warden of these United Counties for the time being, and it is hereby authorized and empowered to appoint some fit and proper person to attend any arbitration, that may hereafter take place in reference to any matter or thing in which this Council is or may be concerned, to attend the sitting or sittings of any such arbitration, to see that the interests of this Council shall not suffer for want of fit and proper witnesses being had in attendance, or for want of fit and proper counsel and advice to any arbitrator or arbitrators acting on the part of this Council, so that justice may be done in the premises.

(Signed,) WM. GARVEY, Warden.

[L. S.]

(Signed,) JAMES JESSUP, Clerk.

No. CLXXIX.—BY-LAW

To confirm a By-Law of the Municipal Council of the Corporation of the Township of Wolford to stop up and sell a certain original allowance for Road in the Township of Wolford.—Passed January 28th, 1860.

Whereas it is expedient and necessary to confirm a By-Law passed by the Municipal Council of the Corporation of the Township of Wolford, on the 27th day of December, in the year of our Lord one thousand eight hundred and fifty-nine, which said By-Law is numbered fifty-five, and intituled, "By-Law to stop up and sell a certain original allowance for road in the Township of Wolford;" Be it therefore enacted by the Municipal Council of the Corporation of the United Counties of Leeds and Grenville, and it is hereby enacted : That the said in part recited By-Law, passed by the said Council of Wolford on the day and year last aforesaid, be, and the same is hereby confirmed. *Preamble.*

By-Law No. 55 confirmed.

(Signed,) WM. GARVEY, WARDEN.

[L. S.]

(Signed,) JAMES JESSUP, CLERK.

———

No. CLXXX.—BY-LAW

To cover certain Grants of Money.—Passed 28th January, 1860.

Be it enacted by the Municipal Council of the Corporation of the United Counties of Leeds and Grenville, and it is hereby enacted, That the several sums of money hereinafter mentioned, shall be paid by the Treasurer to the parties respectively, out of any moneys in his hands applicable to such purposes, viz. : *Sums to be paid to.*

To Adam Anderson the sum of $25 80, for fifty-seven covers for Collectors' and Assessment Rolls. *Adam Anderson.*

To William Howse the sum of $30, for repairing roof of Court House. *William Howse.*

To the County Clerk the sum of $8 42, for postage, freight &c., disbursed by him for the Counties. *County Clerk.*

John McMullen. To John McMullen the sum of $19 74, for stationery and advertising.

Commissioners of County Roads. To each of the Commissioners of the County Toll Roads, the sum of $10, as payment of their expenses while employed as such Commissioners for the last year.

James Kincaid. To James Kincaid the sum of £4 10s. 6d., for services as messenger and stationery furnished.

Abigail Nettleton. That the sum of £11 5s. be deducted from the rent of Abigail Nettleton, keeper of the Toll Gate No. 2, on the Kemptville and Prescott County Road.

Prescott taxes. That the Treasurer be authorized to receive from the Municipality of Prescott, the sum of £400 in full for taxes due by them to these Counties for the year 1859.

(Signed,)   WM. GARVEY, Warden.

[L. S.]

(Signed,)   JAMES JESSUP, Clerk.

No. CLXXXI.—BY-LAW

To authorize a temporary loan until the Assessments for the present year become available.—Passed January 28th, 1860.

(Repealed : see By-Law No. 228, sec. 4.)

No. CLXXXII.—BY-LAW

To raise the sum of £4,500 for the purpose therein mentioned.- Passed 19th June, 1860.

Preamble. Whereas the Municipal Council of the Corporation of the United Counties of Leeds and Grenville, have resolved to pay off the balance of the debt of the said United Counties to Robert Peden, Esq., contracted under the provisions of By-Law numbered one hundred and fifty-six, passed by the said Council on the fifth day of February, in the year of our Lord one thousand eight hundred and fifty-nine, and intituled—" By-Law to authorise an arrangement for the resumption of the County Toll Roads on the terms therein mentioned."

And, whereas, to carry into effect the said recited ob- Preamble. ject, it will be necessary for the said Municipal Council to raise the sum of four thousand five hundred pounds by the issue of debentures in the manner hereinafter mentioned, and which debentures the said Robert Peden hath agreed to receive at par in full satisfaction and discharge of the said debt.

And, whereas, it will require the sum of nine hundred Preamble. and seven pounds ten shillings to be raised annually by special rate for the payment of the said debt and interest, as also hereinafter mentioned.

And, whereas, the amount of the whole rateable pro- Preamble. perty of the said Municipality, irrespective of any future increase of the same, and also irrespective of any income to be derived from the temporary investment of the sinking fund hereinafter mentioned, or any part thereof, according to the last revised Assessment Rolls of the said Municipality, being for the year one thousand eight hundred and fifty-nine was £1,513,256.

And, whereas, for paying the interest and creating an Preamble. equal yearly sinking fund for paying the said sum of four thousand five hundred pounds and interest, as hereinafter mentioned, it will require an equal annual special rate of one-sixth of a penny in the pound, in addition to all other rates to be levied in each year.

Be it therefore enacted by the Municipal Council of the Corporation of the United Counties of Leeds and Grenville, and it is hereby enacted as follows :—

1. That it shall be lawful for the Warden of the said Warden to cause United Counties for the time being, to cause debentures to Debentures to be made. be made, as hereinafter provided, for a sum of money not exceeding in the whole the sum of four thousand five hundred pounds upon the credit of the special rate hereinafter imposed for the purpose and with the object above recited.

2. That the said debentures shall be issued in sums of seven hundred and fifty pounds each, and shall be sealed Each Debenture £750. with the seal of the Municipal Council, and be signed by the Warden, Clerk and Treasurer.

Payable annually.

3. That the said debentures shall be made payable annually, from the day hereinafter mentioned for this By-Law to take effect, at the office of the Treasurer of the said Municipality, and shall have attached to them coupons for the payment of the interest.

Rate of Interest, &c.

4. That the said debentures shall bear interest at and after the rate of six per cent. per annum from the date thereof, which interest shall be payable half-yearly at the office of the Treasurer aforesaid.

special rate.

5. That for the purpose of forming a sinking fund for the payment of the said debentures and the interest, at the rate aforesaid, to become due thereon, an equal special rate of one-sixth of a penny in the pound shall, in addition to all other rates, be raised, levied and collected in each year, upon the rateable property in the said Municipality during the continuance of the said debentures or any of them.

When By-Law to take effect I

6. That this By-Law shall take effect and come into operation upon the twentieth day of June, in the year of our Lord one thousand eight hundred and sixty.

(Signed,) WM. GARVEY, WARDEN.

[L. S.]

(Signed,) JAMES JESSUP, CLERK.

No. CLXXXIII.—BY-LAW

To make provision for the preservation of the Public Morals of the United Counties of Leeds and Grenville.— Passed 20th June, 1860.

(Repealed: see By-Law No. 193.)

No. CLXXXIV.—BY-LAW

Respecting Government allowances for Roads between Municipalities.—Passed 21st June, 1860.

(Repealed: see By-Law No. 213.)

No. CLXXXV.—BY-LAW

To establish a Grammar School in the Village of Farmers- See 29 Vic., Cap.
ville.—Passed 21st June, 1860. 23.

Whereas it appears that the state of the Grammar School Preamble.
fund is at present ample to permit the establishment of
an additional Grammar School in these Counties.

Be it therefore enacted by the Municipal Council of
the Corporation of the United Counties of Leeds and
Grenville, and it is hereby enacted, That a Grammar
School be established at the Village of Farmersville, in the School establis'd.
County of Leeds, according to the statute in that behalf.

2. That James Deming, Harmonious Alguire, Arza
Parish, Thomas Hayes, Lemuel Cornell, John Kincaid,
Wellington Landon, and Henry Green, be appointed
Trustees of the said Grammar School, and that two of such Trustees.
Trustees shall retire from office annually on the thirty-first
day of January in each year, in the order of their appoint-
ment, as hereinafter mentioned.

(Signed,)   WM. GARVEY, Warden.

[L. S.]

(Signed,)   JAMES JESSUP, Clerk.

No. CLXXXVI.—BY-LAW

To confirm a By-Law of the Municipal Council of the
Township of Elizabethtown to sell to James B. Powell,
Esq., the Government allowance of side road between
the front part of Lots numbers thirty and thirty-one, in
the second Concession of the Township of Elizabeth-
town.—Passed 21st June, 1860.

Whereas it is expedient and necessary to confirm a cer- Preamble.
tain By-Law, passed by the Municipal Council of the
Township of Elizabethtown, on the seventh day of November, in the year of our Lord one thousand eight hundred
and fifty-nine, and intituled—"By-Law to sell to James
B. Powell, Esq., the Government allowance of side road
between the front part of lots numbers thirty and thirty-
one, in the second Concession of the Township of Elizabethtown."

Be it therefore enacted by the Municipal Council of the Corporation of the United Counties of Leeds and Grenville, and it is hereby enacted, That the said in part recited By-Law passed by the said Council of Elizabethtown, on the day and year last aforesaid, be and the same is hereby confirmed.

By-law confirmed.

(Signed,) WM. GARVEY, Warden.

[L. S.]

(Signed,) JAMES JESSUP, Clerk.

No. CLXXXVII.—BY-LAW

See By-Law No. 231.

To authorize the completion of the arrangement with Robert Peden, Esq.—Passed 22nd June, 1860.

Warden & Clerk appointed for that purpose.

Be it enacted by the Municipal Council of the Corporation United Counties of Leeds and Grenville, and it is hereby enacted, That the Warden and Clerk of this Council be authorized and empowered to complete the proposed arrangement with the said Robert Peden, Esquire, and to take and receive from him such release or discharge as in the opinion of the Solicitors of this Council may be requisite to fully discharge this Council from any liability under the existing contract with him, after the liquidation of the balance of the debt to the said Robert Peden, as now proposed, and also that the said Warden and Clerk be empowered to sign, seal, and execute on behalf of the Corporation any writings or documents that may be necessary to carry into full and complete effect the said arrangement.

(Signed,) WM. GARVEY, Warden.

[L. S.]

(Signed,) JAMES JESSUP, Clerk.

No. CLXXXVIII.—BY-LAW

To assess the United Counties of Leeds and Grenville for the year 1860.—Passed 22nd June, 1860.

Be it enacted by the Municipal Council of the Corporation of the United Counties of Leeds and Grenville, and it is hereby enacted, That there be raised and levied upon the whole rateable property in the said United Counties for the present year, the sum of £4,000 to defray the ordinary and current expenses thereof, and the further sum of £1,498 to pay the salaries of legally qualified Common School teachers, and the further sum of £3,090 7s., as a special rate authorised to be raised and levied upon the said property, under the provisions of By-Laws numbered eight and thirty-nine, passed respectively on the tenth day of October, 1850, and the seventh day of May, 1852, and the further sum of £882 18s. 8d., as a special rate authorized to be raised and levied upon the said property, under the provisions of By-Law numbered one hundred and twenty, passed on the thirteenth day of October, 1856, and intituled—" By-Law to authorize the negotiation of a loan of money by the issue of debentures, to pay the debt and other liabilities therein mentioned;" and the further sum of £1,030 1s. 6d., as a special rate authorized to be raised and levied upon the said property under the provisions of By-Law numbered one hundred and eighty-two, passed on the nineteenth day of June, 1860, and intituled—" By-Law to raise the sum of £4,500, by the issue of debentures for the purpose therein mentioned;" and that the said several sums shall be raised and levied in addition to all other rates and assessments, and be apportioned to the several Municipalities of the said United Counties in the following manner, viz.:—

Sums to be levied.

County Rate.

Com'on Schools.

Special rate for County Roads.

Special rate for loan.

Special rate under By Law No. 182.

How apportioned to Municipalities.

MUNICIPALITIES.	County Rate.			Common Schools.			Special rate for County Roads.			Special rate for Loan.			Special rate under By-Law 182.		
	£.	s.	d.	£.	s.	d.	£.	s.	d.	£.	s.	d.	£.	s.	d.
Elizabethtown	652	11	4	169	5	0	417	10	7	119	5	10	139	3	6
Bastard and Burgess	247	17	1	126	10	0	196	15	0	56	4	3	65	11	8
Rear of Yonge and Escott	209	19	4	47	15	0	159	5	3	45	10	1	53	1	9
Front of Yonge	169	2	3	71	5	0	123	16	11	35	7	8	41	5	7
Front of Leeds and Lansdowne	284	19	2	110	0	0	219	0	7	62	11	7	73	0	½
Rear of Leeds and Lansdowne	151	19	2	64	10	0	99	16	6	28	10	5	33	5	½
Kitley	235	16	3	125	5	0	199	10	5	57	0	1	66	10	1
North Crosby	94	18	8	68	0	0	68	4	11	19	9	11	22	14	11
South Crosby	135	12	2	59	15	0	98	7	3	38	2	1	32	15	9
Elmsley	76	16	8	36	15	0	59	18	4	17	2	4	19	19	5
Front of Escott	73	15	3	31	0	0	53	13	4	15	6	8	17	17	9
Augusta	423	13	6	188	10	0	355	7	0	101	10	6	118	9	0
Edwardsburgh	367	8	7	146	10	0	246	6	10	70	7	8	82	2	3
Oxford	274	10	6	126	5	0	218	15	8	62	10	2	72	18	6
Wolford	180	10	6	98	15	0	151	14	10	43	7	1	50	11	7
South Gower	94	12	10	28	0	0	76	11	1	21	17	5	25	10	4
Prescott	198	5	8				251	7	11	71	16	6	83	15	11
Kemptville	63	10	3				40	8	9	11	11	1	13	9	7
Mirickville	63	19	10				53	15	10	15	7	4	17	18	7
Totals	4000	0	0	1498	0	0	3090	7	0	882	18	8	1030	1	6

2. That the said several sums hereinbefore directed to be raised and levied in the said Municipalities respectively, shall be placed on the Collector's Roll by the Clerk thereof, in separate columns, and be collected in like manner as all other rates and assessments are by law directed to be collected, and that every Collector shall, on or before the fourteenth day of December next, return his Roll to the Treasurer of the Municipality for which he is appointed, and pay over to such Treasurer the sums hereby directed to be raised, levied and collected therein. *How levied and collected.*

(Signed,) WM. GARVEY, Warden.

[L. S.]

(Signed,) JAMES JESSUP, Clerk.

No. CLXXXIX.—BY-LAW

Respecting the Sale of Lands for Taxes.—Passed 23rd June, 1860.

Whereas it is expedient and necessary to determine the sum for which lands in arrear for taxes may be sold, pursuant to the 127th section of " the Consolidated Assessment Act for Upper Canada." *Preamble.*

Be it therefore enacted by the Municipal Council of the Corporation of the United Counties of Leeds and Grenville, and it is hereby enacted, That no lot or parcel of land shall be sold which is chargeable with a sum less than four dollars, and the Treasurer is hereby directed to include in any warrant he may hereafter issue to the Sheriff, such parcels of land only as are chargeable with an arrear of tax amounting to the said sum of four dollars or upwards. *Lots charged with less than $4 not to be sold.*

(Signed,) WM. GARVEY, Warden.

[L. S.]

(Signed,) JAMES JESSUP, Clerk.

No. CXC.—BY-LAW

To cover certain Grants of Money—Passed 23rd June, 1860.

<table>
<tr><td>Sums paid to.</td><td>Be it enacted by the Municipal Council of the United Counties of Leeds and Grenville, and it is hereby enacted, that the several sums of money hereinafter mentioned, shall be paid by the Treasurer to the parties respectively out of any moneys in his hands applicable to such purposes, viz. :—</td></tr>

<tr><td>David Wylie.</td><td>To David Wylie, Esq., the sum of twenty nine pounds twelve shillings, being the balance due him for printing and advertising.</td></tr>

<tr><td>Maclear & Co.</td><td>To Messrs. Maclear & Co., the sum of four pounds for book for the County Clerk's Office.</td></tr>

<tr><td>James Kincaid.</td><td>To James Kincaid, the sum of seven pounds ten shillings, for six months salary as Keeper of the Court House, and for keeping the same in order from the 13th October, 1859, to 13th April, 1860.</td></tr>

<tr><td>County Clerk.</td><td>To the County Clerk, the sum of one pound one shilling and five pence, for postages disbursed for the Counties.</td></tr>

<tr><td>Rice Mosher.</td><td>To Rice Mosher, the sum of sixteen pounds five shillings as compensation for land taken from him in the construction of the Mirickville and Maitland County Toll Road and for fence, provided the said Rice Mosher shall give to the Corporation a good and sufficient deed of the said land, to be approved of by the Clerk.</td></tr>

<tr><td>Harvey Miller.</td><td>To Harvey Miller, the sum of ten shillings for repairing stove in the Court Room.</td></tr>

<tr><td>James Kincaid.</td><td>To James Kincaid, the sum of two pounds fifteen shillings, for services as messenger of the Council and keeping the Council Chamber in order this session.</td></tr>
</table>

(Signed,)   WM. GARVEY, WARDEN.

[L. S.]

(Signed,)   JAMES JESSUP, CLERK.

No. CXCI.—BY-LAW

To appoint a Trustee of the Grammar School therein men- See 29 Vic., Cap.
tioned.—Passed 7th November, 1860. 25.

Be it enacted by the Municipal Council of the Corporation of the United Counties of Leeds and Grenville, and
it is hereby enacted, That David F. Jones, Esq., be elected David F. Jones.
and appointed a Trustee of the County Grammar School
established at the Village of Gananoque, in the place of
the Hon. John Macdonald, deceased, and that the said
David F. Jones shall hold such appointment until the
thirty-first day of January, in the year of our Lord one
thousand eight hundred and sixty-two.

(Signed,) WM. GARVEY, Warden.
[L. S.]
(Signed,) JAMES JESSUP, Clerk.

No. CXCII.—BY-LAW

To repeal By-Law numbered thirty-four, and to divide the
Counties into School Circuits.—Passed 8th Novem-
ber, 1860.

Be it enacted by the Municipal Council of the Corporation of the United Counties of Leeds and Grenville, and
it is hereby enacted, That By-Law numbered thirty-four,
and intituled, " By-Law to divide the United Counties of
Leeds and Grenville into School Circuits," be repealed, Repeal.
and the same is hereby repealed; and that from and after
the passing of this By-Law the said United Counties shall
be divided in five School Circuits, pursuant to the ninety-
fifth section of " the Upper Canada Common School Act,"
and that the limits and description of the said Circuits
respectively, shall be as follows, that is to say :—

CIRCUIT No. 1.

To include the Town of Brockville, and the Township of Limits of Circ'lts.
Elizabethtown and Front of Yonge. Amended: see
By-law No. 226.

CIRCUIT No. 2.

To include the Townships of Front of Leeds and Lansdowne, and Front of Escott.

Circuit No. 3.

To include the Townships of Oxford, Wolford and South Gower, and the Villages of Kemptville and Mirickville.

Circuit No. 4.

To include the Townships of Edwardsburgh and Augusta, and the Town of Prescott.

Circuit No. 5.

To include the Townships of Rear of Yonge and Escott, Rear of Leeds and Lansdowne, Bastard Burgess, North Crosby, South Crosby, Kitley and Elmsley.

(Signed,)   WM. GARVEY, Warden..

[L. S.]

(Signed,)   JAMES JESSUP, Clerk.

No. CXCIII.—BY-LAW

To repeal By-Law one hundred and eighty-three.—Passed 8th November, 1860.

Repeal.   Be it enacted by the Municipal Council of the Corporation of the United Counties of Leeds and Grenville, and it is hereby enacted, That from and after the passing thereof, By-Law numbered one hundred and eighty-three, and intituled, " By-Law to make provision for the preservation of the Public Morals of the United Counties of Leeds and Grenville," be repealed and the same is hereby repealed.

(Signed,)   WM. GARVEY, Warden.

[L. S.]

(Signed,)   JAMES JESSUP, Clerk.

No. CXCIV.—BY-LAW

*To provide for the preservation of the Public Morals of the
United Counties of Leeds and Grenville.—Passed 9th
November, 1860.*

Be it enacted by the Municipal Council of the Corporation of the United Counties of Leeds and Grenville, and
it is hereby enacted, as follows :—

1. That it shall be unlawful to sell or give intoxicating
drinks of any sort to any child, apprentice or servant,
within these Counties, without the consent of the parent,
master, or legal protector of such child, apprentice, or servant. *Selling liquors to a child, &c.*

2. That it shall not be lawful for any person to post any
indecent placards, writings or pictures, or write any indecent words, or make any indecent pictures or drawings on
any walls or fences, in any street, highway, or public place,
within these Counties. *Posting placards,*

3. That it shall not be lawful for any person to utter any
profane oath, or any obscene, indecent, blasphemous, or
grossly insulting language, in any street, highway, or public place, within these counties. *Profane oaths, &c.*

4. That it shall not be lawful for any person to be drunk,
or guilty of any drunkenness or disorderly conduct, in
any street, highway, or public place, within these Counties. *Drunkenness, &c*

5. That it shall not be lawful for any person indecently
to expose his or her person, or to be guilty of any indecent,
immoral, or scandalous behaviour, in any street, highway,
or public place, within these Counties. *Exposing the per- sons, &c.*

6. That it shall not be lawful for any person to bathe,
or indecently expose his or her person by washing the
person in any public water, within these Counties, near
any public highway, or any dwelling house, between the
hours of six of the clock in the morning and eight of the
clock in the evening, unless provided with and clothed in
a proper bathing dress, sufficient to prevent any indecent
exposure of the person. *Bathing, &c., in public waters*

7. That it shall not be lawful for any tippling to be in
any inn, tavern, or place where intoxicating liquors are sold, *Tippling.*

within these Counties, and no house designated as a tippling house, shall be permitted to exist and to be within these Counties.

House of ill fame. Amended: see By-law No. 248. 8. That it shall not be lawful for any person or persons to keep, support, or maintain any house or place of " ill-fame ;" nor shall there be permitted to be and exist any such house or place within these Counties.

Horse Racing. 9. That it shall not be lawful for any horse-racing, whether or not for hire, gain, wager, money or moneys, value or worth, to be done or practised in any public street, road, or highway, within these Counties.

Bowling Alley. 10. That it shall not be lawful for any bowling alley, kept for hire or profit, (excepting herefrom those already licensed till expiry of license,) to be within these Counties.

Gambling House. 11. That it shall not be lawful for any gambling house or place to be within these Counties, and that it shall be lawful for any Constable of these Counties to seize and destroy all faro banks, rouge et noir, roulette tables, and other devices for gambling, found within such place or house.

Breach of By-law, penalty for. 12. That any person or persons guilty of a violation of any of the provisions of this By-Law shall, upon a conviction before any Justice or Justices of the Peace, having jurisdiction in the said Counties, be liable to a fine of not more than fifty dollars, with costs of conviction, to be collected by distress and sale of the goods and chattels of the said offender or offenders; and in case no goods or chattels are found belonging to the said offender or offenders as aforesaid, on which to levy the fine and costs as aforesaid, it shall be lawful for any such Justice or Justices of the Peace to commit the offender or offenders to the common gaol or lock-up, within the said United Counties of Leeds and Grenville, for a period of not more than twenty days with or without hard labor, as the said Justice or Justices may determine, unless the fine and all costs be sooner paid.

How penalties applied. 13. That all penalties imposed and collected by virtue of this By-Law shall be, when collected, paid, one moiety thereof to the informer or prosecutor, and the other moiety to the said Corporation, unless the prosecution is brought in the name of the Corporation, and in that case the whole of the pecuniary penalty shall be paid to the said Corporation.

14. That this By-Law shall have no force or effect within the incorporated Towns of Brockville and Prescott. *Not in force in Brockville and Prescott.*

15. That any By-Law or part or parts of any By-Law contrary to or inconsistent with any of the provisions of this By-Law are hereby repealed. *By-laws inconsistent repealed.*

(Signed,)   WM. GARVEY, Warden.

[L. S.]

(Signed,)   JAMES JESSUP, Clerk.

No. CXCV.—BY-LAW

To authorize the opening of part of the Town Line or Government allowance for road between the Township of Leeds, in the County of Leeds, and the Township of Pittsburgh, in the County of Frontenac.—Passed 9th November, 1860.

Whereas application has been made to the Municipal Council of the Corporation of the United Counties of Leeds and Grenville, by William Shaw and others, inhabitants of the said Township of Leeds, to open the Town Line or Government allowance for road between the said Townships of Leeds and Pittsburgh, from the centre of the second concession to the centre of the fifth concession of the said Township of Leeds; and whereas, one Luke Connor is in possession of part of the said Town Line or Government allowance, and whereas, notice in writing has been given to the said Luke Connor, at least eight days before the present meeting of this Council, that such application would be made thereat for opening the said Town Line or Government allowance for road: and whereas, it is expedient and necessary to open the same, be it therefore enacted by the Municipal Council of the Corporation of the United Counties of Leeds and Grenville; and it is hereby enacted, that the said Town Line or Government allowance for road be opened for public use and travel, from the centre of the second concession to the centre of the fifth concession of the said Township of Leeds, and the same is hereby declared to be opened for that purpose, according to the statute in that behalf, so far as this Council has a right to do so, having only a joint jurisdiction over the said road with the Council of the Corporation of the United Counties of Frontenac, Lennox and Addington. *Preamble.* *Town Line opened.*

Z

2. That at the first meeting of this Council in each and
every year hereafter, one or more overseer or overseers of
highways shall be appointed by this Council to act jointly
with such overseer or overseers that may be appointed by
the said Council or the Corporation of the United Counties of Frontenac, Lennox and Addington, for the said
Town Line or Government allowance, so ordered to be
opened as aforesaid.

Overseers.

3. That nothing herein contained shall be taken or
construed to mean that this Council intends or intended
to appropriate any money towards the opening of the said
road as aforesaid ; nor shall it bind this Council to make
any appropriation therefor.

Interpretation.

(Signed,)   WM. GARVEY, Warden.

[L. S.]

(Signed,)   JAMES JESSUP, Clerk.

———

No. CXCVI.—BY-LAW,

*To cover certain Grants of Money.—Passed 10th Novem-
ber, 1860.*

Be it enacted by the Municipal Council of the Corporation of the United Counties of Leeds and Grenville, and
it is hereby enacted, That the several sums of money
hereinafter mentioned shall be paid by the Treasurer to
the parties respectively, out of any moneys in his hands
applicable to such purposes, viz. :

Sums paid to.

To Messrs. Sherwood and Steele, Solicitors of the Council,
the sum of seventy-two pounds fifteen shillings, being
the balance of their account for services rendered.

*Messrs. Sher-
wood & Steele.*

To William Fitzsimmons, the sum of one pound thirteen
shillings and ten pence, for work done in the gaol.

*William Fitzsim-
mons.*

To Alfred Poulton, the sum of seventeen pounds two shillings and eight pence, for repairing windows in gaol
and court-house for the year ending 1st October,
1860, and for painting the windows of the Court
House.

Alfred Poulton.

To James Kincaid, the sum of six pounds fifteen shillings and three pence, for fitting up the Court Room and lighting the Court House, on the visit of the Prince of Wales. James Kincaid.

To the County Clerk, the sum of two pounds eight shillings and two pence for postage and other disbursements made by him for the Counties. County Clerk.

To the Board of Education for the Gananoque division, the sum of two pounds six shillings and sixpence, for the expenses of the Board. Board Education Gananoque.

To the Board of Public Instruction for Circuit No. 1, the sum of four pounds fifteen shillings, for the expenses of the Board. Board Public Instruction No. 1.

To James Kincaid, the sum of seven pounds ten shillings, for six months salary to 13th October, 1860, as keeper of the Court House. James Kincaid.

To Reuben Fields, the sum of three pounds five shillings, amount of his account as arbitrator on the claim of John Shephard. Reuben Fields.

To Benjamin Kirker, the sum of three pounds, amount of his account as arbitrator on the claim of John Shephard. Ben. Kirker.

To William Lattimore, the sum of eight pounds fifteen shillings ; N. Gilbert, the sum of three pounds ; M. Chisamore, the sum of two pounds ; Thos. Darling, the sum of ten pounds ; and to John Shephard, the sum of six pounds as compensation awarded by the arbitrators for lands taken from them respectively, for the road between Lansdowne and Escott, provided they shall respectively give to the said Corporation a good and sufficient deed of such land, to be approved of by the Clerk. William Lattimore and others.

To William Garvey, Esquire, the sum of twelve shillings for postage and other disbursements. William Garvey.

To John McMullen, the sum of four pounds fifteen shillings and two pence, for stationery furnished ; and the further sum of fifty pounds on account of his contract for printing and advertising. John McMullen.

F. H. Whitmarsh. To E. H. Whitmarsh, the sum of twelve pounds ten shillings, for services as arbitrator on claims for land taken for the road between Lansdowne and Escott.

James Kirker. To James Kirker, the sum of seven pounds ten shillings, for services as arbitrator on claims for land taken for the road been Lansdowne and Escott.

Auditors. To C. H. Peck and Jacob A. Brown, the sum of ten pounds each, allowed to them for their services as auditors for the present year.

Harvey Miller. To Harvey Miller, the sum of two pounds nine shillings and sixpence, for work done to the gaol and materials furnished.

The Warden. To the Warden, the sum of twenty-five pounds in full for his services out of Council for the current year, in lieu of the sum of £1 per day as per By-Law.

James Kincaid. To James Kincaid, the sum of three pounds two shillings and sixpence for services as messenger.

Visit of Prince of Wales. 2. That the sum of one hundred and twenty-five pounds, ordered to be paid by the Treasurer to the Town of Brockville, to defray in part the expenses attending the late visit of His Royal Highness the Prince of Wales to these United Counties and the Town of Brockville, be granted from the County funds, to cover the said sum so paid by the said Treasurer.

Bonds, Wm. Willoughby. 3. That the Treasurer be requested to return to William Willoughby his bail-bonds as Tollgate keeper, on the Victoria Macadamized Road, in 1858, on the said Wm. Willoughby paying the amount of his tender, deducting therefrom the sum of fifteen pounds.

Prescott taxes 4. That the Treasurer be authorised to receive from the Corporation of the Town of Prescott the sum of three hundred and fifty pounds, instead of six hundred and five pounds, as apportioned to the said Municipality, to be in full for the claim of these Counties for the present year.

Addition to Clerk's Salary. See By-laws Nos. 26 and 80. 5. That the sum of fifty pounds per annum be added to the County Clerk's salary, payable quarterly, on the first days of January, April, July and October, in each year, to enable him to employ assistance in his office, and that the receipt of the said clerk shall hereafter be a sufficient voucher to the Treasurer for the payment of the said salary.

(Signed,) WM. GARVEY, WARDEN.

[L. S.]

(Signed,)   JAMES JESSUP, CLERK.

No. CXCVII.—BY-LAW

To appoint Auditors for the current year.—Passed 23rd January, 1861.

Be it enacted by the Municipal Council of the Corporation of the United Counties of Leeds and Grenville, and it is hereby enacted, as follows :—

1. That Samuel McCammon, of the Village of Gananoque, having been nominated by the Warden, be appointed Auditor for the current year. Samuel McCammon.

2. That Chancey H. Peck, of the Town of Prescott, be also appointed Auditor for the same period. Chancy H. Peck.

3. That the said Samuel McCammon and Chancey H. Peck, be also appointed School Auditors for the current year, pursuant to the Common School Act for Upper Canada. School Auditors.

[Signed,]   WM. GARVEY, WARDEN.

[L. S.]

[Signed,]   JAMES JESSUP, CLERK.

No. CXCVIII.—BY-LAW

To appoint Trustees for each of the County Grammar Schools, and Local Superintendents of Common Schools.—Passed 23rd January, 1861.

Be it enacted by the Municipal Council of the Corporation of the United Counties of Leeds and Grenville, and it is hereby enacted as follows :

1. That the persons hereinafter in this section mentioned, be elected and appointed Trustees of the County Grammar Schools in the said United Counties, as they are respectively assigned to each of the said schools, that is to say :

Trustees for.

For the Grammar School at Brockville.

Brockville Sch'l.

Rev. J. K. Smith, in place of David Robertson, and William Fitzsimmons in place of Robert Fitzsimmons, Jr.

For the Grammar School at Kemptville.

Kemptville Sch'l.

Richard Waugh, in place of Ambrose Clothier, and Robert Kernaban, re-appointed.

For the Grammar School at Prescott.

Prescott School.

Hamilton D. Jessup, re-appointed, and Mathew Dowsley, in place of C. H. Peck, and Charles Shaver, in place of the late John Patton.

For the Grammar School at Gananoque.

Gananoq'e Sch'l.

Rev. John Carroll, re-appointed and Rev. Henry Gordon, re-appointed.

For the Grammar School at Farmersville.

Farmersville School.

James Deming and Harmonious Alguire, re-appointed.

And that the said appointments are to commence and take effect on the thirty-first day of January, A. D. 1861.

2. That the persons hereinafter mentioned, be appointed Local Superintendents of Common Schools for the Municipalities respectively in the section mentioned, that is to say :

Local Superin-tendents.

Augusta.	James Clapperton.
Oxford.	Rev. Joseph Anderson.
Front of Leeds & Lansdowne	Robert McCrum.
Rear of Leeds & Lansdowne.	Rev. John Davison.
Rear of Yonge and Escott.	Seabury Scovil.
Front of Yonge..............	Joshua Lily.
Front of Escott...............	Chas. N. Hagerman.
Elizabethtown..............	Jacob A. Brown.
Edwardsburg.................	Rev. Andrew Melville.

South Gower	Rev. Joseph Anderson.
Wolford	Rev. J. R. Parnell.
Kitley.	William Morin.
Elmsley	John Ferguson.
Bastard and Burgess	Lewis Chipman.
South Crosby	Rev. John Davidson.
North Crosby	James Bilton.

And that the said appointments of Local Superintendents shall commence and take effect on the first day of April next, and not before.

(Signed,)   WILLIAM GARVEY, Warden.

[L. S.]

(Signed,)   JAMES JESSUP, Clerk.

No. CXCIX.—BY-LAW

To amend By-Law number Fifty-five, and intituled " By- See By-Law No·
Law to provide for Regular Meetings of the Municipal 160.
Council of the United Counties of Leeds and Grenville.
—Passed 24th January, 1861.

Be it therefore enacted by the Municipal Council of the Corporation of the United Counties of Leeds and Grenville, and it is hereby enacted.

That the words *" Fourth Monday in January,"* in the First Meeting 4th first Section of said By-Law number fifty-five, be expunged Tuesday in January. therefrom, and the words *" Fourth Tuesday in January,"* be inserted in lieu thereof, as now provided by law for the first meeting of said Council.

(Signed,)   WM. GARVEY, Warden.

[L. S.]

(Signed,)   JAMES JESSUP, Clerk.

No. CC.—BY-LAW

To repeal By-law number 169, and intituled " By-Law to appoint a Keeper of the Court House."—Passed 24th January, 1861.

See By-Laws
Nos. 125 & 169.

Be it enacted by the Municipal Council of the Corporation of the United Counties of Leeds and Grenville, and it is hereby enacted :

Repeal.

1. That the said in part recited By-Law be repealed, and the same is hereby repealed.

Sheriff to have charge of

2. That after the passing hereof, the Sheriff of these Counties shall have the care and custody of the Court House, Garden and Yard attached, provided he enter into a written lease with this Council for the said Garden and Yard, to be held by him during the pleasure of this Council, and pay a yearly rent of five shillings therefor; and provided also, that such lease be executed by the said Sheriff on or before the first day of March next, and be approved of by the Solicitors of this Council, reserving in said lease the use of the shed and out offices attached to the Court House for the public offices.

To be kept in order.

3. That the Sheriff keep the Court Room and Grand Jury Room in proper order at his own expense.

Lease.

4. That the Warden and Clerk be authorized to sign and countersign the said lease, and affix the seal of the Corporation thereto, on behalf of this Council.

(Signed,)   WM. GARVEY, Warden.

[L. S.]

(Signed,)   JAMES JESSUP, Clerk.

No. CCI.—BY-LAW

To appoint a Commissioner for the Kemptville and Prescott County Toll Road, in place of Ambrose Clothier.—Passed 25th January, 1861.

(Repealed : see By-Law No. 231.)

No. CCII.—BY-LAW

To authorize a Temporary Loan until the Assessments for the present year become available.—Passed 25th January, 1861.

(Repealed: see By-law No. 228, Sec. 4.)

No. CCIII.—BY-LAW

To Cover certain Grants of Money.—Passed 25th January, 1861.

Be it enacted by the Municipal Council of the Corporation of the United Counties of Leeds and Grenville, and it is hereby enacted:

That the several sums of money hereinafter mentioned shall be paid by the Treasurer to the parties respectively, out of any moneys in his hands applicable to such purposes, viz: *Sums paid to.*

To the Board of Public Instruction, for Grammar School Circuit No. 3, the sum of Twenty-six dollars for attendance of members and expenses of the Board. *Board Public Instruction No. 3.*

To M. Noodles, the sum of three dollars and fifty cents for removing snow drifts from the County Toll Road near Maitland, which sum shall be deducted by the Warden from the Contractor's next quarterly payment. *M. Noodles.*

To Adam Anderson the sum of twenty-four dollars, for making sixty covers for Assessment and Collectors' Rolls. *Adam Anderson.*

To the County Clerk, the sum of thirteen dollars and seventy cents, for Postage and other disbursements for the Counties. *County Clerk.*

To David Weeks, the sum of three dollars for removing snow drifts from the County Toll Road near Maitland, which sum shall be deducted by the Warden from the Contractors' next quarterly payment. *David Weeks.*

To David Wylie, the sum of twenty-four dollars and fifty cents, for printing and advertising. *David Wylie.*

N. S. Lasher. To N. S. Lasher, the sum of three dollars and twenty-five cents, for advertising for the Board of Education at Gananoque.

John McMullen. To John McMullen, the sum of one hundred and twenty dollars, on account of his contract for printing and advertising.

Commissioners County Roads. To each of the County Toll Commissioners, the sum of ten dollars, as expenses incurred for their services for the past year.

James Kincaid. To James Kincaid, the sum of twenty-eight dollars, and thirty cents, for keeping the Court House in order, attendance as messenger, and stationery and fuel furnished.

Elijah Barnes. To Elijah Bains, the sum of twenty-five dollars, being the amount of his account as keeper of Toll Gate at Sheffield's Corners, for repairing Toll House, &c.

(Signed,) E. H. WHITMARSH, Chairman.
[L. S.]

[Signed,] JAMES JESSUP, Clerk.

No. CCIV.—BY-LAW

To authorize the taking of the Census of the Village of Gananoque.—Passed 28th June, 1861,

Preamble. Whereas David F. Jones and one hundred and thirty-one other resident Freeholders and Householders of the Village of Gananoque, have applied by petition to have the census of the said Village taken, under the direction of this Council, with a view to its incorporation, and Whereas it is expedient to comply with the prayer of the said petition; be it therefore enacted by the Municipal Council of the Corporation of the United Counties of Leeds and Greenville, and it is hereby enacted as follows:—

1st. That the Commissioner hereinafter appointed be authorized and empowered to take the census of the said Village of Gananoque within the time hereinafter limited, and for the purpose of this by-law the boundaries of the

said village shall include and consist of the south halves Boundaries of
and broken fronts of lots number ten, eleven, twelve, Village.
thirteen, fourteen, fifteen, sixteen, and the west half of seventeen in the first concession of the Township of Leeds.

2nd. That the said census shall be taken and completed When cencus to
before the first day of October next, and a return thereof be taken.
made by the Commissioner to this Council at its meeting
in the month of October next.

3rd. That William Rodgers be appointed Commissioner Wm. Rodgers ap-
to take said census for the purpose aforesaid, and that all pointed to take
costs and charges for taking the said census be paid by same.
the petitioners.

(Signed,) WM. GARVEY, Warden.

[L. S.]

(Signed,) JAMES JESSUP, Clerk.

No. CCV.—BY-LAW

To cover certain Grants of Money.—Passed 29th June, 1861.

Be it enacted by the Municipal Council of the Corporation of the United Counties of Leeds and Grenville, and
it is hereby enacted, That the several sums of money here- Sums paid to.
inafter mentioned shall be paid by the Treasurer to the
parties respectively, out of any moneys in his hands
applicable to such purposes, viz:—

To John McMullen the sum of one hundred and thirty- John McMullen.
four dollars and sixty-four cents for Stationery,
Printing and Advertising, as per contract,

To County Clerk the sum of seven dollars and eighty- County Clerk.
three cents for postage and express charges.

To the Board of Examiners of Prescott circuit the sum of Board of Exami-
fifteen dollars and fifty cents, as per account. ners.

To the Board of Public Instruction the sum of three Board Public In-
pounds fourteen shillings and ten pence half-penny struction.
for attendance of members and expenses of the Board.

To J. G. Elwood the sum of four pounds ten shillings, as J. G. Elwood.
per his account.

2. That the sum of twenty-five pounds having been granted by the Council of Frontenac, Lenox and Addington for improving the eastern boundary line of the Township of Pittsburgh, between the Counties of Leeds and Frontenac, extending from the Montreal road to the front of the fourth concession, that a like sum of twenty-five pounds be granted by this Council for the same purpose, provided that the by-law of the Council of Frontenac, Lenox and Addington is in force, the sum of twenty-five pounds is still applicable for that purpose, and that Robert Anderson be appointed Commissioner for expending the sum hereby granted.

Town line Road between Leeds & Pittsburgh.

3. That the sum of seventy-five pounds be granted to build a new bridge at North Augusta on the County Toll Road, and that the Warden, E. H. Whitmarsh, and William Humphries, be authorized to expend the same in building of the said bridge.

North Augusta Bridge.

4. That the sum of seventy-five pounds be granted to build a bridge on the Victoria County Toll Road across Otter Creek where the old bridge now stands, and that James Shanks, John Riddle and John Moorhouse, be appointed Commissioners to build said bridge.

Otter Creek Bridge.

5. That the sum of fifteen dollars and fifteen cents be granted to James Kincaid for Stationery furnished, and attendance as messenger of the Council.

James Kincaid.

6. That the sum of eight dollars be granted to Allen Hunter for services as Arbitrator for this Council.

Allen Hunter.

7. That the following sums be paid to the parties:—

To Thomas Bell the sum of twenty dollars, William Young the sum of twenty dollars and William Humphries the sum of thirty-four dollars, in full payment as Commissioners on the County Toll Roads.

Thomas Bell and other commissioners.

8. That the sum of twenty-five pounds be granted to build a fence on the Court House premises agreeably to the second report of the Standing Committee on County property, and that the Warden and Mr. John Anderson be appointed Commissioners for expending the same.

Court House fence.

(Signed,)   WM. GARVEY, WARDEN,

[L. S.]

(Signed,)   JAMES JESSUP, CLERK.

No. CCVI.—BY-LAW

To Assess the United Counties of Leeds and Grenville, for the year 1861.—Passed June 29, 1861.

Be it enacted by the Municipal Council of the Corporation of the United Counties of Leeds and Grenville, and it is hereby enacted, That there be raised and levied upon the whole Rateable Property in the said United Counties for the present year, the sum of £4,500, to defray the ordinary and current expenses thereof, and the further sum of £1,484 15s., to pay the salaries of legally qualified common school Teachers, and the further sum of £781 12s. 10d., as a special rate, authorized to be raised and levied upon the said property, under the provisions of By-law numbered thirty-nine, passed on the seventh day of May, 1852, and the further sum of £893 6s. 5d., as a special rate, authorized to be raised and levied upon the said property, under the provisions of By-law numbered one hundred and twenty, passed on the thirteenth day of October, 1856, and a further sum of £1,042 4s. as a special rate authorized to be raised and levied upon the said property under the provisions of by-law numbered one hundred and eighty-two, passed on the nineteenth day of June 1860, And that the said several sums shall be raised and levied in addition to all other rates and assessments, and be apportioned to the several Municipalities of the said United Counties, in the following manner, viz:—

Marginal notes: Sums to be levied. County Rate. Com'on Schools. Special rate for County Roads. Special rate for loan. Special rate under By-Law No 182. How apportioned to Municipalities.

MUNICIPALITIES.	County Rates.			Common Schools.			Special Rate for County Roads.			Special Rate for Loan under by-law 120.			Special Rate under By-law 182.		
	£	s.	D.	£	s.	D.	£	s.	D.	£	s.	D.	£	s.	D.
Elizabethtown	737	11	4	156	15	0	112	15	10	128	18	1	150	7	9
Bastard and Burgess	280	6	10	128	15	0	49	8	9	56	10	1	65	18	4
Rear of Yonge and Escott	237	9	8	71	0	0	39	18	8	45	12	10	53	4	11
Front of Yonge	190	11	7	55	5	0	29	9	3	33	13	5	39	5	8
Front of Leeds and Lansdowne,	322	3	1	107	15	0	54	14	11	62	11	4	72	19	11
Rear of Leeds and Lansdowne,	171	13	9	62	5	0	28	6	11	32	7	11	37	15	11
Kitley	266	10	8	99	10	0	49	11	2	56	12	9	66	1	7
North Crosby	107	5	3	72	0	0	17	13	1	20	3	6	23	10	9
South Crosby	153	4	5	55	0	0	25	15	6	29	9	2	34	7	4
Elmsley	86	16	3	42	5	0	15	2	2	17	5	4	20	2	11
Front of Escott,	83	6	10	45	10	0	13	2	1	14	19	6	17	19	5
Augusta	487	1	6	169	10	0	90	11	9	103	10	7	120	15	8
Edwardsburgh	415	3	0	145	5	0	60	3	8	68	15	7	80	4	10
Oxford	310	3	7	131	5	0	57	2	10	65	6	2	76	3	10
Wolford	207	1	8	110	10	0	36	12	10	41	17	7	48	17	2
South Gower	106	18	8	31	15	0	19	8	11	22	4	6	25	18	7
Prescott	224	0	8				63	10	3	72	11	8	84	13	8
Kemptville	71	15	2				10	8	10	11	18	9	13	18	6
Merrickville	44	6	1				7	15	5	8	17	8	10	7	3
Totals	£4,500	0	0	£1,484	15	0	£781	12	10	£893	6	5	£1,042	4	0

2. That the said several sums hereinbefore directed to be raised and levied in the said Municipalities respectively, shall be placed on the Collector's Roll by the Clerk thereof in separate columns, and be collected in like manner as all other rates and assessments are by law directed to be collected, and that every Collector shall, on or before the fourteenth day of December next, return his roll to the Treasurer of his Municipality, and pay over to such Treasurer the sums hereby directed to be raised, levied and collected therein.

How levied and collected.

(Signed,)   WM. GARVEY, Warden.

[L. S.]

(Signed,)   JAMES JESSUP, Clerk.

No. CCVII.—BY-LAW

To confirm a certain By-Law of the Municipal Council of the Corporation of the Township of Rear of Leeds and Landsdowne.—Passed 15th October, 1861.

Whereas it is expedient and necessary to confirm a certain By-Law passed by the Municipal Council of the Corporation of the Township of Rear of Leeds and Lansdowne, on the twenty-fifth day of February, in the year of our Lord one thousand eight hundred and sixty-one, and entituled "By Law No. 32, to vest in Thomas Sheffield, Esquire, the Government allowance of road in rear of Lot No. 10, in the twelfth concession of Lansdowne." Be it therefore enacted by the Municipal Council of the Corporation of the United Counties of Leeds and Grenville, and it is hereby enacted, That the said in part recited By-Law, so passed by the said Council of Rear of Leeds and Lansdowne, be and the same is hereby confirmed.

Preamble.

By-law No. 32 confirmed.

(Signed,)   WM. GARVEY, Warden.

[L. S.]

(Signed,)   JAMES JESSUP, Clerk.

No. CCVIII.—BY-LAW

To confirm a certain By-law of the Municipal Council of the Corporation of the Township of Rear of Leeds and Lansdowne.—Passed 15th October, 1861.

Preamble.

Whereas it is expedient and necessary to confirm a certain By-law passed by the Municipal Council of the Corporation of the Township of Rear of Leeds and Lansdowne, on the twenty-fifth day of February, in the year of our Lord one thousand eight hundred and sixty-one, and intituled " By-Law No. 33, to vest in Alpheus R. Howard, Esq., a certain Government allowance of Road as hereinafter mentioned," whereby the Government allowance of Road in rear of Lot No. nine, in the twelfth concession of Lansdowne, lying east of the Macadamized Road, is vested in the said Alpheus R. Howard, Esq., in lieu of the present travelled road running across said lot. Be it therefore

By-law No. 33 confirmed.

enacted by the Municipal Council of the Corporation of the United Counties of Leeds and Grenville, and it is hereby enacted, that the said in part recited By-law, so passed by the said Council of Rear of Leeds and Lansdowne, be and the same is hereby confirmed.

(Signed,) WM. GARVEY, Warden

[L. S.]

(Signed,) JAMES JESSUP, Clerk.

No. CCIX.—BY-LAW

To appoint a Committee for the purpose therein mentioned.—Passed 18th October, 1861.

To arrange claim against Brockville.

Be it enacted by the Municipal Council of the Corporation of the United Counties of Leeds and Grenville, and it is hereby enacted, that a Committee of the members of this Council be appointed to arrange with the Council of the Town of Brockville the terms upon which the payment of the Execution in the Sheriff's hands against said Town in favor of these Counties shall be made, also of the costs incurred thereon, and the costs in the chancery suit connected therewith, and that the basis of such agreement shall be that the said Town of Brockville shall pay not less than one thousand dollars, with interest on the whole

sum remaining unpaid, annually, at the rate of seven per
centum per annum, and that on the completion of such
agreement with said Town of Brockville the above referred to execution to be withdrawn, and that the said
Committee be authorized to receive on behalf of this
Council Debentures of the said Town of Brockville, falling
due at or about the times when the above payments shall
be payable, at the current value of said Debentures, provided that the Counties' Solicitors are of opinion that this
Council would be safe in accepting such Debentures.

2. That the said Committee consist of Messrs. Garvey,
Kirker and Waugh, and that the said Committee do
nothing without the concurrence of the said Solicitors as
to the legality of their proceedings. *Messrs. Garvey, Kirker & Waugh.*

3. Be it further ordained and enacted that the said
Committee have full power to settle the said debt by any
other means they may deem right and expedient, but
with the sanction of the Solicitors aforesaid, as regards the
legality of their proceedings. *Power of Committee.*

(Signed,) WM. GARVEY, WARDEN.
[L. S.]
(Signed,) JAMES JESSUP, CLERK.

No. CCX.—BY-LAW

*To Cover certain Grants of Money.—Passed October 19,
1861.*

Be it enacted by the Municipal Council of the Corporation of the United Counties of Leeds and Grenville, and it
is hereby enacted, That the several sums of money hereinafter mentioned shall be paid by the Treasurer to the
parties respectively, out of any moneys in his hands
applicable to such purposes, viz: *Sums paid to.*

To John McMullen the sum of sixteen dollars and eighty-
two cents for extra advertising and for stationery. *John McMullen.*

To A. Robertson the sum of three dollars for repairs upon
Toll Gate No. 3 on the Prescott and Kemptville Toll
Road. *A. Robertson*

A 1

386

Gananoque Board Public Instruction. To the Board of Public Instruction for the Gananoque Circuit the sum of seven dollars and thirty-seven cents, for attendance, advertising, stationery, &c.

Prescott Board Public Instruction. To the Board of Public Instruction for the Prescott Circuit the sum of nine dollars and seventy-five cents for attendance, advertising, &c.

County Clerk. To the County Clerk the sum of seven dollars and sixteen cents for postage and cartage of Statutes.

John McMullen. To John McMullen the sum of thirty pounds, in part payment on his contract for printing and advertising for the current year.

Alfred Poulton. To Alfred Poulton the sum of six pounds five shillings, for repairing windows in Gaol and Court House from 1st October, 1860, to 1st October, 1861, and for painting, &c., in the Office of the Clerk of the Peace.

Claim against Prescott. That the Treasurer be authorized to receive from the Municipality of the Town of Prescott the sum of three hundred pounds, in full for the claim of these Counties for the present year.

William Fitzsimmons. To William Fitzsimmons the sum of eight pounds and nine pence, for work done and materials furnished for the Clerk's Office.

Brockville Board Public Instruction. To the Board of Public Instruction for Brockville Circuit the sum of forty-eight dollars for attendance of members at Meetings of the Board.

Seabury Scovil. To Seabury Scovil the sum of five dollars and forty cents for attendance at meeting of Board of Public Instruction as Local Superintendent of Schools for the Rear of Yonge and Escott.

Auditors. To the Auditors of this Council the sum of forty dollars each for the present year.

Clerk. To the Clerk the sum of six dollars to purchase one copy of Messrs. G. R. & G. M. Tremaine's Map of Upper Canada, when the same is published.

John Carlow. To John Carlow the sum of two pounds ten shillings for digging and building a cellar at the Maitland Toll Gate.

The Commissioners for building the fence on the Court House property are hereby authorized to give an order on the Treasurer for the expense of painting the said fence when completed. *Court House fence.*

To Richey Waugh the sum of twelve dollars and seventy- *Richey Waugh.* five cents for attendance at meeting of Gaol Inspectors as one of the Special Committee appointed by this Council.

To James Kirker the sum of twelve dollars for attendance *James Kirker.* at meeting of Gaol Inspectors, as one of the special Committee appointed by this Council.

To Walter H. Denaut the sum of seven pounds for making *Walter H. Denaut.* a railing on the bridge at Delta, on the Westport and Farmersville Toll Road.

To each of the Commissioners of the County Toll Roads, *Road Commissioners.* who have made their reports, the sum of five pounds to cover disbursements made by them.

To James Kincaid the sum of two pounds sixteen shillings *James Kincaid.* and three pence for attendance as messenger and for stationery furnished.

To James G. Elwood the sum of fifteen shillings for clean- *Jas. G. Elwood.* ing County buildings and wood furnished.

To William Garvey the sum of twenty-five pounds for his *The Warden.* services as Warden out of Council, in lieu of one pound per day as per By-Law, and the further sum of twelve pounds and ten shillings for services as Commissioner on behalf of this Council on several occasions.

(Signed,) WM. GARVEY, WARDEN.

[L. S.]

(Signed,) JAMES JESSUP, CLERK.

388

No. CCXI.—BY-LAW

To appoint Auditors for the current year.—Passed 29th January, 1862.

Be it enacted by the Municipal Council of the Corporation of the United Counties of Leeds and Grenville, and it is hereby enacted, as follows :—

Samuel McCammon. 1. That Samuel McCammon, of the Village of Gananoque, having been nominated by the Warden, be appointed Auditor for the current year.

Chancy H. Peck. 2. That Chancy H. Peck, of the Town of Prescott, be also appointed Auditor for the same period.

School Auditors. 3. That the said Samuel McCammon and Chancy H. Peck be appointed School Auditors for the current year, pursuant to the Common School Act for Upper Canada.

(Signed,) WM. GARVEY, Warden.

(L. S.)

(Signed,) JAMES JESSUP, Clerk.

No. CCXII.—BY-LAW

To appoint Trustees for each of the County Grammar Schools, and Local Superintendents of Common Schools.—Passed 29th January, 1862.

Be it enacted by the Municipal Council of the Corporation of the United Counties of Leeds and Grenville, and it is hereby enacted, as follows :—

Trustees for. 1. That the persons hereinafter, in this section, mentioned, be elected and appointed Trustees of the County Grammar Schools in the said Counties, as they are respectfully assigned to each of the said Schools, that is to say—

Brockville Sch'l. For the Grammar School of Brockville—Richard F. Steele, and the Reverend Edward J. Senkler, re-appointed, and Reverend F. R. Tane in place of Reverend Dr. Lewis, resigned.

For the Grammar School at Kemptville,—Reverend J. C. Quinn, and Robert Leslie, re-appointed Kemptville Sch'l.

For the Grammar School at Prescott—William Hillyard and Charles Shaver, re-appointed. Prescott School.

For the Grammar School at Gananoque—David F. Jones, re-appointed, and David F. Britton, in place of Thomas Richmond. Gananoq'e Sch'l.

For the Grammar School at Farmersville—Arza Parish, re-appointed, and Wm. W. King, in place of Thomas Hayes. Farmersville School.

And that the said appointments are to commence and take effect on the 31st day of January, A. D. 1862.

2. That the persons hereinafter mentioned be appointed Local Superintendents of Common Schools for the Municipalities respectively in this section mentioned, that is to say :

Augusta..............................James Clapperton. Local Superintendents.
Oxford...............................Rev. J. C. Quinn.
Front of Leeds and Lansdowne. . Robert McCrum.
Rear of Leeds and Lansdowne... Rev. John Davison.
Rear of Yonge and Escott........Seaberry Scovili.
Front of Yonge............... ......John Dickey.
Front of Escott.   ....Charles N. Hagerman.
Elizabethtown.....................Jacob A. Brown.
Edwardsburgh.....................Rev. A. Melville.
South Gower.......................Rev. Joseph Anderson.
Wolford.............. ....Rev. T. R. Parnell.
Kitley............. ....William Morin.
Elmsley ....John Ferguson.
Bastard and Burgess......·.......Lewis Chipman.
South Crosby..... .... Miles Young.
North Crosby..............James Bilton.

And that the said appointments of Local Superintendents shall commence and take effect on the first day of April next, and not before.

(Signed,)   WM. GARVEY, WARDEN.

[L. S.]

(Signed,)   JAMES JESSUP, CLERK.

No. CCXIII.—BY-LAW

To Repeal By-Law numbered One Hundred and Eighty-four.—Passed 30th January, 1862.

Repeal.

Be it enacted by the Municipal Council of the Corporation of the United Counties of Leeds and Grenville, and it is hereby enacted, That from and after the passing hereof, By-law Numbered One Hundred and Eighty-four, passed on the twenty-first day of June, in the year one thousand eight hundred and sixty, and intituled "By-law respecting Government Allowances for Roads between Municipalities," be repealed, and the same is hereby repealed.

(Signed,)   WM. GARVEY, WARDEN.

[L. S.]

(Signed.)   JAMES JESSUP, CLERK.

No CCXIV.—BY-LAW

To sell to James P. Ferguson Part of the Original Allowance for Road between Yonge and Escott.—Passed 30th January, 1862.

Preamble.

Description of Road.

Warden to convey.

Whereas James P. Ferguson has applied to this Council to purchase that part of the Original Allowance for Road between the Townships of Yonge and Escott, opposite to the rear half of Lot No. 24, in the fifth concession of the said Township of Escott; and whereas the Council has agreed to sell and convey to the said James P. Ferguson the above described part of the said Allowance for Road at or for the price or sum of $50. Be it therefore enacted by the Municipal Council of the Corporation of the United Counties of Leeds and Grenville, and it is hereby enacted, That the Warden be authorized and empowered to convey to the said James P. Ferguson, by Deed, in fee simple, that part of the said allowance for Road, as above described, on payment of the sum of $50; which Deed or Conveyance shall be signed by the Warden on behalf of this Council, and countersigned by the Clerk, who is hereby authorized to affix the Seal of the Corporation thereto.

2. That the Warden be authorized to pay the said $50 to Francis Fortune, according to the arrangement made between this Council and the said James P. Ferguson and Francis Fortune, for the sale of that part of the said allowance hereinbefore described.

Warden to pay Francis Fortune $50.

        (Signed,)   WM. GARVEY, Warden.

[L. S.]

(Signed,)   JAMES JESSUP, Clerk.

No. CCXV.—BY-LAW

To appoint Commissioners for the County Toll Roads therein mentioned.—Passed 31st January, 1862.

(Repealed ; see By-law No. 231.)

No. CCXVI.—BY-LAW

To Authorize a Temporary Loan until the Assessments for the present year become available.—Passed 1st February, 1862.

Part repealed · See By-Law No. 228.

Be it enacted by the Municipal Council of the Corporation of the United Counties of Leeds and Grenville, and it is hereby enacted, That for all sums of money borrowed from the Commercial Bank of Canada, or which may be borrowed from that institution, or any other Bank, by the Treasurer. to meet any claims upon the said Corporation, required to be paid by that Officer, under the provisions of any By-law of this Council, or any Act of Parliament, before the Assessments for the present year become available, the said Treasurer is hereby authorized and empowered to make a Promissory Note or Notes for the same, and to renew them from time to time, until the said Assessments become available, and to pay them out of the said Assesments, which are hereby charged with such payment, and that the Clerk, on the presentation to him of the said Note or Notes, or the renewal or renewals thereof, by the said Treasurer, shall countersign the same and affix the seal of the Corporation thereto.

Treasurer to make notes.

2. That the sum to be raised under this By-law shall be limited to Eight Thousand Dollars, to be drawn from time to time as required.

(Signed,)   WM. GARVEY, Warden.

[L. S.]

(Signed,)   JAMES JESSUP, Clerk.

No. CCXVII.—BY-LAW

See By-law No.
231.

To Authorize the Cancelling of the Contract with Thomas Woods, on the terms therein mentioned, and for other purposes.

Preambles.

Whereas, by agreement under Seal, bearing date the tenth day of March, A. D. 1859, made between Thomas Woods of the first part, Hamilton Nelson Sherwood and John Woods of the second part, and the Corporation of the United Counties of Leeds and Grenville of the third part; it was agreed that the said Thomas Woods should keep in repair the Four County Toll Roads therein mentioned, for a period of five years from the date of said agreement, and that in consideration thereof this Council should pay him yearly the sum of four pounds five shillings for each and every mile of the total length of said Roads, to be kept in repair by the said Thomas Woods; and whereas the said Thomas Woods has applied to this Council to be relieved from the said agreement, and that it should be cancelled; And whereas it is expedient for this Council to comply therewith, and that the said agreement should be surrendered and cancelled by the parties thereto : Be it therefore enacted by the Municipal Council of the Corporation of the United Counties of Leeds and Grenville, and it is hereby enacted as follows :

Contractor to execute release, &c.

1. That if the said Thomas Woods shall, on or before the day hereinafter mentioned for the completion of this arrangement, execute a release, discharging this Council from all and every claim or claims for money or otherwise he may now have or pretend to have against the said Corporation for and in respect to the said agreement, and shall deliver up all materials now on the said roads, or either of them, to the Commissioners of the said Roads

respectively, without charge or cost to this Council, and free from any incumbrance thereon, then the said agreement shall be surrendered and cancelled by the parties thereto.

2. That the Warden and Clerk of this Council are hereby authorized to Seal, Sign and Execute, on behalf of this Council, all such documents and papers as shall, in the opinion of the Solicitors of this Council, be requisite to carry out the foregoing arrangement for cancelling the said agreement.

Warden & Clerk to sign papers.

3. That unless the said arrangement be completed within fifteen days from the date of this By-Law, the Warden shall take no further action thereon.

To be completed in 15 days.

4. In case the said arrangement, for cancelling the said agreement, shall be fully completed as aforesaid, it is hereby further enacted, that each Commissioner of the County Toll Roads be authorised and empowered to expend a sum on the average not exceeding seventeen dollars per mile, for the repairs of the Road under his control, and that he give out no Contract to any one party which shall extend over a greater distance than five miles, and that the said Commissioners be authorised to draw orders on the County Treasurer for any work done on the said Roads respectively, not exceeding the before mentioned sum of seventeen dollars per mile.

Commissioners to expend $17 per mile.

(Signed,) WM. GARVEY, Warden.

[L. S.]

(Signed,) JAMES JESSUP, Clerk.

No. CCXVIII.—BY-LAW

To Cover certain Grants of Money.—Passed 1st February, 1862.

Be it enacted by the Municipal Council of the Corporation of the United Counties of Leeds and Grenville, and it is hereby enacted, That the several sums of money hereinafter mentioned shall be paid by the Treasurer to the parties respectively, out of any monies in his hands applicable to such purposes, viz:

Sums paid to.

394

Messrs. Sherwood, Steele & Wethey. To Messrs. Sherwood, Steele & Wethey, the sum of £52 19s. 8d., for costs incurred in the case of these Counties against the Hon. James Morris.

County Clerk. To the County Clerk, the sum of $5 79 cents, for postages and other disbursements for the Counties.

Adam Anderson. To Adam Anderson, the sum of £4 16s., for Covers for Assessor's and Collector's Rolls.

William Garvey and others. To William Garvey, Esq., the sum of $5, and to James Kirker and Richey Waugh, Esquires, the sum of $10 each, for services in attending on behalf of these Counties to arrange with the Town of Brockville the terms of payment of the execution against Brockville.

Kemptville B'rd Public Instruction. To the Kemptville Board of Public Instruction, the sum of £28, for attendance of Members, Stationery and Expenses of the Board.

John Hutton. To John Hutton, the sum of $14, expended on the Kemptville and Prescott County Toll Road for cleaning Snow off the road and repairs on the Toll House; and that the sum of $10, part of the above sum for cleaning off the snow, be deducted from the Contractor of the County Toll Roads.

Adiel Sherwood. To Adiel Sherwood, Esq., the sum of $9, for 100 Rules and Regulations for Gaols.

David Wylie. To David Wylie, the sum of $8 40c. for Advertising for Board of Public Instruction for Circuit No. 5, and Teachers' Certificates furnished the Board.

Lewis Chipman. To Lewis Chipman, the sum of $15 30c., for attending the Board of Public Instruction for Circuit No. 5, as Secretary and Local Superintendent, and for Stationery, &c., furnished.

Seabury Scoville. To Seabury Scoville, the sum of $2 40c., as incidental expenses for attending the Board of Public Instruction for Circuit No. 5.

Jas. G. Elwood. To James G. Elwood, the sum of £2 11s. 7d., for articles furnished for the Court House, as per account.

James Kincaid. To James Kincaid, the sum of £2 8s. 9d., for services as Messenger and Stationery furnished.

2. That the sum of £387 10s., be granted from the County funds for the purpose of making certain alterations and additions to the Gaol, and for Roofing the Court House, as recommended by the Standing Committee on County Property. Alterations to Gaol.

(Signed,)   WM. GARVEY, Warden.

[L. S.]

Signed,)   JAMES JESSUP, Clerk.

No. CCXIX.—BY-LAW

To appoint Commissioners for the purpose therein mentioned.
—Passed 1st February, 1862.

Be it enacted by the Municipal Council of the Corporation of the United Counties of Leeds and Grenville, and it is hereby enacted, as follows:—

1. That Wm. Garvey, Wm. H. Fredenburgh and Richey Waugh, Esquires, be appointed a Board of Commissioners to superintend, advertise and let out all the work, at such prices as they, or a majority of them, shall deem just and reasonable for the Construction, Erection, Building and Improving the Court House and Gaol, in conformity with the Plan finally agreed upon by the Committee and the Inspectors of Prisons, &c., submitted to this Council by E. A. Merredith, Esq., and approved by His Excellency the Governor General, in Council; and also to contract with any party or parties, on behalf of the said Corporation, for the performance of the said work, and to give orders on the County Treasurer, as the work progresses, for such sum or sums of money as may become due, and may be satisfactory to the said Commissioners, not exceeding in the whole, the amounts coming from Government, and granted by this Council for that purpose; and also to do and perform all such other acts, matters and things as they shall consider necessary in the prosecution and completion of the said work. Messrs. Garvey and others appointed.

2. That the said Commissioners, or a majority of them, are hereby also authorised and empowered to sign and duly execute all contracts, or other instruments that may be necessary in the premises, for and on behalf of the said To execute contracts, &c.

Corporation, and the Clerk shall countersign the same and affix the seal of the Corporation thereto whenever requested by the said Commissioners or a majority of them.

(Signed,)   WM. GARVEY, Warden.

[L. S.]

(Signed,)   JAMES JESSUP, Clerk.

No. CCXX.—BY-LAW

To appoint a Local Superintendent of Common Schools for the Township of Edwardsburgh.—Passed 18th June, 1862.

Preamble.

Whereas, since the last meeting of the Council, a vacancy has occurred in the office of Local Superintendent of Common Schools for the Township of Edwardsburgh, by the resignation of the Rev. Andrew Melville, and by virtue of the power given him by the statute in that case made and provided, the Warden appointed William B. Imrie, Esquire, to supply such vacancy, until the present meeting of the Council ; Be it therefore enacted by the Municipal Council of the Corporation of the United Counties of Leeds and Grenville, and it is hereby enacted that William B. Imrie the said Wm. B. Imrie be and he is hereby appointed and appointed. continued in office as such Local Superintendent of Common Schools for the said Township of Edwardsburgh until the first day of April, in the year of our Lord One Thousand Eight Hundred and Sixty-three.

(Signed,)   WM. GARVEY, Warden.

[L. S.]

(Signed,)   JAMES JESSUP, Clerk.

No. CCXXI.—BY-LAW

To authorize Settlement of a certain claim on the Town of Brockville.—Passed 19th June, 1862.

Preamble.

Whereas, by By-Law No. 209, entitled, "By-Law to appoint a Committee for the purposes therein mentioned," a Committee was appointed to arrange with the Town

Council of Brockville the terms upon which the payment of the execution in the Sheriff's hands against said Town, in favor of these Counties, should be made, and also of the costs therein referred to upon the basis mentioned in said By-Law.

And whereas it was thereby further enacted that the said Committee should have full power to settle the said debt by any other means they may deem right and expedient, but with the sanction of the Counties' Solicitors as regards the legality of their proceedings.

And whereas the said Committee, with the sanction of the Counties' Solicitor, accepted and received in full satisfaction of the said debt and costs, the bond of the Corporation of the Town of Brockville, bearing date the seventh day of April, A. D. One Thousand Eight Hundred and Sixty-two, in the penal sum of three thousand pounds payable to the Corporation of the United Counties of Leeds and Grenville, and conditioned for the payment of the said last mentioned Corporation of One Thousand Eight Hundred and Nineteen Pounds and Seven Shillings, with interest, by annual instalments of One Thousand Dollars, in manner and as therein mentioned.

And whereas the acceptance of said bond in satisfaction as aforesaid was made with and under the sanction of the Counties' Solicitors aforesaid, and the same has been approved and adopted by this Council of these Counties.

And whereas the Council of the Town of Brockville have proposed to the Council of the said United Counties to pay the sum of One Thousand Four Hundred Pounds at once in cash in full satisfaction of the said debt, execution and costs, and in discharge of said bond and the condition thereof, and of the said sum so payable by instalments as therein and herein aforesaid. Brockville to pay £1400.

And whereas the said Council of the said United Counties have upon consideration agreed to accept the said offer.

Be it therefore enacted, and it is hereby enacted by the Council of the Corporation of the United Counties of Leeds and Grenville, that immediately upon and after the payment of the said sum of One Thousand Four Hundred Pounds of lawful money of Canada to the Warden of these Counties for and on account of the said Council of these Counties by the Council of the Corporation of the Town of Brockville, the said Warden be and he is hereby authorized and empowered to make, sign, seal, execute and deliver on behalf of the Corporation of the United Counties of Leeds and Grenville, to the Council of the Corporation of the Town of Brockville, a full, effectual and sufficient discharge and release of the said debt, execution and costs, and of the said bond and of the condition thereof and payments therein mentioned or referred to, and to surrender the said bond and condition to be cancelled, and to cancel the same and to withdraw the said execution from the Sheriff of these Counties, and to put a final end and conclusion to the same and utterly discharge the said Corporation and Council of the Town of Brockville therefrom, and that the Clerk of this Council do set the seal of this Corporation to and countersign all such documents as may be required to be executed in giving effect to this By-Law. But the Warden is not to act upon this By-Law unless the said money be paid within five days from the passage hereof.

Discharge on payment.

(Signed,)   WM. GARVEY, Warden.

[L. S.]

Signed,)   JAMES JESSUP, Clerk.

No. CCXXII.—BY-LAW

See 29 Vic., Cap. 23.   *To establish a Grammar School in the Village of Mirickville.—Passed 19th June, 1862.*

Preamble.   Whereas it appears that the state of the Grammar School fund is at present ample to permit the establishment of an additional Grammar School in these Counties : Be it therefore enacted by the Council of the Corporation of the United Counties of Leeds and Grenville, and it is hereby *School establish'd.* enacted that a Grammar School be established at the Village of Mirickville, in the County of Grenville, according to the statute in that behalf.

Trustees appointed.   2. That Mills K. Church, Reverend T. Parnell, Dr. J. R. Cousens, John Muir, John Burchill and Samuel Jakes, be appointed Trustees of the said Grammar School, and that two of such Trustees shall retire from office annually on the Thirty-first day of January in each year, in the order of their appointment as hereinbefore mentioned.

(Signed,)   WM. GARVEY, Warden.

[L. S.]

(Signed,)   JAMES JESSUP, Clerk.

No. CCXXIII.—BY-LAW

To assess the United Counties of Leeds and Grenville for the year 1862.—Passed 20th June, 1862.

Be it enacted by the Council of the Corporation of the United Counties of Leeds and Grenville, and it is hereby enacted, That there shall be raised and levied upon the whole rateable property in the said United Counties for the present year, the sum of £2,500 to defray the ordinary and current expenses thereof, and the further sum of £1,457 5s. to pay the salaries of legally qualified Common School teachers, and the further sum of £893 6s. 8d., as a special rate authorised to be raised and levied upon the said property, under the provisions of By-Law numbered one hundred and twenty, passed on the thirteenth day of October, 1856, and the further sum of £1,042 4s., as a special rate authorized to be raised and levied upon the said property, under the provisions of By-Law numbered one hundred and eighty-two, passed on the nineteenth day of June, 1860, and that the said several sums shall be apportioned to the several Municipalities of the said United Counties in the following manner, viz. :— *Sums to be levied. County Rate. Com'on Schools. Special rate for loan. Special rate under By-Law No. 182. How apportioned to Municipalities.*

MUNICIPALITIES.	County Rate.			Common Schools.			Special rate for Loan under By-Law No. 120.			Special rate under By-Law No. 182.		
	£.	s.	D.	£.	s.	D.	£.	s.	D.	£.	s.	D.
Elizabethtown	409	13	6	174	10	0	128	18	1	150	7	9
Bastard and Burgess	155	14	0	114	15	0	56	10	1	65	18	4
Rear of Yonge and Escott	131	18	6	64	10	0	45	12	10	53	4	11
Front of Yonge	105	17	7	51	10	0	33	13	5	39	5	8
Front of Leeds and Lansdowne	178	19	6	123	15	0	62	11	4	72	19	11
Rear of Leeds and Lansdowne	95	7	8	71	15	0	32	7	11	37	15	11
Kitley	148	1	6	99	0	0	56	12	9	66	1	7
North Crosby	59	11	10	60	15	0	20	3	6	23	10	9
South Crosby	85	2	6	60	15	0	29	9	2	34	7	4
Elmsley	43	4	7	40	5	0	17	5	4	20	2	11
Front of Escott	46	6	1	45	15	0	14	19	6	17	9	5
Augusta	270	11	0	158	15	0	103	10	7	120	15	8
Edwardsburgh	230	12	10	152	10	0	68	15	7	80	4	10
Oxford	172	6	0	128	0	0	65	6	2	76	3	10
Wolford	113	7	7	79	5	0	41	17	7	48	17	2
South Gower	59	8	2	31	5	0	22	4	6	25	18	4
Prescott	124	9	0				72	11	8	84	13	8
Kemptville	39	17	4				11	18	9	13	18	6
Mirickville	24	12	3				8	17	8	10	7	3
Totals	2500	0	0	1457	5	0	893	6	8	1042	4	0

2. That the said several sums hereinbefore directed to be raised and levied in the said Municipalities respectively, shall be placed on the Collectors' Rolls by the Clerk thereof, in separate columns, and be collected in like manner as all other rates and assessments are by law directed to be collected, and that every Collector shall, on or before the fourteenth day of December next, return his Roll to the Treasurer of his Municipality and pay over to such Treasurer the sums hereby directed to be raised, levied and collected therein. *How levied and collected.*

(Signed,) WM. GARVEY, WARDEN.

[L. S.]

(Signed,) JAMES JESSUP, CLERK.

No. CCXXIV.—BY-LAW

To cover certain Grants of Money.—Passed 20th June, 1862.

Be it enacted by the Council of the Corporation of the United Counties of Leeds and Grenville, and it is hereby enacted, that the several sums of money herein-after mentioned shall be paid by the Treasurer to the parties respectively, out of any moneys in his hands applicable to such purposes, viz :— *Sums paid to.*

To Messrs. Sherwood and Steele, the sum of twenty-three pounds fifteen shillings, for professional services, as the Solicitors of the Council. *Messrs. Sherwood & Steele.*

To James Kirker, the sum of five pounds for attending meeting of Commissioners to arrange settlement with the Town of Brockville in February last. *James Kirker.*

To Richey Waugh, the sum of five pounds for attending meeting of Commissioners to arrange settlement with the Town of Brockville in February last. *Richey Waugh.*

To John McMullen, the sum of thirty-two pounds and seven pence, for balance of contract for printing and advertising and for stationery furnished. *John McMullen.*

To William Smith, the sum of two pounds ten shillings, for attending meeting of Gaol Inspectors as one of the special Committee appointed by the Council, *William Smith.*

B 1

Board Public Instruction No. 1. To the Board of Public Instruction for Circuit No. 1, the sum of six pounds nine shillings and sixpence, for expenses of the Boards as per account.

Adam Anderson. To Adam Anderson, the sum of one pound four shillings for covers for Collectors Rolls.

Jns. G. Elwood. To James G. Elwood, the sum of two pounds three shillings and nine pence for cleaning Court House Rooms other than the Court Room, by order of the Warden.

Wm. Dunn. To William Dunn, the sum of five shillings and seven pence for glass furnished for Toll House.

Wm. Moran. To William Moran, Local Superintendent of Schools for Kitley, the sum of one pound fifteen shillings, for services in attending the Board of Public Instruction for circuit No. 5.

Wm. Garvey. To William Garvey, Esq., the sum of three shillings and seven pence half-penny, for brick of Wm. Simpson, for Maitland Toll House, and paid by him.

County Clerk. To the County Clerk, the sum of one pound and nine-pence for postage, disbursed for the Counties.

William Fitzsimmons. To William Fitzsimmons, the sum of five pounds eighteen shillings and sixpence, for work done and repairs on the Court House, Jail and Registry Office.

E. H. Whitmarsh. To E. H. Whitmarsh, the sum of two pounds ten shillings to cover his travelling expenses as Commissioner of the Mirickville and Maitland County road in the years 1860 and 1861.

Prescott Board Public Instruction. To the Board of Public Instruction for Prescott Circuit, the sum of nine dollars for expenses of the Board, as per account.

Wm. Weir To William Weir, the sum of one hundred and fifty dollars for re-building the bridge across the Nation River, at Lawrences, on the line of the County Toll Road, in Edwardsburgh, as per contract with the Commissioner of the road.

Wm Willoughby. To William Willoughby, the sum of fourteen dollars and twenty-five cents for removing snow from the Westport and Farmersville County Road, and the further sum of twelve dollars, for repairs on the Toll House at Farmersville on the said road.

To James Kincaid, the sum of two pounds twelve shillings and sixpence for services as messenger, and for stationery furnished. *James Kincaid.*

     (Signed,)   WM. GARVEY, WARDEN.

[L. S.]

(Signed,)   JAMES JESSUP, CLERK.

No. CCXXV.—BY-LAW

To appoint Trustees for the Grammar School at Merrickville, and a Local Superintendent for the rear of Leeds and Lansdowne.—Passed 15th October, 1862.

Be it enacted by the Council of the Corporation of the United Counties of Leeds and Grenville, and it is hereby enacted, that Aaron Merrick, Esquire, and the Reverend Mr. McGill, be appointed Trustees of the County Grammar School at Merrickville, in the place of Mills R. Church and John Burchill, who decline to act as Trustees. *Trustees A. Merrick and Rev. Mr. McGill.*

2. That the Reverend Christopher F. Denroche be appointed Local Superintendent of Common Schools, for the Township of the rear of Leeds and Lansdowne, in the place of the Reverend John Davison, resigned, and that the said appointment shall expire on the first day of April next. *Superintendent. Rev. Christopher F. Denroche.*

     (Signed,)   WM. GARVEY, WARDEN.

[L. S.]

(Signed,)   JAMES JESSUP, CLERK.

No. CCXXVI.—BY-LAW

To amend By-law No. 192, and to form a new School Circuit.—Passed 15th October, 1862.

Be it enacted by the Council of the Corporation of the United Counties of Leeds and Grenville, and it is hereby enacted, That the Township of Wolford and the village

**Wolford & Mer-
rickville new
Circuit.**

of Merrickville be detached from School Circuit number three, and formed into a new and separate Circuit and be called and known as School Circuit number six.

(Signed,)   WM. GARVEY, Warden.

[L. S.]

(Signed,)   JAMES JESSUP, Clerk.

No. CCXXVII.—BY-LAW

To erect the village of Gananoque, in the County of Leeds, into an Incorporated Village.—Passed 15th October, 1862.

Preamble.

Whereas, from the return of the census of the unincorporated village of Gananoque, with its immediate neighbourhood, taken under the direction of the Council of the United Counties of Leeds and Grenville, (within which Counties the said village and its said immediate neighborhood are situate) by the Commissioner appointed under the provisions of By-law numbered two hundred and four, passed on the twenty-eighth day of June, in the year of our Lord one thousand eight hundred and sixty-one, and intituled " By-law to authorize the taking of the Census of the village of Gananoque." It appears that the said village and neighborhood as hereinafter described and bounded, contain over seven hundred and fifty inhabitants : and whereas the residences of said inhabitants are sufficiently near to form an Incorporated village ; and whereas one hundred and upwards of the resident freeholders and householders of the said village and neighborhood, have, by their petition prayed that the said village and neighborhood may be erected into an Incorporated village, and it is desirable to grant the prayer of the said petition. Be it therefore enacted by the Council of the Corporation of the United Counties of Leeds and Grenville and it is hereby enacted as follows :

**Declared an
Incorporated
Village.**

1. That the said village and neighborhood and the inhabitants thereof, shall be and are hereby declared to be an Incorporated village, apart from the Township of the Front of Leeds and Lansdowne in which the same are situate, by the name of the Corporation of the Village of Gananoque.

2. That the boundaries of said incorporated village shall Limits.
be as follows : That is to say, the said incorporated village
shall comprise and consist of the south halves of Lots
numbers ten, eleven, twelve, thirteen, fourteen, fifteen,
sixteen and the south half of the west half of Lot number
seventeen, in the first concession of Leeds, being part of
the said Township of the Front of Leeds and Lansdowne,
together with the broken fronts of the said lots and part lot
respectively.

3. That the old stone School House in the said Incorpo-
rated Village of Gananoque shall be the place for holding When first elec-
the first Election for the said Incorporated Village, and that tion to be held.
James Kirker, Esq., shall be and he is hereby appointed Returning offi-
to be the Returning Officer to hold the same. cer.

(Signed,)   WM. GARVEY, Warden.

[L. S.]

(Signed,)   JAMES JESSUP, Clerk.

No. CCXXVIII.—BY-LAW

*To regulate the countersigning of the Notes and Checks
therein mentioned.—Passed 15th October, 1862.*

Be it enacted by the Council of the Corporation of the
United Counties of Leeds and Grenville, and it is hereby
enacted, That so much of By-law No. 216, passed on the first Part By-Law No.
day of February, A. D. 1862 ; and intituled, By-law to auth- 216 repealed.
orize a temporary loan, until the assessments for the present
become available," as requires the Clerk to countersign
any note or notes authorized by the said in part recited
By-Law, to be made by the Treasurer, shall be, and the
same is hereby repealed.

2nd. That hereafter every such note or notes shall be
countersigned by the Warden for the time being, before Warden to coun-
the same shall be discounted or renewed at the Bank, and tersign notes.
that the Warden shall make full inquiry for what emer-
gency or purpose such note or notes are to be discounted
or renewed ; and shall keep a memorandum of each transaction, and report to the Council at each Session the
numbers and amount, and for what particular purpose,
each such note shall be made and discounted.

3rd. That all checks made by the County Treasurer to draw out of the Bank, the avails of every such discounted note or notes, shall be countersigned by the Clerk; and that he shall keep a book in which he shall enter the date of any such check or checks, to whom paid and for what purpose, and for what amount; and shall lay such book before the Finance Committee at each session of the Council, for them to report thereon.

Checks countersigned by Clerk.

4th. That all other By-Laws heretofore passed to authorize temporary loans until the assessments become available, shall be, and the same are hereby repealed, saving and excepting from the operation of this section, so much of the said By-law No. 216, as is not repealed by the first section of this By-law.

By-Laws repealed, saving part No. 216.

(Signed,) WM. GARVEY, Warden.

[L. S.]

(Signed.) JAMES JESSUP, Clerk.

No. CCXXI.X--BY-LAW

To authorize the execution of the Lease therein mentioned. —Passed 16th October, 1862.

Preamble.

Whereas at the last meeting of this Council, the Mayor of the Town of Brockville applied for leave to erect an Engine House on the County property, at the intersection of Church and Wall Streets, in the said Town of Brockville, and by resolution passed thereat, the said application was referred to the Special Committee for making alterations and improvements on the Gaol property, and that full authority and power were given to them to act in the matter as they might deem best for the interest of the Counties.

Be it therefore enacted by the Council of the Corporation of the United Counties of Leeds and Grenville, and it is hereby enacted, That the said Committee, or a majority of them be authorized and empowered to arrange with the Corporation of the Town of Brockville, for the leasing of the land required for the erection of a Brick or Stone Engine House similar to the one being now erected on Main Street, in the East Ward of the said Town of Brockville, for a term not

Lease to Corporation of Brockville.

exceeding fifty years at a yearly rent of one shilling and three pence; the said Engine House to be erected and completed within two years from this date, and that the Warden and Clerk are hereby authorized to Seal, Sign and Execute, on behalf of this Council, the Lease of the said land to the Corporation of the Town of Brockville, such lease to be drawn by the Solicitors of this Council at the expense of the Corporation of the Town of Brockville.

Term not exce'd-ing 50 years.

Rent.

(Signed,) WM. GARVEY, Warden.

[L. S.]

(Signed,) JAMES JESSUP, Clerk.

No. CCXXX.—BY-LAW

To confirm a By-Law of the Council of the Township of Elizabethtown to sell and convey to Michael Green eleven chains in length of the Government allowance of side road between Lot number eighteen and the centre Commons in front of the fourth Concession.—Passed 16th October, 1862.

Whereas it is expedient and necessary to confirm a certain By-Law, passed by the Council of the Corporation of the Township of Elizabethtown, on the sixteenth day of December, A. D. 1861; whereby it is enacted, that eleven chains length, supposed width forty feet, be sold and conveyed to Michael Green, for the sum of five shillings, commencing at the south angle of said lot and running on said road allowance, eleven chains aforesaid to the travelled road: Be it therefore enacted by the Council of the Corporation of the United Counties of Leeds and Grenville, and it is hereby enacted, That the said in part recited By-Law passed by the Corporation of the Township of Elizabethtown, on the day and the year aforesaid, be and the same is hereby confirmed.

Preamble.

By-Law con-firmed.

(Signed,) WM. GARVEY, Warden.

[L. S.]

(Signed,) JAMES JESSUP, Clerk.

No. CCXXXI.—BY-LAW

To repeal By-Laws respecting County Roads, and to transfer the same to the several Municipalities interested.—Passed 16th October, 1862.

Be it enacted by the Municipal Council of the Corporation of the United Counties of Leeds and Grenville, and it is hereby enacted, as follows :—

After 1st Jan., 1863, By-Laws repealed.

1. That on and after the first day of January next so much of the several By-Laws or parts of By-Laws hereinafter specially named and designated, and of every other By-Law or portion of By-Law—although not herein named or specially designated—whereby any Roads or Highways or portion of Roads or Highways, within the United Counties of Leeds and Grenville, have been assumed as County or Toll Roads ; or whereby any powers, duties, or obligations on the part of this Council over or respecting any such roads or portions of roads, have been assumed or reserved to or by this Council, or whereby or by virtue where of any Toll Gates or Toll Gate, in, upon or near any of such roads or portions of roads have been established, or whereby or by virtue whereof any Tolls or Fees for passing through, upon, over, or across said roads, portions of roads, or gates, or any of them, are exigible, demandable, or collectable, be and the same are hereby repealed.

By-Laws and parts of By-Laws repealed and specially designated, are as follows :—

By-Law No. 4. To repeal By-Laws therein mentioned, and to make further provisions than are at present by Law made for the construction of four Toll Roads in the United Counties of Leeds and Grenville.

By-Law No. 8. To amend By-Laws Nos. 4 and 5, passed on the 14th day of March, 1850.

By-Law No. 69. By-Law to assume, open, and establish the County Toll Road therein mentioned.

By-Law No. 97. By-Law to provide for the inspection of the County Toll Roads, and for other purposes therein mentioned.

By-Law No. 101. By-Law to provide for the Macadamizing the roads therein mentioned.

By-Law No. 112. By-Law to repeal part of the third section of By-Law numbered 63.

By-Law No. 114. By-Law to establish Toll Gates and Toll Houses on the four County Toll Roads.

By-Law No. 116. By-Law to amend part of the tenth section of By-Law numbered 47.

By-Law No. 146. By-Law to change the location of Toll Houses and Gates therein mentioned, and to provide for a more satisfactory method of leasing the Toll Houses and Gates upon the four County Toll Roads. Passed 14th October, 1858.

By-Law No. 201. By-Law to appoint a Commission for the Kemptville and Prescott County Toll Road in the place of Ambrose Clotheir.

2. On and after the first day of January next, so much of the several Roads or Highways, and portions thereof herein aforesaid, as lie within the several and respective Municipalities within these Counties, shall be and the same are hereby transferred and made over to the several Municipalities respectively, within which or within whose jurisdiction they respectively lie, free and clear of and from all Tolls and Gates, so far as regards the Council. *Roads transferred to Municipalities.*

3. The repeal of the said By-Laws and portions of By-Laws shall not repeal, defeat, or disturb or invalidate, or prejudicially affect any matter or thing whatsoever had done, competed, existing, or pending at the time of such repeal; or render invalid any debenture issued under or by virtue of any of said By-Laws:—provided always that nothing herein contained shall be taken to revive any By-Law or part of By-Law repealed by any of the By-Laws or parts of By-Laws hereinbefore repealed. *Repeal not to effect Debentures, &c.*

[Signed,]   WM. GARVEY, Warden.

[L. S.]

[Signed,]   JAMES JESSUP, Clerk.

No. CCXXXII.—BY-LAW

To cover certain Grants of Money.—Passed 16th October,
1862.

Sums paid to.

Be it enacted by the Council of the Corporation of the United Counties of Leeds and Grenville, and it is hereby enacted, That the several sums of money hereinafter mentioned, shall be paid by the Treasurer to the parties respectively, out of any moneys in his hands applicable to such purposes, viz.:

Alfred Poulton.

To Alfred Poulton, the sum of twenty dollars, for repairing Windows of Gaol and Court House, as per contract.

County Clerk.

To the County Clerk, the sum of nine dollars and nine cents, for postages disbursed.

William Moran and others.

To William Moran, the sum of thirteen dollars and thirty cents, for attendance as member of the Board of Public Instruction of School Circuit No. 5; also to Seabury Scovil, the sum of three dollars; and to John Furguson, the sum of four dollars and fifty cents, for services rendered the same School Circuit.

H. H. Horsey.

To H. H. Horsey, the sum of one hundred and fifty-five dollars, for plans and specifications for the Gaol, as per account.

Board Public Instruction No. 1.

To the Board of Public Instruction for School Circuit No. 1, the sum of twenty-one dollars and forty cents, as per account.

Rev. Jno. Davidson.

To the Rev. John Davidson, the sum of sixteen dollars and sixty cents, for attending the meetings of the Board of Public Instruction for School Circuit No. 5.

Prescott Board Public Instruction.

To the Board of Public Instruction for the Prescott Circuit, the sum of seven dollars, for attendance of Members and Secretary, as per account.

Board Public Instruction No. 2.

To the Board of Public Instruction for School Circuit No. 2, the sum of twenty dollars and seventy-five cents, for attendance of Members and incidental expenses, as per account.

Jas. G. Elwood.

To James G. Elwood, the sum of three dollars and twenty-five cents, for work at Court House, as per account.

To R. W. Kelly, the sum of seventy-five dollars, on account R. W. Kelly. of his contract for printing and advertising.

To Messrs. John McMullen & Co., the sum of fifteen dollars and thirty cents, for stationery and advertising. Messrs. Jno. McMullen & Co.

To the Commissioners of County Toll Roads, the sum of thirty dollars each, for their services during the year 1862; and to John Johnston, one of the said Commissioners, the further sum of three dollars and forty cents, for balance in cash. Commissioners County Roads.

To Nelson Shaver, the sum of four dollars and seventy-five cents, for building Gate at Toll House No. 1, on the Kemptville and Prescott Road. Nelson Shaver.

To William Garvey, Esq., the sum of one hundred dollars, for his services as Warden; and the further sum of one hundred dollars for his attendance as Commissioner on the various special committees to which he was appointed, over and above the sum to which he is entitled as Councillor. William Garvey.

To David Wylie, the sum of ten dollars, for attending and reporting the proceedings of the Council during the current year. David Wylie.

To James Kincaid, the sum of two pounds one shilling and three pence, for services as messenger and stationery. James Kincaid.

To James G. Elwood, the sum of fifteen shillings and nine pence for materials furnished the Judge's room. Jas. G. Elwood.

To Richey Waugh and William H. Fredenburgh, the sum of ten dollars each, for services as Commissioners for making repairs and alterations to the Gaol. Messrs. Waugh & Fredenburgh.

2. That the sum of eighty dollars be granted towards the re-building of a bridge at Burritt's Rapids, across the Rideau river: the Corporation of the County of Carlton having granted a like sum for that purpose—and that John Meikle, Richey Waugh, and Silas Andrews, Esqrs., be Commissioners to expend the same. Bridge, Burritt's Rapids.

3. That the sum of four hundred dollars be granted in aid of the fund for the relief of the Lancashire distressed operatives, and that the said amount be sent by the Treasurer to the Provincial Secretary for transmission to England. Lancashire distressed operatives.

4. That the Treasurer be authorized to receive from the Corporation of the Town of Prescott, the sum of eight hundred dollars in full of all County Taxes for the year 1862.

5. That the sum of eight hundred pounds be placed at the disposal of the Commissioners for repairing the Gaol and Court House.

6. That the sum of two hundred dollars be granted to the Municipality of the Front of Yonge, to aid in rebuilding three bridges, carried away last Spring by the Freshet.

(Signed,)   WM. GARVEY, WARDEN.

[L. S.]

[Signed,]   JAMES JESSUP, CLERK.

No. CCXXXIII.—BY-LAW

To appoint Auditors for the Current year.—Passed 29th January, 1863.

Be it enacted by the Municipal Council of the Corporation of the United Counties of Leeds and Grenville, and it is hereby enacted as follows :—

1. That Samuel McCammon, of the Village of Gananoque, having been nominated by the Warden, be appointed Auditor for the current year.

2. That Chancey H. Peck, of the Town of Prescott, be also appointed Auditor for the current year.

3. That the said Samuel McCammon and Chancey H. Peck, be appointed Auditors of School monies and accounts for the current year, pursuant to the Common School Act for Upper Canada.

(Signed,)   JAMES KEELER, WARDEN.

[L. S.]

(Signed,)   JAMES JESSUP, CLERK.

No. CCXXXIV.—BY-LAW

To appoint Trustees for each of the County Grammar Schools and Local Superintendents of Common Schools.
—Passed 30th January, 1863.

Be it enacted by the Council of the Corporation of the United Counties of Leeds and Grenville, and it is hereby enacted as follows :

1. That the persons hereinafter, in this Section mentioned, be elected and appointed Trustees of the County Grammar Schools, in the said United Counties, as they are respectively assigned to each of the said Schools. That is to say :— *Trustees for. See 89 vic. Cap. 23.*

For the Grammar School at Brockville :   Brockville Sch'l.

The Rev. F. R. Tane, re-appointed.
John Ross, re-appointed.

For the Grammar School at Kemptville :   Kemptville Sch'l.

The Rev. Joseph Anderson, re-appointed, and the
Rev. James Harris, in the place of Samuel Christie, resigned.

For the Grammar School at Prescott :   Prescott School.

John Reid and William Dunn, in the place of William Ellis and John Easton.

For the Grammar School at Gananoque :   Gananoq'e Sch'l.

Wm. S. MacDonald and James Kirker, re-appointed.

For the Grammar School at Farmersville :   Farmersville School.

Dr. A. Chamberlin and Aaron Wright, in the place of Samuel Connell and John Kincaid.
Thomas Hays in the place of James Deaning deceased.

For the Grammar School at Merrickville :   Merrickville School.

Aaron Merrick and the Rev. Thos. Parnell, re-appointed.
And that the said appointments of Trustees are to commence and take effect on the 31st day of Jan., A.D., 1863.

2. That the persons hereinafter mentioned, be appointed Local Superintendents of Common Schools, for the Municipalities respectively in this section mentioned. That is is to say :—

Local Superintendents.

Augusta........................ James Clapperton.
Oxford .. .. Rev. James Harris.
Front of Leeds and Lansdowne.. Joel Landon.
Rear of Leeds and Lansdowne .. Rev. C. E. Denroche.
Rear of Yonge and Escott...... Seaberry Scovill.
Front of Yonge............... John Dickie.
Front of Escott.............. Charles N. Hagerman.
Elizabethtown .... Jacob A. Brown.
Edwardsburgh .... William B. Imrie.
South Gower .... Rev. Joseph Anderson.
Wolford .... Rev. Thomas Parnell.
Kitley .... William Moran.
Elmsley...................... John Ferguson.
Bastard and Burgess.......... Lewis Chipman.
South Crosby........ . .... Miles Young.
North Crosby.................. Isaac Read.

And that the said appointments of Local Superintendents shall commence and take effect on the first day of April next, and not before.

(Signed,) JAMES KEELER, Warden.

[L. S.]

(Signed,) JAMES JESSUP, Clerk.

No. CCXXXV.—BY-LAW

To cover certain Grants of Money—Passed 31st January, 1863.

Sums paid to.

Be it enacted by the Council of the Corporation of the United Counties of Leeds and Grenville, and it is hereby enacted, that the several sums of money hereinafter mentioned, shall be paid by the Treasurer to the parties respectively out of any moneys in his hands applicable to such purposes, viz. :—

John Burchill.

To John Burchill, the sum of twelve dollars, for services as County Engineer, in inspecting part of the Merrickville and Maitland road.

To Adam Anderson, the sum of twenty-four dollars and eighty cents, for Assessors and Collectors portfolios. Adam Anderson.

To Seaberry Scovil, the sum of two dollars and forty cents; Lewis Chipman, the sum of eighteen dollars and fifty-two cents; Rev. Mr. Denroche, two dollars and fifty cents, James Bilton, four dollars and sixty cents; William Moran, three dollars and ten cents; John Ferguson, four dollars and fifty cents; Miles Young, three dollars and seventy cents; John McMullen & Co., four dollars and forty cents; W. H. Denant, four dollars; and David Wylie, two dollars and seventy cents, as incidental expenses attending the Board of Public Instruction for Circuit No. 5. Seaberry Scovil and others.

To the Board of Public Instruction, for School Circuit No. 6, the sum of twenty-two dollars and forty-five cents, for attendance and incidental expenses of the Board as per accounts. Board Public Instruction No. 6.

To C. N. Hagerman, the sum of twelve dollars, as incidental expenses attending the Board of Public Instruction for Circuit No. 2. C. N. Hagerman.

To the County Clerk, the sum of five dollars and five cents for postages disbursed for the counties since its last meeting. County Clerk.

To James G. Elwood, the sum of four dollars and fifty cents, as per account. J. G. Elwood.

To the Board of Public Instruction at Kemptville, the sum of twenty-seven dollars, for attendance and incidental expenses. Kemptville Bo'rd Public Instruction.

To the Board of Public Instruction for Circuit No. 1, the sum of twenty-five dollars and eighty cents, for attendance and incidental expenses. Board Public Instruction No. 1.

To William Fitzsimmons, the sum of twelve dollars and ninety-three cents for work at the Court House. William Fitzsimmons.

To R. W. Kelly, the sum of forty dollars, on account of his contract for printing and advertising. R. W. Kelly.

To David Wylie, the sum of ten dollars, for attending and reporting the proceedings of this Session of the Council. David Wylie.

416

Grenville Registry books. To the Special Committee appointed to inquire respecting the books of the Register Office, Prescott, the sum of fifty pounds, if the said Committee find it necessary to draw on the Treasurer for that amount.

James Kincaid. To James Kincaid, the sum of ten dollars for attendance as messenger of the Council, and stationery furnished.

(Signed.) JAMES KEELER, Warden.

[L. S.]

(Signed,) JAMES JESSUP, Clerk.

No. CCXXXVI.—BY-LAW

To appoint Inspectors of Weights and Measures.—Passed 2nd July, 1863.

Be it enacted by the Council of the Corporation of the United Counties of Leeds and Grenville, and it is hereby enacted as follows:

Wm. Stitt for Grenville. 1. That William Stitt, of the Village of Spencerville, be, and he is hereby appointed Inspector of Weights and Measures for the County of Grenville, one of the United Counties aforesaid, during the pleasure of the said Council, pursuant to the fifth section of the Consolidated Statute for Upper Canada, chaptered 58.

Wm. Smith for 2. That William Smith, of the Village of Frankville, be, and he is hereby appointed Inspector of Weights and Measures for the County of Leeds, one of the said United Counties during the pleasure of the said Council, pursuant to the said section of the said Act.

Senior Inspector. 3. That the said William Stitt is hereby appointed to be the senior Inspector, according to the sixth section of the said Act.

Brockville and Prescott excluded. 4. That the Incorporated Towns of Brockville and Prescott be, and they are hereby excluded from the operation of this By-Law.

(Signed,) JAMES KEELER, Warden.

[L. S.]

(Signed,) JAMES JESSUP, Clerk.

No. CCXXXVII.—BY-LAW

To Assess the United Counties of Leeds and Grenville for the year 1863.—Passed 3rd July, 1863.

Be it enacted by the Council of the Corporation of the United Counties of Leeds and Grenville, and it is hereby enacted, that there shall be raised and levied upon the whole rateable property in the said United Counties for the present year, the sum of £3,500, to defray the ordinary and current expenses thereof, and the further sum of £1,458 10s., to pay the salaries of legally qualified Common School Teachers, and the further sum of £857 4s. 5d., as a special rate authorized to be raised and levied upon the said property, under the provisions of By-Law numbered one hundred and twenty, passed on the 13th day of October, 1856, and the further sum of £1,000 2s. 3d., as a special rate authorized to be raised and levied upon the said property, under the provisions of By-Law numbered one hundred and eighty-two, passed on the nineteenth day of June, 1860, and that the said several sums shall be apportioned to the several Municipalities of the said United Counties in the following manner, viz. :—

[marginal notes:] Sums to be levied. County Rate. Com'on Schools. Special rate for loan. Special rate under By-Law No. 182. How apportioned to Municipalities.

MUNICIPALITIES.	County Rates.			Common School Rates.			Special Rate for Loan under By-law No. 126.			Special Rate under By-law No. 182.		
	£	s.	D.	£	s.	D.	£	s.	D.	£	s.	D.
Elizabethtown	505	0	9	174	10	0	118	12	2	138	7	6
Bastard and Burgess	221	7	6	114	15	0	55	5	6	64	9	9
Rear of Yonge and Escott	178	16	4	61	10	0	44	11	9	52	0	5
Front of Yonge	131	18	6	51	10	0	31	19	5	36	9	8
Front of Leeds and Lansdowne	168	3	8	130	5	0	43	19	10	51	6	6
Rear of Leeds and Lansdowne	126	17	11	65	5	0	31	18	10	37	5	4
Kitley	221	18	3	99	0	0	55	7	9	64	5	6
North Crosby	79	1	2	60	15	0	19	17	8	22	3	11
South Crosby	115	8	4	60	15	0	29	13	6	34	12	5
Elmsley	67	13	2	40	15	0	17	5	3	20	2	10
Front of Escott,	58	13	5	45	15	0	13	12	6	15	17	11
Gananoque	76	19	2	00	0	0	103	16	8	11	12	9
Augusta	405	12	6	158	15	0	67	14	2	121	2	9
Edwardsburgh	269	9	7	148	0	0	60	7	5	78	19	11
Oxford	255	17	5	128	5	0	41	7	5	70	8	8
Wolford	164	1	7	85	0	0	20	19	6	48	5	4
South Gower	87	1	7	31	5	0	64	16	1	24	9	6
Prescott	284	7	9	00	0	0	10	3	7	75	12	1
Kemptville	46	13	3	00	0	0	16	15	11	11	17	7
Mirrickville	34	16	2	00	0	0				19	11	11
Totals	3500	0	0	1458	10	0	857	4	5	1000	2	3

2. That the said several sums hereinbefore directed to
be raised and levied in the said Municipalities respectively,
shall be placed on the Collector's Roll by the Clerk
thereof in separate columns, and be collected in like manner **How collected.**
as all other rates and assessments are by law directed to
be collected, and that every Collector shall, on or before
the fourteenth day of December next, return his roll to
the Treasurer of his Municipality, and pay over to such
Treasurer the sums hereby directed to be raised, levied and
collected therein.

(Signed,)　　JAMES KEELER, Warden.

[L. S.]

(Signed,)　　JAMES JESSUP, Clerk.

No. CCXXXVIII.—BY-LAW

*To Authorize a Loan of Money from the Commercial Bank
of Canada.—Passed 3rd July, 1863.*

Whereas by a certain By-Law, passed the third day of **Preambles.**
July, 1863, by the Council of the Corporation of the
United Counties of Leeds and Grenville, it was enacted that
there should be raised and levied upon the whole rateable
property of the said United Counties for the said year the
sum of £3,500 to defray the ordinary and current expenses
thereof, and the further sum of £1,458 10s., to pay the
salaries of legally qualified Common School Teachers, and
the further sum of £857 4s. 5d., as a special rate authorised
to be raised and levied upon the said property under the
provisions of By-Law numbered one hundred and twenty,
passed on the thirteenth day of October, 1856, and the
further sum of £1,000 2s. 3d., as a special rate authorised
to be raised and levied upon the said property, under the
provisions of By-Law numbered one hundred and eighty-
two, passed on the nineteenth day of June, 1860, apportioned to the several Municipalities of the said United
Counties, as therein set forth.

And whereas the said Corporation of the said United
Counties is liable for and may be called upon to pay certain portions of the said several amounts before the same
can be levied by the said several Municipalities, and it is

therefore necessary to raise in anticipation, from time to time sufficient sums of money to pay the same.

And whereas the Commercial Bank of Canada has agreed to advance to the said Corporation, from time to time, on account of the said sums of money so to be raised and levied as aforesaid, a sum of money not exceeding in the whole the sum of £2,500, to be repaid on the second Monday in January, 1864, with interest at seven per cent. per annum, payable on the last day of the month of Nov. next, and on the said second Monday in January.

Be it therefore enacted by the Municipal Council of the Corporation of the United Counties of Leeds and Grenville aforesaid, that the Treasurer of the said United Counties may and is hereby authorised to raise by way of loan from the said The Commercial Bank of Canada, from time to time, sums of money not exceeding in the whole the sum of £2,500 for the purpose aforesaid.

2. That the interest, to be computed on each sum from the date of its advance, shall be paid upon the said loan, at the rate of seven per cent. per annum, on the last day of November next, and the second Monday in January next, and the said loan shall be repaid to the said The Commercial Bank of Canada on the said second Monday in January next.

3. That to secure the payment of the said sum so to be borrowed from the said The Commercial Bank of Canada, the said Treasurer shall deposit from time to time, as received by him, in the office at the said Bank at Brockville, in the said United Counties, all such sum or sums of money as shall or may be paid on account of the several By-Laws in the hereinbefore in part recited By-Law mentioned, which may be retained by the said bank for the repayment of the amount of the principal and interest of said advances as aforesaid.

4. That the Bond of the said Corporation, signed by the Warden of the said United Counties, and countersigned by the clerk, and sealed with the seals of the Corporation, in the penal sum of £5,000, shall be given to the said bank, with a condition thereunder written, for the payment of any sum or sums of money so to be advanced, with interest as aforesaid, upon the days and times above specified, and for the depositing with the said bank, on

(margin notes) Treasurer to loan £2,500. Amended; see By-law No. 242.

Rate of Interest.

Treasurer to deposit money in bank.

Bond to be giv'n.

the times aforesaid, by way of security, the sum or sums to be received by the said Treasurer on account of the assessments hereinbefore mentioned.

(Signed,)   JAMES KEELER, Warden.

[L. S.]

(Signed,)   JAMES JESSUP, Clerk.

No. CCXXXIX.—BY-LAW

To cover certain Grants of Money.— Passed 3rd July, 1863.

Be it enacted by the Council of the Corporation of the United Counties of Leeds and Grenville, and it is hereby enacted, That the several sums of money hereinafter men- Sums paid to. tioned shall be paid by the Treasurer to the parties res- pectively, out of any moneys in hands applicable to such purposes, viz. :—

To Messrs. John McMullen & Co., the sum of eighteen Messrs. Jno. Mc- dollars and forty-nine cents, for stationery and adver- Mullen & Co. tising.

To County Clerk, the sum of six dollars and seventy-six County Clerk. cents, for postages and other disbursements.

To R. W. Kelly, the sum of twenty-four dollars and fifty R. W. Kelly. cents, being balance due him on his contract for printing and advertising.

To Wm. Smith, the sum of twenty dollars, for superintend- William Smith. ing repairs on County Roads as Commissioner.

To the Board of Public Instruction, for the Prescott Prescott Board School circuit, the sum of eight dollars and twenty- Public Instruc- five cents, as expenses of the Board. tion.

To J. G. Elwood, the sum of six dollars and forty cents, J. G. Elwood. for cleaning court-room, &c., as per account.

To R. W. Kelly, the sum of three dollars and fifty cents, R. W. Kelly. for advertising.

To William Garvey, the sum of one hundred dollars, for William Garvey. services as chairman and commissioner for getting the roof on the Court-house, and also alterations, repairs and improvements in the gaol and yard, and letting out contracts, &c.

J. R. Cousens To J. R. Cousens, the sum of twenty dollars, for visits to the Registry Office at Prescott, by order of the Council, relating to the application of the Register to purchase certain books for the use of the office.

Robt. Anderson. To Robert Anderson, the sum of ten dollars, for services rendered in 1862 as Commissioner appointed by the Council to superintend the improvement of the town-line between Leeds and Frontenac.

Board Public Instruction No. 2. To the Board of Public Instruction for School Circuit No. 2, the sum of twenty-two dollars and forty-five cents, for attendance of members and stationery furnished.

John Johnston. To John Johnston, the sum of twenty dollars, for balance due for services as Commissioner of the Prescott and Kemptville County Toll Road.

R. W. Kelly. To R. W. Kelly, the sum of forty dollars, as an extra payment on account of the great rise in the value of paper after he took the contract for printing for the Council.

James Kincaid. To James Kincaid, the sum of three pounds five shillings, for attendance as messenger and stationery furnished.

Premium of Insurance. 2. That the sum of fifty dollars be granted to cover the premiums of insurance paid by the Treasurer on the order of the Clerk for Mechanics' risks during the repairs to the roof of the Court-house, as recommended in the second report of the Standing Committee on County Property.

(Signed,) JAMES KEELER, WARDEN..

[L. S.]

(Signed,) JAMES JESSUP, CLERK.

No. CCXL.—BY-LAW

*To appoint a Local Superintendent of Common Schools for
the Township of Wolford.—Passed 15th October, 1863.*

Be it enacted by the Council of the Corporation of the
United Counties of Leeds and Grenville, and it is hereby
enacted.

That the Reverend Charles Forrest of the Village of Rev. Chas. For
Merrickville be, and he is hereby appointed Local Super-rest.
intendent of Common Schools for the Township of Wolford, in the place and stead of the Reverend T. A. Parnell,
resigned ; such appointment to take effect from the passing
thereof, and continue in force until the first day of April,
A. D., 1864.

(Signed,)   JAMES KEELER, Warden.

[L. S.]

(Signed,)   JAMES JESSUP, Clerk.

No. CCXLI.—BY-LAW

*To confirm a certain By-Law of the Council of the Town-
ship of North Crosby—Passed 15th October, 1863.*

Whereas it is expedient and necessary to confirm a Preamble.
certain By-Law passed by the Council of the Corporation
of the Township of North Crosby, on the twenty-eighth
day of September, A. D. 1863, and intituled " By-Law to
grant and convey to James M. Rorison, a part of the original allowance for road in front of lots numbers twelve
and thirteen, in the seventh concession of the township of
North Crosby."

Be it therefore enacted by the Council of the Corporation of the United Counties of Leeds and Grenville,
and it is hereby enacted, That the said in part recited By-law con-
By-Law, so passed by the said Council of North Crosby, firmed.
be and the same is hereby confirmed.

(Signed,) JAMES KEELER, Warden.

[L. S.]

(Signed,)   JAMES JESSUP, Clerk.

No. CCXLII.—BY-LAW

To amend By-Law numbered two hundred and thirty-eight.—Passed 16th October, 1863.

Preamble.

Whereas it is necessary and expedient to amend the first section of By-Law numbered two hundred and thirty-eight, passed on the third day of July, A. D., 1863, and intituled " By-Law to authorise a loan of money from the Commercial Bank of Canada ;" Be it therefore enacted by the Council of the Corporation of the United Counties of Leeds and Grenville, and it is hereby enacted, that all checks drawn by the Treasurer on the said Bank, for any loan of money effected under the provisions of the said in part recited By-Law, shall be drawn to the order of and

Warden to endorse checks.

endorsed by the Warden, anything in the said By-Law to the contrary notwithstanding.

(Signed,)   JAMES KEELER, Warden

[L. S.]

(Signed,)   JAMES JESSUP, Clerk.

No. CCXLIII.—BY-LAW

To repeal By-Laws numbers Seventy-seven, Eighty-five and Ninety-two.—Passed 16th October, 1863.

Be it enacted by the Council of the Corporation of the United Counties of Leeds and Grenville, and it is hereby enacted, that from and after the passing hereof, By-Law numbered seventy-seven, passed on the twenty-second day of June, A. D. 1854, and intituled " By-Law to assume the Bridge in the Village of Gananoque as a County work," and also By-Law numbered eighty-five, passed on the thirteenth day of October, A. D. 1854, and intituled " By-

Repeal.

Law to amend By-Law numbered seventy-seven ;" and also By-Law numbered ninety-two, passed on the twenty-seventh day of January, A. D. 1855, and intituled " By-Law to appoint additional Commissioners for re-building the Gananoque Bridge," be repealed, and the same are hereby severally repealed.

(Signed,)   JAMES KEELER, Warden.

[L. S.]

(Signed,)   JAMES JESSUP, Clerk.

No. CCXLIV.—BY-LAW

To cover certain Grants of Money.—Passed 17*th October*,
1863.

Be it enacted by the Council of the Corporation of the
United Counties of Leeds and Grenville, and it is hereby
enacted, That the several sums of money hereinafter
mentioned shall be paid by the Treasurer to the parties
respectively, out of any moneys in his hands applicable
to such purposes, viz. : Sums paid to.

To the County Clerk, the sum of seven dollars and forty-
six cents for postages and express charges disbursed
by him. County Clerk.

To Alfred Poulton, the sum of twenty dollars, for repairing windows of the Court House and Gaol, as per
contract. Alfred Poulton.

To the Board of Public Instruction for circuit number six,
the sum of fifteen dollars, for attendance of members
and advertising. Board Public In-
struction No. 6.

To the Board of Public Instruction for circuit number one,
the sum of twenty-eight dollars and thirty cents, for
attendance of members and secretary, as per account. Board Public Instruction No. 1.

To E. H. Whitmarsh, the sum of twenty dollars, for services as Commissioner of the County Roads. E. H. Whitmarsh.

To David Jones, the sum of ten dollars to carpet the floor
of his office. David Jones.

To the Board of Public Instruction for the Prescott circuit,
the sum of eight dollars for attendance of members. Prescott Board
Public Instruc-
tion.

To Dr. Scott, of Prescott, the sum of seventy-five cents for
searches in Registry office. Dr. Scott.

To R. W. Kelly, the sum of two dollars and seventy cents,
for advertising. R. W. Kelly.

To James G. Elwood, the sum of seventeen dollars
and thirty cents, as per account. Jas. G. Elwood.

To William Fitzsimmons, the sum of fifteen dollars and
seven cents, as per account. William Fitzsimmons.

James Kincaid. To James Kincaid, the sum of eleven dollars and sixty-three cents, for services as messenger and stationery furnished, as per account.

James Keeler. To James Keeler, Esq., the sum of $100 for his services as Warden, and the further sum of $100 for his services as Commissioner on various accounts, besides the sums to which he is entitled as a member of the Council.

David Wylie. To David Wylie, the sum of $10 for reporting the proceedings of this Council.

Taxes of Prescott and other Corporations. 2. That the Treasurer be authorised to receive from the Corporation of the Town of Prescott the sum of eight hundred dollars, in full of all County Taxes for the year 1863, the sum of two hundred and eighty dollars from the Corporation of Gananoque, the sum of two hundred and sixty dollars from the Corporation of Kemptville, and the sum of two hundred and forty dollars from the Corporation of Merrickville, for the same purposes.

Gananoque Bridge. 3. That the sum of two hundred dollars be granted to the Municipality of the Village of Gananoque to aid in repairing the Gananoque bridge.

Insurance Premiums. 4. That the sum of one hundred dollars be granted to cover the premiums of Insurance paid by the Treasurer on the order of the Clerk, for Mechanics' Risks during the repairs and alterations to the Court House and Gaol, as directed at the last meeting of the Council.

(Signed,) JAMES KEELER, Warden.

[L. S.]

(Signed,) JAMES JESSUP, Clerk.

No. CCXLV.—BY-LAW

To appoint Auditors for the current year.—Passed 2nd February, 1864.

Be it enacted by the Council of the Corporation of the United Counties of Leeds and Grenville, and it is hereby enacted as follows:—

1. That Norton Marshall, of the Township of Kitley, Norton Marshall. having been nominated by the Warden, be appointed Auditor for the current year.

2. That Chancey H. Peck, of the Town of Prescott, be Chanc'y H.Peck. also appointed Auditor for the current year.

3. That the said Norton Marshall and Chancey H. Peck be appointed Auditors of School moneys and accounts School Auditors. for the current year, pursuant to the Common School Act for Upper Canada.

(Signed,)   H. McCREA, Warden.

[L. S.]

(Signed,)   JAMES JESSUP, Clerk.

No. CCXLVI.—BY-LAW

To appoint Trustees for each of the County Grammar Sec 39 Vic. Cap. *Schools, and Local Superintendents of Common* 23. *Schools.—Passed 4th February, 1864.*

Be it enacted by the Council of the Corporation of the United Counties of Leeds and Grenville, and it is hereby enacted as follows :—

1. That the persons hereinafter in this section named be elected and appointed Trustees of the County Grammar Trustees appointed. Schools in the said United Counties as they are respectively assigned to each of the said Schools, that is to say:

For the Grammar School at Brockville—Rev. J. K. Brockville Sch'l. Smith and William Fitzsimmons re-appointed.

For the Grammar School at Kemptville—Richey Waugh Kemptville Sch'l. and R. Kernahan, re-appointed.

For the Grammar School at Prescott—William Ellis in Prescott School. place of Hamilton D. Jessup, and Dr. John Easton, in place of Matthew Dowsley.

For the Grammar School at Gananoque—The Rev. Gananoq'e Sch'l. John Carroll and Rev. Henry Gordon re-appointed, and the Rev. P. Walsh in place of Wm. S. McDonald, left the Province.

Farmersville School.

For the Grammar School at Farmersville—Henry Green re-appointed, and Joseph Wiltse, in place of Wellington Landon.

Merrickville School.

For the Grammar School at Merrickville—Dr. J. R. Cousens re-appointed, and Michael Kelly in place of John Muir, the Rev. C. Forrest in place of the Rev. T. Parnell, removed to Kingston, and Robert Gwynne in place of Aaron Merrick, resigned; And that the said appointments of Trustees are to commence and take effect on the 31st day of January, A. D. 1864.

Local Superintendents.

2. That the persons hereinafter mentioned in this section, be appointed Local Superintendents of Common Schools for the Municipalities respectively herein mentioned, that is to say : Augusta, James Clapperton ; Oxford, Rev. James Harris ; Front of Leeds and Lansdowne, David C. Read ; Rear of Leeds and Lansdowne, Rev. C. Denroche ; Rear of Yonge and Escott, Wm. W. King ; Front of Yonge, Henry Lillie ; Front of Escott, Charles N. Hagerman ; Elizabethtown, Jacob A. Brown ; Edwardsburgh, William B. Imrie ; South Gower, Rev. Joseph Anderson ; Wolford, Heman McCrea; Kitley, Rev. D. J. McLean ; Elmsley, John Ferguson ; Bastard and Burgess, Samuel Babb; South Crosby, Miles Young; North Crosby, James Bilton. And that the said appointments of Local Superintendents shall commence and take effect on the first day of April next, and not before.

(Signed,)   H. McCREA, Warden.

[L. S.]

(Signed,)   JAMES JESSUP, Clerk.

No. CCXLVII.—BY-LAW

To authorise a Loan of Money from the Commercial Bank of Canada.—Passed 4th February, 1864.

Preambles.

Whereas the Corporation of the United Counties of Leeds and Grenville is liable for and may be called upon to pay certain portions of the several rates or assessments to be raised and levied upon the whole rateable property of the said United Counties for the present year, to defray the ordinary and current expenses thereof, and to pay the salaries of legally qualified Common School teachers, and the special rates under the provisions numbered one hundred and twenty and one hundred and eighty-two, passed respectively on the thirteenth day of October, 1856, and the nineteenth day of June, 1860, before the said rates or assessments can be levied by the several Municipalities of the said united Counties, and it is therefore necessary to raise in anticipation, from time to time, sufficient sums of money to pay the said liabilities.

And whereas the Commercial Bank of Canada has agreed to advance to the said Corporation, from time to time, on account of the said rates or assessments so to be raised and levied as aforesaid, a sum of money not exceeding in the whole the sum of £2,000, to be repaid on the second Monday in January, A. D., 1865, with interest at seven per cent. per annum, payable on the last day of the month of November next, and on the said second Monday in January.

Be it therefore enacted by the Council of the Corporation of the United Counties of Leeds and Grenville, and it is hereby enacted : That the Treasurer of the said United Counties may and is hereby authorised to raise by way of Loan, from the said The Commercial Bank of Canada, from time to time, sums of money not exceeding in the whole the sum of £2,000 for the purpose aforesaid, and that all checks drawn by the said Treasurer on the said Bank for any loan of money raised under the provisions of this By-law shall be drawn to the order of and endorsed by the Warden. *Treasurer to loan £2000.*

2. That interest, to be computed on each sum from the date of its advance, shall be paid upon the said loan at the rate of seven per cent. per annum, on the last day of November next and the second Monday in January next, and the said loan shall be repaid to the said The Commercial Bank of Canada, on the said second Monday in January next. *Rate of Interest.*

3. That to secure the payment of the said sum so to be borrowed from the said The Commercial Bank of Canada, the said Treasurer shall deposit from time time, as received by him, in the office of the said Bank at Brockville, in the said United Counties, all such sum or sums of money as shall or may be paid on account of the said rates or assessments hereinbefore mentioned, which may be retained by the said bank for the payment of the amount of the principal and interest of said advances as aforesaid. *Treasurer to deposit money in bank.*

4. That the bond of the said Corporation, signed by the Warden of the said United Counties and countersigned by the clerk, and sealed with the seal of the said Corporation in the penal sum of £4,000, shall be given to the said bank with a condition thereunder written, for the payment of any sum or sums of money so to be advanced, with interest as aforesaid, upon the days and times above specified, and for the depositing with the said bank, on the terms aforesaid, by way of security, the sum or sums to be received by the said Treasurer on account of the assessments hereinbefore mentioned.

Bond to be giv'n:

(Signed,) H. McCREA, Warden.

[L. S.]

(Signed,) JAMES JESSUP, Clerk.

No. CCXLVIII.—BY-LAW

To Amend By-Law numbered one hundred and ninety-four.
—Passed 5th February, 1861.

Preamble.

Whereas it is expedient for the more effectual suppression of houses or places of "ill-fame," that persons frequenting them should be liable to the same penalties as persons keeping, supporting or maintaining the same: Be it therefore enacted by the Council of the Corporation of the United Counties of Leeds and Grenville, and it is hereby enacted, that the eighth section of By Law numbered one hundred and ninety-four, passed on the ninth day of November, in the year of our Lord one thousand eight hundred and sixty, and intituled "By-Law to provide for the preservation of the Public Morals of the United Counties of Leeds and Grenville," is hereby amended and extended by the addition of the word "frequent," which word is hereby incorporated in the said section of the said in part recited By-Law, and shall be read as part of the said section immediately after the word "support," where such last mentioned word occurs in the said section.

8th section, amended.

(Signed,) H. McCREA, Warden.

[L. S.]

(Signed,) JAMES JESSUP, Clerk.

No. CCXLIX.—BY-LAW

To cover certain Grants of Money.—Passed 6th February,
1864.

Be it enacted by the Council of the Corporation
of the United Counties of Leeds and Grenville, and
it is hereby enacted, That the several sums of money here- Sums to be paid
inafter in this section mentioned shall be paid by the to.
Treasurer to the parties respectively, out of any moneys
in his hands applicable to such purposes, viz:—

To the Board of Public Instruction for School Circuit No. Board Public In-
1, the sum of $25.30 for attendance of members, salary struction No. 1.
of Secretary and incidental expenses.

To the Board of Public Instruction for School Circuit No. Board Public In-
2, the sum of $1.60 for advertising meeting of Board. struction No. 2.

To the Board of Public Instruction for School Circuit No. 5, Board Public In-
the sum of $100.89 for attendance of members, salary struction No. 5.
of Secretary, printing, advertising and other incidental
expenses.

To the Board of Instruction for School Circuit No. 6, the Board Public In-
sum of $41 for attendance of members, salary of Secre- struction No. 6.
tary and incidental expenses.

To the County clerk the sum of $2.50 for postages and County Clerk.
other disbursements.

To Adam Anderson, the sum of $24.80 for covers for As- Adam Anderson.
sessors' and Collectors' Rolls.

To McMullen & Co., the sum of $56.88 for printing and Messrs. McMul-
stationery furnished. len & Co.

To John McMullen, the sum of $160 on account of his John McMullen.
contract for printing and advertising.

To the Board of Public Instruction for School Circuit No. 2, Board Public In-
the sum of $22 for attendance of members and inci- struction No. 2.
dental expenses.

To J. G. Elwood, the sum of $8.75 as per account. J. G. Elwood.

To Adiel Sherwood, Esq., the sum of $59.90 for sundry Adiel Sherwood.
articles furnished on the introduction into the gaol of
the dietary system, as per account.

Wm. H. Freden-
burgh.

To William H. Fredenburgh, the sum of $20 for services as Commissioner of the Wesport road.

Bridge over Hut-
ton's Creek.

To the Reeves of Wolford and Elmsley, and the Deputy Reeve of Kitley, the sum of $95, to be expended on the covering of the bridge over Hutton's Creek, and that this grant is with the distinct understanding that any further amount required for the completion of the said bridge shall be raised by local means.

Committe suit,
Roe vs. Counti's.

That the sum of $400 be placed at the disposal of the Special Committee appointed to confer with the County Solicitors respecting the suit of Roe against these counties, to be drawn upon as required in the progress of the said suit, for the purposes mentioned in the second clause of the fourth report of the Standing Committee on Finance and Assessments.

James Kincaid.

To James Kincaid the sum of $15.10 for attendance as messenger and stationery furnished.

David Wylie.

To David Wylie, the sum of $10 for attending and reporting the proceedings of this session of the council.

(Signed,)   H. McCREA, Warden.

[L. S.]

(Signed,)   JAMES JESSUP, Clerk.

No. CCL.—BY-LAW

To appoint Local Superintendents of Common Schools for the Townships therein mentioned.—Passed 23rd June, 1864.

Be it enacted by the Council of the Corporation of the United Counties of Leeds and Grenville, and it is hereby enacted, as follows:—

South Crosby.

1. That Car Lee Ripley be appointed local Superintendent of Common Schools for the Township of South Crosby in the place of Miles Young, resigned.

Rear of Yonge &
Escott.

2, That Seaberry Scovil be appointed local Superintendent of Common Schools for the Township of Rear of Yonge and Escott in the place of Wm. W. King, resigned.

3. That Robert E. Brown be appointed local Superin- Augusta
tendent of Common Schools for the Township of Augusta,
in the place of James Clapperton, deceased.

4. That the said appointments shall continue in force Till 1st April
until the first day of April next, and no longer. next.

(Signed,) H. McCREA, Warden.

[L. S.]

(Signed,) JAMES JESSUP, Clerk.

———

No. CCLI.—BY-LAW.

To cover certain Grants of Money.—Passed 25th June,
1864.

Be it enacted by the Council of the Corporation of the
United Counties of Leeds and Grenville, and it is hereby
enacted, That the several sums of money hereinafter men- Sums to be paid
tioned shall be paid by the Treasurer to the parties to.
respectively entitled to the same, out of any moneys in
his hands applicable to such purposes, viz:

To the Board of Public Instruction for Kemptville School Kemptville
  Circuit, the sum of twenty-eight dollars for attend- Board Public In-
  ance of members and incidental expenses in 1862. struction.

To Bryan Leary, the sum of fifteen dollars and seventeen Bryan Leary.
  cents, for repairing cornice and plastering in the
  Court House.

To County Clerk, the sum of ten dollars and four cents, County Clerk.
  for postages and other disbursements.

To the Board of Public Instruction for School Circuit No. Board Public In-
  6, the sum of twenty-nine dollars and forty cents, for struction No. 6.
  attendance of members and incidental expenses.

To John McMullen, the sum of thirty-three dollars and John McMullen
  thirteen cents, for stationery, printing and the balance
  due on contract.

To Alfred Poulton, the sum of ninety-two dollars, for Alfred Poulton.
  whitewashing the Court Room, Treasurer's, Sheriff's
  and Jailor's Rooms.

D 1

William Fitzsim- To William Fitzsimmons, the sum of ninety dollars and
mons. seventy-seven cents for work in Gaol and Court
House.

R. W. Kelly. To Robert W. Kelly, the sum of nine dollars and thirty-
nine cents, for advertising.

C. N. Hagerman. To C. N. Hagerman, the sum of eight dollars, for attendance as a member of the Board of Public Instruction.

Chas. Dickenson. To Charles Dickenson, Esq., the sum of seventy-four
dollars, to aid in furnishing his office, as Sheriff of
these Counties.

County Clerk to To the County Clerk, the sum of thirty-seven dollars and
buy Municipal fifty cents, to purchase from George Gregg, Esq., the
Guide. Municipal Guide, to be published by him.

Jas. G. Elwood. To James G. Elwood the sum of six pounds and three
pence, in full of his account.

David Wylie. To David Wylie, the sum of ten dollars, for reporting the
proceedings of this session.

James Kincaid. To James Kincaid, the sum of eleven dollars and seventy-
five cents, for attendance as messenger and stationery
furnished.

2. That the sum of fourteen hundred and thirty-five dollars
be granted to pay the verdict and costs in the case of Roe
Verdict, &c., in vs. these Counties, and the expenses attending the defence
Roe vs. Counties. of the said suit, less the sum of five hundred and sixty
dollars advanced by the Treasurer, on account thereof,
and that the same be paid by the said Treasurer to the
parties mentioned in the report of the Special Committee
appointed to enquire into the case of Roe vs. Leeds and
Grenville, as the said parties are respectively entitled to
the same.

(Signed,)   H. McCREA, Warden.

[L. S.]
(Signed,)   JAMES JESSUP, Clerk.

No. CCLII.—BY-LAW

To assess the United Counties of Leeds and Grenville for the year 1864.—Passed 25th June, 1864.

Be it enacted by the Council of the Corporation of the United Counties of Leeds and Grenville, and it is hereby enacted, That there shall be raised and levied upon the whole rateable property in the said United Counties for the present year, the sum of £3,500 to defray the ordinary and current expenses thereof, and the further sum of £1,475 10s. to pay the salaries of legally qualified Common School teachers, and the further sum of £858 7s. 4d., as a special rate authorised to be raised and levied upon the said property, under the provisions of By-Law numbered one hundred and twenty, passed on the thirteenth day of October, 1856, and the further sum of £1,001 5s. 4d., as a special rate authorized to be raised and levied upon the said property, under the provisions of By-Law numbered one hundred and eighty-two, passed on the nineteenth day of June, 1860, and that the said several sums shall be apportioned to the several Municipalities of the said United Counties in the following manner, viz. :—

Sums to be levied.

County Rate.

Com'on Schools.

Special rate for loan.

Special rate under By-law No. 182.

How apportion'd to Municip'lities.

MUNICIPALITIES.	County Rates.			Common School Rates.			Special rate for Loan under By-Law No. 120.			Special rate under By-Law No. 192.		
	£.	s.	d.	£.	s.	d.	£.	s.	d.	£.	s.	d.
Elizabethtown	485	16	7	182	0	0	117	5	9	136	16	8
Bastard and Burgess	226	5	6	119	15	0	51	15	11	63	18	9
Rear of Yonge and Escott	181	16	9	67	5	0	41	6	9	48	4	5
Front of Yonge	128	0	2	55	15	0	29	10	6	31	8	10
Front of Leeds and Lansdowne	183	8	1	90	10	0	44	12	4	52	1	0
Rear of Leeds and Lansdowne	130	14	6	68	0	0	31	17	7	37	0	11
Kitley	226	8	4	103	5	0	54	12	7	63	14	7
North Crosby	81	0	3	63	10	0	19	16	1	22	2	1
South Crosby	121	9	6	63	10	0	31	15	7	37	1	4
Elmsley	70	13	6	42	0	0	17	10	5	20	8	10
Front of Escott	55	15	8	47	15	0	14	3	4	16	10	7
Gananoque	48	4	3				10	0	11	11	14	5
Augusta	425	7	5	165	15	0	110	9	11	128	18	2
Edwardsburgh	277	3	5	155	15	0	68	11	1	79	19	6
Oxford	247	5	9	131	10	0	59	7	9	69	5	8
Wolford	169	7	0	88	15	0	40	15	5	47	11	3
South Gower	85	17	5	32	10	0	21	5	3	24	16	1
Prescott	245	6	4				65	17	4	76	16	10
Kemptville	43	12	6				10	7	3	12	1	8
Mirickville	66	6	7				14	6	1	16	13	9
Totals	3500	0	0	1475	10	0	858	7	4	1001	5	4

2. That the said several sums hereinbefore directed to be raised and levied in the said Municipalities respectively, shall be placed on the Collectors' Rolls by the Clerk thereof, in separate columns, and be collected in like manner as *How collected.* all other rates and assessments are by law directed to be collected, and that every Collector shall, on or before the fourteenth day of December next, return his Roll to the Treasurer of his Municipality and pay over to such Treasurer the sums hereby directed to be raised, levied and collected therein.

(Signed,)   H. McCREA, Warden

[L. S.]

(Signed,)   JAMES JESSUP, Clerk.

No. CCLIII.—BY-LAW

To Regulate the Proceedings of the Council.—Passed 13th October, 1864.

Be it enacted by the Council of the Corporation of the United Counties of Leeds and Grenville, and it is hereby enacted, that a certain By-Law numbered one hundred and *By-law No. 160 repealed.* sixty, passed on the twentieth day of June, in the year of our Lord one thousand eight hundred and fifty-nine, and intituled " By-Law to regulate and govern the proceedings of the Council," and all and every of the Standing Rules of the Council, made on the fourth day of May, in the year of *Rules made in May, 1850, repealed.* our Lord one thousand eight hundred and fifty, be repealed, and the same are hereby repealed.

2. That after the passage of this By-Law, it is hereby declared and enacted that the following shall be the Standing Rules and Regulations for governing the proceedings of the said Council, and be numbered consecutively as follows :

MEETINGS AND ADJOURNMENTS.

1. That the Council do meet at the hour of ten o'clock in the forenoon, unless otherwise specially provided, and *New rules.* if at that hour there is no quorum the Warden do take the chair and adjourn, with the consent of the majority then present, but that on the first day of each session it do meet at the hour of two o'clock in the afternoon.

2. That when the Council adjourns, the members shall keep their seats until the Warden leaves the chair.

3. That on the appearance of a quorum, the Warden shall take the chair and call the members to order.

MINUTES.

4. That immediately after the Warden shall have taken the chair, the Minutes of the preceding day shall be read by the clerk, in order that any mistakes therein may be corrected by the Council.

5. That during the reading of the Minutes the doors shall be closed.

WARDEN.

6. That the Warden shall preserve order and decorum, and shall decide all questions of order, subject to an appeal to the Council.

7. That when the Warden is called upon to explain a point of order or practice, he shall state the rule applicable to the case without argument or comment.

MEMBERS.

8. That every Member, previous to his speaking, shall rise from his seat and address himself to the Warden.

9. That when two or more Members shall rise at once, the Warden shall name the member who is first to speak.

10. That every Member who shall be present when a question is put shall vote thereon, and shall not after the question is put and before the division takes place leave the Council.

11. That a Member called to order shall sit down until the question of order is decided by the Warden.

12. That no Members shall speak beside the question in debate.

13. That each Member may of right require the question or motion in discussion to be read for his information at any period of the debate, but not to interrupt a Member speaking.

14. That no Member, other than the one proposing a question or motion, [who shall be permitted to reply,] shall speak more than once on the same question, except in explanation, or by leave of the Council.

15. That a motion of adjournment shall always be in order.

16. That no motion shall be debated upon or put, unless the same be written with ink and seconded.

17. That no motion, prefaced by a preamble, shall be admitted in the Council.

18. That every motion when seconded, must be read by the Member standing in his place, and also by the Warden, and it shall then be deemed to be in the possession of the Council, but may be withdrawn at any time before decision or amendment by consent of Council.

19. That no Member shall speak to any motion until it is read by the Warden, except the introducer, and when the question has been finally put by the Warden, no Member is to speak thereon before voting.

20. That when a motion on question is under debate, no motion shall be received, unless to amend or commit, or postpone it to a certain day, or to adjourn, or to lay it on the table.

21. That a motion for commitment, until it is decided, shall preclude all amendments of the main question.

22. That all questions shall be put in the order they are moved, except amendments and in filling up blanks, when the shortest time and the lowest sum shall be put first, but no amendment shall be received to a motion for appointment to office.

23. That it shall be the duty of the Warden, whenever he shall conceive that a motion read by the introducer may be contrary to the Rules of the Council, to apprise the Council thereof before the motion shall be read by by him, and to tell the rule applicable to the case.

24. That every By-Law shall be introduced by a motion
of leave, specifying the title of it, or a motion to appoint
a committee to prepare and bring it in, or by an order
from the Council on the report of a Committee.

25. That no By-Law shall be committed or amended
until it shall have been twice read.

26. That every By-Law shall receive three separate
readings previous to its being finally passed.

27. That all By-Laws shall be read and passed in Committee of the whole between the second and third reading.

28. That all amendments made in Committee shall be
reported to the Council, and by it adopted, before the question to engross shall be put.

29. That each time a By-Law is read, the Clerk shall
certify the reading and the time, on the back thereof.

30. That in Committee of the Whole, all By-Laws shall
be read by the Chairman, and be debated upon clause by
clause, and put by the Chairman as read by him, leaving
the preamble and title to be last considered.

31. That when a By-Law passes the Council, the Warden and Clerk shall sign it, and put the date and seal of the
Corporation thereto.

32. That By-Laws of a private nature shall be introduced by a petition, to be presented by a member.

PETITIONS AND PETITIONERS.

33. That petitions, memorials, and other papers, addressed to the Council shall be presented by a member in
his place, who shall be answerable to the Council that they
do not contain improper or impertinent matter.

34. That every petition, memorial, &c., may be delivered
to, and presented by any member, but not after the third
day of any general meeting, unless it shall arise out of a
matter before the Council.

35. That whenever any petition or By-Law shall have been referred to a Committee to examine the matter thereof and report upon the same, the Council will not admit any petitioners to be heard against such a petition or By-Law until the matter thereof shall have first been reported to the Council by the Committee to whom it was referred.

COMMITTEE OF THE WHOLE.

36. That in forming a committee of the whole Council, the Warden shall leave the chair, and shall, before doing so, appoint one of the members to preside, who shall have the same authority in the chair of the committee as the Warden in the chair of the Council.

37. That the motion in Committee to rise and report the question shall always be in order.

38. That the rules of the Council shall be observed in Committee of the whole, as far as they may be applicable, except the rules limiting the number of times of speaking.

COMMITTEES.

39. That the mode of appointing a Special Committee shall be, first to determine the number it shall consist of, then each member naming one, which shall be written down by the Warden, those who have the most names shall be taken successively until the number is completed.

40. That of the number of members appointed to compose committees, such number thereof as shall be equal to a majority of the whole number chosen shall be a quorum.

41. That every member who shall introduce a By-Law, Petition, or Motion, upon any subject, which may be referred to a select committee, shall be one of the committee without being named by the Council.

STANDING COMMITTEES.

42. That at the first session of the Council in each and every year, standing committees to consist of five members each, shall be appointed for the following purposes, viz. : 1st, Finance ; 2nd, Assessments ; 3rd, Roads and Bridges ; 4th, Education and Schools ; 5th, County Property, to

whom all matters relating to these objects shall severally be referred.

43. That it shall be the duty of the Clerk, so soon as such Committees are appointed to post the names of the members of each in some conspicuous place in the Council Chamber, and so at each other session throughout the year.

YEAS AND NAYS.

44. That upon a division of the Council, the names of those who vote for and of those who vote against a motion shall be entered upon the minutes, if one member requires it.

ORDERS OF THE DAY.

45. That the orders of the day shall always have the preference to any motion before the Council.

46. That when any order, resolution, or question, shall be lost by the Council or Committee breaking up for want of a quorum, the order, resolution or question so lost, shall, after the routine business, be the first business to be proceeded with and disposed of at the next meeting of such Committee or Council.

FINANCE.

47. That if any motion shall be made in the Council for any charge upon the people, the consideration of the debate thereof shall not presently be entered upon, but postponed till such further time as the Council should think fit to appoint, and shall first be referred to a Committee of the whole.

TEMPORARY CHAIRMAN.

48. That all rules applicable to the Warden shall, in his absence, apply to the temporary chairman.

THE BAR.

49. That the limit formed by the rails on either side of the Court Room and the front of the Grand Petit Jury boxes, shall constitute the bar of the Council Chamber.

50. That no person other than the members and officers of the Council shall be allowed within the Bar unless

upon special leave of the Council, and that it shall be the
duty of the Messenger to see that this rule is strictly observed.

(Signed,)   JAMES KEELER, Chairman.
[L. S.]
(Signed,)   JAMES JESSUP, Clerk.

No. CCLIV.—BY-LAW

To cover certain Grants of Money.—Passed 15th October,
1864.

Be it enacted by the Council of the Corporation of
the United Counties of Leeds and Grenville, and it is
hereby enacted, that the several sums of money herein- Sums to be paid
after mentioned shall be paid by the Treasurer to the to.
parties respectively, out of any moneys in his hands applicable to such purposes, viz :—

To W. A. Schofield, Coroner, the sum of three dollars, W. A. Schofield.
the expense of burying a pauper woman.

To Alfred Poulton, the sum of twenty dollars for repair- Alfred Poulton.
ing the windows in Court House and Gaol from the
first of October, 1863, to the first of October, 1864,
as per contract.

To the Board of Public Instruction for School Circuit No. Board Public In-
1, the sum of thirty-three dollars and ten cents, for struction No. 1.
attendance of members and incidental expenses.

To John Burchell, the sum of thirty-nine dollars, for sur- John Burchill.
veying part of the Town Line between Augusta and
Wolford, and the Town Line between Kitley and
Elmsley.

To Messrs. Sherwood and Steele, Solicitors of the Council, Messrs. Sher-
the sum of two hundred and fifty-four dollars and wood & Steele.
twenty-five cents, being amount of bill of costs in the
case of Roe against the Counties.

To James Jessup, Esq., the sum of two hundred and fifty James Jessup.
dollars for account of revision of the By-laws.

James Turner. To James Turner, the sum of twenty dollars for support of an idiot.

James Jessup.⌐ To James Jessup, per account, eleven dollars twenty-eight cents.

School Circuit No. 2. To School Circuit No. 2, thirty-three dollars thirty-three cents.

School Circuit No. 6. To School Circuit No. 6, six dollars forty cents.

John McMullen. To John McMullen, per account, ten dollars thirty-one cents.

John McMullen. To John McMullen, on account of contract for printing, eighty dollars.

James Kincaid. To James Kincaid, for services, eleven dollars and fifty cents.

Harvey Miller.⌐ To Harvey Miller, for work at Registry Office, twenty-five dollars.

Jas. G. Elwood. To James G. Elwood, for cleaning Court Room, four dollars fifty cents.

(Signed,)   H. McCREA, WARDEN.
[L. S.]
(Signed,)   JAMES JESSUP, CLERK.

No. CCLV.—BY-LAW

To make provision for the opening, improving, and maintaining of County Roads.—Passed 9th November, 1864.

Preamble. Whereas it is expedient to make provision for opening, improving and maintaining County Roads, Be it therefore enacted by the Council of the Corporation of the United Counties of Leeds and Grenville, and it is hereby enacted by the authority of the same, that all local Municipalities in these United Counties be, and they are hereby

Local Municipalities to open, &c. required jointly to open, improve and maintain every road and section of road dividing any two local Municipalities, although such road deviates so as in some places to be partly or wholly within one of such Municipalities.

2. And be it further enacted, That such local Municipalities be, and they are hereby required to remove, or Obstructions to
cause to be removed, all obstructions lying or being in any be removed.
road dividing such Municipalities, and any costs incurred
thereby shall be paid by each of such Municipalities in
proportion to the interest they may have in such road.

3. Provided always, That nothing in this By-law shall Proviso.
apply to any private road or bridge in the possession of
or owned by any incorporated road or bridge company.

(Signed,)   H. McCREA, WARDEN.

[L. S.]

(Signed,)   JAMES JESSUP, CLERK.

No. CCLVI.—BY-LAW

To accept and confirm the arrangement therein mentioned.— See By-laws Nos.
Passed 9th November, 1864.   259 and 264.

Whereas the Committees appointed by the Council of Preambles.
the United Counties of Leeds and Grenville and the Council of the Town of Brockville, have agreed upon the sum
to be paid annually hereafter by the Corporation of the
Town of Brockville to the Corporation of the United
Counties of Leeds and Grenville for the purposes hereinafter
mentioned, and have reported the same to the said Councils respectively ; and whereas by a certain By-law, bearing date the seventh day of November, A. D. 1864, of the
Council of the Town of Brockville, and intituled, "By-
law to complete and confirm the arrangement made by the
committee appointed for the purpose therein mentioned,"
it is amongst other things enacted, that the said the Corporation of the Town of Brockville, agree to pay to the
Corporation of the United Counties of Leeds and Grenville, the sum of one thousand dollars annually on the
fifteenth day of January in each and every year hereafter for and during the term and period of five years, to
be computed from the 15th day of January, A. D. 1864,
for the expenses of the Administration of Justice, (including jury expenses) and the use of the gaol, and as compensation for the use of the buildings referred to in the
405 section of the consolidated Statutes of Upper Canada,
chaptered 54, and for the care and maintenance of prison-

ers, and that the first payment should be made and paid on the 15th day of January next ensuing, the date of the passing of the said By-law ; And whereas it is expedient to accept and agree to the said arrangement as contained in the said in part recited By-law of the Council of the Town of Brockville ; Be it therefore enacted by the Council of the Corporation of the United Counties of Leeds and Grenville, and it is hereby enacted, that the said arrangements made by the said committees and confirmed by the Council of the Town of Brockville as set forth in the said By-law, be and the same is hereby accepted and confirmed by the Council of the Corporation of the United Counties of Leeds and Grenville.

Arrangements with Brockville confirmed.

Warden & Clerk to sign agreement. 2. That the Warden and Clerk are hereby authorized to sign and countersign any agreement that may be necessary to carry out the said arrangement on behalf of the Corporation of the United Counties of Leeds and Grenville, and affix the seal of the Corporation thereto.

Copy of By-law to be furnished Corporation of Brockville. 3. That a copy of this By-law duly certified by the Clerk be furnished to the said the Corporation of the Town of Brockville.

(Signed,)　　H. McCREA, Warden.

[L. S.]

(Signed,)　JAMES JESSUP, Clerk.

No, CCLVII.—BY-LAW

Respecting the Security of the Treasurer.—Passed 10th November, 1864.

Preamble. Whereas it is expedient to accept a certain policy, bearing date the seventh day of September, in the year of our Lord one thousand eight hundred and sixty-four, of the European Assurance Society for the sum of eight thousand dollars as a guarantee to the Corporation of the United Counties of Leeds and Grenville for the fidelity of James Lancaster Schofield, Esq., as the Treasurer of the said Corporation ; be it therefore enacted by the Council of the Corporation of the United Counties of Leeds and Grenville, and it is hereby enacted, that the said policy of the European Assurance Society be and the same is hereby accepted as such guarantee upon the terms and conditions expressed and endorsed thereon, as by reference thereto will more fully and at large appear. *Guarantee European Society accepted.*

2. That in addition to such guarantee policy, the said Treasurer shall execute a bond individually to the said the Corporation of the United Counties of Leeds and Grenville in the penal sum of eight thousand dollars, for the faithful performance of his duties as such Treasurer, and especially for duly accounting for and paying over all moneys belonging to the said Corporation which may come into his hands as such Treasurer, and that the existing bonds of the said Treasurer and his sureties be not cancelled until after the next audit of his accounts, and the report of the Auditors be submitted to and adopted by the Council. *Additional security. Existing Bonds, &c.*

(Signed,) H. McCREA, Warden.

[L. S.]

(Signed,) JAMES JESSUP, Clerk.

No. CCLVIII.—BY-LAW

To provide for the payment of certain sums of money.—
Passed 11th November, 1864.

Be it enacted by the Council of the Corporation of the United Counties of Leeds and Grenville, and it is hereby enacted, that the several sums of money hereinafter mentioned, shall be paid by the Treasurer to the parties respectively entitled to the same out of any moneys in his hands applicable to such purposes, viz. :— *Sums to be paid to.*

To the Board of Public Instruction for Prescott Circuit, the sum of fourteen dollars and twenty-five cents for attendance of members, printing, advertising and stationery. *Prescott Board Public Instruction.*

To R. Byrne, the sum of two dollars and four cents, for advertising in the Prescott *Telegraph*, meeting of the Board of Education for the Prescott Circuit. *R. Byrne.*

To Messrs. Hall and Wright, the sum of ten dollars for printing and advertising for the Board of Public Instruction in Circuit number six, *Hall & Wright.*

J. G. Elwood. To J. G. Elwood, the sum of eleven dollars and two cents for whitewashing, repairing Court House, and cleaning building as per account.

Thomas Wallace.
See 2 Sec: By-
law No. 267. To Thomas Wallace, the sum of twenty dollars, as compensation for land taken on lot number two, broken front concession of Escott, for the road laid out and established by the Council, as described in By-law passed on the twenty-third day of June, A. D. 1859, and intituled, "By-law to establish a road between the Townships of Lansdowne and Escott," provided the said Thomas Wallace shall by a good and sufficient deed in law and equity, convey the land so taken on the said lot for the said road to the Corporation of the United Counties of Leeds and Grenville.

J. G. Elwood. To J. G. Elwood, the sum of twelve dollars being the amount of his account rendered in June last.

John McMullen. To John McMullen, the sum of ten dollars for reporting the proceedings of the Council at the present meeting.

David Wylie. To David Wylie, the sum of ten dollars for reporting the proceedings of the Council at the present meeting.

Hiram McCrea. To Hiram McCrea, the sum of one hundred dollars for his services as Warden, and the further sum of one hundred dollars for extra services as Commissioner, &c., on various occasions, besides the sum to which he is entitled as a member of the Council for 1864.

James Kincaid. To James Kincaid, the sum of eight dollars, for services as messenger and stationery furnished as per account.

C. J. Hynes. To C. J. Hynes, the sum of three dollars and ten cents for printing and advertising for the Prescott Board of Education.

William Fitz-
simmons. To William Fitzsimmons, the sum of three dollars, for a coffin for a poor woman.

2. That the Treasurer is hereby directed to pay to the Sheriff such sum or sums of money as it may be necessary for him to disburse in the purchase of a stove for his The Sheriff, wood office, and also of thirty-three cords of wood, by tender, for offices. for the use of the several Courts held in this Court House (except the Division Court,) and for the County Council, offices of the Sheriff, Clerk of the Peace, Treasurer and

Deputy Clerk of the Crown, as recommended in the fourth
report of the Standing Committee on Finance, and that
the receipts of the Sheriff shall be sufficient ;vouchers to
the Treasurer for such payments.

(Signed.)　　　H. McCREA, Warden

[L. S.]

(Signed,)　　JAMES JESSUP, Clerk.

No. CCLIX.—BY-LAW

To repeal By-law numbered two hundred and fifty-six.— — Repealed: see
Passed 11th November, 1864. By-law No. 261.

Be it enacted by the Council of the Corporation of the
United Counties of Leeds and Grenville, and it is hereby
enacted, that By-law numbered two hundred and fifty- By-law No. 256
six, passed on the ninth day of November, in the year one repealed.
thousand eight hundred and sixty-four, and intituled " By-
law to accept and confirm the arrangement therein mentioned," be and the same is hereby repealed.

(Signed,)　　　H. McCREA, Warden.

[L. S.]

(Signed,)　　JAMES JESSUP, Clerk.

No CCLX.—BY-LAW

*To appoint Auditors for the current year.—Passed 24th
January, 1865.*

Be it enacted by the Council of the Corporation of
the United Counties of Leeds and Grenville, and it is
hereby enacted, as follows:—

1. That Chancey H. Peck, of the Town of Prescott, Chanc'y H.Peck.
having been nominated by the Warden, be appointed
Auditor for the current year.

2. That William Thomson, of the Township of Lans- Wm. Thomson.
downe, be also appointed Auditor for the current year.

E 1

3. That the said Chancey H. Peck and William Thomson be appointed Auditors of School Accounts pursuant to the Common School Act of Upper Canada.

School Auditors.

(Signed,)   JAMES KEELER, WARDEN.

(L. S.)

(Signed,)   JAMES JESSUP, CLERK.

No. CCLXI.—BY-LAW

To confirm a certain By-Law of the Corporation of the Township of Oxford, conveying an allowance of Road therein——Passed 25th January, 1865.

Preamble.

Whereas the Corporation of the Township of Oxford, has passed a By-Law bearing date the sixth day of August, in the year of our Lord one thousand eight hundred and sixty-four, and intituled "By-Law to convey to Joseph Bowen, the allowance of Road between Lot No. 25 and 26, in the 2nd Concession of the Township of Oxford, whereby it was ordained and enacted by the said the Corporation of the Township of Oxford, that the said allowance for road be conveyed to and given to him the said Joseph Bowen, his heirs and assigns, for and in consideration of the land taken from him on said lot number twenty-six, and occupied for the road leading from Kemptville to the Rideau river; Be it therefore enacted by the Council of the Corporation of the United Counties of Leeds and Grenville, and it is hereby enacted, that the said By-Law be and the same is hereby confirmed.

Confirmed.

(Signed,)   JAMES KEELER, WARDEN.

[L. S.]

(Signed,)   JAMES JESSUP, CLERK.

No. CCLXII.—BY-LAW

*To confirm a certain By-Law of the Council of the Town-
ship of Elmsley, numbered one hundred and sixty-
three.—Passed 25th January, 1865.*

Whereas the Council of the Corporation of the Town- _{Preamble.}
ship of Elmsley has passed a By-Law bearing date the
thirtieth day of May, in the year of our Lord one thousand
eight hundred and sixty-four, and intituled "By-Law for
the purpose of selling that part of allowance of said road
running from Otter lake to the Portland road, and appointing commissioners to sell the same," whereby it
was ordained and enacted by the said Council of the
Township of Elmsley, that the said allowance for side
road on Government allowance for road, commencing at
Otter Lake and running to the Portland road between lots
twenty-four and twenty-five, be sold by public sale on
Wednesday, the first day of June, at the hour of two
o'clock, p. m. Be it therefore enacted by the Council of
the Corporation of the United Counties of Leeds and
Grenville, and it is hereby enacted, that the said By-Law ^{Confirmed.}
be and the same is hereby confirmed.

(Signed,)   JAMES KEELER, Warden.
[L. S.]

(Signed,)   JAMES JESSUP, Clerk.

No. CCLXIII.—BY-LAW

To appoint Trustees of the County Grammar Schools, _{See 29 Vic., cap}
and also Local Superintendents of Common Schools. _{23.}
—Passed 26th January, 1865.

Be it enacted by the Council of the Corporation of the
United Counties of Leeds and Grenville, and it is hereby
enacted, that the persons hereinafter, mentioned, in this _{Trustees ap-}
section, be and they are hereby appointed Trustees of _{pointed.}
the Grammar Schools to which they are severally and
respectively assigned, as follows :

Brockville Grammar School, Richard F. Steele and Rev. _{Brockville Sch'l.}
E. J. Senkler, reappointed.

Kemptville Sch'l. Kemptville Grammar School, Robert Leslie, reappointed, and W. R. Anderson.

Prescott School. Prescott Grammar School, Hamilton D. Jessup and Stephen B. Merrill.

Gananoq'e Sch'l. Gananoque Grammar School, D. Ford Jones, and D. F. Britton, reappointed.

Farmersville School. Farmersville Grammar School, Arza Parish and Wm. H. Giles.

Merrickville School. Merrickville Grammar School, Dr. C. Leggo and H. D. Smith.

And that the said appointments of Trustees are to commence and take effect on the 31st day of January, 1865.

2. That the persons hereinafter mentioned be, and they are hereby appointed Local Superintendents of Common Schools for the Townships to which they are severally and respectively assigned, as follows:

Local Superintendents.

Augusta...........,..................Robert E. Brown.
Oxford.............................Rev. James Harris.
Front of Leeds and Lansdowne..David C. Read.
Rear of Leeds and Lansdowne...Rev. C. Denroche.
Rear of Yonge and Escott........Rev. Wm. Magill.
Front of Yonge.............. ......Rev. Mr. Morton.
Front of Escott. ....Charles N. Hagerman.
Elizabethtown.....................Jacob A. Brown.
Edwardsburgh.....................Wm. B. Imrie.
South Gower.......................Rev. Joseph Anderson.
Wolford.............................Heman McCrea.
Kitley.............................Rev. D. J. McLean.
Elmsley ....John Ferguson.
Bastard and Burgess......·.......Samuel Rabb.
South Crosby..... ....Rev. L. A. Betts.
North Crosby..............James Bilton.

And that the said appointments of Local Superintendents shall commence and take effect on the first day of April next, and not before.

(Signed,)   JAMES KEELER, WARDEN.

[L. S.]

(Signed,)   JAMES JESSUP, CLERK.

No. CCLXIV.—BY-LAW

*To repeal By-Law numbered two hundred and fifty-nine
and to revive By-Law numbered two hundred and fifty-
six.—Passed 27th January, 1865.*

Be it enacted by the Council of the Corporation of the
United Counties of Leeds and Grenville, and it is hereby
enacted, that By-Law numbered two hundred and fifty- By-law No. 259
nine, passed on the eleventh day of November, in the year repealed.
one thousand eight hundred and sixty-four, and intituled
" By-Law to repeal By-Law numbered two hundred and
fifty six," be repealed and the same is hereby repealed.

2. And be it further enacted, that By-Law number two
hundred and fifty-six, passed on the the 9th day of November, in the year one thousand eight hundred and sixty-
four, and intituled " By-Law to accept and confirm the
arrangement therein mentioned," and all and every of its
recitals, agreements and provisions, shall be revived and By-law No. 256
the same are hereby revived, and shall be in force and revived.
effect on the passing hereof as fully and effectually to all
intents and purposes as if the said last mentioned By-Law
and all and every of its recitals, agreements, and provisions
were severally embodied and re-enacted herein, anything
in any other By-Law to the contrary notwithstanding.

(Signed,)   JAMES KEELER, Warden.

[L. S.]

(Signed,)   JAMES JESSUP, Clerk.

No. CCLXV.—BY-LAW

*To provide for the Printing and Advertising of the Council.
—Passed 27th January, 1865.*

Be it enacted by the Council of the Corporation of the
United Counties of Leeds and Grenville, and it is hereby
enacted, that the printing and advertising of the Council
for the year commencing on the third Monday in the
month of June next, and ending on the same day in the To be given out
month of June, A. D. 1866, be given out by tender to the by tender.
lowest bidder, and the Clerk advertise for tenders in some
newspaper published in these Counties.

When tenders received.

2. That such tenders be received by the Clerk until 12 o'clock, noon, on the 17th day of June next, and that they state a gross sum for such printing and advertising.

Sample paper.

3. That samples of the quality of paper to be used for the printing with specifications of the whole work required to be furnished and preformed, shall be exhibited by the Clerk at his office to parties desirous of tendering for such printing and advertising.

Warden & Clerk to contract for.

4. That the Warden and the Clerk be authorized to enter into a contract with the lowest bidder for such printing and advertising, and to sign and countersign the same, and affix the seal of the Corporation thereto.

The whole or separate.

5. That the Warden and the Clerk may, if they see fit, call for tenders for such printing and advertising separately, or for the whole work, as they in their discretion may consider for the interest of the Counties.

(Signed,)   JAMES KEELER, WARDEN.

[L. S.]

(Signed,)   JAMES JESSUP, CLERK.

No. CCLXVI.—BY-LAW

To authorize a loan of money from the Commercial Bank of Canada.—Passed 28th January, 1865.

Preambles.

Whereas the Corporation of the United Counties of Leeds and Grenville is liable for and may be called upon to pay certain portions of the several rates or assessments to be raised and levied upon the whole rateable property of the said United Counties for the present year, to defray the ordinary and current expenses thereof, and to pay the salaries of legally qualified Common School Teachers, and the special rates under the provisions of By-Laws numbered one hundred and twenty and one hundred and eighty-two, passed respectively on the thirteenth day of October, A. D., 1856, and the nineteenth day of June, A. D., 1860, before the said rates or assessments can be levied by the several Municipalities of the said United Counties, and it is therefore necessary to raise in anticipation, from time to time, sufficient sums of money to pay the said liabilities.

And whereas the Commercial Bank of Canada has agreed to advance to the said Corporation, from time to time, on account of the said rates or assessments so to be raised and levied as aforesaid, a sum of money not exceeding in the whole, the sum of £2,500, to be repaid on the second Monday in January, A. D., 1866, with interest at seven per cent per annum, payable on the last day of the month of November next and on the said second Monday in January : Be it therefore enacted by the Council of the Corporation of the United Counties of Leeds and Grenville, and it is hereby enacted, that the Treasurer of the said United Counties, may and is hereby authorized to raise by way of loan from the said the Commercial Bank of Canada, from time to time, sums of money not exceeding in the whole, the sum of £2,500, for the purpose aforesaid, and that all checks drawn by the said Treasurer on the said Bank for any loan of money raised under the provisions of this By-Law, shall be drawn to the order of and endorsed by the Warden.

Treasurer to borrow £2,500.

2. That interest to be computed on each sum from the date of its advance, shall be paid upon the said loan, at the rate of seven per cent per annum, on the last day of November next, and the second Monday in January next and the said loan shall be repaid to the said the Commercial Bank of Canada on the said the second Monday in January next.

Rate of Interest.

3. That to secure the payment of the said sum so to be borrowed from the said the Commercial Bank of Canada, the said Treasurer shall deposit from time to time, as received by him, in the office of the said Bank at Brockville, in the said United Counties, all such sum or sums of moneys as shall or may be paid on account of the said rates or assessments hereinbefore mentioned, which may be retained by the said Bank for the repayment of the amount of principal and interest of said advances as aforesaid.

Treasurer to deposit money in bank.

4. That the bond of the said Corporation signed by the Warden of the said United Counties, and countersiged by the Clerk, and sealed with the seal of the said Corporation in the penal sum of £5,000, shall be given to the said Bank, with a condition thereunder written, for the payment of any sum or sums of money so to be advanced, with interest as aforesaid, upon the days and times above specified, and for the depositing with the said Bank on

Bond to be giv'n.

the terms aforesaid by way of security, the sum or
sums to be received by the said Treasurer on account of
the assessments hereinbefore mentioned.

(Signed,) JAMES KEELER, Warden.

[L. S.]

(Signed,) JAMES JESSUP, Clerk.

No. CCLXVII.—BY-LAW

To authorise the payment of certain sums of Money.—
Passed 28th January, 1865.

Be it enacted by the Council of the Corporation of the
United Counties of Leeds and Grenville, and it is hereby
enacted, That the several sums of money hereinafter mentioned shall be paid by the Treasurer to the parties
respectively entitled to the same, out of any monies in his
hands applicable to such purposes, viz:

Sums to be paid to.

County Clerk. To the County Clerk the sum of twelve dollars and eighty-nine cents for postages and other disbursements.

R. W. Kelly. To R. W. Kelly, the sum of six dollars, for publishing Professor Buckland's essay on drainage.

Ogden Foxcroft. To Ogden Foxcroft, the sum of twenty-four dollars and thirty-seven and a half cents, for making Port-folios for Assessors' and Collectors' Rolls.

Kemptville Bo'rd Public Instruction. To the Kemptville Board of Public Instruction, the sum of twenty-eight dollars and fifty cents, for attendance of members and Incidental expenses.

Messrs. Jno. Mc-Mullen & Co. To Messrs. John McMullen & Co., the sum of six dollars and forty-nine cents, for stationery furnished for the Clerk's office.

John McMullen To John McMullen, Esq., the sum of sixty dollars, on account of his contract with the Council for printing and advertising.

Prescott Board Education. To the Board of Education for Prescott Circuit, the sum of sixteen dollars for attendance of members at the examination.

To the Council of the Municipality of Bastard and Burgess, the sum of thirty-five dollars to aid in sending George Canton of Bastard, to the Deaf and Dumb Institution in the City of Hamilton. *Council Bastard and Burgess for Geo. Canton.*

To the Treasurer, the sum of two hundred dollars, for transferring the non-resident lands from the old book to the new books. *County Treasurer.*

To Messrs. Hall & Wright, the sum of six dollars, for publishing Professor Buckland's essay on Farm Drainage. *Messrs. Hall & Wright.*

To David Wylie, the sum of six dollars, for publishing Professor Buckland's essay on Farm Drainage. *David Wylie.*

To Harvey Miller, the sum of two dollars and forty-three cents, for work done in the Gaol. *Harvey Miller.*

To J. G. Elwood, the sum of two dollars and sixty-five cents, for cleaning County property. *J. G. Elwood.*

To William Fitzsimmons, the sum of eight dollars and twenty cents. *William Fitzsimmons.*

To David Wylie, the sum of ten dollars for reporting the proceedings of this session of the Council. *David Wylie.*

To John McMullen, the sum of ten dollars, for the same purpose. *Jno. McMullen.*

To James Kincaid, the sum of ten dollars and ten cents, for attendance as messenger and stationery furnished. *James Kincaid.*

To the Board of Public Instruction for Circuit No. 5, the sum of sixty-three dollars and seventy-four cents, for attendance of members and incidental expenses, as per account. *Board Public Instruction No. 5.*

To the Board of Public Instruction for Circuit No. 5, the sum of forty-one dollars and ten cents, for attendance of members and incidental expenses as per account. *The same.*

2. That the sum of twenty dollars granted to Thomas Wallace at the last meeting of this Council, shall not be paid [his title being disputed] until he produces satisfactory *Grant to Thomas Wallace suspended. See By-law No. 263.*

proof to this Council that he is owner of the land taken
for the road between Lansdowne and Escott and for which
the said grant was made.

(Signed,) JAMES KEELER, Warden.

[L. S.]

(Signed,) JAMES JESSUP, Clerk.

No. CCLXVIII.—BY-LAW

*To appoint a Local Superintendent of Common Schools for
the Township of Leeds and Lansdowne.—Passed, 22nd
June, 1865.*

Rev. Jno. Carroll.

Be it enacted by the Council of the Corporation of the
United Counties of Leeds and Grenville, and it is hereby
enacted, that the Reverend John Carrroll be, and he is hereby appointed Local Superintendent of Common Schools for
the Township of the Front of Leeds and Lansdowne, in
the place of David C. Read who has left the Province, and
that the said appointment shall take effect on the passing
hereof and continue in force until the first day of April,
next, anything in any other By-Law to the contrary notwithstanding.

(Signed,) JAMES KEELER, Warden.

[L. S.]

(Signed,) JAMES JESSUP, Clerk.

No. CCLXIX—BY-LAW.

*To appoint a Local Superintendent of Common Schools
for the Township of Front of Yonge.—Passed 23rd
June, 1865.*

Dr. E. B. Haight.

Be it enacted by the Council of the Corporation of the
United Counties of Leeds and Grenville, and it is hereby
enacted, that Dr. E. B. Haight be, and he is hereby
appointed Local Superintendent of Common Schools for
the Township of Front of Yonge, in the place of Rev.

William Morton who has resigned, and that the said appointment shall take effect on the passing hereof, and continue in force until the first day of April next, anything in any other By-Law to the contrary notwithstanding.

(Signed,)   JAMES KEELER, Warden.

[L. S.]

(Signed,) JAMES JESSUP, Clerk.

No. CCLXX.—BY-LAW

To open part of the Town Line between the Township of Edwardsburgh and Augusta.—Passed 24th June, 1865.

Whereas application has been made to this Council by D. C. Wilkinson and other inhabitants to open a portion of the Town Line or original allowance for road between the Township of Edwardsburgh and Augusta; and whereas due notice of such application has been given according to law; and whereas it is expedient and right that so much of the said Town Line as is hereinafter mentioned and described should be opened accordingly; be it therefore enacted by the Council of the Corporation of the United Counties of Leeds and Grenville, and it is hereby enacted, that that part of the Town Line or original allowance for road between the said Townships of Edwardsburgh and Augusta, extending from the River St. Lawrence to the Rear of the first Concession of the said Township of Augusta, be opened and the same is hereby required to be opened for public use and travel.

Preambles.

Open to rear of 1st Con. Augusta.

2. That Christopher Farley be appointed and he is hereby appointed Overseer of the said portion of the said Road hereby directed to be opened for public use and travel, with full power and authority to open the same according to law.

Chris. Farley appointed overse'r.

(Signed,)   JAMES KEELER, Warden.

[L. S.]

(Signed,) JAMES JESSUP, Clerk.

No. CCLXXI.—BY-LAW

To Assess the United Counties of Leeds and Grenville for the year 1865.—Passed 24th June, 1865.

Be it enacted by the Council of the Corporation of the United Counties of Leeds and Grenville, and it is hereby enacted, that there shall be raised and levied upon the whole rateable property in the said United Counties for the present year, the sum of £3,500, to defray the ordinary and current expenses thereof, and the further sum of £1,468 15s., to pay salaries of legally qualified Common School Teachers, and the further sum of £858 7s. 4d., as a special rate authorized to be raised and levied upon the said property, under the provisions of By-Law numbered one hundred and twenty, passed on the 13th day of October, A.D.1856, and the further sum of £1,001 5s. 4d., as a special rate authorized to be raised and levied upon the said property, under the provisions of By-Law numbered one hundred and eighty-two, passed on the nineteenth day of June, 1860, and that the said several sums shall be apportioned to the several Municipalities of the said United Counties in the following manner, viz. :—

Marginal notes:
Sums to be levied.
County Rate.
Com'on Schools.
Special rate for loan.
Special rate under By-Law No. 182.
How apportioned to Municipalities.

MUNICIPALITIES.	County Rates.			Common School Rates.			Special Rate for Loan under By-law No. 120.			Special Rate under By-law No. 182.		
	£	s.	d.	£	s.	d.	£	s.	d.	£	s.	d.
Elizabethtown,............	485	16	7	182	0	0	117	5	9	136	16	8
Bastard and Burgess,......	226	5	6	119	15	0	54	15	11	63	18	9
Rear of Yonge and Escott,..	181	16	9	64	0	0	41	6	9	48	4	5
Front of Yonge,............	128	0	2	53	15	0	29	10	6	34	8	10
Front of Leeds and Lansdowne,	183	8	7	90	10	0	44	12	4	52	1	0
Rear of Leeds and Lansdowne,	130	14	6	68	0	0	31	17	1	37	0	11
Kitley,....................	226	8	4	103	5	0	54	12	7	63	14	7
North Crosby,.............	81	0	3	63	10	0	19	16	1	23	2	1
South Crosby,.............	121	9	6	63	10	0	31	15	7	37	1	4
Elmsley,..................	70	13	6	42	10	0	17	10	5	20	8	10
Front of Escott,...........	55	15	8	47	15	0	14	3	4	16	10	7
Gananoque,...............	48	4	3	0	0	0	10	0	11	11	14	3
Augusta,..................	425	7	5	165	15	0	110	9	11	128	18	2
Edwardsburgh,.............	277	3	5	152	15	0	68	11	1	79	19	6
Oxford,...................	247	5	9	131	0	0	59	7	9	69	5	8
Wolford,..................	169	7	0	98	15	0	40	15	3	47	11	3
South Gower,..............	85	17	5	32	10	0	21	5	3	24	16	1
Prescott,..................	245	6	4	0	0	0	65	17	3	76	16	10
Kemptville,...............	43	12	6	0	0	0	10	7	3	16	1	8
Merrickville,..............	66	6	7	0	0	0	14	6	1	12	13	9
Totals,............	3500	0	0	1468	15	0	858	7	4	1001	5	4

2. That the said several sums hereinbefore directed to be raised and levied in the said Municipalities respectively, shall be placed on the Collector's Roll by the Clerks thereof in separate columns, and be collected in like manner as all other rates and assessments are by law directed to be collected, and that every Collector shall, on or before the fourteenth day of December next, return his roll to the Treasurer of his Municipality, and pay over to such Treasurer the sums hereby directed to be raised, levied and collected therein.

How collected.

(Signed,)   JAMES KEELER, WARDEN.

[L. S.]

(Signed,)   JAMES JESSUP, CLERK.

No. CCLXXII.—BY-LAW

To authorize the payment of certain sums of Money.—Passed 24th June, 1865.

Be it enacted by the Council of the Corporation of the United Counties of Leeds and Grenville, and it is hereby enacted, That the several sums of money hereinafter in this section mentioned shall be paid by the Treasurer to the parties respectively, entitled to the same, out of any moneys in his hands applicable to such purposes, viz. :—

Sums to be paid to.

John McMullen. To John McMullen the sum of sixty-six dollars and sixty-seven cents, for balance of his printing contract and stationery furnished.

Prescott Board Public Instruction. To the Prescott Board of Public Instruction the sum of nineteen dollars, for attendance of members and incidental expenses.

Board Public Instruction No. 2. To the Board of Public Instruction for School Circuit No. 2, the sum of twenty-two dollars and fifty-five cents, for attendance of members and incidental expenses.

Board Public Instruction No. 1. To the Board of Public Instruction for School Circuit No. 1 the sum of thirty dollars and six cents, for attendance of members and incidental expenses.

Chas. J. Hynes. To Charles J. Hynes the sum of six dollars for publishing Professor Buckland's paper on Farm drainage.

To the County Clerk the sum of fifteen dollars and nine County Clerk.
cents, for postage and other disbursements for the
Counties.

To P. Byrne the sum of four dollars and seventy cents for P. Byrne.
printing and advertising for the Prescott Board of
Public Instruction.

To P. Byrne the sum of six dollars for publishing Professor The same.
Buckland's paper on Farm drainage.

To William Fitzsimmons the sum of twenty-one dollars William Fitzsim-
and ten cents for work done on the Gaol. mons.

To J. G. Elwood the sum of twenty-eight dollars and fifty Jas. G. Elwood.
cents for a stove furnished the Gaol. work on pump
and cleaning Court House.

To the Registrar of the County of Leeds the sum of five Register County
dollars to provide shelves and pigeon holes for papers of Leeds.
in his office.

To the Board of Public Instruction for School Circuit No. Board Public In-
6, the sum of forty-three dollars and sixty cents, for struction No. 6.
attendance of members and incidental expenses as
per accounts for 1864 and 1865.

To James Kincaid the sum of eleven dollars and sixty cents, James Kincaid.
for services as Messenger and stationery furnished.

To Messrs. Wylie and McMullen the sum of ten dollars Messrs. Wylie &
each for attending and reporting the proceedings of McMullen.
the Council during the session.

2. That the sum of twenty-five dollars be paid to David David Jones, Esq.
Jones, Esquire, late Registrar of the County of Leeds, provided he accepts the same in the satisfaction for that part
of the furniture belonging to him and left in full at the
Registry Office of the said County by him as detailed in the
account annexed to his petition, but in case he refuses to
accept the said sum hereby granted in full satisfaction for the
said furniture, then the said David Jones is at liberty to
remove the same from the said Registry Office so far as
the Council is concerned.

(Signed,) JAMES KEELER, Chairman.
[L. S.]
(Signed,) JAMES JESSUP, Clerk.

No. CCLXXIII.—BY-LAW

Granting a sum of money to repair the County Bridge at Kilmarnock.—Passed 12th October, 1865.

Be it enacted by the Council of the Corporation of the United Counties of Leeds and Grenville, and it is hereby enacted that the sum of one hundred and twenty dollars be granted to repair the Bridge across the River Rideau, at Kilmarnock, provided the Council of the Corporation of the United Counties of Lanark and Renfrew grant a like sum for the same purpose.

$120 granted.

Proviso.

2. That Abraham Brundige, Joseph Ferguson, jun., and Charles Tollman, jun., be appointed Commissioners to superintend the expenditure of the said sum of money hereby granted for the repairs of the said Bridge.

Commissioners to expend money.

(Signed,) JAMES KEELER, Warden.

[L. S.]

(Signed,) JAMES JESSUP, Clerk.

No. CCLXXIV.—BY-LAW

Granting a sum of money to repair the County Bridge at Burritt's Rapids.—Passed 12th October, 1865.

Be it enacted by the Council of the Corporation of the United Counties of Leeds and Grenville, and it is hereby enacted, that the sum of twenty dollars be granted to repair the Bridge across the River Rideau, at Burritt's Rapids, the Council of the County of Carlton having appropriated a like sum for the same purpose.

$20 granted.

2. That the money hereby granted be expended under the supervision of the Council of the Township of Oxford, and be paid to the Reeve of the said Township of Oxford at the close of the present session of this Council.

To be expended by Council of Oxford.

(Signed,) JAMES KEELER, Warden.

[L. S.]

(Signed,) JAMES JESSUP, Clerk.

465

No. CCLXXV.—BY-LAW

To authorise the payment of certain sums of money.—
Passed 14th October, 1865.

Be it enacted by the Council of the Corporation of the United Counties of Leeds and Grenville, and it is hereby enacted, That the several sums of money hereinafter ^{Sums to be paid} in this section mentioned shall be paid by the Treasurer^{to.} to the parties respectively entitled to the same, out of any moneys in his hands applicable to such purposes, viz.:

To the County Clerk the sum of thirteen dollars and County Clerk. two cents for postages disbursed for the Counties.

To the Board of Public Instruction for School Circuit Board Public In-No. 5, the sum of fifty-one dollars and thirty cents struction No. 5. for attendance of members and incidental expenses.

To the Board of Public Instruction for School Circuit No. Board Public In-2, the sum of seventeen dollars and fifty cents for struction No. 2. attendance of members and incidental expenses.

To Dr. Yates, of the City of Kingston, the sum of sixteen Dr. Yates. dollars for attendance as a witness at the trial in the case of Roe vs. Leeds and Grenville, on the part of the defence.

To William Fitzsimmons the sum of twenty-eight dollars Wm. Fitzsim-and seventy-five cents for materials furnished and mons. work done to the Court House and Gaol.

To J. G. Elwood, the sum of eleven dollars and ninety-J. G. Elwood. seven cents for material furnished and work done in the Gaol.

To Richard Poulton, the sum of twenty dollars for repair-Richard Poulton. ing windows in the Court House and Gaol for the year ending the first day of October, 1865, as per contract.

To D. Ford Jones, Esq., the sum of seventy dollars to aid D. Ford Jones. in sending George and Hannah Canton, (both having been blind from infancy) to the Educational Institution in the City of Hamilton, for the education of the blind.

F 1

Thomas Wood. To Thomas Wood, the sum of one hundred dollars in full of all claims for and in respect to his contract, for keeping the County Toll Roads in repair.

Board Public Instruction No. 1. To the Board of Public Instruction for Circuit No. 1, the sum of twenty-eight dollars and fifteen cents for attendance of members and incidental expenses.

Wm. H. Flynn. To William H. Flynn, the sum of one hundred and twenty-five dollars as one of the Special Committee in the investigation of the Treasurer's accounts.

George Tennant. To George Tennant, the sum of one hundred and twenty-five dollars for services as one of the said Committee.

D. Ford Jones. To D. Ford Jones, the sum of seventy dollars as one of the said Committee.

James Kincaid. To James Kincaid the sum of eleven dollars and seventy-five cents for services as messenger and stationery furnished.

James Keeler. To James Keeler, Esq., the sum of one hundred dollars for his services as Warden, and the further sum of one hundred dollars for extra services as Commissioner, &c., on various occasions.

David Wylie. To David Wylie, the sum of ten dollars for reporting the proceedings of this session of the Council.

(Signed,) JAMES KEELER, Warden.

[L. S.]

(Signed,) JAMES JESSUP, Clerk.

INDICES.

INDEX

TO

BY-LAWS OF THE DISTRICT COUNCIL.

A

K

L

M

N

O

INDEX

BY-LAWS OF THE COUNTY COUNCIL.

C

xiv. INDEX.

www.ingramcontent.com/pod-product-compliance
Lightning Source LLC
Chambersburg PA
CBHW031812270326
41932CB00008B/400